*Praise fo*

# *SGT. ROCK:*
# *THE LAST WARRIOR STANDING*

"Sgt. Rock is the quintessential memoir of the Vietnam War…A brilliantly told story."

Tom Haroldson
*Writer/Newspaper Editor*

"Excellent story teller – too bad it was all true."

Jonathan Tibbets

Your book was a real page turner – especially for me (an Infantry officer).

Dan Miller
*LTC, USAR (ret)*

"This book is awesome! …fascinating reading, full of adventure, tragedy and triumph."

Tamera Wursten

"I felt as if I were there with you observing the scenes as they graphically unfolded. …very well written."

James M. Ashworth
*Captain, USAF (ret)*

"As an American living in Post WWII battleground Okinawa, Japan, I am reminiscent not only of the devastation of war, but the true stories of courage and sacrifice of young soldiers. Rocky writes in such a way that one can imagine walking in his boots through the dense Vietnam jungle."

Holly Bailey

**Rocky Olson**

"I was able to 'watch your story' more that read your story. You showed the human side of war and the toll it takes on one's body – very well written. I Salute You."

Bart Wood
*LTC, ANG (ret)*

"Sgt. Rock is a gripping book about an incredible soldiers' experience in Vietnam. BAND OF BROTHERS & PACIFIC are the spirit of this book."

Mike Amos

"…Sgt. Rock was fascinating. Thank you so much".

Lisa Coles

"Riveting, well written. Sorry I took this long" (to review the draft manuscript) "but I read it twice."

Carol Operhal

"…very real and compelling. It was hard to put down."

Thomas Funk

"Great book. I am having my wife read the book to try and help her understand".

Leland K. Nielson
*Petty Officer Third Class USN (Vietnam)*

"Great expression of a grunts frustration with Nam. I read selected episodes to my grandson."

David Glen Anderson
Former Navy journalist

"I gained a greater appreciation for soldiers and what they experience to protect freedom. Thank you".

Tim LaRue

"Thank you for your strength and example".

Ancil Young
Vietnam veteran

"Your style of writing is excellent. I could actually feel, see, and hear your story. …I've read other books" (about Vietnam) "but your book is the best".

Kelly Mathias
*Veteran*

Published by
Zeroed-In Press

ISBN 978-0-9831489-0-6

First edition, first printing November 2010

Send all correspondence to:
Zeroed-In Press
P.O. Box 122
Roy, Utah 84067

www.sgtrockbook.com

Printed in the United States of America

# SGT. ROCK: THE LAST WARRIOR STANDING

by

ROCKY OLSON

# CONTENTS

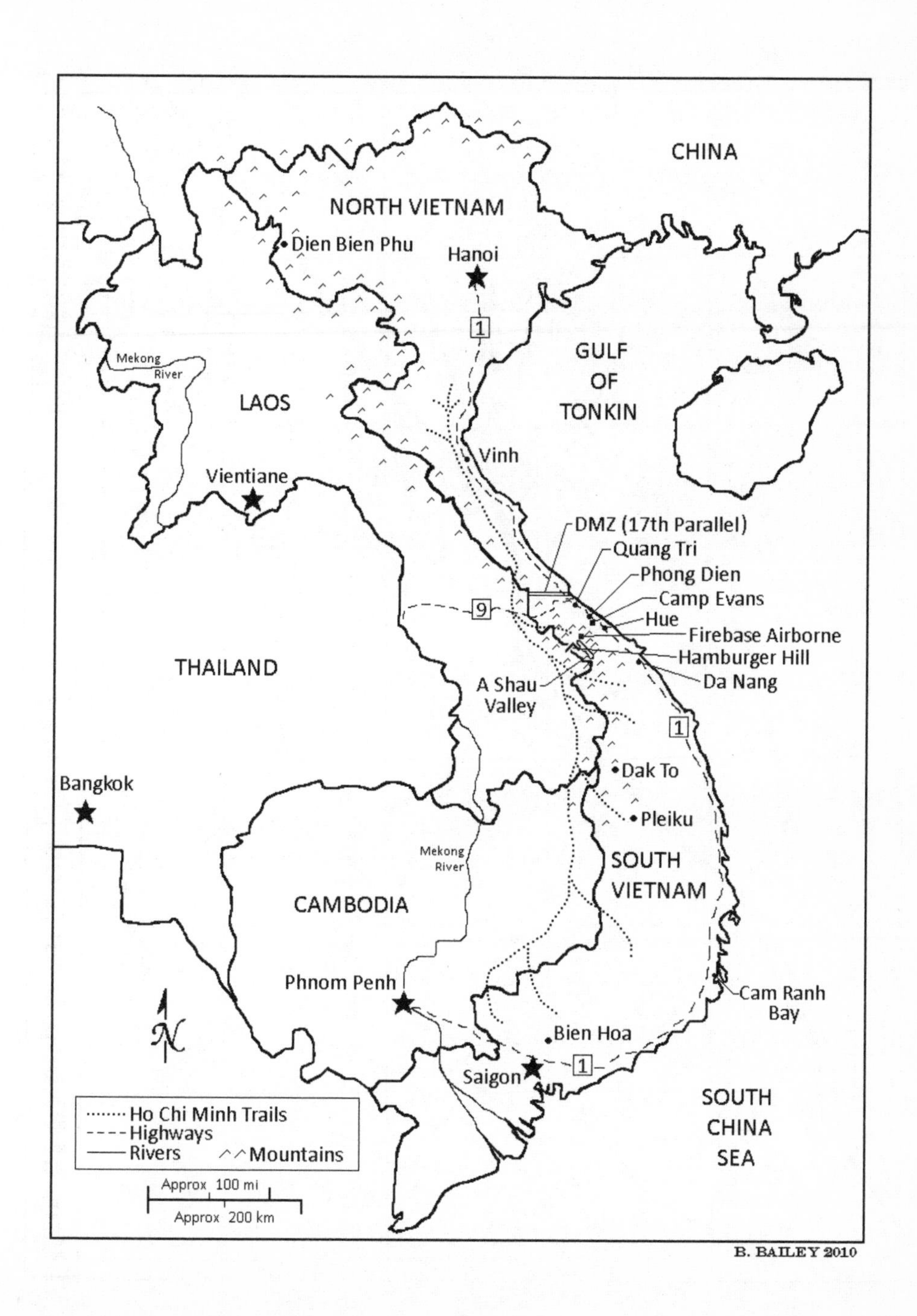


B. BAILEY 2010

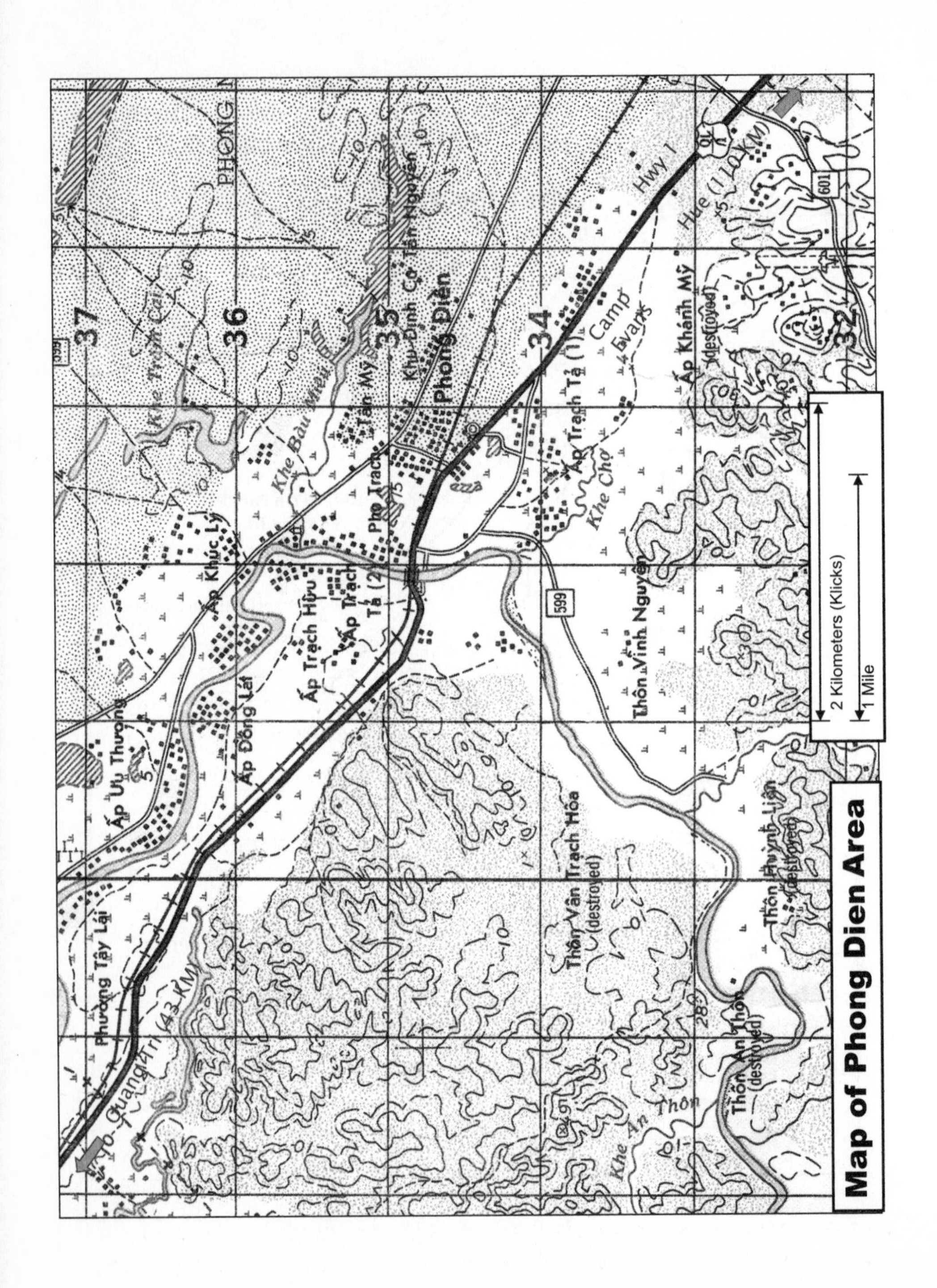
Map of Phong Dien Area
2 Kilometers (Klicks)
1 Mile
Phong Điền
Camp Evans
Hwy 1
Hue (1 LO KM)
Quang Tri (43 KM)
Áp Trạch Tả (1)
Áp Trạch Tả (2)
Áp Trạch Hữu
Áp Khúc Lý
Áp Đông Lái
Áp Ưu Thượng
Phương Tây Lại
Thôn Vĩnh Nguyên
Thôn Văn Trạch Hòa (destroyed)
Thôn Huỳnh Liên (destroyed)
Thôn An Thôn (destroyed)
Áp Khánh Mỹ (destroyed)
Khe Chợ
Khe An Thôn
Khe Bàu Miêu
Tân Mỹ
Phò Trạch
599
601
37
36
35
34
32
PHONG

## ACKNOWLEDGEMENTS

There has never ever been a book presented to the public for literary consumption that was not a collaborative effort. If the text was the author's first attempt or one-hundredth, the same principle applies; no one can do it alone. Authors sometime depend on the talents of researchers, historians, ghost writers, typists, editors, agents, artist, publisher, critics and a host of other professionals. Among the most important to a writer are those who give unending support and encouragement.

Typically, within the first few pages of most books we consume for the pleasure of the experience, is a page entitled "Acknowledgments," which is a long word that summarizes an even larger desire to say "thank you." Family members, or friends, are quite often mentioned in the lead paragraph. Though these special people are usually not literary professionals, they are often the very reason the work was undertaken in the first place and completed at last.

I wish to thank the many people who have listened to my stories (including my children Holly, Breck, Cody and Colt) and in turn asked, "When are you going to write a book?" Individually I must recognize my wife, Shaunna, for her encouragement and computer skills. She kept me going even though she knew that her support meant hundreds of evenings alone, while I toiled in the den with elevated thoughts on the mysteries of "Do I use a question mark after the quotation mark of before it?" I could not have done this without her.

Thank you, Kevin and Chad. These guys are my brothers and invaluable to my writing process. They spent a great deal of their own office time tending to my needs while they could have been paying attention to their growing business. They were "walls" to bounce ideas off, "fingers" for hundreds of pages of word processing, and "caffeine" when I needed a surge of confidence.

My father a WWII infantry veteran, probably understood my feelings and hesitancy (for the first few years) to talk about Vietnam better than anyone.

There have been many unpaid, but valued, critics over the years who have suggested better ways to say things. I will not attempt to name names for the fear of leaving a significant contributor off the list. Thank you all.

# FOREWORD

Every combat soldier's story is unique. Some experiences are so private they will never be told. Others stories, like the one you are about to read, require years of seasoning in the heart before their teller can relive them. Sometimes only time will mellow the harshness of miserable days, weeks, or years, and transpose them into valuable learning lessons for others.

I wrote most of this book years ago. I cried as I recorded for the first time, longhand on yellow legal pads, some of my mind's forbidden stories. Abrasive fingers dragged their way across my tender heartstrings, and I shelved the book for a long time. I was not ready; the project would wait.

If anything was "typical" about an infantryman's varied experiences in Vietnam, it was that they were almost universally bad. So, in the telling of these true events, I speak generally for everyone and at the same time specifically for no one except myself.

The longer memory holds a fact, the less likely it is to be one. A natural tendency of storytellers is to expand the experience, make it more exciting, and himself a hero. I have relied on personal letters, pictures, and research of facts in establishing this effort. Using a file of almost 100 pieces of correspondence written during my tour and several hundred personal photographs, I have recounted my experiences.

To protect the anonymity of those about whom I have written, I have generally given my comrades-in-arms fictitious names and home states. For the sake of continuity, many individuals described herein are really compilations of several real-life soldiers that came and went as tours and combat dictated.

Because the 101st Airborne Division was "Air Mobile," our areas of operation were many and varied. We were continuously shuttled by helicopter from gooey rice paddies and friendly (or hostile) villages to dense sweaty jungles, sometimes daily. If the exact date or sequence of an incident was of no consequence to its significance, I have included it with others that occurred in the same general area during another time.

Most of my days were filled with doing nothing. I would bore you very quickly telling those stories, and I know that is not what you paid your buck to read. Days of "action" got the emphasis, while time sitting under a bush reading a paperback has mercifully been deleted, for the most part.

Quotations contained herein represent the gist of conversations from years ago, but are typical of what I often heard. The volatile language commonly used, especially by combat soldiers in Vietnam, ranged somewhere between spicy and vulgar. Although I have tried to give the reader a true feeling of what life was like, I have taken a great deal of liberty concerning our harsh way of communicating. Most generally I have avoided using the four-letter-word language that warriors commonly employed in almost every sentence. Sometimes, however, nothing will substitute for the dynamics of what was actually said.

Typically, because of a new occupation or a move to another region, one acquires the vernacular of one's new associates. Words and phrases can be cliquish in nature and thus allow that certain feeling of belonging. In Vietnam, our occupation and environment were crude; consequently, expletive-filled sentences were the norm for many soldiers. If any readers, particularly current or former soldiers, are disappointed in my way of editing war language, sorry.

I wrote this work from the point of view of those who filled the lower infantry ranks of the United States Army. We were expendable. We came a dime a dozen. Though our heads had been force-filled with the glories of being the tip of the spear, we were not ignorant of the fact that even the most hardened steel breaks when used incorrectly or when it is pounded upon by an equal or superior force. It is a fact that no matter how efficient the air or sea powers are, boots in the mud still have to go in and take control.

Sometimes those who waved the tip of the spear so freely gave little consequence to the replaceable parts. We charged ahead, as ordered, not immune to lousy tactics or poor decisions made by our superiors. Usually, our only recourse was to profanely badmouth everyone of at least a rank higher—usually sergeants or officers—behind their backs. That we did with relish, even though those soldiers may have been under the same order we were. Most officers, I will admit, were of the highest caliber, yet even they found opportunity to criticize (more privately) the inept decisions of others. That is the nature of man, I guess, no matter what our professions may be.

Aristotle said: "War must be for the sake of peace." Although that may be true, I wish it were not. Almost a complete generation of American soldiers fought in Vietnam. This editorial comment, however, does not detail the real pain and suffering, and the death and destruction, experienced by those courageous American defenders of Vietnamese freedom.

Combat is always bloody, dirty, and mind altering, and its aftermath sickens those involved in policing up the battleground for the remains of missing best friends. An infantry soldier's senses can be supremely offended, even by the "successful and commendable" results of their own acts. High-powered rifle bullets, hand grenades, claymore mines, artillery, and highly explosive booby-traps did not kill with surgical precision as the WW II black and white movies had portrayed to me. And there was never any patriotic music playing in the background.

As those veterans who earned the "Combat Infantry Badge" in any war gain political and military power and in turn control our national destiny, their commitment to lasting peace must be in memory of those who have paid the price. "Freedom is the taste the protected will never know," and no one should treasure it more than a war's survivor.

Civilian politics (for the most part) directed this long melodrama. Not everyone capitulated to the direction the director took with the player's parts. There was a great deal of supporting sentiment in the cast that those "evil, lying, Communist North Vietnamese S.O.B.s" had played too prominent a role for too long. It was now time for the mighty U. S. of A. to shove the damn "gooks" out of the spotlight and erase their names from the program. There would be no communist domino effect in this play if the cast had anything to do with it. Rebellion, however, of any military against its incompetent civilian leadership is done on the slippery road to military dictatorship.

Concerning this work, I want you to understand some things: I was involved in everything I've written about. It all really happened. This work is not fiction. I have not attempted to develop a leading character to which you can grow attached as the plot thickens. A series of subplots, overcome at the last minute, which allows the hero to solve the ultimate problem (saving the heroine or the country) are not contained herein.

It was not my intent to cover the entire war saga, just my piece of the complicated puzzle. What I have attempted to do is allow you to live, through my story, one brutal year of combat in war-torn Vietnam.

This writing is autobiographical. The book details my thoughts and actions, hopefully providing you with a greater insight concerning this sad era in American history.

**Note: If you are not familiar with Military acronyms or jargon, please refer to the GLOSSARY in the back of the book for help.**

## CHAPTER 1

# THE BEACH

Several minutes passed before I remembered the thundering blast that cratered the earth. "They're going to kill me!" flashed through my head. It was about the 6th of November, 1968—or was it? Keeping track of the days of the week was impossible, except for Mondays, when Doc gave each of us a big orange malaria pill.

I was one of 12 new guys, "in-country" just two weeks, with orders that assigned us all to the 101st Airborne Division. My unit, Alpha Company 2/506 Infantry, patrolled the beaches about twenty-four kilometers (15 miles) south of the Demilitarized Zone (DMZ) along the Gulf of Tonkin, Vietnam. My primary job was that of a travel agent: I was extensively trained and equipped to send enemy soldiers on long trips to meet their beloved ancestors.

Just a few years earlier, reporters back home had been calling this the "Vietnam conflict," wherein U.S. soldiers were fighting some "insurgent Viet Cong guerillas." Everyone here in Nam, however, emphatically told me that this was indeed a full-blown war already. Well-armed, -trained, and -uniformed communist armies were marching from North Vietnam in huge numbers to destroy us. Early in the conflict, U.S. soldiers were tasked to quickly defeat the bunch of rag-tag Viet Cong guerillas. Recently, however, this new and much more formidable North Vietnamese Army had started to kill Americans. It was not clear who would be doing the shooting at me. I guessed I would just have to see for myself.

The two enemy armies had the same political/military goals but, like the Axis armies of World War II, they were quite independent of each other. Maybe evil is too strong a word, but it was clear to me that they were bad guys.

Typical of our first two weeks, we humped our rucksacks all night through boot-sucking rice paddies. Just before sunrise, 120 of us quietly surrounded (on three sides—open toward the ocean) a little Vietnamese fishing village and waited. Although the temperature had not dipped below 90 degrees all night, the sand felt cool. I plowed my fingers through the smooth unspoiled beach where I sat. With me were my new squad leader Jim Pearson, the machine gunner Eddie Zorn, and another FNG (f---ing new guy) with whom I had gone through Basic and Advanced Infantry Training, "Major" Poulsen. In his case, Major was not a military rank, but a nickname that a hard-driving drill sergeant had given him during our training days. Poulsen was a "Major" screw-up. Anything learned just once, Major could never successfully repeat.

Sergeant Pearson crawled over and quietly reminded me that since our position was the only one on the flat low-lying beach and in the open, it would be wise to pay close attention. I trusted his instincts. Pearson was a born leader: smart, handsome, and—most importantly—he seemed to know his way around. I began to think of the sergeant as the kind of soldier I could really learn from. As for Zorn, I didn't know much about him. Physically, Zorn was maybe 240 pounds, a square jawed, hairy armed prototypical infantryman. He looked like the type of soldier the Army put on all their recruiting posters. The machine gun that hung from his broad shoulders swung with the rhythm of his long stride. Zorn also had a quick temper that matched the fiery red of his hair. The gunner intimidated everyone. If I were a gook soldier intending to harm Zorn, I'd try to do it from long distance.

As the sun's early rays began to streak skyward from the ocean's grey horizon, three brilliant white starburst flares burst into full bloom high in the sky above me. They lit up the beach for a few seconds. The prearranged signal told us, and any NVA or VC (easier to say than North Vietnamese Army or Vietnamese Communists) inside the surrounded area that we were about to begin the search for them.

I saw them almost immediately in the fading luminance of the flares: four enemy soldiers in full North Vietnamese battle uniform with rifles in hand. They ran down the beach from the village, toward the ocean. While I sat there thinking that my first encounter with the enemy would be easy, the old-timers Pearson and Zorn were already aiming their weapons at the running targets, allowing the NVA to come a little closer.

The gooks, who had begun their sprint in the little cluster of fishing huts about 400 meters away, got closer to us with every footprint they left in the wet sand. They ran parallel with the ocean's waves and were soon within 300 meters of our semi-hidden position behind a very small mound of sand and sea grass. That's when Zorn opened fire with the M-60 machine gun. The surprised gooks did an immediate about face and attempted to *didi mau*—run away—from our fire. Soon they began taking fire from the other side of the little ville as well. Back towards our little fire-team they came again, as fast as they could run. It reminded me of my visits to the pinball arcade back home. Every time I shot that mechanical bear it turned around and ran back through the machine again as if to say, "Lucky shot. Bet you can't do that again."

Captain Becker, the no-guff company commander who was personally directing the cordon and search of the *ville*, came running through short brush to our rear. As he broke onto the beach, he stepped on one of our rucksacks lying in the sand and did a sloppy one-point landing on his face right at my feet. I stopped firing just long enough to make sure that he had not been shot.

"What the hell are you shooting at?" he mumbled, spitting wet sand from his mouth.

Before I could answer, he rose to one knee and fired a perfect three-round burst in the general direction of the fleeing soldiers. He did not need to be told what to do.

"Follow me!" he yelled to the four of us.

Our shooting at the long-range targets was quite ineffective in the early morning darkness. The captain's idea (and it sounded good to me at the time) was for the fire-team to run parallel with the gooks. A kilometer away the ocean swept in toward the trees, narrowing the beach to about fifty meters. At the bottleneck we could intercept and capture the NVA soldiers. That was the commander's plan.

Several other soldiers who usually followed the captain also responded to the excitement and quickly spilled onto the beach. My heart raced, but I was thinking how easy combat was going to be. Hey, maybe I can do this. The enemy was not as ferocious as I had been told. My brave thoughts however, were about to be dashed. The romance of war can be quickly shattered by the crack of a bullet passing in close proximity.

A crushing roar turned the world upside down. A sharp blow to my chest, like a ten-pound sledgehammer, collapsed my lungs. The very air molecules themselves hit me with such force they stung my exposed skin. So this is it, I thought. After all the time I've waited, and the training I've endured, I've gotten myself killed in my first contact with the enemy. I waited for the dark tunnel and the "being of light" that was supposed to greet me.

Moments after my 'death,' I involuntarily opened my mouth and sucked the sweetness of morning air back into my collapsed chest. Maybe I wasn't … I could see stars, both imaginary and real. I ran my trembling hands along the length of my body, fearing what I might find. All of my parts were still intact. No wet spots, so I was not bleeding and I had not (yet) defecated in my new green jungle pants. I did find, however, that the blast had caked the right side of my body with sand. Semi-conscious, it took me a few more seconds to notice the screaming. I rolled onto my stomach and faced the waist-high brush that concealed the rest of my company to our rear. Slowly my brain responded and I realized what had happened. I then joined the terrified chorus of American soldiers lying in the sand around me, screaming "CEASE FIRE!"

M-16 and M-60 muzzle flashes expelled long lines of bright red tracers that raced each other toward us. The supersonic fireflies smashed into the beach around us and the ocean waves beyond. Between each of the burning fireflies, five other fireless bearers of death also zipped by, searching for a home, some of them whining far out into the sea after impacting the sand. Bright white flashes and deafening concussions soon followed the muffled thumping of M-79 grenades that were being launched blindly toward us from the dark trees. The unseen 40 millimeter high-explosive grenades arched high into the dark sky before returning to earth and detonating on the beach. "CEASE FIRE, CEASE FIRE!" we continued to yell.

Fifty meters away, the other half of my squad—Martinez, Jakes, Cosby and Washington—were pumping out lead and M-79 grenades as fast as they could toward us. They thought they had a squad of NVA soldiers pinned on the beach, and they were not about to let them return fire.

In the early morning darkness, the excitement generated by our initial contact with the enemy had drawn the "friendly" attention to us. To their rear, where no one should be, the other fire-team suddenly saw black figures running across the beach. Not recognizing the profiles as American, they opened fire on us. All we could do was pancake ourselves in the moist sand and scream. Bright red tracer bullets ripped the air inches over our prostrate bodies. The rhythm of the machine gun was as smooth and fast as the company clerk's new electric typewriter.

We were in a hopeless situation. We had no place to hide, and we could not return the fire. It seemed like an eternity that we lay in the sand, screaming to our buddies to cease the cursed shooting!

Ten or 15 seconds after that first grenade had detonated and knocked me down, the other fire-team finally heard our pleas and stopped firing. Captain Becker made our identities perfectly clear, using explicit Army four-letter language, and we cautiously stood up.

I did a quick survey of the guys around me. To my surprise, none of us had been hit. The captain peered down toward the ocean and the now empty beach. In a voice several octaves above normal he cursed several more times and then commanded us to return to our original positions. The order suited us perfectly. We were not eager to charge across an open beach in search of a foe who was by then prepared and waiting somewhere back in the trees with AK-47s locked and loaded. I suddenly realized that I could get killed in this dangerous new profession of mine, and it might even be my friends who do it.

We cleaned the grit from our ears and eyes as we retraced the long strides of our sandy bootprints. When we had rejoined the rest of our apprehensive squad, Zorn's temper nearly resulted in several Americans getting KIA—killed in action. Pearson and I were really pissed, but Zorn was almost out of control. The captain and several of his command post personnel had to physically restrain the raging bull. Later, after an uneventful search of the *ville*, Sergeant Pearson got the guys together and "expressed" his intense displeasure to the trigger-happy fire-team. He liberally used descriptive terms my Christian ears were not accustomed to hearing—but they were quickly becoming used to it. I mentally seconded every word he said.

It took Zorn several days to cool down from the morning's fiasco. I stayed away from the big guy, and no one else dared talk to him much the whole time.

# CHAPTER 2

# THE BUNKER

We established our day defensive position (DDP) several kilometers from the fishing village, near two natural waterholes. Footprints revealed that the small semi-fresh oasis had been used for some time by man and animal. Several armored personnel carriers, or APCs, joined us from a nearby cavalry unit and stood guard while the entire company tried to sleep. Physically drained as we were, daytime sleep was still difficult. Our steel helmets protected our heads from the sun's direct rays, but they also baked our brains. The high humidity and 100-plus-degree days had turned the night's cool sand into a reflector oven.

Pearson, seeing my inexperience, called to me.

"Sergeant Rock, come over here!"

Sooner or later most grunts picked up a nickname. My squad leader had started calling me "Sergeant Rock," after the famous but fictitious World War II comic book hero. He was a popular cartoon character among the budding warriors of the 1960s. My actual military rank was private first class, which is toward the bottom of the military hierarchy.

"I'm going to teach you an old-timer's trick," he said.
He stripped a spare communications battery of its plastic bag cover. The sergeant then tied the small bag over the flash suppresser of my M-16 and shoved the rifle, muzzle first, into the soft sand. Next, he opened my poncho and draped it over the butt of the rifle, creating a little tent.

The small teepee provided three feet of "hot" shade in the middle of an otherwise shadeless beach. Pearson's idea quickly caught on, and soon our little DDP looked like a graveyard, with the poncho markers forming a circle around our perimeter. The sand was still hot, but now we had just enough shade to protect our heads from the merciless sun.

We continued the cordon and search operations for the next week or two. Sergeant Pearson said that the NVA and VC were scarcer than pork ribs in a kosher butcher shop. Days and nights were pretty boring, except for the hassles the new guys (myself included) got from some of the old-timers. I guess someone up the chain of command could not believe we were not successful at finding anything, so he had us persist with the waste of time. We continued doing nothing day after day, because we had not finished doing nothing the day before. Army wisdom.

Traditionally, the 101st Airborne Division was manned only by those who were "jump qualified." For whatever reason—maybe parachute landings were very difficult and impractical in the jungle environment, or because helicopters had come of age and jumping skills were not required in Vietnam—the division was instead designated as "air mobile" by the Army. Now we could be transported by air, usually helicopter, and delivered where required much more efficiently. At a moment's notice, a fully armed squad, platoon, or company of combat-ready infantry soldiers could be dropped by chopper onto a North Vietnamese Army doorstep.

Because the air mobile concept did not require infantry ground-pounders to be jump qualified, most of the new replacements, like me, were not. It took a while for us "legs" to become adopted by our jump-qualified brothers. Zorn and a few of the others took pride in making life even more miserable than it already was for us. Carrying an extra load of machine gun ammo, or standing guard an extra hour at night, or walking point more than our share, were hassles we lived with. Sometimes Sergeant Pearson would come to our aid, but most of the time we just lived with the harassment. Eventually us legs became the majority, and the badgering stopped.

When we finally received word that our area of operation (AO) was changing, my initial apprehension was quickly overridden. I learned that Pearson had selected Zorn to be the point man for the day's particularly dangerous assignment. I got a great deal of satisfaction in knowing that the big Kansas farmer was teed-off about his new role. Machine gunners normally did not lead patrols. I think his dislike for walking point was the reason he had volunteered to carry the heavy gun.

Lieutenant DeWitt, our platoon leader, went into unusual detail as he explained the day's operation and our individual squad assignments to us. Spreading the map on the ground, the tanned officer made grease-pencil X's at each of the platoon landing zones, or LZs. Arrows pointed in our direction of travel. What the map did not show, the lieutenant explained, was that the whole area was heavily mined.

"These mines are extremely old and fragile. They are the deadliest thing since cholera. Stay away from 'em."

Before North Vietnam's defeat of the French in 1954, the area was a heavily defended outpost belonging to the French. The mines they had laid 15 years earlier were still there, and most would be capable of blowing a leg off a careless or unlucky soldier. Lieutenant DeWitt told us to leave our rucksacks behind and to travel light. It was just going to be a short one-day operation.

"No sweat," he promised. "It'll be no sweat; just watch what you're doing and keep your intervals."

I had no reason to distrust the young officer. Everyone in the platoon looked to him for guidance, and as far as I could tell he had never betrayed their trust. Lieutenant DeWitt was from Portland, Oregon, and during his senior year of college he was president of the state's Young Republicans. We jokingly accused him of being our "political officer." Unlike the political officers in the North Vietnamese and Viet Cong armies, however, the lieutenant kept his politics to himself. There were many opportunities to verbally blast the unpopular Democrats in the White House, but he never did.

Within an hour of our briefing, the radio/telephone operator (RTO) at the company command post yelled, "Choppers inbound!"

I hurriedly tied three bandoleers of M-16 ammo around my waist, and put a red smoke grenade in my left shirt pocket and a yellow one in my right. I then put two fragmentation grenades in my leg pockets, grabbed my rifle, and ran to join my squad at the pickup point. The lightweight jungle uniform was much cooler than the heavy cotton pants and blouse we all wore during training days. We also loved the many large pockets.

We fought swarming flies for two long hours in the 115-degree sun before our transportation finally arrived. Typical Army, I thought, hurry up and wait. The choppers gently settled in the soft sand and we all scrambled aboard.

*Aircraft technology had improved greatly since WWII and Korea. This war was ideal for rotary-winged helicopters. We knew them by a variety of names. The UH-1 Iroquois, for example, was unofficially called a "Huey" by everyone. Depending on what the "bird" was designed to do, it may have also been called a Gunship (with external weapons), Slick (no external weapons), Log (logistics) bird, Dust-off or Medevac (medical evacuation), or it may just be called by the general term "chopper".*

It was refreshing for me to sit in the Huey's open doorway and feel the morning air penetrate my already sweaty jungle fatigues. A few feet above me the chopper's blades beat a soothing rhythm against the air. Two thousand meters below me the green and tan countryside was deceptively peaceful. The terrain was flat, with small groups of mostly destroyed huts clustered beside the once fertile but now bone-dry rice paddies. Coconut palms and banana trees were probably still producing fruit, which would likely be harvested by the VC or NVA.

The helicopters, each loaded with anxious infantry soldiers, followed the preceding bird at 45-degree angles above and behind. Pilots hesitated to land on "new" ground. The tall grass often hid hazardous obstacles like tree stumps or landmines. When they were all trying to land on the same little LZ, it was also important not to blow the air cushion out from under each other. Without the cushion the helicopter would fall, mostly uncontrolled, until the earth suddenly broke its rapid decent. A falling chopper never killed anyone; it was the sudden impact with the earth that turned a good day bad.

As it turned out the landing zone was cold (we were not fired on) this time. As quick as a hiccup we scattered out into defensive positions in the tall grass. We were all safely in place, except for "Major" Poulsen. Sergeant Pearson had to go back, grab the confused soldier by the sleeve, and drag him away from the whirling helicopter blades.

This terrain looked identical to much I had already seen. I could see no obvious place "Victor Charlie" would be hiding, but one of the first things the Army taught me upon my arrival in-country was that Charlie was very deceptive. He was quite often where you thought he was not.

On Lieutenant DeWitt's command, each of the squads lined up in columns and headed to various assigned destinations. With Zorn in the lead, my squad walked along a hard-packed dry rice paddy dike for two kilometers, or klicks, in a semi-northerly direction. When we got to coordinates 773 291 on the map, we turned due east for another klick, and then headed south. This route would bring us in the back door of a vacated little *ville* that we had paid little attention to and passed by two hours earlier. Meanwhile, the other two squads in the platoon openly established their presence in front of the *ville* to draw any hostile attention away from us.

At 1500 hours we started across an old sun-baked rice paddy, heading toward the *ville*. Fifty meters into the recon, Zorn froze in his tracks and held both hands high above his head. We all read his signal to stop in place.

Without moving his feet, he slowly turned his head and shoulders and shouted to Pearson, "This place's frigging mined! We gotta get out of here!"

Following Zorn's example, each of us did a quick visual search around our feet. This was my first real experience with mines, and I was not sure what I was supposed to be looking for.

Pearson reached back without moving his feet and snatched the radio headset from Washington's shoulder.

"Blade, this is King of Hearts, over."

We all heard the radio's speaker box answer back.

"Roger King of Hearts, this is Blade Actual. I've got you Loose Change; what's your sit rep, over?"

*"Lima" and "Charlie" are the correct military phonetic words for "L" and "C" in the American alphabet. Phonetic words were developed to clarify alphabet letters that may sound similar over garbled radio transmissions and result in deadly miscommunications. Sometimes radio users got creative and invented other non-military words for these (and the other) letters of the alphabet. In non-emergency situations one might hear substitutes for these letters, like "Lumpy Chicken" or "Loose Change." The non-standard words were a violation of strict radio protocol, but what was the Army going to do, send the violator to Vietnam?*

Pearson wiped his sweaty face with the dirty olive-colored towel he had draped over his shoulders and answered.

"We're in a frigging mine field. The only thing we can do is to back outta here and find another way to the target, over."

"Roger that King of Hearts. Mark the field on the map and back out. If you can't make the target by 1600 hours, return by alternate route two and rejoin the Queen and Jack, over."

"Roger that," answered Pearson adding, "And keep the pill pusher handy in case we break one of these things. King of Hearts out."

"All right, here's the thing," Pearson shouted, as if we were all deaf. "Coz, do an about face and lead us out of this hell hole. Major Poulsen, I want you to follow Cosby and step only where he steps, or so help me I'll kick your butt so hard you'll have to pull down your zipper to drink a cup of coffee."

We carefully retraced our steps one at a time. Several of the old-timers pointed to rusty brown discolorations in the earth, indicating very old mines—could be French. They hesitantly confessed that they should have noticed them earlier.

When Pearson was sure that we were safely out of the mine field, Zorn took the lead again. I still didn't like the man very much, but I had to admit that he had probably just saved someone's life. We gave wide berth to the old contaminated paddy and headed back toward the *ville*.

Army intelligence officers had identified this area as a resupply point for a local Viet Cong paramilitary contingent, and that was one of the things we were supposed to check out. There were a few broken-down hootches scattered around as we entered the remains of the once-active *ville*. I found it difficult to believe mosquitoes could find enough to eat, let alone an enemy force of 10 to 30 soldiers. We fought our way through shoulder-high grass and hacked apart "wait-a-minute vines," which made us do just that. It didn't look to me like anyone had been here for a long time.

During our search of the old family bunkers located beneath each hootch, a single M-16 blast broke the quiet. I quickly dropped to one knee and faced the direction from which the shot had come. I could see nothing except tall slender blades of green elephant grass. After paying close attention for a few more seconds, and regaining control of my rapid breathing, I slowly stood up. Instinctively my thumb rotated the safety selector past "semi-auto" to "auto" and I was ready to play some "rock and roll" on my M-16.

Major Poulsen began yelling, "I saw one! I saw one!"

I cautiously ran over to Poulsen, whose sweaty face had allowed his thick glasses to slip to the end of his nose.

"What did you see?" I asked, not believing he could see anything.

"I seen a leg right there," he said, pointing to the small opening of a mostly overgrown bunker.

Still disbelieving, I listened as he cleaned his glasses on his filthy shirttail and repeated the sentence to Sergeant Pearson, who had just arrived. Washington and Martinez also ran up, and the excited soldier repeated his short story a third time. Pearson quickly called the lieutenant on the radio, again asking for instructions.

"Blade ordered us to check it out; who volunteers to go in?"

Pearson had just asked exactly what we did not want to hear. After eyeballing each other for a few moments, we all settled on

Martinez. We selected him not only because "Minnie" was the smallest, but also because he was the most gung ho. "Minnie" was the name his friends tagged him with back home on the streets of New York City. Minnie stood five foot four and weighed 115 pounds with a six-pack in his hand. He was a real terror of a soldier, as he must have been as a street fighter back in the projects. Minnie's eyes were always bloodshot, and he just looked mean.

Minnie shrugged his shoulders.

"It don't mean a thing," he said. "I'll be the tunnel rat. There ain't no bullet in Nam with my name on it."

Before entering the black hole, Minnie threw a frag into the entrance of the bunker. It didn't do much more than fill the air with grey dust and dirt. The little tunnel rat borrowed Sergeant Pearson's flashlight, checked his M-16, and carefully crawled in. Forty-five seconds after his feet had disappeared around a corner we heard a muffled shot that we recognized as coming from an AK-47. The shot was quickly followed by six rock and roll blasts from an M-16. Minnie's feet reappeared first as he hurriedly exited the bunker opening.

"Holy shit, there's at least two of 'em in there," he said, "and my damn rifle jammed!"

Pearson turned to me and in a command voice announced, "Sergeant Rock, you're next."

I guess everyone thought I was brave, because I immediately dropped to my knees at the bunker's entrance. The truth was that my knees were just suddenly very weak, and I had almost collapsed in a heap. This business of crawling into a bunker that contains armed enemy soldiers who intend to kill you would put fear in anyone. Our squad's grenadier, Milo Jakes, now joined us, and I asked to borrow the .45 caliber pistol he carried. With his pistol in one hand and Pearson's flashlight in the other, I cautiously crawled into the black hole.

The squared tunnel, with its walls of split bamboo, made two right-angle turns, and then opened into a large chamber. Before I rounded each corner, I pushed the flashlight ahead of me to see if it drew fire. When nothing happened, I slowly eyed the next few feet and crawled forward again.

I reached the main chamber and pushed the flashlight in. I heard several metallic clicks. Not waiting for a grenade to come bouncing around the corner, I shoved the pistol into the room and fired blindly until the .45 was empty. In the tight confines of the small tunnel, the concussion of the exploding bullets pounded against my ears and caused dirt to begin to fall from overhead. Fear of a collapse almost caused me to panic, but the tunnel roof held. I quickly regained my composure and backpedaled to daylight and safety.

Thirty seconds after I exited the bunker, one of its frightened occupants crawled into the entrance, pleading, "*Chu Hoi*." Pearson cautiously accepted his surrender, tied his arms and legs with some green nylon cord, and then allowed the medic to work on a large bullet hole in his upper left arm. Torn muscle protruded from the gaping hole. The pain must have been intense, but our prisoner said nothing.

Fifteen or 20 grunts were by now milling around the area, including the company's Vietnamese interpreter, Trung. He began to interrogate the prisoner. "*Khong Biet*" was the reply to every question Trung asked. This was my first experience with a prisoner, but I guessed he was claiming to know nothing. Frustrated, the interpreter grabbed the M-16 from his shoulder and fired a three-round burst next to the VC's head. The muzzle blast unevenly parted the soldier's dirty black hair. Trung then pointed the barrel of the rifle between the prisoner's deeply set brown eyes and rested the flash suppressor on the bridge of the VC's nose. The three-round burst and the weight of the warm rifle barrel crossed all language barriers. Even I understood what the inquisitor wanted. The next round of questions produced successful results.

Sergeant Smith, from the third platoon, entered the bunker after the questioning was over. He dragged out a dead body that had been hit three times in the chest by Minnie's M-16. Unlike the first soldier, who was dressed in black pajamas, this one wore dirty green uniform pants and a worn khaki shirt. Sergeant Pearson said that the guy was a Viet Cong tax collector. "You got the rights to his ears," Smith said to Minnie. Several old-timers in the company still displayed shriveled "souvenirs" of their first kill. Minnie declined the offer.

Many soldiers wore love beads around their necks. The neckwear represented a contradiction in our moral attitudes. Most of us did not want to come to Vietnam, and some of us were totally opposed to the war. However, after a few months of watching close friends die, killing to save one's own life and killing to get revenge became acceptable to us. By fighting against us, the VC or NVA were committing themselves to an eventual battlefield death. We were only providing the exact moment.

To a few, the M-16 was a scepter of authority. Sovereign power, unlike anything experienced back in the world, belonged to he who carried the black staff with a dragon's breath. Most of us hated the life to which we had been forced to adapt; putting a peace symbol on one side of a helmet and "born to kill" on the other was not uncommon. Perhaps that can be understood only by another grunt.

Alpha Company continued to search the old *ville.* By evening, we had captured one AK-47 rifle, seven stick-handled grenades, 40 mortar rounds, 300 pounds of rice, and the two Vietnamese Communists—one dead.

We were all feeling really good about the day's activities when Captain Becker walked up to our position, and with a smile on his face just looked at us. I was expecting some kind of unpleasant detail. His grin widened.

"Tomorrow is Thanksgiving, and we are getting a hot kick-out."

Hot food, outta sight! I had not eaten mess hall food for several weeks, and it seemed like months. The canned combat rations (C-rations) we were forced to swallow day after day were really quite bland (even with small amounts of Tabasco sauce added) and they were getting very boring. The rations were designed to be consumed "for short durations in the field" when soldiers were not able to use the regular military chow halls. Yeah, right. On the positive side, the old C's, many of which had been canned 20 years before, made me appreciate little things, even Army cooking.

Alpha Company's morale rose immediately in our anticipation of what the good news would bring us. Little did we realize how much pain and suffering the captain's good news would really afford us.

## CHAPTER 3

# THANKSGIVING?

The company left the old *ville* and humped into a flat grassy expanse of terrain early Thanksgiving Day. The area was a safe place to chow down in celebration of the American holiday. Most of us migrated toward a stream that flowed gently through the center of our position on its way to the larger Song O Lau River. We were waiting for the supply choppers to bring us the much anticipated Thanksgiving feast. Grunts passed the time by throwing rocks into the stream or by playing a few hands of poker.

Around 1400 hours we heard the choppers off in the distance, and hungry soldiers started running toward the kick-out point. Several guys in third platoon followed a trail that led across a shallow crossing in the stream. Just as the third man entered the tributary, the water exploded around him, making a heavy *twump* sound. The soldier fell to his back in the shallow water and began to scream. His two companions immediately froze. The water had been booby-trapped.

The two soldiers carefully settled to their hands and knees and crawled to their wounded comrade, feeling their way for dangerous obstacles in the mud as they went. Other members of the platoon at the stream's edge called for the medic. They also inched toward the soldier, who was still thrashing around in blood-red water. Someone yelled that the downed soldier was the third herd RTO, Martini. I didn't know the guy, but because infantry grunts bond in a special way, he was my friend. The first of the rescuers carefully began to pull the screaming soldier out of the water. I could see that most of his left foot was missing. I watched as his buddies cut the remnants of his boot off, revealing the messy remains of his foot, held together by torn muscle.

The medic gave Martini a shot of morphine and put a tourniquet above the compress-wrapped wound. The RTO’s screams of pain lessened as the morphine did its job. One of the Thanksgiving choppers, now off-loaded, set down on that side of the river. Martini's friends carried him over and carefully set him on the bird's wide aluminum floor. The door gunners pulled him inside.

Thousands of miles from home, all we had that we could depend on was each other, and now one of us was going home. For the RTO this was not a day to give thanks. A few of Martini's closest friends yelled avenging oaths toward the olive-green bird as it lifted off and carried him away.

Metal canisters that once stored individual artillery shells now produced food. Marmite insulated food cans were in short supply, I guess. REMFs (rear echelon mother f---ers—pronounced rimph) were trying to feed a lot of soldiers, all at once. Someone must have had the bright idea to have the cooks at Camp Evans fill empty metal artillery canisters with the hot chow.

We anxiously scooped real Thanksgiving dinner onto thin paper plates. It was food like people "back in the world" were eating. I eagerly consumed turkey, potatoes, yams, dressing, and corn. The log birds had also off-loaded large stores of iced beer, soda water, and pumpkin pie. I thought I'd died and gone to heaven, until that evening when my guts were twisted in knots by food poisoning. Within minutes almost everyone in the company had joined me in the pangs of extreme intestinal misery. Perhaps the meat hadn't been cooked enough, or maybe the insides of the metal artillery canisters weren't cleaned properly. Whatever those REMFs did or did not do, Alpha Company was paying the price. My stomach went through contortions as it tied itself in complicated lumberjack knots with every breath I took. I lay on the ground rolled up in a fetal ball, hoping some gook would come out of nowhere to stick a live grenade in my pocket and end the pain.

Suddenly I had an overwhelming urge to defecate. I tried to get away from our perimeter before my rumbling bowls burst, but I did not make it. As I ran, my intestines voided themselves in a diarrheic flood. To make matters even worse, I discovered that I had no C-ration toilet paper. I usually kept several of the very small rolls in my shirt pocket, but since I had not been expecting anything unusual I just wasn't prepared. Pleading with my best buddies brought no results, as they were in the same hopeless condition. Toilet paper was suddenly worth its weight in gold nuggets. Desperately, I cut a sleeve from my shirt with my bayonet to sop up the mess from my backside and out of my jungle pants.

Since nearly all of the men in the company (125 of us) were sick with gut-wrenching dysentery, Captain Becker cancelled our assignments for recon patrols or ambushes. The captain did, however, call in an order for new jungle fatigues, as all of ours were now short-sleeved and attracting flies.

The weather continued hot and dry, opposite the cold I was accustomed to in the Rocky Mountains of Utah this time of year. Two years before, I had been a ski salesman in a large sporting goods store in Ogden City. The snow around my parents' home could be a foot deep, and at the ski resorts just a half an hour away there could be six feet of Utah's world-famous powder. Sitting on Vietnam's hard warm earth, I daydreamed of a million things I'd rather be doing in the soft snow. Early December was a great time of year for some serious after-work runs down the pure white sparkling slopes.

I grew up in a middle-class family, as did many other soldiers now transplanted to Vietnam. My father was a World War II vet; he did five years in the army infantry and cavalry, earning a Bronze Star and the Purple Heart medal. He knew jungle fighting well from those years in the Philippines, New Guinea, and Biak. After The Big One, he worked for 30 years procuring supplies and weapon systems for the U.S. Air Force—things that were now saving my life. His job was not as exciting as storming an island's coral beach, but the pay and life expectancy was better, for both of us.

My family was large, four boys and four girls, and we were very close. During my 19th and 20th years, I had been a full-time ordained missionary for my church. I taught Christian values such as peace, harmony, love, and charity. Two years later, I was fully trained in the art of war and very competent at causing death and destruction.

The fact that I was now a paid professional killer caused a certain amount of confusion in my Christian mind and heart. A Bible scripture I learned during my missionary days taught me, "To every thing there is a season, and a time to every purpose under the heaven." Several of the next verses in the third chapter of Ecclesiastes helped to ease my conflicted conscience: "A time to be born, and a time to die, a time to kill, and a time to heal, a time to weep, and a time to laugh; a time to mourn, and a time to dance. The eighth verse says: "A time to love, and a time to hate; a time of war, and a time of peace."

The receipt of my draft notice in February was unwelcome, although I had made the decision to accept it long before it came. I believed in the necessity of fighting for my country. Besides, while investigating the possibility of "joining up," the Army recruiter told me that it took eight soldiers in the rear to support every infantry soldier in the field. I guess he put that positive possibility into my head to distract me from the probable truth. Even a third-grade student could grasp the concept that the odds of becoming a ground-pounding grunt were only one out of nine. Those were good odds; the recruiter had even told me so. And even if I was selected for the infantry, I still had a good chance of being assigned to stateside duty, or maybe even Europe. He painted a pretty picture about a future of "good duty" in the Army. I could not comprehend (at the time) that the well-dressed recruiter, with colorful medals all over his chest, was leading me by the hand down the yellow brick road to a grand fairytale.

Seven months later, here I was, camping out every night, hunting and learning survival skills. I had managed to beat (or lose to) those one-in-nine odds. I had been quickly grouped with other naive dreamers, stripped of my physical individuality, and trained to be a basic front row one-move-at-a-time pawn on the United States Army's vast chess board of warriors. Unlike any other piece, I could move in just one direction: forward. Only these pawns were never really lost in the game. We were, in fact, interchangeable. If my space was taken by an enemy pawn, the Army simply replaced me with another, and continued with the game. If I stubbornly and cleverly fought my way straight ahead, all the way to the last row, and survived my encounters with the opposing army, I would be changed into a more valuable soldier (rank advancement) and turned loose on the board again with added powers to defeat the opposition.

My first pawn (infantry) duty station orders contained the famous V word.

# CHAPTER 4

# PRISONERS

The entire company spent the morning of December 2 lying around a sandy old Vietnamese graveyard. The ambush we set the night before was uneventful, so we just tried to catch up on some long-lost sleep. About noon, Captain Becker announced that some armored personnel carriers (M-113s) were on their way to pick us up and take us to a new area of operation. His news was met with some excitement, because we were not getting much sleep in the hot sun anyway, and riding on an APC sure beat humping our heavy rucks any day.

The M-113 was often called a "Green Dragon" by the VC. The vehicle was originally designed to carry a 10-man ground-pounding squad inside its inch and a half of aluminum armor, where they would be protected from small-arms fire. Actual experience in Vietnam however, changed its combat role. Soldiers were better protected from landmine injuries and the heat by riding on top of the APC. The track's greatest value to us was its effectiveness as a quick, close-support, hedgerow-busting weapons platform.

Upon the arrival of the M-113s we threw our heavy rucksacks up on the top of the tracked vehicles and climbed aboard. The APC that my squad occupied took the lead in the column of 20 noisy vehicles. The "tracks" ride was rough. Our chariots bounced over the hot, drifted sand at almost 20 miles per hour. I chose to ride on the front of the APC, in the V created after the launch bridge was lowered. I leaned back against the aluminum armor and dozed off, I guess. The next thing I heard was a burst of fire coming from the .50 cal machine gun just inches over my head.

The driver of the Armored Personnel Carrier applied the brakes quickly. In my still disoriented state, I was almost thrown from the front of the vehicle. Finally I spotted the target the .50 was pointed at. Dead ahead, about 300 meters away, I could see a Viet Cong soldier dressed in black pajamas with his hands held high. I guess the machine gunner had just fired warning shots, because it was obvious the soldier was surrendering. Behind the VC was a small jungle-covered hill about 200 meters long and 50 meters wide. The hill provided so much concealment, with the possibility of ambush, that our APC driver would not advance toward the soldier. I could hear the enemy combatant yelling the words of surrender, "*CHU HOI*! *CHU HOI*!" Trang, on a second track that had pulled up to our side, yelled a few Vietnamese words that I did not recognize, and the apparently unarmed VC soldier began walking toward us. When he got a little closer, we could see a fresh bullet wound in his side, and blood was flowing down his leg onto his Ho Chi Minh sandals. The wound was bad, but nothing like the huge hole a .50 cal bullet would have made.

After Pearson and Jakes searched the scrawny little Vietnamese communist soldier for hidden weapons and removed his web belt, the interpreter began to question our new prisoner. We learned that this guy was from one of several squads of VC hidden on the hill to our front. He said that he and a comrade were attempting to surrender to our column when they were shot from behind by their commander.

Captain Becker ordered the armored vehicles to quickly cordon the hill to prevent anyone from escaping, just in case the gook's story was true. He then called in our map coordinates to the artillery folks back at Camp Evans. That done, he gave us the order to go in and "make contact with the enemy." Alpha Company quickly assembled at the north end of the hill. On line almost shoulder to shoulder, we entered the hill's thick green jungle. Up and down the line, the safety selectors on our rifles clicked off. Most of us had rotated the switch a second click to rock and roll. We knew that at any second the jungle in front of us could erupt into a volcano of fire and red-hot lead.

Major Poulsen, standing close to me, said that he hoped the bullet with his name on it was not out there somewhere ahead in the jungle.

Pearson replied, "Don't worry about the round with your name on it; there's nothing you can do about it anyway. Just watch out for the ones marked 'To Whom It May Concern'!"

It took the company just 30 minutes to completely sweep the hill. Except for one dead VC with a bullet in his back, our search results of the undergrowth were negative. We turned around and beat our way through the thick green vegetation again, 124 jungle-experienced soldiers having found nothing.

The captain's news that we would sweep that mosquito-infested island for a third time drew much verbal defiance. Zorn was pissed off, and many of the guys rallied behind him. Most of us felt that we were wasting our time. If Luke the gook was in fact on the hill, we were lucky to be alive. The consensus was that we should fall back and call in the prearranged artillery, crater up the hill a little bit, and then leave. Contrary to our bitches and wishes, Captain Becker ordered us in a third time.

Just ten meters into the jungle, someone on the far side of the hill excitedly yelled, "I found one, I found one!" Word quickly passed up the line to look for small holes under the thick bushes we had been carefully stepping over. No sooner had we been told that than Pearson on my left and Zorn on the right each pulled up bushes revealing small openings in the earth. The holes were so small that they could have been covered by a large Frisbee. I felt my heart begin to throb as my finger gently caressed the trigger in anticipation of what the earth might produce. Simultaneously, hands appeared first at each of the two holes, quickly followed by black-haired, dark-skinned Viet Cong soldiers. I shoved the flash suppressor of my weapon firmly, hard enough to cause a bruise, against one soldier's forehead, and began yelling, "*Lai day, lai day*." It was the closest Vietnamese I knew to "Get out of the hole!"

I leaned him up against a tree, kicked his legs far apart, and searched him thoroughly, as if he may be hiding a secret gum wrapper with which he could later attack me. My search between his legs revealed that he was a she. Surprise! Her black pajama-style clothing, hairstyle, and lack of facial hair were just like that of a young VC man. I was not immediately sure what to do with a female captive. The company commander detailed major Poulsen to quickly deliver the two gooks to the nearest APC while we continued to search the area. Other American soldiers with us wanted to "search" the female themselves, in case I had missed anything.

We discovered that under each of the two entrance holes was a room roughly one square meter in size. The skinny little soldier had squeezed down into their spider holes and simply pulled thick thorny bushes over the top of them to conceal the entrances, thus disappearing from possible detection. It was a clever way to hide. Now that we'd figured it out, we located and captured a total of 16 Vietnamese communists, including another woman, in our next two sweeps. They just kept popping up as we kicked small vegetation out of the way.

We found a cache of 27 rusty old 20-gallon tin cans full of rice, and a large assortment of medical supplies. We also recovered an AK-

47 assault rifle and a pistol of an unknown make. The two weapons were all we found. These were poorly armed local-yokel Viet Cong. *The derogatory name Viet Cong became the norm long before I arrived in country, even among the Vietnamese communists themselves.*

It was obvious why they had elected not to fight—no firepower. The find dealt a considerable blow to the enemy's manpower and logistics in the area. Within an hour of our last sweeps, several chopper loads of senior Army officers and their armed security landed. A senior officer getting wounded, or Lord forbid killed, in a combat zone was not acceptable, hence the security. The officers paraded around for a while and then congratulated us on a job well done. An Army photographer traveling with them took pictures of the officers and the prisoners "they" had captured. The REMF officers would undoubtedly earn fancy medals—something they could wear on their dress uniforms—for what we had accomplished. As far as I know no grunt was awarded anything.

# CHAPTER 5

# LEECHES

By 2200 hours, on the fourth day after capturing the hill prisoners, the captain had organized the company into platoon-size ambushes. Our platoon's position was in an old abandoned *ville* 15 or 16 klicks northwest of our base, Camp Evans. The jungle had reclaimed the entire area, except for the narrow trail, originally a small dirt road, that led through the center of the hamlet. The dirt path was well beaten, evidence of substantial foot traffic.

Upon reaching the designated ambush site, after a two-hour hump, the fatigued platoon collapsed along the trail and waited for further instructions. Soldiers leaned against their sweaty rucks and alternately watched the darkness on each side of the trail. I inverted my helmet and sat in it. My brain needed cooling more than my butt did.

In groups of three, Lieutenant DeWitt guided us to our specific ambush areas of responsibility. The platoon leader placed me with Haskell and Bennett, both from third squad, as rear security for the rest of the platoon, spread out 20 meters off the trail's north side. Our position was in a small clearing about 40 meters off the path, about the same distance from the closest fire-team. The three of us were surrounded by a thicket of old dried bamboo that creaked and groaned in protest every time a slight breeze tried to fight its way through.

Bennett was a tall soul brother from St. Louis. We were both fans of the Cardinals baseball and football teams and we would collaborate when arguing with other team fans. I had every confidence in his ability to protect Haskell and myself while we slept. Haskell was a different story. He was a full-blooded Choctaw Indian from Oklahoma and, contrary to the stereotype that Indian braves are excellent warriors, the "Chief" was a dud. He was all right during daylight hours, but at night we could not keep him awake. By the time we had settled in and got our claymore mines out, only six hours of darkness remained.

*A claymore is a highly explosive mine designed to throw all of its deadly projectiles in one direction. Rather than being buried in the ground like most anti-personnel mines, this defensive weapon stands upright on edge facing the direction of the oncoming enemy. The front of the mine is filled with hundreds of small steel balls. The plastic explosive (C4) behind the projectiles is detonated remotely by a firing device connected to the blasting cap via a long wire. When a soldier squeezes the firing device (clacker) and the claymore explodes, all of the deadly steel shrapnel flies in a fan-shaped spray toward the intended targets (enemy ground soldiers) up to 50 meters away. Newton's third law demanded that the mine be placed as far away from the clacker as possible to avoid the back-blast. American claymores were about as thick and tall as a 500-page paperback book and three times wider. The North Vietnamese equivalent, shaped like a discus, could measure up to three feet across.*

After a brief whispered discussion, the three of us decided to each take two one-hour guard shifts, and since the Chief was already awake, we let him start. It was very unlikely that enemy soldiers would attempt to stumble through the thick bamboo that Bennett, Haskell, and I were in. Any nighttime traffic would follow the easy route, the trail we now had heavily ambushed.

I lay back on the spongy damp earth, using my helmet for a pillow, and quickly fell asleep. Two hours later, Bennett woke me up by gently shaking my foot.

"Sergeant Rock, it's your turn for guard," he whispered.

I sat up, cradling my M-16 in my arms. It had been lying across my chest, as it did every time I slept. After a brief stretch, I quietly duck-walked the five steps to where the claymore firing devices lay on the ground and sat down beside them. The night was still, but a three-quarter moon was directly overhead. It provided great night vision for anyone on the move, and for we who ambushed them.

After half an hour of staring into the moonlit darkness and listening to the small animal noises coming from the dry bamboo, my tongue started playing with a water blister that had somehow formed inside my cheek while I slept. I decided to examine the blister a little closer. I found my two-by-three inch mirror in one of the rucksack pockets and then quietly pulled my poncho from the sleeping area to the guard point. I slowly covered myself with it. Once enshrouded, I tore a paper match from the others in the book and struck it. I then bit down on the blister. Blood splattered all over my little mirror. It was not a water blister in my mouth but a slimy land leech! I guess it had crawled into my mouth while I was sleeping. It had attached itself to the blood-rich flesh inside my cheek. That inch-long leech was what I had been sucking on as I sat on the ground intently watching nothing.

A month earlier and back home, touching a leech would have scared me half to death. But after just three weeks in the jungles of Vietnam, I was no longer afraid of the little buggers. Wisdom came from the lessons I'd learned. I tried to pull the leech out of my mouth with my fingers, but it was much too slippery. Nothing left to do but chew it off in pieces and spit it out.

Because of my preoccupation with the leech, I had failed to keep track of the time. When I finally pulled my watch out from under my shirtsleeve, I was angry to find I had already sat through 15 minutes of the Chief's watch. To make matters even worse, I knew it would take at least another 15 minutes to get him up.

I reasoned that if I could get a cup of hot coffee in his hands my job would be easier. Digging into my rucksack again, I found a foil-sealed heat tablet and a paper box of C-rations. In the box, I located a B-1a unit. I opened the can with my trusty P-38 can-opener and dumped the desiccated crackers into my shirt pocket. As best I could in the darkness, I poured a packet of instant coffee into the empty can and added a half cup of water from my canteen. A jolt of hot, caffeine-rich black coffee was what the chief needed. With two fingers, I scratched a small trench three inches deep into the soft black earth and placed the heat tab in it. Again I covered myself with my poncho before tearing off and striking the paper match.

The heat tab gave off a soft blue flame; the glow was almost impossible to see above my finger's micro-excavation. With the can resting on the ground above the trench, I impatiently waited for the coffee to steam. When the tab finally burned itself out, I picked the can up by its peeled-back lid and carried the boiling coffee over to the sleeping Chief. I shook him gently at first, but quickly got more violent when he failed to react.

"Huh!" he finally said, rather loudly.

The yawning Chief then mumbled some spicy language about being awake and sat up. I handed him the coffee. He again muttered several four-letter words when he touched the sides of the hot can. At last, he stumbled over to the guard post and took a sip of the black brew. I lay back on my poncho and went to sleep.

I was abruptly awakened by Bennett's voice in my ear breaking the morning calm.

"You jackass, you're sleeping on guard!"

I sat up so quickly my rifle flipped off my chest and its full weight landed on my right shin. I grabbed my leg and began to rub the soon-to-be bruise as I tried to remember the night's sequence of events. Bennett, who had been sleeping next to me, rose up on one elbow with a pissed-off stare. It finally registered that he was not looking at but past me. I turned my head to see where he was looking. The sun's early morning rays filtered through the tall bamboo, revealing the prostrate Chief still at the guard post. Slowly Haskell sat up and sleepily looked around at us. He immediately received another verbal blast from Bennett that began with, "You S. O. B . . . !" The droopy-eyed Chief at first claimed the FNG (me) didn't wake him up. The fact that he was at the guard post with a nearly empty can of coffee proved my counter-argument, and finally he just shrugged his shoulders. Before Bennett had a chance to express any more expletives, Lieutenant DeWitt walked up from our rear.

"Saddle up; we're moving out."

While we rolled up the claymore wires, I told Bennett about my experience with the leech during the night. He suggested we take our shirts off, drop our pants and check each other for more of the blood suckers. We did. Bennett and I were free of the carnivorous critters, but the Chief was not. An inch-long leech had attached itself right on the end of Chief's pecker. I took the little plastic bottle of mosquito repellent off my helmet and gave the leech a liberal squirt. It wiggled and squirmed and eventually fell off. Then, due to the repellent's sharp sting, good ol' Chief also wiggled and squirmed, but nothing else fell off . . . darn! Bennett and I looked at each other and grinned.

# CHAPTER 6

# NVA

Several days after my experience with the leeches, helicopters off-loaded us at the edge of a heavy stand of tall trees covering several square kilometers. Supposedly inside the cordon we were forming around the trees that afternoon were several VC who had decided to *chu hoi*. We were there to make sure they could not do otherwise.

As one of three companies participating in the cordon, Battalion ordered Captain Becker to spread Alpha's men along a wide rice paddy dike separating the yet-to-be planted bogs. The captain positioned my platoon along the raised dike first. It was six meters wide and thick with waist-high foliage. A trail ran down its middle. Behind us for about a klick and a half was nothing more than vacant but knee-deep paddies of brown water, separated by elevated dikes like ours. To our front was a single 50-meter-wide paddy. Beyond that was the heavily wooded area containing the VC soldiers. Since we were attempting to take prisoners, the captain ordered us not to fire unless we were fired upon.

It looked like this was going to be a slow day. Three companies of American soldiers were tasked with capturing two or three little gooks, and we had to wait for them to come to us. We could handle that. Welcoming the chance to rest, many soldiers crawled into the shade of small bushes and began to re-read mail or old paperbacks.

About 2100 hours, I stood up to stretch and check out the paddy in our front. As usual, nothing was happening. I turned around to sit back down. Suddenly in front of me there were six NVA soldiers with packs on their backs and AK-47s on their shoulders. They were behind where we were watching, walking along a narrow dike that paralleled ours, just 50 meters away. They had not seen us yet. I dropped to my knees behind cover and frantically hand-signaled what I had seen to the rest of the squad. Pearson quickly told Lieutenant DeWitt, who immediately got on the radio; he requested permission to fire. The company RTO responded that Captain Becker was not at the command post but he would find him and get back to us ASAP. We did not want the NVA to have the advantage of firing first, so we just continued peeking through the foliage watching the gooks walk and walk and walk . . .

Fifteen minutes later, when it was too late to engage the North Vietnamese soldiers with our small arms, we received permission to "light 'em up." The NVA were a klick and a half to our rear by then. They were just entering another wooded area when our artillery shells began landing in the vicinity. It was too dark for us to judge the effect. The way our luck had been lately, we probably missed them anyway. The captain's "no fire" order had prevented us from blowing a good ambush on the gooks. They never knew how close they had been to becoming rice paddy fertilizer.

The captain immediately called a staff strategy meeting, to include the all platoon leaders and platoon sergeants. Captain Becker was really irritated that Lieutenant DeWitt could not tell the difference between two surrendering VC and a squad of armed North Vietnamese combat soldiers, and for not taking the responsibility to make the "obvious" decision "and kill the damn gooks." That was all the lieutenant would tell us when he returned from the dress-down session. I think he still blamed the captain for the situation, but he would not say it in front of us. I guess he and the other lieutenants had gotten their butts chewed real good by the irate red-faced company commander.

Captain Becker was a graduate of West Point, and he spoke with the authority his black captain's bars and the company's leadership responsibility gave him. He was only 28 years old, but we often called him the "The Old Man." The phrase was a respectful one. Captain Becker's word was the law, and the poor lieutenants now had to decide when it was safe to countermand his orders.

Lieutenant DeWitt passed down the captain's order to maintain our cordon through the night. We stomped down the vegetation and set up poncho tents. We kept our rucks mostly packed, in case we received middle-of-the-night orders to move out and sure enough, we did.

I guess the REMFs decided that o-dark-thirty would be a good time to check on the six gooks. Lieutenant DeWitt came around to each position and ordered us to leave everything behind except our weapons and our basic loads of ammo. Dropping most of our stuff, we fumbled our way in the dark to the rally point where 10 huge M-48 Patton tanks met us.

This was my first experience working with the 50-ton

behemoths. Their physical size and appearance were awesome, and feelings of invincibility swept over me when I eagerly climbed aboard and found a place to sit.

I had seen these big boys racing down the dirt road in front of Camp Evans, clearing the highway of any landmines that may have been placed there during the night. Their successful mine detection sometimes resulted in the loss of a rubber-shoed track and maybe a steel road wheel, but both could easily be fixed or replaced; damage to a tank beyond that seldom happened. Previously, morning sweeps down the highway involved brave soldiers with handheld mine detectors. That was a slow and very dangerous process, sometimes delaying for many hours the truck convoys of desperately needed supplies.

As we rumbled off into the night, it struck me that we were going in the wrong direction from the cordoned area. I leaned over and asked Pearson what was going on. He hollered above the deep roar and sharp clanks of the tank that we were circling to come in the back door. We hoped to force the gooks out of hiding and into the open rice paddies.

After an hour of riding and sleeping, we dismounted the lumbering chariots and began a ground sweep of the area. Spotlights mounted above the big guns on the tanks lit up, piercing the blackness. The light exposed everything to our front, everything that is, except a well-hidden booby-trap. Almost immediately an explosion seventy-five meters to my left brought cries of "Medic!" and "Doc!" In the darkness I could not see what was happening or who had been hit, but within 60 seconds the grunt grapevine answered both questions.

Sergeant Smith—Smitty—was the only soldier I knew of the four unlucky men who got hit. He was a soft-spoken squad leader, much respected by his men. The left side of his body looked like a shotgun had blasted it. Several medics rushed to his side and cut his jungle fatigues off. The first aid practitioners tried to plug all the little holes and stop the flow of blood. Even though Smitty was only semi-conscious, it took four big soldiers to hold him down while Doc Bayne gave him a morphine shot.

The other three soldiers who were hit by the booby-trapped grenade were in much better shape, I thought. The squad leader had taken the brunt of the blast. Smitty's wounds would get him sent back to the world (but he would be OK.)

"The others," Doc confirmed, "will be back on the line in a

couple of weeks."

Within 10 minutes of the blast, a medevac chopper hovered above us, awaiting landing directions. My hate for booby-traps had just taken another giant leap.

After the medevac had evacuated Smitty and the other three, we resumed our search, but we found nothing. The element of surprise had been lost. Several hours had passed since we had begun the misadventure, and we were anxious to get back to our rucks where it was safe and we could get some sleep. Again the tanks rumbled off into the black night with their parasite cargo of infantry. A few tiny stars peeking through the cloudy sky provided very little illumination for the drivers. I was glad I did not have the responsibility of keeping the mammoth tanks out of the rice paddies.

Upon reaching our original rally point, everyone in the squad jumped off the armored vehicle and began walking back down the dike toward our previous position. We quickly discovered that one of the M-48s had evidently rumbled down this same dike. It had crushed vegetation on both sides of the narrow trail. As we continued, we passed several other squad positions that had been destroyed by the tracked monster. Our own spot on the trail was no luckier. Our bamboo and poncho tents lay flat against the earth, as did the rucksacks and everything else we had left behind. My once bulging ruck was unrecognizable; its magnesium frame was twisted like a pretzel. Everything in the nylon sack was smashed. Even the green boonie towel that I used to cushion my shoulders from the rucksack straps and wipe the salty sweat from my eyes was shredded.

The tank had destroyed my light antitank weapon (LAW), claymore, machine gun ammo, flares, and smoke grenades. Cans of C-rations were pancaked against each other. Everything was covered by greasy, gooey globs of beans and franks, ham and eggs, peanut butter, beef and potatoes, and who knows what else.

Early in the morning, after his conversation with Captain Becker, Lieutenant DeWitt told Sergeant Pearson, who (following the chain of command) then instructed us to burn all of the mashed ordnance. We piled everything on the dike. Pearson lit a piece of C4 from a destroyed claymore, threw it into the pile, and ran. From 100 meters away, behind an earthen dike, we watched the intense fire burn. Occasionally there were the popcorn sounds of machine gun ammo "cooking off." When it was safe, Pearson verified that nothing remained except scorched earth and a mix of melted metals. Still an

FNG, I got the detail to bury the mess.

Since we were going to get new rucks and ammo, Sergeant Pearson asked me if I would carry the M-79 grenade launcher. He said Jakes had carried the launcher for several months and had requested a change of weapons. I recognized the need for a ‘79 in the squad, so I agreed. Shooting grenades might even be fun, I thought. The weapon only weighed 6.5 lbs, which was less than an 8.5-pound M-16 rifle. During the exchange I discovered that the M-79 also came with a 10-pound basic load of high- explosive grenades. I hadn’t counted on that.

Later that morning the lieutenant walked down to our position and informed us that our cordon was "successful." At 0630 three gooks surrendered to Delta Company on the far side of the encircled trees. We never again brought up the subject of our encounter with the NVA squad. Some stories were like gooks: they were better left dead.

"It cost us four wounded to capture the three gooks," the platoon leader confided. "At this rate every male in America can get drafted and sent to Vietnam, and we'll still end up short of soldiers to fight this damn war."

For the next week or ten days, we "worked" in the same general area. Nothing much got accomplished during the day. My squad lay around in the shade of bushes, playing cards, smoking bowls of grass, or writing letters. At night we set up our ambushes on the little-used trails. This area was "safe” for us, there hadn’t been any real gook activity anywhere near this place for a long time. We stayed alert for booby-traps but found no more of them. Our suntans got darker and our spirits got lighter; Christmas was just around the corner.

## CHAPTER 7

# CHRISTMAS

A few days before Christmas, a resupply chopper brought us a new target for Sir Charles to shoot at. The captain assigned him to our squad. He introduced himself as Ed Moran, but said that friends called him "Bugs." He claimed he was a Hell's Angel from Las Vegas, Nevada and, based on pictures he showed us of himself with his Harley Hog and the "Born to Raise Hell" tattoo on his left shoulder, I supposed he really was.

The first thing he wanted to know was where he could get a little grass and if it was good stuff. Jakes answered both questions:

"Almost anywhere. It's good shit."

Maybe 60 percent of the guys were pot-smoking "Heads." They disappeared frequently to "socialize" around a bowl (marijuana pipe.) Beer chugging "Juicers" comprised another 80 percent. Obviously, many of the guys were both, and a few, like me, did neither. I could see that the Heads had just increased by one. Jakes took Bugs under his wing and introduced him to the other Heads. That evening when I saw him next, he had drawn a skull and crossbones on his helmet. The skull was smoking a joint.

On our last day in the area, I got a package from home. It contained some goodies I had requested in one of the first letters to my parents. The squad gathered around and we feasted on homemade sugar cookies, Jiffy Pop Popcorn (popped over heat tabs), licorice, sardines, and Tang drink mix. The most prized object in the box was a pair of thick, soft, green socks. I shared that prize with no one. The one and only pair of Army-issue socks I owned had been on my feet for over a month. They were wet and had never been in the company of soap. Most of the old-timers were suffering from jungle rot because their feet were never dry. Now that I had new dry socks, I thought I could postpone the inevitable. I peeled the stiff aromatic old stockings off my feet and tied them to the back of my rucksack. I'd save them for when I needed a "fresh" pair.

I stretched the new socks over my wet, wrinkled feet. They felt as fine as the fur-lined leather gloves I'd gotten for Christmas the year before. I delayed putting on my muddy boots for as long as possible. Pearson's order, however, to "Pack it up, we're moving out," hurried the decision.

Pearson said that a medevac chopper pilot had spotted gooks in a rice paddy two klicks away from us, and we had been elected to check out the report.

"Several Hueys are on the way to pick us up. Sergeant Rock, get those boots on and let's break those civilian socks in right."

Choppers delivered the squad to the proper map coordinates, but we could see nothing from the air except sunlight reflected off the rice paddies. The Hueys settled to water level and we reluctantly jumped into mud and water up to our chests. My new, dry socks were history. We sloshed around for about an hour looking for breathing tubes sticking out of the water, but none existed. Tired, wet and muddy, we re-boarded the Hueys, and the chopper jockeys flew us back to the day defense position.

That evening at 1930 hours we were flown to the outskirts of Phong Dien. It was a sleepy little village of about a hundred families, on Route 1, just a klick from Camp Evans. Because the Christmas "stand down" was only a few days away, some personnel logistics needed to be done a little ahead of time.

Phong Dien was unusually quiet, considering that there was a huge U.S. military facility next door. The usual black market activity went on, but the bars and whorehouses (called boom-boom houses in local slang) typically found next to bases were not as visually prominent as in the big cites. Children 5 to 12 years of age were everywhere. They were "businessmen," out to hustle a buck from the G.I.s. Whatever a soldier was in the market for, children could procure and deliver. It was not unusual to see the kids holding sandbags full of hash, marijuana, and whiskey as they bargained with a soldier. In 15 minutes, these young hustlers could return with an order for cocaine, heroin, or a beautiful young prostitute. They were wise to the ways of the world way beyond their years.

The male head of a household, a papa san, did well if he earned 50 cents a day while working for some Vietnamese enterprise. By trading with the G.I.s fresh from many long days in the jungle, the children could quickly make enormous amounts of money by Vietnamese standards. At five dollars a quickie, a prostitute could afford to live well and look good.

We enjoyed the few days spent in and around the village, for all the right and wrong reasons. The village people seemed to like us, and they treated us well. Children told us the communists were "number frigging ten thousand" (the scale went from one down to ten as a measurement of popularity, with an automatic jump to ten thousand if someone really wanted to make a negative point.) The area was semi-secure from enemy soldiers, and we liked that also.

In Phong Dien I could get all the local Vietnamese food I could eat, and American soda water was cheap. They were great supplements to canned C-rations and river water. On one of the days in the *ville*, Minnie, our New York City tunnel rat, caught a convoy truck back to the base camp, where Doc had sent him to get a penicillin shot for the clap. When he returned, Minnie passed out six duffel bags that he had "midnight requisitioned" from the supply shack. We took the pilfered duffel bags to a local Vietnamese tailor shop. For a couple of bucks the tailor cranked up his pedal-operated sewing machine and turned them all into ammo vests, each holding 21 M-16 magazines—the basic load for a rifleman. The six of us were the envy of the entire company, and the supply sergeant at Camp Evans had to put the remaining bags under lock and key.

Christmas Eve was like every other hot and humid day, except on this particular day the REMFs allowed us *en masse* on their hallowed ground. At noon, trucks took us to Alpha Company headquarters at Camp Evans. All of the company headquarters buildings (Alpha, Bravo, Charlie, Delta, and Echo) looked the same, and they were all neatly lined up on one side of the dirt street. Each hootch was identified by its own company flag on a tall pole and its “original” display of painted white rocks. The small white rock path in front of Alpha Co. made the area real homey and comfortable. The rocks and paint also gave the new guys something to do while awaiting their chance to end the war.

Officers slept in little cubicles behind a plywood wall separating them from the working end of the HQ building. Behind the headquarters and supply buildings were the tin-roofed hootches that provided sleeping places for the junior NCOs and enlisted men when they came in for stand-downs such as this. It was first come, first served for the wood and canvas cots—everyone else slept on the plywood floor. Way out in the back was the six-hole latrine.

Across the street from Alpha and Bravo HQs was the battalion mess hall. It was the closest building to the fighting bunkers and concertina wire that surrounded the Camp Evans perimeter.

Everything was nice and orderly.

The supply sergeant said he wasn't ready to assign hootches yet, so he told us to go get some chow. With rifles still in our hands, we beelined it to the mess hall. A big barrel-chested, pizza-faced mess sergeant stood protectively at the door. In one long sentence, containing at least 20 expletives, he informed us that we were not welcome in his building. I have to admit the guy had guts, even if he wasn't too bright. He told 125 armed jungle animals that we "smelled like shit!" I had not had a bath for over a month, and for some of us it had been a lot longer than that. Considering where we had just come from, with its scarcity for the finer things of life, we thought he should show us a little consideration and make an exception. He didn't and wouldn't. We angrily wandered back to company HQ, threatening to get even.

Captain Becker announced to the company that REMFs were assembling portable showers over the hill, but that they would not be ready for at least another two hours, so he said to just hang loose. Only 30 seconds away from hot mess-hall food, we sat Indian style on the ground and ate our cold and greasy 20-year-old C-rats.

At the showers we peeled off our crusty green uniforms. We threw the filthy sun-bleached jungle fatigues into a pile, and they were burned. The same supply sergeant that sent us to chow then opened several cases of disinfectant scrub. He issued a bottle of the 12-ounce liquid soap to each of us and told us to *use it all*! After we exited the shower and dried ourselves in the afternoon sun, the sergeant gave us new olive-drab fatigues. He then sent us to the Vietnamese barbers who were standing by with orange-crate chairs and manually operated hair clippers. When the assembly-line procedure was finished, we looked good, but a lion with a poodle trim is still a lion. Our dispositions remained the same: a lot of pent-up frustration, anger, and youthful energy was waiting to explode, and the REMFs chow line fiasco had not helped.

Captain Becker turned us loose for the next few hours. The only orders he gave us were to stay within the Camp Evans perimeter and return to the company compound by 1800 hours. There was no way he could keep track of us. It would be like stepping on a hill of angry red ants and then trying to organize them into formation. Some of the guys smuggled themselves outside the wire, looking for girls despite the order. Most of us headed for the Post Exchange (PX) or one of the several clubs.

The PX was packed with soldiers from the many different units all in for the two-day Christmas stand-down. I loaded up on snack foods and film for my camera, and then returned to the hootch where I had thrown my gear. I stuffed my prized goods into my rucksack, to be eaten during leaner times.

By 1800 hours, our officers and a few REMFs had assembled some old oil drums that had been cut in half and converted into large barbecue cookers. The company area smelled of thick steaks as they sizzled over the charcoal. A trailer loaded with ice, beer, and soda water was left for us to do with as we pleased. Someone had hung green and red paper ornaments on a communications antenna to remind us that this was Christmas Eve. A scratchy phonograph record, "I'm Dreaming of a White Christmas," played repeatedly from the compound loudspeakers. We picked the steaks off the hot cookers with our hands and devoured them like a pack of starved dogs. Civilities be damned.

The sky that had begun to cloud up in the late afternoon broke loose with heavy rain about sundown. The downpour caused cancellation of the "skin flick" scheduled for 2100 hours behind the mess hall. By midnight, 75 percent of the battalion was drunk and/or stoned. Soldiers were scattered in little groups around their hootches and bunkers.

One group of inebriates from Bravo Company decided they would steal the flags that flew above each of the five company headquarters in the battalion. They were successful down at Echo Company, but when they tried it at our sandbagged building, some Alpha Company drunks caught them. I stood outside the opposing mobs that quickly formed, not as unwisely brave as some of the whiskey-fortified guys were. Words of challenge from the drunken soldiers were hurled back and forth. When an unseen face with a big mouth from Alpha Company shouted, "Pinprick is an a--hole," Sergeant Pincock from Bravo Company took it personally. The center of the mobs became a pile of swinging and kicking humanity. With no consideration at all, they completely messed up our militarily-aligned little white rocks.

Just about the time I thought I would become involved, Captain Becker burst through the clerks' office screen door and fired three single rounds from an M-16 up into the blackened rain-filled sky.

The yelling stopped and bodies unpiled. With fire (maybe they were just bloodshot) in his eyes, the company commander pronounced an expletive-filled Scotch blessing. It began with, “What the hell is going on out here?” and ended with, "Save your damned energy for Victor Charlie. All five companies are moving out at 0900 tomorrow!"

None of the combatants were really mad at anyone; it was just a way of releasing built-up emotion. Soldiers who fight one night may risk their lives for each other the next.

Everyone soon drifted off in little groups again to revel in their bravery. By first light, both sides would have invented stories of pugilistic superiority. I don't know when the others figured it out, but the thought hit me as I walked back to my hootch to get some sleep: Captain Becker said we were moving out in the morning. That meant they had just cut our two-day stand-down in half. Not knowing whether it was our fault or if they had planned it all along, I stood in the pouring rain pissed off at all officers, REMFs, the Army and even my drunk buddies—everybody.

Long before I reached my hootch, I could hear Motown sounds blasting away from inside. The room was full of celebrating soul brothers, and two of them jumped me as I walked in the door.

"Stay in your own territory, Whitey,” said the bigger of the two "bloods" as he violently shoved me against the door frame.

Before I had the time to make an unwise decision that would have resulted in my face blocking a few fists, I was saved!

"Leave 'em alone! He's OK!" someone shouted from the far side of the candle-lit room.

I recognized Bennett's voice. Figuring it was a good time to do an about face, I grabbed the poncho and a bag of mashed potato chips out of my rucksack and executed a strategic retreat.

Determined to get some sleep, I wandered around visiting other hootches. They were all rockin with partying soldiers. My soda water-filled stomach could not compete with their beer bellies, so I refused any more invitations to party. Finally, I joined some guys who were lying on a four-foot tall sandbag wall that surrounded the supply hootch. The sandbags were rock hard from years of rain and baking in the sun, but I was too tired to care. I pulled the poncho over me and went to sleep in the rain.

I had not been sleeping long when M-16 rifle fire blew the sandman's dust from my eyes. Instinctively, I rolled off the wall and splashed into the mud on the ground between the hootch and the sandbags. My rifle was lying on my cot in my hootch, and I suddenly felt naked without it. Rain poured off the corrugated steel roof and down my neck as I carefully peered (Kilroy was here) over the wall.

Thirty-five meters away, behind our hootches were 8 or 10 grunts. I was relieved to see that the shooting was not incoming. My partying buddies were shooting tracer bullets into the sky and laughing. Too much whiskey, beer, and cheap wine had led to dangerous celebrating. Soon they started tossing fragmentation grenades into a large grass field behind our company area. They "grooved" on the flashes of light and the concussions. I didn't want any of my friends to get hurt, but I also did not want to accidentally get shot trying to stop them. I decided to stay where I was in the mud, and go back to sleep. They would pay for their drinking in the morning. A hangover is the wrath of grapes.

During the morning formation and roll call, Lieutenant Colonel Capalitti, the battalion commander, stood us at attention for an hour while he expressively chewed our butts. To put it mildly, he was "upset" with the night's activities. Besides everything else that had happened, someone had fragged the mess sergeant. A grenade tossed onto the floor of his plywood hootch had blown it apart. The double mattress cot he'd been sleeping on saved his life. The REMF had never heard the sound of combat or even seen smoke on the horizon. He would now go home with hero stories about war being hell. And he would have grenade wounds to prove it.

The irate commander said that he suspected Alpha Company was involved in the fragging. He told us that there would be a full military investigation into the incident (if there was an investigation nothing ever came of it.) He finally released us to go about our business of preparing for the field.

Everyone in Vietnam carried dangerous weapons and knew how to use them. Officers or NCOs, who may have otherwise tended to obnoxiously showcase their rank authority, were much more cautious about needlessly and unwisely flaunting that behavior. Sometimes those who would dangerously grandstand found themselves the recipient of "friendly fire." The judge and jury were in the hands of he who packed the weapon. In a combat zone, strict military law is often relegated to the backseat of the slow-moving jeep of justice.

## CHAPTER 8

# THE AMBUSH

Four huge Chinook helicopters airlifted the company 12 klicks west from Camp Evans to the base of the Annamite Mountains. Captain Becker briefed us that the area was heavily booby-trapped and that we should be unusually careful where we walked. A South Vietnamese company had taken heavy casualties while on a recon mission in the same area just a short time earlier.

Gunships prepped the LZ moments before we were inserted. Our Chinooks then quickly settled into the freshly blasted grey haze, and we charged down the rear ramp door. No opposition—so far so good. We were on the ground only a few hours, however, when the Charlie Company RTO called to warn us that they had just lost two men to a booby-trapped frag. Not so good. Charlie Company had been inserted several klicks north of us.

The terrain was mostly flat, dried-up rice paddies. Sharp-edged elephant grass grew up to our elbows in most places, so we kept our shirt sleeves rolled down to prevent the stinging "paper cuts." One of our point men found several well-worn trails and still-warm ashes from a cooking fire. We knew there were gooks in the area. At dusk, the three platoons in the company separated and formed independent NDPs. The night defensive positions were about a klick apart. The night was uneventful for each of the platoons—at least, that was the report just before sunup. When it came time to move out, the third platoon found the wires to two of their claymores cut and the mines missing.

The fact that Luke the gook was brave enough to crawl up and steal our claymore mines prompted the lieutenant to order the normal guard doubled for the next few nights. He also decided to divide the third squad so that first and second squads each got half of the men, figuring it was better to have two full-strength squads than three weak ones. He assigned Haskell, Wood, Jacobs, and Sonognini to our squad. Jacobs and Sonognini carried M-79 grenade launchers like I did; the other two soldiers were riflemen. The squad now totaled thirteen men.

We carried out normal squad patrols all that second day but saw no fresh signs of enemy activity. About 1700 hours, our squads rejoined to eat our C-rats. Just before dark, my squad left to set up our own NDP. We quietly followed a narrow little path that led us into a thick entanglement of gnarled jungle vines and broadleaf trees. It was supposed to be an uneventful little hump of 300 meters, but the calm we expected was broken by the unmistakable thump, thump, thump, of a mortar tube just 50 meters away.

"Get down, incoming!"

Thinking we were about to be the recipients of three mortar shells, Sergeant Pearson yelled the warning and dove into the undergrowth. The rest of us scattered to both sides of the trail. The mortar shells swooshed overhead but exploded back by the other squad we had just left.

The jungle was too thick for us to see to see more than 10 or 15 meters.

Pearson whispered, "Stay low, and we'll ambush them if they come this way."

We quietly backed into the palm fronds on the right side of the trail and squatted, listening for movement. We waited for half an hour until it got dark, then moved about 100 meters in the opposite direction of the noisy mortar and quietly set up for the night.

While I was standing my first guard watch, Lieutenant DeWitt called us on the radio from the other squad's location. He informed us that they had suffered no casualties. The enemy mortar rounds had fallen short.

"I've got a really bad feeling about this area," he said, "so pay attention."

The morning sun was a welcome sight, now we could safely catch up on the sleep we had missed during the night. We laid low in our jungle hideaway until about noon, and then joined the other squad searching for Sir Charles and his mortar tube. During the early afternoon hump, major screw-up Poulsen collapsed from heat exhaustion or some kind of flu. He went into convulsions, so we called in a medevac chopper to take him to the hospital. The dust-off arrived right on the map coordinates we had given it. Sonognini threw a yellow smoke to identify the exact landing spot we had selected. Drifting smoke identified the upwind approach to the fast-approaching pilot. The big Hawaiian stood in the center of the LZ with his arms extended skyward like he was praising the Lord at a Mississippi tent revival. Using a few hand and arm signals, he gave landing instructions to the sky jockey, who brought the bird in for a smooth landing.

Sonognini was a powerfully built kid, typical of many island football athletes that were beginning to show up on my home state (Utah) collegiate teams. The guy could run through a bunker wall; we would then have to call a medevac for the poor sandbags.

The bright yellow smoke and the landing helicopter quickly gave away our position to anybody watching, but we had no other choice; we had to get Poulsen out. The extraction proved uneventful. We were two klicks from the mountains, so it would be difficult for an enemy force to attack us and then retreat to the safety of their sanctuaries, all under the cover of darkness. To make that scenario even less likely, Pearson decided to move us into our final ambush destination after sundown.

An hour and a half before the sun disappeared over the horizon, we took a break between six water-filled bomb craters blasted into the earth maybe two years earlier. Bugs Moran, sitting on the edge of one of the stagnant ponds, motioned for me to come over.

"Sergeant Rock, come here and look at this," he said.

I dropped my rucksack and walked over to him. In the pond were dozens of two-inch-long fish. When he threw a few grains of sand in the water, the fish all swarmed to that spot.

Pearson, who had been on the radio most of the time, signed off and sauntered over to Bugs and me.

"Stay here with the rest of the squad," he said. "Zorn, Washington, and I are taking the radio. We're going to check out the hill over there."

He pointed to a small brush-covered rise identified as hill "51" on the map. The number told us the height of the hill (or any other terrain feature) in meters. The little knob was the highest ground in the area, 51 meters above sea level.

"If it looks good, we'll set a tiger (ambush) there after dark."

Realizing that this was going to be an extended break, I walked back to my rucksack and found a B-1a unit. I took a couple of crackers out of the can and returned to Bugs and the fish pond. We crumbled pieces of the crackers in our fingers and threw them into the water. The tiny fish again swarmed after the bits of food as it settled in the mud. It was like feeding goldfish in a bowl.

While Bugs and I sat there entertained by the fish, two F-4 jet fighters suddenly roared over our heads at treetop level. Halfway up the mountain, 10 seconds in front of the fighters, a puff of white smoke filtered up through the triple-canopy jungle. We then looked for and found a tiny spot high in the sky, the forward air controller (FAC) plane.

The small Cessna 01 "Bird Dog" had just fired a white phosphorous rocket to mark the target for the F-4s. The trailing jet peeled off to the right and climbed, getting in position to cover the first as it pulled away from its bomb run. It was too far for us to see what the first F-4 dropped, but the ground erupted at the target and jungle debris flew high into the sky. The second F-4 now made its run as the first moved into a covering position. There was no doubt what the second streaking aircraft dropped. The sky filled with a giant orange napalm fireball, its fiery brilliance turning to coal black as it rolled up into the early evening sky. My eyes followed the second plane as it climbed up toward the evening's marshmallow clouds and circled behind me.

That is when I saw them, behind me, sneaking from one clump of bushes to another.

"Gooks! I can see gooks!"

I pointed and counted one, two, three. "There's three of 'em—no, wait—four, five, six, seven!"

My excited warning had the guys scrambling for their weapons.

They were Viet Cong soldiers, carrying AK-47 rifles. The soldiers were uniformed in black pajamas, cinched at the waist with green web belts that contained cloth pouches probably full of 40-round magazines and personal items. They wore the traditional tan conical hats that the villagers wore and they had linen tubes of dry rice over their shoulders like bandoliers.

The VC were about 400 meters away, a little far to be accurately engaged with our M-16s and M-79s. Zorn had the machine gun, and he was off with Pearson looking for a tiger site. I yelled for someone to get on the radio but then remembered that Washington had the radio, and he was also off with Pearson. Bugs and Jakes each cut loose with long bursts from their '16s. The gooks, now aware that they had been discovered, gave up trying to hide and began to run for their lives.

In a matter of seconds, the three missing members of the squad came running back to our location from the base of Hill 51. Pearson, gasping for air, reported our situation to Captain Becker and requested air support from the Phantom jets that were above us.

We quickly found the correct frequency and got the FAC pilot on line with us. Pearson gave map coordinates for our position and that of the VCs. We then watched as the FAC plane rolled on its side and dove to the earth. The first white phosphorus rocket hit exactly on target. As the ball of white smoke rose to meet the sky, one of the F-4s came in low, screaming out of the late evening sun.

The pilot's ordnance release altitude needed to be high enough for the bomb to arm itself, which would also allow the fast-moving airship the distance required to avoid the bomb's lethal fragments, traveling at 1,300 feet per second. Release too high and accuracy is degraded, however. It had to be done just right.

Just short of the target the big twin-engine jet leveled off momentarily and dropped its remaining ordnance. Four large fins on each of the two 250-pound bombs flipped open to create drag and retard their forward momentum, allowing the F-4 time to escape. The high explosives fell almost straight to earth. The resulting detonation was almost a hundred meters short of the target, however.

The red-hot shrapnel ripped through the brush, reminding us that bombs had a large kill zone and they had no respect for nationality. (*Henry Shrapnel must have been rolling over in his grave. Modern inventors have greatly improved on the British officer's basic idea of exploding cannon balls. They have turned it into a profoundly efficient tool for the destruction of man. Every time something explodes, his name will be connected to that horrible destruction. Thanks Henry.*) Everyone scrambled for cover. Dirt and vegetation from the blast hung, suspended for a moment, and then fell into and around the new crater.

The second jet came screaming out of the sun at an even lower altitude. Fins did not open on this ordnance; the dark 750-gallon cylinders of jellied gasoline tumbled end over end to the earth. We all knew what to expect and jumped up to watch the napalm canisters impacting with the ground. A 200-meter-long swath of grass and brush burst into bright orange fire. We cheered spontaneously. This second drop was right on target. I held my weapon up to protect my face from the first few seconds of intense heat. I was sure that a ton of super-hot hurt had just been dropped on the gooks. Within minutes, the napalm-fueled blaze died down to a little grass fire. There was no more enemy movement.

Pearson radioed his intentions to the company HQ and then announced to the rest of us, "All right gentlemen, let's go see what we've got. And hurry up; this war ain't going to last forever."

We spread out 10 meters apart "on line" and cautiously advanced to the target. It was getting dark, so we made just one quick sweep of the burnt area and found no sign of the enemy. Realizing that we were asking for trouble wandering around after dark, Pearson put his hand on my shoulder and said, "Sergeant Rock, take point and get us the hell outta here. Take us to Hill 51. We'll set up our tiger there tonight. With any luck we'll surprise them when they come back to collect their dead."

Pearson organized the defensive perimeter by designating four guard posts on top of the little knoll; three of us manned each position. We agreed that at least two must be awake at each position during the night. We were all very tired, but the area had potential to be disastrous. The earlier ordnance drop had looked good, but in our quick search we found no bodies, rifles, mortar tubes, or blood trails. The same Vietnamese communist soldiers may now be watching us again, waiting for dark to crawl back and attack.

Pearson, Washington, and I took the guard position overlooking the trail we had just climbed. The well-beaten path made it obvious that we were not the only soldiers who liked the high ground. Pearson and Washington talked on the radio to our artillery support in the rear, and mapped out possible target coordinates. I took our three claymores 20 meters down the trail and hid them in the bushes. Two of them covered the trail, and the third was aimed toward a small opening in the ground cover. Satisfied all avenues of approach were covered, I ran the wires back and connected them to the electrical firing devices. Pearson thought it was more important for the twelve of us to keep quiet than to dig foxholes, so again my entrenching tool rested. In-country a little more than six weeks, and I had yet to dig a hole except to bury trash.

Quietly I rummaged around in my rucksack and found a can of beef and potatoes. The canning date on the bottom of the olive green can told me it was only 19 years old. Aged beef is how I chose to look at it. Considering our situation, heat tabs were out of the question. I slowly opened the can with my new P-38 can opener and flipped some of the solidified grease off with my well-used white plastic spoon. I was glad it was dark because the congealed slick at the top of the can always made me want to puke.

The first spoonful of potatoes made it unpleasantly clear to me that much of the grease was still there. It smeared my lips like beef-flavored Chapstick. When I finished eating, I used my sleeve as a napkin and cleaned the spoon on my pant leg. The rest of the squad finished eating about the same time I did, so we worked out a guard schedule. I got to sleep first, which was good because I was dead tired. The sky was clear so I didn't bother with my poncho; I just left it rolled up and tied on the bottom of the ruck.

The ground seemed exceptionally hard, and I could not find a comfortable position for sleeping. I pulled my entrenching tool off the rucksack and very quietly scraped an inch of rocks and soil away, customizing a hip hole. Semi-comfortable, I listened to the sounds of the night: the crickets, lizards, birds and mice, but no Charlie, thank goodness no Charlie. The guys let me sleep for three hours. When Washington woke me up to sit with Pearson, I knew that was the last sleep I would get for at least the next 20 hours.

I fumbled through my rucksack looking for a tin of peanut butter . . . finally found it, then crawled on my hands and knees over to Sergeant Pearson. Even though silence is a critical part of an ambush, idle whispering between two guards is sometimes necessary. We had just worked through several hot days of hard patrols, including two minor contacts with Sir Charles, and for three straight nights, including Christmas Eve, we had not had much sleep.

Trying to keep us both awake, Sergeant Pearson leaned over and whispered, "Being from Utah, you must be a Mormon, right?" I answered that I was. He told me that he was a Baptist. For the next three hours we discussed the differences in what we and others believed, politics, hometowns, girlfriends, and a host of other subjects. He observed that it was ironic that we Christians went back to war the day after we had celebrated the birth of the Prince of Peace.

The time really flew. Conversation with Pearson was intellectually stimulating, unlike other conversations I had previously had with most of the other guys.

I learned that Jimmy Pearson was born and raised in Fort Lauderdale, Florida. His father, who owned several auto parts stores, was from the "old school": he believed in a strong work ethic. Like his two older brothers and one sister, Pearson began working in one of the parts stores when he was just fourteen years old.

“What do you want to be when you get out of Vietnam and the Army?” I asked.

"Alive!" He responded without a second's hesitation.

He said he was expected to work and pay his own way through college before joining the family business. His story seemed to parallel my own experience. He explained that attending school "full time" (to avoid the draft), doing homework, working full time, attending college activities and spending time with his pretty girlfriend, Julie, was more than he could handle, so he had decided to let the draft get him, do his two years, then get on with his life. He said that Julie was faithfully writing and waiting. It was obvious that he was eager to get back home to her. She had wanted to get married before he left for Nam, but he promised her a big church wedding if she would wait a year.

With an old-timer's pride and smile, he stuck a finger in my ribs and whispered, "DEROS (date of estimated return from overseas) in just 63 days."

When Pearson looked at his watch and announced that it was "sack time," I held my watch close to my face, hoping it would indicate that we had a few more minutes to talk; it didn't. While watching Pearson crawl over to Washington, I thought about the vacancy the company would have in just 63 days. We wouldn't miss his rank or position, for those could be easily filled; what we would miss was his leadership. Soldiers with his natural talents were few and far between. I knew that he'd be successful whether he stayed in the military or if he returned to the family business.

I spent the rest of the night with our squad RTO. Washington's conversation was not as interesting as Pearson's had been, but we did manage to keep each other awake. Washington was from Georgia; he never did say exactly where. He was really into the hippie scene. His conversation was punctuated with "Far out," "Yeah man," and "Peace" buzz words. As a symbol of his rebellion against the military in general, the RTO wore three strands of colorful plastic "love beads" around his neck.

When the early morning sun turned the horizon a soft orange, Washington made the last of our hourly situation reports back to company HQ. I crawled over and woke our squad leader up. Pearson sat up, stretched, and then asked me to check on the other guys.

"Tell them we're moving out soon, so if they want a cup of coffee they better get busy. And tell them to get their claymores in."

I quickly moved around to the other three positions and passed on the messages. Within 45 minutes, we were all packed and sitting together at the top of the hill. We listened to Pearson's briefing on how he wanted us to go about searching the bomb and napalm drop site.

"When we get to the target, stay spread out so we can cover the area in one sweep. Minnie, you and Bugs take the lead and watch for newly placed booby-traps. The rest of us will fall in. Stay alert!"

Before swinging the heavy rucksack up onto my shoulders, I stretched my sore back and took one last look at the old rice fields and hedgerows below. Everything was quiet for as far as I could see. This was probably going to be another of those hot, boring Vietnam days. Minnie started down off the hill and each of us found a place in the line. I stepped in behind Washington, sixth in the line of 12. As we approached the flat ground at the base of the hill, we began to spread out in 10-meter intervals per the sergeant's instructions.

The old rice paddy we were about to cross had been dry for years; it now supported razor-edged elephant grass that was thigh high. The field was about 50 meters square and surrounded on three sides by tall hedgerows, which in earlier days served as windbreaks for the growing rice plants.

Just as Sonognini, our last man, came down off the high ground, an AK-47 in the hedgerow to our front cut loose with the familiar CRACK-CRACK-CRACK of a weapon on full automatic. The AK was immediately joined by half a dozen other AKs in the hedgerow to our right. We had been caught in a textbook L-shaped ambush! We could not see our attackers and we had no place to hide. I did not even have time for a last desperation prayer to flash through my mind. This was not a good day to die!

I did a one-quarter turn to my right and dove to the ground. In the process of seeking safety in the arms of mother earth, I managed to fire the grenade from my M-79 in the general direction of the hedgerow I faced. Impacting with the ground, the heavy rucksack on my back flew forward and its metal frame bashed against the back of my head, sending my helmet flying somewhere ahead of me in the grass. Half-dazed, I rolled onto my left side, grasped the quick-release tabs on the rucksack shoulder straps, and yanked. The pack and I separated as designed. My breathing was instantly heavy and a bass drum echoed in my chest. Random bullets began to impact the ground around me.

I broke the grenade launcher open, dumped the empty casing and quickly shoved another grenade into the chamber. Enemy fire had by then greatly increased in intensity. I could identify the cracking sounds of 25 to 30 AK rifles and the more methodical fire of several enemy RPD light machine guns, all concentrating on the 12 of us scattered around the flat rice field.

I licked the salty sweat and dirt from my lips and popped up to my knees, facing the closest hedgerow. Forty feet away I could see three Viet Cong soldiers concentrating their fire on someone in the field to my left. I brought the '79 to my shoulder, took quick aim, and launched my grenade at the three. The VC on the right took a direct hit. The grenade detonated. Thousands of tiny pieces of jagged steel ripped into the thick hedgerow, and a gunpowder-grey cloud immediately filled the area. Not even waiting to watch the pieces of the soldier fall, I returned as flat as a collapsed ironing board to the grassy earth and loaded another round in the tube. The other two grenadiers, the eight riflemen in the squad, and Zorn on the '60 were all answering the challenge, but we were at a definite disadvantage.

*See the front cover of this book for a view of Hill 51 and the old rice paddy. The picture of the author was taken a month after the ambush, on the exact site.*

The last seconds of our young lives were flashing by. Everything we did was probably for the last time. Besides our being outnumbered maybe three to one, the Viet Cong soldiers were well hidden in the bushes, while we were trapped in the open field. We were in deep trouble. The thigh-high grass provided a little cover but certainly no protection. I could hear Washington 10 feet off to my left yelling into the radio headset for air cover and medics. He screamed that he had been hit, and that we needed help right now!

A VC machine gun only eight meters from me began its RATA-TAT-TAT death song. It sounded as if the barrel of the gun was in my ear. I could feel the concussions of the exploding powder on the side of my face. The first several rounds tore my rucksack apart. The next 10 or 15 shots sailed inches over the length of my flattened body and impacted in the ground somewhere behind me. The VC gunner was too close for me to shoot at because the detonator in my M-79 grenade could not unwind and arm itself in such a short distance. Not armed, it was only a giant, very slow bullet. The shotgun rounds, each loaded with 20 pellets of #4 buckshot, designed for close-up combat, were safely packed inside my rucksack—a mistake I would never make again.

The VC gunner did not know exactly where I was. He was waiting for me to roll or crawl and move the grass; then he could concentrate his fire. When I didn't move, he got impatient and took a guess. The next burst of lead from his weapon slammed into the hard earth next to me. One of the bullets cut the stem of a small red flower that was standing tall just inches from my nose. The dew-covered flower fell over and rested against my sweaty face. I could smell the beauty of Mother Nature and the ugliness of mankind at the same moment. I still did not move. The man behind the hot machine gun was sure he had killed me so he shifted his attention to Washington. In the middle of a plea for help I heard the sickening *thump thump* as bullets penetrated his body. A short involuntary cry came from his lips, the last sounds of a dead man.

Our only chance to survive was if the message had made it out before Washington and the radio had been killed. Left for dead, I lay motionless in the grass. Bullets continued to tear holes in the air over my head at distant targets. There was a lot of noise and a great deal of confusion. After a long 30 seconds, I could hear several Vietnamese communist soldiers suddenly running through the hedgerow. Instantly I decided that if they were charging me I would jump to my feet and meet them head on. I would not die hiding in the grass. I immediately unsnapped the sheath that held my bayonet on my waist and quickly stuck my head and M-79 above the grass, but there was nothing to see. Returning to the hard ground, I began using the '79 like a mortar. By shooting the grenades almost straight up, they returned to the earth 10 seconds later and detonated in the VC's cover nearby. I fired as fast as I could, about 6 rounds per minute, walking the grenades up and down the VC-filled windbreak closest to me.

I could hear cries of pain all around me. Somewhere far to my left Bugs was screaming. I didn't know how badly he was hurt. It must have been very severe or he would have kept quiet. Obviously he was beyond the fear of being heard by enemy gunners. To my right, Jakes was pleading for the medic which we did not have. Beyond him, I could hear a high-pitched whine and someone thrashing around in the dry grass.

During my childhood, I had those bad dreams where the monster would be breathing down my neck, but because I was running in sticky mud up to my knees, I could never get away. I felt that sense of total frustration again and wished that I could just wake up from this nightmare and find myself safe in my bed. The whole world was exploding around me and at any second I would be caught up in the destruction. An ocean of death surrounded my tiny island of life. Just when I was conceding my life to the inevitable, another island verbally mated with mine.

"Sergeant Rock, are you all right?"

It was Pearson! He was alive! Somehow with Pearson alive I knew I had a chance.

I yelled back "I'm OK; are we alone?"

Without responding to my question, he gave the command that normally would strike immeasurable fear in me but I was now eager to obey.

"Let's go get them!" he screamed above the pounding gunfire.

Without hesitation, we each jumped to our feet and charged the nearest hedgerow. The fear of dying was gone. Side by side, we would fight until we were dead. It was like we were in another dimension. This was our last chance to resist, and we would not do it hiding in the grass. Most of the guys in the squad were already dead or dying, and we were about to join them anyway. We had nothing to lose. Revenge had chased our fear away. This was a good day to die.

Unbelievably, we received supporting fire from several '16s and the '60. Supporting fire meant that a few of the guys were still able to fight back. It seemed like an eternity between the grenades I launched, but I was loading and firing them as quickly as I could. Not having the time to look for individual targets, I fired randomly into the hedgerow as the two of us charged it. Because Pearson's weapon was firing on full automatic, I knew he was doing the same.

I heard a whistle blow, and suddenly the roar of combat died; we were no longer receiving fire. The intense noise and explosion of hostile lead stopped. Doubtful that our two-man charge had scared anyone, I figured the enemy must be attempting a preplanned retreat into the mountains before our air support arrived. The idea that I was chasing fleeing enemy soldiers pumped another shot of high-octane adrenaline into my already charged system; I felt unstoppable, like I could personally destroy the entire Viet Cong army. I crashed into the hedgerow, totally oblivious to the possibility that a gook might be standing in there with bayonet, waiting.

I broke through into the next field. Several VC soldiers were just entering a brush-covered flatland that continued for two klicks to the mountains. I fired one of the remaining four grenades in my last bandoleer at them, about 50 meters ahead, and continued the charge. Halfway through the field I heard Pearson screaming my name.

"Rock! Rock! Get your butt back here!"

Twenty-five meters to my rear I could see Sergeant Pearson,

still standing in the hedgerow. I suddenly realized that I was alone. In the excitement, I had run out into the field all by myself. I was chasing 30 Viet Cong soldiers and I had forgotten to even reload the grenade launcher. Rocky, what are you doing? I thought to myself.

"Rocky, what are you doing?" yelled Pearson.

In that instant my adrenaline high crashed, and my superhuman body turned to mush. Running back to the safety of the windbreak, I no longer felt invincible—quite the opposite. I was back in the mud again with the monster breathing down my neck. This time it was not a dream.

The hedgerow seemed miles away. Every vine and blade of grass seemed to reach out and grab at my jungle boots. It was a notable accomplishment just to get one foot in front of the other. I expected a bullet to rip into the flesh of my back at any second. "Dear God," I quickly prayed, "get me out of here!" Each step seemed to be in slow motion, but I kept going. Finally . . . finally I made it.

Collapsing in the dirt behind the cover of the hedgerow, Pearson and I just looked at each other. We were both breathing hard, too exhausted to speak. Two Huey gunships arrived just then and began to rocket and machine gun the area around us. At last I felt safe; maybe I would not die today. Now I could take care of my friends—my dead and dying friends.

Looking back toward Hill 51, I could see nothing but dry grass peacefully swaying in the early morning breeze. The sun was shining, and a bird sang somewhere in the distance. Mother Nature seemed to be totally oblivious to this little ambush, as if, in the grand scheme of things, it really didn't matter much.

My attention quickly refocused when Zorn's head popped up in the grass and then disappeared again. When it came up a second time, I could tell that he was feverishly working on a fallen comrade. With the gunships "working out" around us, Sergeant Pearson and I hurried out into the grass, looking for survivors. I found Washington with the radio still on his back, rolled up in the fetal position. He was dead. Several bullets had entered his side and exited through his stomach. Handfuls of vital organs were lying exposed on the ground. His bloody left foot was grotesquely twisted and lying next to his knee. Large green flies made a steady hum as they flew around the remains of my friend. I thought I should cover him with my bullet-riddled poncho out of respect and to keep the flies off, but the wounded required my assistance first.

In the distance I could hear more yelling. I looked up from Washington's body to see Lieutenant DeWitt leading Sergeant Tew and his squad as they ran toward us. The RTO, trying to talk on his radio and run at the same time, shouted between gasps of air to the lieutenant, "Medevacs . . . are inbound. ETA (estimated time of arrival) . . . is three minutes."

I zigzagged around the field searching for bodies, looking for places where the grass appeared to be mashed down. First I found Jacobs, one of the other two '79ers. He was lying on his side, motionless. I could see he had a messy head wound. I gently rolled him onto his back, exposing the damage. A bullet had blown open the side of his skull, exposing his brain. I lifted his still-warm body to remove a bandoleer of grenades. He had only managed to fire three of them before being killed. I draped the blood-soaked grenades around my shoulders.

Next, I found Sonognini, the other grenadier. The big 18-year-old Hawaiian grunt was laying face-up in the grass; he had been hit in the left leg. His femur penetrated his bloody fatigue pants just above the knee. The soldier, so physically powerful, had been stopped by a single steel-jacketed piece of lead weighing just ounces. I wiped my bloody hands on my shirt, then knelt down and placed my fingers on the side of his throat. Sonognini was alive. My bloody fingerprints remained on his neck as I checked the rest of his body for wounds. Doc Bayne, arriving with the other squad, ran up and asked if I needed him. I told him I was OK, but if Sonognini regained consciousness I would need some help with the big guy. Doc ran off in search of the more seriously wounded.

Using one of my empty bandoleers, I applied a tourniquet above the wound. Inserting the barrel of Sonognini's grenade launcher into the bandoleer, I twisted the tourniquet tight enough to stop the flow of blood. I then tore open the plastic bag Doc had given me; it contained a green compress bandage. I loosely tied it over the exposed bone, mostly to keep the flies and dirt out. Another squad member, Jim Wilson, and I covered the bloody Hawaiian with a poncho in anticipation of flying debris from the three medevacs that were now landing.

Sergeant Pearson hollered from across the field, "Sergeant Rock, is he ready to go?"

"Yes," I answered, "but he's unconscious. We'll need some help carrying him."

"Screw you two," said Zorn, quietly walking up behind us.

Cradling him like a baby, Zorn picked up Sonognini's limp body and carried him to the closest medevac chopper, then returned with a grunt of disrespect.

Wilson and I then rushed over to Pearson to help him carry good ol' Chief. The Chief had taken a hit through the calf muscle on his right leg. He was lying back in the grass, hands behind his head, blowing cigarette smoke rings at us. It was his way of saying, "I'll see you dudes later. This little flesh wound is going to take me back to the world, all the way home to Oklahoma." Obviously Doc's morphine shot had the Chief higher than a short-tailed kite. Pearson leaned over and made eye contact with me.

"Did you strip him?"

Knowing that he meant Sonognini, I answered, "He was clean."

Pearson was making sure none of his guys would get caught with a little marijuana stuffed in their pockets when the hospital orderlies were prepping them for surgery. He hated the use of drugs by his men, but getting shot in Vietnam was a big enough price to pay. No one needed drug charges against them back home.

I watched as Bugs and Wood were carried to one of the medevacs. Both had bad stomach wounds, but Doc said they would live. I did not see Jakes get carried aboard, but after the choppers had lifted off, Pearson told me that Jakes had been hit at the base of his neck and might be paralyzed. Of the 12 of us who were caught in the field just an hour earlier, Washington and Jacobs were KIA; Jakes, Moran, Sonognini, Haskell, and Wood had been hit so badly that we would never see them again. It all happened so fast.

We hardly had time to mourn their loss before a resupply chopper landed. Understandably, the pilot and his crew did not want to hang around the hostile battlefield. The door gunner kicked several cases of ammo out the door, and the resupply bird quickly took off to a safer environment. The chopper left enough M-79 grenades behind for three grenadiers, but I was now the only one left. Pearson said I would have to carry them all.

"We are going after the son-of-a-bitch that did this, and you may wish you had all the grenades you could get."

I still didn't like the idea of carrying three basic loads of ammo—90 rounds of high explosives—but I had no other choice. I tied most of the cotton bandoleers so they crisscrossed my chest, like the machine gunners did with their belts of ammo, and secured the remaining bandoleers around my waist. I stuck three M-79 shotgun rounds in a leg pocket; lesson learned. Zorn sarcastically remarked to Pearson that he didn't want to be around me when the shit hit the fan: "Sergeant Rock is a walking bomb."

Lieutenant Colonel Capalitti flew over in his observation helicopter and ordered Lieutenant DeWitt to get the troops moving.

"You're falling behind," he said.

Once everyone was loaded up, the lieutenant commanded us to advance "on line." Side by side, five meters apart, we pushed forward, searching for blood trails or bodies in the bush-covered terrain between us and the mountains. One hundred meters into our advance, a booby-trapped grenade detonated on the far side of the line. The morning's quiet was again violated by screams from wounded soldiers. Sergeants Pearson and Tew posted security while the rest of us assisted our downed buddies. Cosby, Hernandez, and another guy I didn't know had been hit pretty badly by the shrapnel.

I ran over to Coz. He was thrashing around on the ground and screaming in pain. Blood covered the vegetation all around the shrapnel-shredded soldier. Doc Bayne quickly gave Coz a shot of morphine, then went to work on Hernandez, who was in worse shape than the other two. As I cut the bloody jungle fatigues off Coz with my bayonet, I watched Doc's desperate attempt to save Hernandez.

Doc was applying his best external heart massage to the seriously wounded soldier, who was lying motionless in the wet red Vietnam dirt. Bennett and Sergeant Tew took turns at mouth-to-mouth resuscitation between compressions. Each breath of air forced into the soldier's lungs just bubbled out again through the shrapnel holes in his chest. Doc tried to use the plastic bags that had contained field compresses to seal the sucking chest holes, but there were just too many to cover. His gurgling breath got shallower and shallower until there was silence. Hernandez died long before the medevac could reach us, too many of them to cover.

With Hernandez dead, Doc went to work on Coz and the other guy. We used most of our canteen water to wash the scarlet-colored blood off the soldier's body so the medic could and evaluate the seriousness of the holes in his flesh. Doc tried to seal the larger wounds and stop the most serious bleeding.

Coz kept asking, "Rock, am I going to die?"

I told him he was fine and that he would be going home. I lied.

He might be going home, but there was a good chance it would be in one of those black rubber body bags like Washington, Jacobs, and now Hernandez. Soldiers of past wars, going back as far as Old Testament times, were buried where they fell. This war offered the benefit of having one's remains (what was left, anyway) shipped all the way home from Southeast Asia to be cried over again. It was also a wonderful opportunity for television to repeat to everyone just what a terrible war this was. As if anyone needed that reminder.

Our battalion commander, safe and secure in his little Command and Control (C&C) observation chopper flying high overhead, seemed to be getting tired of waiting to get us all killed. It was obvious we were in a heavily booby-trapped area, and that our catching Sir Charles before he reached the mountains was impossible. Still, he ordered us to find and engage the enemy. I could tell that Lieutenant DeWitt was really frustrated about his options in this situation. To proceed would almost surely cause more suffering and death to his men. But to disobey the order of a superior officer, especially during a combat operation, would bring personal condemnation and end his promising military career.

*During my short Army experience, it had been impressed very strongly upon me that a direct military order is not to be refused, no matter how idiotic it may seem. The reasoning made sense. If subordinates were allowed to countermand an officer's orders, the military could never be controlled. One of the favorite phrases used by drill instructors during my basic training was, "When I say jump, you had better ask 'How high?' on the way up!" Because all sergeants were bilingual, the sentence was usually punctuated liberally with "French." We were taught to salute and execute, not to rethink an order.*

With the wind from the departing medevac still whipping our blood-stiffened fatigues, Lieutenant DeWitt gave the command:

"Pick up your crap, we're moving out!"

The lieutenant had made the only logical decision, although I did not like it.

"We're going to form two columns, one on either side of the trail," he said, pointing to a little-used path that meandered through the low brush.

"Cannon, you take the lead in one of the columns. Sergeant Rock, I want your '79 up front, so you'll be number two. Wilson, you and Sergeant Pearson will head up the other column."

Since our squad of 12 was now only four, I was hoping he would let someone else have a turn up front. No such luck.

"Follow these four—they know what to look for." he yelled to Sergeant Tew's squad. I thought to myself that if what the lieutenant had just said was true, most of our squad would not be in black body bags and medical evacuation helicopters right now.

"I want them to stay off but parallel with the trail. Walk only where they walk and stay out of the brush."

Cannon and I had pulled several tigers together. During one of those tigers we discovered we'd grown up just 200 miles apart. He was married and worked on his uncle's large potato farm outside of Idaho Falls, Idaho. Because of our Western kinship we had quickly become friends. We walked to the front of the column, stooped with our loads of equipment, and waited for everyone else to get saddled up in their rucksacks. We were brave soldiers who were now immeasurably terrified. Walking point and getting killed in the next few minutes were almost synonymous. Cannon turned around and looked at me. I could see the fear that he was also seeing in my eyes. The dude was a doing a brave thing. Cannon always did whatever was asked of him, no matter how hard or dangerous it was. It was just his nature. After a small moment's pause, his dirty right hand reached out for mine.

"Well Rocky, I guess this is it." he said.

The strength of his handshake gave me courage, like Dad's arm around my neck had when I was a kid.

Cannon turned back around, took one step, and the ground beneath him exploded. The blast blew me off my feet and onto my back. Immediately the earth shook again as another stunning explosion from across the trail threw human debris into the air. The gooks are throwing hand grenades! I thought. I have to get out of their killing zone, or I'll die! For the second time that morning I knew that my life would be over in seconds.

I tried to roll over but couldn't. I felt paralyzed. My mind was fuzzy. I could not concentrate. I could hear yelling and shooting around me, but it didn't seem to matter. Dying was easy. Nothing seemed important. I had no problems. It was all just so mind-numbing. Slowly . . . very slowly . . . my mind began to clear from the brain-rattling concussions of the "up-close and personal" blasts. I fought the desire to slip back into that black Never-Never Land.

Consciousness gradually took control of my brain, and I

discovered that I was not dead or dying after all. I was still breathing and I could see. I tried to move again, but the heavy ruck on my back and the grenades on my chest pinned me to the earth. For the second time in three hours I yanked on the quick release tabs and broke free of the rucksack. With some effort, I sat up, found the launcher that I had somehow managed to hold on to, and fired my loaded grenade into the bushes nearby. Dizzily I rolled onto my stomach and again tried to low-crawl out of hand grenade range. My head was still a little fuzzy, but my instincts told me to get outta there. I slowly crawled toward better cover until someone behind me yelled, "Mines!"

I froze momentarily; this was a new danger that required a different physical reaction. I stopped dragging myself forward through the dirt. Hesitantly rising to my hands and knees, I began a visual search for any indication of the hidden devices. The shooting had stopped. We were not receiving any incoming fire; in fact, we never had been fired upon. All the shooting had been outgoing, I was beginning to remember.

The enemy had simply followed a precise, prearranged escape route, cleverly leading us into their mine field. There probably weren't any gooks within a klick of our position. Yet again, for the third time, we had been ambushed and taken serious casualties.

Before I dared move toward Cannon, who was screaming in pain just six feet to my left, I had to visually and maybe physically clear the area between us. When I looked toward the soldier's cries, my cheek made contact with a warm, tacky substance on my shoulder. I cocked my head to one side to see what I had felt. What I saw further sickened my already nauseated stomach. I twitched my shoulder forward, causing a bloody, raggedly torn, two-pound human steak to slide to the ground between my hands. My chest heaved. I gagged and then vomited up the C-ration can of ham and eggs I had eaten for breakfast.

I quickly searched my own body for wounds but found none. The body part lying in the dirt beside me did not belong to me. Although my face, chest, and arms were all covered with fresh blood, none of it was my own.

Still on my hands and knees, I turned left. Cannon was quiet now. I looked over to see if he was dead. My eyes met his again.

"Rock, I . . . I . . . my leg is gone."

I was amazed that he was so composed after what he had just seen. From his right knee down there was nothing. His left leg was also mangled. I was sure it would have to be amputated. I tried to say, "You're going to be OK," but this time the lie caught in my throat. How could he be OK? If he lived, it would be without his legs. I hated Vietnam and I just wanted to go home. I thought that I couldn't take anymore. I didn't know it then, but even worse was just minutes away. Cautiously, watching the ground to my front, I crawled toward my wounded friend.

Doc Bayne, on a dead run, hurdled over me.

"Are you all right, Rock?" he hurriedly asked as he knelt by Cannon's side.

"Yes, but you'd better get to work on Cannon," I said, as if I was telling him something he didn't already know.

In complete disregard for his own life, our medic had run through the mine field. He had run from the rear of the column up to where Cannon and I lay on the ground. With the rest of the squad frozen in their tracks, Doc had heroically risked his life to provide immediate assistance to a wounded soldier. Dang, that was brave! I felt a little stupid and guilty at not showing more courage myself.

The even worse then came.

"Pearson's dead!" someone yelled.

I jumped to my feet, screaming "Noooo!"

From where I stood, I could not see the squad leader. He had disappeared. I then did another visual search of where I had seen him last, and found him. His head and arms lay in a pile beneath a tall bush. That was it—all of him. Oh God, don't let it be Pearson, I prayed. Not Pearson, not Pearson, please dear God, not Pearson. But it was. Pearson was dead, just blown apart. All I could do was stare at his remains. Completely devoid of strength, I finally collapsed back to the earth, physically and emotionally exhausted.

Minnie, upon hearing the news, dropped his weapon and ran like a crazy man to Pearson's remains. Falling to his knees next to our dead leader, he began to sob and pray. Minnie slowly removed a rosary made of thick green string with a white plastic cross from around his neck. He then made the sign of the cross.

"Hail Mary, full of grace . . ."

As he prayed, the knots in the string slowly slipped through his fingers. Minnie's tears tore down the dam that had been holding back my emotions all day. I cried, only semi-conscious of the danger that might still be around me. Crying was not an unsoldierly thing to do. Dead soldiers deserved to be wept over.

Most of us were incapacitated by grief. Warm tears left clean streaks on our dirty faces, only to be wiped dirty again by our shirt sleeves. Several soldiers cleared paths to the casualties. Doc continued to work on Cannon, but it was hard for him to see through his tears. It was only after Cannon was safely aboard a medevac that Doc allowed himself time to cry and pray.

After the area immediately around us was more carefully probed with our bayonets and one unexploded mine marked, we began the grim task of assembling body parts. Sergeant Tew spread his poncho on the ground and we laid all the bits of flesh and bone we could find onto it. There was not much. Pearson had either dived or was blown onto the second mine. His stomach and hips had detonated the explosive. To this point, Minnie had not allowed anyone to touch the bloody pile where he knelt.

Finally, with the huge metallic green flies zeroing in, Minnie motioned for me to come to him. Our squad leader's head, still connected to his arms by strips of neck muscle, dragged on the ground momentarily as we lifted the sergeant's cold mangled arms. I dared not touch his head or the fingers that he had teasingly poked in my side just a few hours earlier.

The flies buzzed their disapproval when we moved these last remains of body over to the poncho. They quieted again as they settled back on the warm pile. No one spoke. We were all deep in prayer or thoughts of vengeance. In an occupation where our choices were few, Sergeant Pearson had been given no opportunity to say good-by. He had died instantly. Minnie gently laid his rosary on our leader's remains, then thought again and put the rosary back around his own neck. Doc picked up the four corners of the poncho, shook Pearson's dog tags and everything else into the center and tied it off like a hobo's knapsack. I could not remember ever having felt so sick.

The medevac landed and we carried Cannon aboard. The door gunner recognized us from three hours earlier and just shook his head. He then threw a rubber body bag onto the ground for our KIA. Two of Sergeant Tew's men placed Sergeant Jim Pearson's body in one end of the black bag and folded the empty half over on top. They reverently placed it on the floor of the chopper. Minnie stood at the side of the medevac, holding onto a corner of the bag until the chopper lifted off.

As the bird broke contact with the earth, PFC Cannon raised himself up on one elbow and bravely flashed the two-fingered peace sign to us all. Words could never describe what we had just seen, or the mix of love and hate we were feeling. It was difficult for me to accept that so many of my friends—my entire squad—had been so violently and quickly taken from me. I was the only one left, and I felt a great emptiness within me. These valiant young men, all my brothers, were gone. They were going home, back to the world or to God. Never would I see them again.

Helicopters flying off into the sky with black body bags containing the remains of best friends was a horrific way to say goodbye. Memorial services for the departed may have been conducted by soldiers in the rear, but we who had been protected by the heroics of these dead were never given the privilege to attend. We just continued with our jobs and hoped we had seen the last buddy pay the supreme price.

Death was a reality that I knew I must face, especially in Vietnam, but I was never ready for it. Although we were violently separated, the spirits of these guys would remain with me forever. The bonds of our brotherhood could never be broken. I take solace in my religious faith that one day we will meet again, and that we will wrap our arms around each other in a long soldierly embrace.

"Dear Mr. and Mrs. Pearson,

In behalf of the United States Government, I am sorry to inform you that your son, Sgt. Jim Pearson, was . . . " My mind could not erase the vision of the local Army chaplain standing on the doorstep of his parents' home, hat in hand, trying to express sincere sympathy to, and about, a soldier he didn't even know. And then there was Julie . . . back home planning a wedding that would never happen.

Lieutenant Colonel Capalitti, still flying high overhead in his C&C ship, again ordered over his radio, "Get after them . . . advance . . . advance!" Lieutenant DeWitt put the radio handset close to his lips so he would not be misunderstood and distinctly said, "F--- you, we're going back!"

And we did.

## CHAPTER 9

# FIREFIGHT ACROSS THE RIVER

After the ambush at Hill 51, the entire company was flown by chopper back to the outskirts of Phong Dien, where for several days we were allowed to lick our emotional wounds. Half of the platoon and nearly my entire squad had been eliminated. Some serious mental and physical reorganization was necessary. I was given a medal for surviving the ordeal and promoted to Specialist 4, which meant a few more dollars going home to my bank account each month. Living away from civilization gave me little opportunity to spend much of it. I kept $15 from each monthly paycheck; that was plenty to buy sodas or Vietnamese candy from the locals whenever we happened to be close to a village.

The second day at Phong Dien we got the first of the many replacements required to bring the platoon back to full strength. Sergeant Taylor did not qualify as an FNG because he transferred to us from an engineering unit that had been disbanded. He'd been in-country almost nine months, involved in military construction the whole time, but he told war stories with the best of us. Taylor was a tall soul brother and weighed maybe 200 pounds. He looked like the kind of guy who could provide the stability and leadership that the squad and platoon desperately needed.

Lieutenant DeWitt assigned the sergeant as our new squad leader—what there was left of it—and that really pissed Zorn off. Zorn was the senior Spec. 4 in the platoon, and he thought he deserved the leadership position—and the money. He wandered around the company for the rest of the day bitching to everyone. I thought Zorn had gotten the shaft, but he had bullied so many of us for so long that I wasn't interested in joining his verbal rebellion.

Lieutenant DeWitt asked me to be his RTO, and I consented. Thus I became part of the platoon command post consisting of Platoon Sergeant Wardle, the medic Doc Bayne, and the platoon leader Lieutenant DeWitt. The new radio job had its advantages and disadvantages. The Prick 25 (PRC-25) weighed about 25 pounds, and its easily identifiable antenna would make me a special target. On the other hand, I liked the lieutenant, I would always know what was going on, and I would never have to walk point.

I had to give up the '79 and instead was issued a brand-new M-16 with the seven magazines of ammo that RTOs customarily carried. My new responsibility was to talk, not shoot. The radio was my primary weapon.

A resupply truck from Camp Evans, escorted by two armored personnel carriers, arrived at our defensive position and most of us were detailed to unload it. From the number of Meal, Combat, Individual (C-rations) cases we off-loaded, it was evident that Alpha Company was going somewhere soon and we would be gone for about a week.

On the front seat of the truck were several unmarked wooden boxes that we were not allowed to touch. Later, one by one, each of the squad leaders were called forward by the supply sergeant and issued, by serial number, a highly classified AN/PVS-2 starlight scope. The six-pound night vision device amplified the faintest light up to 40,000 times and had a range of 400 meters. It was about 14 inches long and as big around as a softball on the rifle muzzle end. It looked like a flashlight that was serious about taking its vitamins. I could see that it would be awkward to carry, but its capabilities rendered that little disadvantage meaningless. When it was so dark that seeing 10 meters was difficult, this new battery-operated starlight scope would allow us to count the buttons on Charlie's uniform shirt at one hundred meters. That gave us a great advantage. With each starlight scope issued came the supply sergeant's warning:

"You *will not* allow this device to fall into enemy hands! You *will* destroy it before you die!"

In the evening of the second day, Lieutenant DeWitt boldly told us to prepare for a combat assault (CA) back into the Hill 51 area. I knew he hated the idea of going back into the AO. He had a bad feeling the first time we were there, but could not prevent the causalities that ensued. His boldness was an act, I was sure, but he was our leader and could act no other way.

Choppers were going to pick us up at 0700 hours the next morning. Because I was the bearer of the bad news, my popularity among my peers dropped dramatically. To make matters even worse, it began to rain like crazy. The guys hastily built some rickety lean-to shelters, using bamboo for the framework and large banana leaves as shingles. The ground underneath the shelters quickly turned to gooey mud anyway.

In addition to the usual Phong Dien children, several Vietnamese women, or mama sans, from the *ville* hung around our encampment trying to sell us a variety of local canned and home-cooked foods. They were very successful. I bought a small loaf of hard-crusted bread, a can of mackerel in tomato sauce, and some little bite-size things that looked like fried eggrolls. The eggrolls were filled with rice, some kind of vegetable greens and whole half-inch-long minnows. I stood a heat tab on end in the black mud and warmed the can of mackerel over the flame.

Thanks to my new position as the platoon RTO, I knew exactly what was going to happen when the choppers arrived. The company was going to be airlifted to the base of the Annamite Mountains, two klicks west of Hill 51.

An ARVN (Army of the Republic of Vietnam) company had arrived in the Hill 51 area the day after we left to get the VC body count from our firefight the previous day. In Southeast Asia getting a body count was a measurement of combat success. It was important since capturing land was seldom a priority. We were professional killers, not homesteaders. In all the ARVN's searching, however, they only found one gook body. He had taken a direct hit by an M-79 grenade, and there really wasn't much of a body for the VC's comrades to drag away. Now this ARVN Company was going to act as a blocking force as we approached the old ambush area. Hopefully we could trap some Viet Cong between us and extract a bit of revenge.

Everything and everyone was so miserably wet that Captain Becker's 0530 wake-up call to the lieutenants found no one sleeping. We each ate a C-ration breakfast, or leftover mackerel, then packed our rucks and sloshed through the mud several hundred meters to the helicopter pick-up point. Our hopes were that the bad weather would ground the birds, but they arrived on time. Lieutenant DeWitt, Doc Bayne, Platoon Sergeant Wardle, two riflemen, and I all climbed on the fourth chopper. The rain felt like hail as it was whipped against my legs by the invisible rotors. Sitting in the doorway at liftoff, I quickly decided, was not a good idea. I leaned back and pulled my legs inside the rotary-winged airship, but I couldn't quite get out of the turbulent air and the stinging rain.

We flew about 20 minutes and landed as planned in an area

that had just been prepped by artillery. The smell of the expended explosives was strong. As we unloaded from each of the choppers the landing zone expanded. Finally, when the company, all 80 of us, was on the ground, we began the patrol back toward Hill 51.

The rain stopped and the sun peeked out occasionally to warm my chilled body and wet uniform. I was beginning to think the day might not be so bad when someone in the front of the long column tripped a booby-trapped grenade. I immediately thought, "Here we go again." From my position near the rear I couldn't see what was going on, but the radio traffic was busy, and I learned that the explosion had messed up three guys pretty bad. While listening to the RTO's conversation with the medevac I heard that one of the three soldiers had lost his leg. Each of the wounded were new guys and, thankfully, I hardly knew them. The distance of our friendship made the loss easier to live with. There were always new guys coming into the company, and quite often these uninitiated were the recipients of Charlie's terrible tricks.

After the medevac had departed, Captain Becker called on the radio for all platoon leaders and platoon sergeants to meet with him for a short briefing. DeWitt and Wardle returned to the platoon after their short ten minute absence and called the squad leaders together.

"We're going back the way we came," the lieutenant said. "The captain has decided the area is still too heavily booby-trapped. The only body count we're getting is our own."

It was a great decision. Hill 51 was not worth one more life.

Since the order of march was going to be reversed, the lieutenant and the squad leaders broke out their terrain maps and black grease pencils. They planned a zigzagging route to our next objective, hoping to avoid any hastily engineered ambushes.

We humped our rucksacks most of the rest of the day, winding through the tall razor-edged elephant grass. About 1600 hours, we broke out onto the banks of the Rao Cao River. The captain told us to look for a suitable place for a company-sized night defensive position, so several first platoon squads were sent out to recon the area. While the rest of us waited for their return, a chopper landed bringing "Major" Poulsen back from his "vacation" in the hospital. His collapse the day before the ambush at Hill 51 had been the result of heat exhaustion, as we had suspected. It probably kept him from getting killed. He told us all about the New Year's party and the "dancing" girls at the enlisted men's club. Only then did I realize that we had begun a new year—1969.

After the recon squads had returned and had given their reports, we proceeded to hump up the lazy river about a klick. Just as one of the patrols had reported, we found several large fields of short grass surrounded by hedgerows. The captain selected one of the fields for our NDP. The three platoon leaders and the company commander each organized their command centers in one of the three thick windbreaks. The fourth side of the field was bordered by the river. Second platoon's portion of the perimeter included all of the river and part of the east hedgerow.

I dropped my equipment on the bank of the river six feet above the waterline and began digging a fighting hole. Since there were no trees or other cover along this side of the Rao Cao's edge, and there was a jungle-covered hill on the other side, I wanted a good place to fight from if I needed it.

Like an army of ants, second platoon busily dug holes up and down the river's raised banks. The lieutenant didn't help me much with our hole, but that was all right because he was spending most of his time organizing the fields of fire along the perimeter.

I was just finishing a can of cold spaghetti after several hours of digging the new two-man hole when the lieutenant walked up and dropped an M-79 and a load of grenades in my lap.

"I'm sending four of the guys from first squad out on an all night listening post. They need to have your radio and weapon. Also, I've decided to move down the river a bit, toward the middle of the platoon. Tony will man the hole with you tonight."

Tony Salvetti came to the Screaming Eagles shortly after I did, and he was a really cool dude. Salvetti was about my size, a soft-spoken brown-eyed Italian kid. We clicked at our first meeting. He walked up to my position about 10 minutes later with his 60 on his shoulder; he also carried two ammo cans full of linked rounds. Salvetti was proud to be a squad gunner.

While preparing for the night, our conversation wandered to the good times back in the world. Tony began talking about his home in Binghamton, New York, and how the Rao Cao reminded him of the gentle Susquehanna River. As I listened to him talk, I realized he did not have the same New York accent as Minnie. When I questioned him about that, he explained that where he lived was "worlds away" from the big city confusion; his home town was surrounded by rolling, tree-covered hills and farms. Having never lived east of the

Mississippi, I guess I just assumed New York State was all city. Salvetti was happy to correct that assumption. He talked about fishing for bass and bullheads off the bridges almost in the center of town.

"You know," he said, "I'll bet there are some good fish right here in this river if we only had some line and a hook."

"What if," I said, "the captain let us throw a frag in the water tomorrow morning? Fresh fish would sure be good for breakfast."

We dreamed on for another hour until it began to rain again. Tony and I worked out a guard schedule with the two guys next to us, then rolled up in our ponchos and went to sleep.

We each stood two one-hour guard shifts, wrapped in our ponchos in the rain. It finally stopped raining about the same time the morning sun came up, lighting the grey sky and giving us good reason to be happy. Wet soldiers built fires at every third or fourth position. Some of the guys dried their fatigue shirts and pants on bamboo poles they held over the smoky flames. Since most of us wore no underwear, looking around the perimeter exposed the amusing sight of eighty naked soldiers wearing only helmets and jungle boots.

Enemy soldiers had not been seen in this area for some time, and we got a little lax. Of more concern to us at that moment was the necessity to get dry. Long before we arrived, Vietnam soldiers had learned that the fewer clothes that were worn, the more quickly the body dries. It was important for us to stay as dry as possible to ward off jungle rot and to allow our cuts and scrapes to heal.

About an hour after sunrise, when almost everyone was either drying their clothes or making coffee, Tony wandered off toward the company HQ. A few minutes later he came running back; I could see he was pretty excited.

“Captain said we’re going to stay here for a couple of days. If we want to do a little fishing with frags this afternoon, it’s OK with him!”

Squad-size patrols were sent out that morning, and they returned about noon with mostly negative reports. One squad had found a booby-trapped North Vietnamese artillery round, and they destroyed it in place. Another one of the squads had stolen a sampan from a small village two klicks down river and triumphantly paddled it up to our DDP. No one could master the single oar in the rear of the boat, like even the smallest Vietnamese child could, so they used their rifle butts as American style paddles.

Rain clouds began to threaten us again, so a few poncho tents sprang up in the hedgerows. Some of the fires were just getting rekindled when suddenly a half a dozen rifles opened up from the hill across the river—and we had no men on that side of the water. Like a bed of red ants that had just been stepped on, American soldiers suddenly ran in every direction. Some were looking for weapons, and everyone was looking for cover. Shooting was quickly increasing from the hill. I grabbed the '79 and rolled into the hole I'd dug the night before. I landed with a splash; the hole had filled with muddy rain water during the night. Tony splashed in beside me and cut loose with a 15-round burst from the '60, then dropped for cover. I waited a second, then stood up and fired a grenade across the Rao Cao into the thick hillside jungle.

Soon 80 weapons from our side of the river were shredding the deep green foliage on the far side. Our fire was answered by an equal number of automatic arms. Tony and I took turns popping up out of the hole to fire our weapons. The rapid concussions and expended gas of his exploding bullets next to my left ear kept blowing my hair around and deafening me. I continued to fire the '79 in rhythm with the '60 except once when several hot casings from his machine gun fell down my shirt collar. I jumped up, hitting Tony's elbow, causing him to blast half a dozen rounds into the water directly in front of us. I began rapidly flapping my shirttail as the empty brass cartridges sizzled their way down my back. Gravity did its job and the casings fell into the mud, hissing.

We didn't seem to be taking any incoming rounds, but there definitely was massive shooting coming from the hill. It was not just an echo of our own firing either, because we had not fired the first shots. Since I had no idea of where the shots were coming from, it almost became a game to return the fire. I picked trees and large bushes for targets and blew them away, Tony was doing the same. Due to the alert actions of one of the RTOs, Huey gunships soon arrived and began their rocket and machine-gun runs up and down the hill, parallel with the river.

After several minutes of intense shooting, one of the two gunship pilots requested that we hold our fire. When we stopped firing our weapons, the shooting on the other side of the river quit also. The captain stood up in his foxhole, dropped the radio handset, and began waving his arms back and forth across his chest as if he were polishing the hood of his new Ford Mustang.

"Cease fire! Cease fire!" he yelled. "There are U.S. forces on the back side of the hill."

I could not hear what he said, so I popped up and launched another grenade at the hill. Salvetti grabbed me and yelled into my ringing ears, “CEASE FIRE, NO GOOKS!”

Within 10 minutes, we all knew what had happened. One of our sister companies, Bravo, had humped into the area during the late morning. After setting up their day defensive position, they decided to sight in some of their new weapons. It was just going to be a little innocent target practice. However, the echo of their M-16s sounded just like the cracking of AK-47 fire to us, so we quickly "returned" the fire. Bravo Company then thought they were being fired upon so they "returned" our fire. We were each harmlessly blasting our own sides of the jungle-enshrouded hill that separated us. Finally, the gunship jockeys figured out what was going on.

Everyone felt a little dumb about what happened, but only Captain Becker had to go back, a few days later and explain it to the brass in battalion. At that dress-down the colonel used a great many descriptive four-letter words and threatened to make Captain Becker “a forward observer in downtown Hanoi” if friendly fire like that ever happened again. He then sent the appropriately censured captain back to us. I guess even company commanders got their butts chewed occasionally.

At 1500 hours, the captain walked over to Tony and me. Following his lead were another 30 or so guys. I wondered what was going on.

"I think its time to do some fishing. Who's got a frag?" he asked me.

I still had problems hearing, so the captain repeated the question, louder this time. Finally understanding, I quickly produced one from my shirt pocket.

"OK SERGEANT ROCK, LET ’ER GO!"

"Fire in the hole" I yelled, and threw the frag into the middle of the river.

It entered the water with a *ploop* and quickly sank to the bottom. In four seconds the river burped up a giant bubble. A geyser then shot about 15 feet into the air and threw its warm spray over us. The muffled *twump* indicated that the river was deep. A dozen or so bystanders took their boots off and jumped into the shallow edge of the river. Using bamboo poles, they guided half a dozen dead fish to within grabbing range. They then threw them up onto the bank to the cheers of the growing crowd.

Within the next half hour, soldiers yelled "Fire in the hole!" a dozen more times up and down the river. The grinning captain, quite enjoying what was going on, got on the radio and ordered a resupply of ammo and frags . . . and a case of concussion grenades.

An hour later when the resupply chopper landed, three FNGs climbed off and looked around, not knowing where to go. Everyone totally disregarded them, focusing instead on the wooden crate of concussion grenades. One "fisherman" standing near the box unsheathed his hunting knife and pried the lid off. There were two dozen black canisters about the size of soup cans in the box. But wait a minute . . . there were no blasting caps in them. The dim-witted REMFs in supply did not know enough about grenades to send us the blasting caps! Without the caps the concussion grenades were useless. We were all pissed off at not being able to detonate the explosives, until the captain got an idea.

"Let's tie a claymore to the top of the case and we'll blow the mine and all 24 grenades at once."

I was reasonably sure that a claymore and 24 concussion grenades would empty the river of fish and its water, but what the heck, it sounded like fun. I walked to the far side of the perimeter, however, to get away from the explosion as I still had a massive headache from the M-60. Tony Salvetti and one of the guys from third platoon tied a claymore to the case and paddled the bomb to the middle of the river in the pilfered sampan. Before the explosive package was dumped into the water, Tony inserted the blasting cap into the claymore. When everyone was safely on the bank and prepared, the captain connected the firing device to the wire. His hand was now connected to the homemade bomb that had disappeared into the river's dark depths. His warning of "Fire in the hole!"—I plugged my ears—was followed by a click on his firing device. Nothing happened. Click, click, click, and still nothing. The captain raised his head out of the foxhole and pushed his helmet back off his forehead.

"Something's wrong;" he said. "Do I have any volunteers to swim down and check it out?"

Everyone observed the age-old military adage: "Never volunteer for anything." The captain shrugged his shoulders and stood up.

He looked at the river for a few seconds in thought and then said, "And I don't blame ya."

He yanked several times on the wire and finally it broke off down next to the claymore. We never did attempt to recover the highly explosive package.

None of us were familiar with the kinds of fish that we had caught, but it really didn't matter; we were willing to try almost anything once. Some of the inventive soldiers fried their fish, sans cooking oil, in their steel helmets over red hot coals. Other men tried to roast their catch on bamboo poles held over the fire. Still others rolled their fish in banana leaves and tried to bake them. Nothing worked very well, and we ate most of the fish a little raw, or dark and crispy.

With our cooking experiment out of the way, card games and reading used up the last hours of daylight. Doc's pills had lessened my pounding head, so I decided to use the time to check out the "fresh meat" that had arrived on the resupply chopper. I found the three men clustered together near the company command post. They felt awkward and self-conscious as we veterans eyeballed them. Their uniforms were fresh and green; ours were ragged and brown. Their clean-shaven boyish faces reflected the innocence of youth, while ours showed the maturity gained by physical suffering and combat.

Staring at them, I realized that I was no longer a FNG. To them I might even be considered an old-timer. The sleepless days and nights, and Vietnam's harsh physical elements were conspiring to take away my youth. Although I didn't think that I had yet acquired the "thousand-yard stare" that the real old-timers like Washington, Cosby, and Pearson had had, I knew it would come. It was as if they were peering into eternity, and seeing nothing. I just needed to experience a little more pain and see a little more suffering and death.

I really didn't want to talk to the new cherries (and it wasn't because I was afraid to make friends that may later die), but I remembered the cold disregard shown when I was new, so I spoke up.

"Where are you from, Polansky?" I asked, using my best command voice.

His stitched name boldly stood out on the green cloth patch above his right breast pocket.

"Scranton, Pennsylvania, Sergeant," he replied.

As if it were important to me, I asked where Scranton was. "Northeastern part of the state, Sergeant," he loudly answered, as though I were a drill instructor.

I told him to knock off the "Sergeant" stuff, because, although the name was right, he used it wrong. I explained about my nickname and real rank (few of us wore our rank because we had no access to the cloth patches or equipment to sew them on.) Polansky said he had called me Sergeant just in case. He said he didn't want to do any pushups. It was obvious that this grunt had basic training drilled into his head.

"Is Scranton anywhere near Binghamton, New York?"

"Yes, Sarge . . . er . . . just 50 miles away." His eyes lit up in anticipation of what I was going to say next.

"Tony, come over here," I called. "I've got one of your home boys here!"

Tony was squatting over a freshly dug slit trench just outside the perimeter, and was doing what comes naturally.

"Be there in a minute!" he yelled back.

In exactly one minute, Tony walked up and I introduced him to Polansky. The machine gunner finished wiping his hands with toilet paper and pushed the right one forward. The FNG was not eager to touch it so they didn't shake hands. Tony and the new guy began to talk about girls they knew in each other's home towns and things they had in common. I could see they were going to be friends.

The other two new soldiers, not daring to speak until spoken to, jumped at the chance to tell me their names when I asked. Brostrom and West were finally getting their turn to talk when Captain Becker walked over to the five of us. The three new troops snapped to attention.

"Salvetti, do you know Polansky?" he asked in his usual deep command voice.

"Well, I kind of do, sir," he replied. "We're from the same part of the world."

"Good. Take him over and introduce him to Sergeant Martindale. He's now part of your squad. Sergeant Rock, take Brostrom and West over to Sergeant Taylor. They are now part of third squad."

The three cherries awkwardly tossed their heavy rucksacks up onto their backs. West winced as the straps dug into his soft untempered shoulders. Brostrom had an ace of spades tucked under his helmet band. The Vietnamese saw it as the symbol of death, but the new guy didn't know that yet.

We worked the river area for another week, patrolling during the day and setting up our tigers at night. We made no contact with Sir

Charles, and we were not eager to do so. Contact resulted in death, or bloody wounds that made you wish you were dead.

When Captain Becker was told that we were all moving to a new AO, our map coordinates indicated a ten-klick hump to the helicopter pick-up point. Zorn instigated a great deal of complaining around the perimeter. The general consensus was that ten klicks was a long way to hump when we had a perfectly good LZ right where we were. The Army never did promise life would be easy, and common sense only got in the way of orders. Zorn's bitching did not change a thing.

When the company began to move out, I watched the FNGs. Their first week of extended exposure to Nam's sun had turned their pale white backs to a nice lobster red. Remembering my first sunburn, I felt a bit of sympathy pain when they tossed the heavy rucksacks up onto their blistered shoulders. This was going to be an especially long hump for them.

We patrolled up the Rao Cao for a klick, then searched for a place to cross but could find none. Swimming to the other side would be impossible with the heavy loads we carried. Sergeant Martindale's squad found a place where the bottom of the river appeared firm and it was only six or seven feet deep. Captain Becker decided that we could cross it by walking underwater the short distance to the other side. When my turn came, I did as everyone else had done. Everything I wanted to keep dry (wallet, matches, toilet paper, letters etc.) went into my inverted helmet. As the water rose over my head, I held the helmet and my rifle as high as I could and just kept walking across the gravel river bed. Soon the water level dropped below my chin, and I continued up and out the other side.

On the bank, I turned to watch the next two or three guys wade through. Brostrom walked in up to his waist in the water, then stopped to remove his glasses. The lenses were thick enough to be used as paperweights, and I wondered if he could see anything without them. He secured the glasses in his shirt pocket and disappeared into the river, but as soon as the water was over his head, he did something unusual. I watched Brostrom make a left-hand turn and begin to walk upstream, underwater. I was not the only one to notice what was happening; several of the guys shouted, almost in unison, "Watch the FNG!"

Five meters and fifteen seconds upstream Brostrom dropped his helmet and rifle. His hands disappeared into the river and for three seconds the water's surface was calm. When his hands and head finally burst above the water, he inhaled with such gusto that the grass at the river sides seemed to lean toward him. Each time he exploded to the surface gasping for air, a small rodent-type shriek escaped his lips. To everyone but him, his pogo-stick bobbing and high-pitched squeals were hilarious. I'm sure he was fighting for his life, but to us safely on the bank, it was the funniest thing we'd seen for ages. Our roars of laughter thundered up and down the river. So much for our noise discipline.

My sides were splitting from the entertainment, but I dropped my waterlogged ruck and quickly waded chest-deep into the river. I held my rifle out for the cherry to grab. He clamped onto the flash suppressor with both hands, and I quickly pulled him ashore. His dark brown hair glistened in the early afternoon sun. Because he couldn't see without his glasses, his little round eyes squinted, creating whisker-like lines above his cheeks.

Lieutenant DeWitt, after watching the entire episode from the bank, yelled down to me, "Well Sergeant Rock, looks like you just saved a half-drowned muskrat."

Sergeant Taylor asked for a volunteer swimmer to go back into the water after Brostrom's equipment, because, he said, "We've got a muskrat that can't swim." Piece by piece all of his gear, including the helmet with the death card, was retrieved from the river, and the company moved out again. From that time forward the name Brostrom disappeared from our vocabularies—it was replaced by Muskrat.

# CHAPTER 10

# THE CHURCH

After a long all-day hump we finally arrived at the extraction point. We napped while we waited until several hours after dark. Finally the choppers arrived to take us to an unknown insertion and a new area of operation. When my turn came to board I stepped on the skid and spun my back toward the Huey's side opening. The momentum of my heavy rucksack pulled me thru the doorway and onto the metal floor. Within five minutes the entire company was airborne—just like the patch on our shoulders said.)

The sky above was as black as a bucket of roofing tar. We felt, rather than saw, the heavy water-laden sky. The jungle, the *villes*, and the ocean that passed below us were also black. There was not a spark of light anywhere. I had no reference to tell me where we were. The coordinates that Lieutenant DeWitt gave me just as the Hueys lifted off told me where the company was going. DeWitt also said that we would be making several false stops, trying to confuse the listening enemy. We, and they, could tell by the beating of the rotors against the humid air whether the Hueys were gaining or losing altitude, or just hovering. The scenario of false stops at potential landing zones proceeded as planned. The skids never touched the ground; we saw nothing and we were not fired upon.

After an hour in the air, we felt the familiar bump that told us we had made it back to mother earth. The lieutenant and I jumped out of the chopper and ran together for 20 meters through the blackness, half expecting to run into a tree. We then waited to be joined by the rest of the platoon. I could hear the other birds landing and taking off but couldn't really see them; they were all just shades of black. As soon as the rhythm of the rotors faded into the distance we found each other and organized back into platoons and departed for individual tigers.

My platoon quietly humped four klicks in a northwestern direction following the dirt highway—Route 1—that the choppers had landed on. According to the luminous hands on my watch, it was 0115 when we veered southwest onto communal road 601 and began another one-klick hump. At 0200 hours, the lieutenant called for a break, studied his map, and plotted our position.

"OK Rock, we're here," he whispered. "Call in our sit rep" (situation report).

I dialed the frequency for the HQ RTO who was traveling that night with the third platoon, and advised him that we were deploying our tiger. With that accomplished, we spread out just off the road and deployed the claymores. In groups of three, we backed into the short roadside elephant grass and waited.

Everyone was extremely tired from the many klicks we had humped since early the previous morning. What little nighttime was left was much too short to get the rest our bodies needed. We took turns and each got one hour of sleep.

The morning sun was blood red—maybe a portent of the near future? The road quickly filled with local Vietnamese civilians heading out for a long day in the rice fields. We stayed in that same position all day. We occasionally stepped onto the road and searched a handcart or two just to break the monotony. Most of us napped on and off until the midday heat made that impossible.

At 1700 hours, we received new tiger coordinates on the radio from Captain Becker. Lieutenant DeWitt wanted to get a head start and scout out the new area before it got dark, so we quickly saddled up into our rucksacks and moved out. It took 45 minutes to reach the ambush site, a once well-established but now empty village. The *ville* must have once been the center of activity in the area. Most of the buildings had weathered grey masonry walls, but the elephant grass roofs had all either caved in or burnt down. It was a Vietnamese ghost town.

The one prominent building in the two-block *ville* was still mostly intact, and the old Catholic church stood proudly at the end of the footpath. Upright oblong holes where stained glass windows had once allowed colored shafts of sunlight to penetrate the church's dark interior were now empty. The old building's smooth exterior concrete was pockmarked, indicating that the church had stopped its share of bullets and shell fragments over the years. The mossy tile roof was still sound, however, and it still protected the inside of the chapel from the monsoon's wind and rain.

As in many of the villages, the occupants of this once

**Chapter 1:**
From this position we opened fire on the fleeing V.C.

**Chapter 1:**
Sgt. Rock with his beach-front accommodations.

**Chapter 2:**
Tired Soldier (rear) sleeps in the shade of his poncho-draped M-16.

**Chapter 2:**
Day defensive position on the beach.

**Chapter 2:**
Sgt. Rock (kneeling) and the Vietnamese interpreter pose at the bunker that hid the two V.C. soldiers.

**Chapter 6:**
Sgt. Rock sits with his new M-79.

**Chapter 6:**
You can tell how long these grunts have been in Vietnam by their suntans.

**Chapter 9:**
We divide up the C-rations.

**Chapter 9:**
Sgt. Rock takes a break from carrying the heavy radio.

**Chapter 9:**
Vietnamese Mama-san sells us bags of cooked rice.

**Chapter 11:**
Minnie sharpens his bayonet at the gravel pit.

**Chapter 11:**
Phong Dien's marketplace.

**Chapter 11:**
Ducklings for sale.

**Chapter 11:**
Typical Phong Dien family grass hootch.
Mama-san's water cans in front of the dwelling

**Chapter 11:**
The bus from Hue to Quang Tri needs a push.

**Chapter 13:**
Sgt. Rock stands beside a new Cobra gunship.

**Chapter 15:**
Rappelling training at Camp Evans.

**Chapter 15:**
Descending the Chinnok chain ladder at Camp Evans.

**Chapter 15:**
Alpha Company burns.

**Chapter 15:**
The supply hootch is burned to the ground.
Unidentified soldier.

**Chapter 17:**
Capt. Becker and Lt. DeWitt eye-ball
the dead V.C. tax collector.

**Chapter 17:**
The squad stops patrol to take baths.

**Chapter 17:**
Vietnamese boy herds his water buffalo.

**Chapter 19:**
Sgt. Rock examines a V.C. cache of documents and Russian-made blasting caps he'd just discovered.

**Chapter 19:**
Wilson displays the AK-47 he just found hidden in the pond.

**Chapter 23:**
View across Fire Base Airborne.

**Chapter 23:**
Soldier waits for feces to burn, while two others "occupy" the outhouse.

**Chapter 23:**
A log bird delivers new supplies, including the orange mail bag.

**Chapter 26:**
Soldier wearing his salt-encrusted shirt smokes marijuana and watches Co Pong mountain.

prosperous hamlet had been evicted for their own protection, and sent to resettlement camps. During the day the people were allowed into their fields, but at sundown the area became a free fire zone, and we were instructed to "shoot to kill" anything that moved.

We wandered around the *ville* checking the buildings and hootches for signs of recent use, but we found none. The little farming community was as quiet as a one-room school on the first day of summer vacation. With just an hour of light remaining, the platoon patrols meandered back to the church to warm up some canned dinners and organize for the night. Lieutenant DeWitt divided us into four-man teams, wisely making sure "Major" Poulsen and Muskrat were not together.

"Tonight we're going to dig," he said, then added as an afterthought, "and dig 'em deep."

The church presented such a good target that he wanted everyone on the outside in fighting holes. The platoon command post, consisting of the lieutenant, Sergeant Wardle, Doc Bayne, and myself, would be the only ones inside the building.

"If it starts to rain," he said, "everyone can come in."

The ground was dry and soft compared to the hard cement floor of the chapel, so most preferred staying in the cooler air outside anyway.

The interior of the church had been totally gutted. Nothing remained but dust in the 100-by-50-foot room. I leaned my rifle and ruck against the wall below one of the empty window openings. I then unrolled my quilted nylon poncho liner and spread it out on the dusty floor. With my bed now made, I found three chips of concrete and arranged them in a small triangle. I ripped the foil from a heat tab and placed it in the center of the chips. After lighting the tab with matches that had seen a little too much moisture, I opened a can of turkey loaf and put it on my makeshift stove. Before long the bottom of the pressed turkey began to sizzle. It was as done as it was going to get; I was hungry.

By the time supper was over, the inside of the church was black. The stars between the clouds provided just enough light for me to see that everyone outside was preparing for sleep. The night was going to be a warm one. In the church, the four of us divided the radio monitoring into two one-hour shifts each. At midnight, Doc woke me for my first shift of listening to soldiers calling negative sit reps to company HQ. The back of my shirt was soaked with sweat, as was the poncho liner on the warm floor where I had slept.

I stretched, trying to loosen up my aching muscles, and slowly walked over to the radio, sat down next to it, and leaned my sore back against the wall. The sun's heat, trapped in the foot-thick cement, was now dissipating into the building. The heat created a stifling environment, and the humid, warm air wrapped itself around my body like a heavy wool blanket. It was hard to even breathe. Droplets of sweat trickled down my ribs. I unbuttoned my shirt and stood up, hoping to find fresher air.

A slight night breeze gently blew through the window nearest me, so I walked over and sat down in the opening. Outside I could see three of the guard positions. Watching closely, I could also see at least one man moving at each of the guard posts. I closed the collar of my shirt so my three-day beard would not irritate my sweaty neck, and then rested my heavy head on my chest.

With a jerk, I sat up and looked around, realizing I had just dozed off. Lifting my watch close to my face I could see the hands were only nine minutes past straight up, so my nap was just a momentary one. I realized I would sleep again if I sat there any longer, so I stood up and felt my way along the smooth interior wall from window to window around the old church. At the four window openings on each side, I paused and took deep breaths of the humid night air and did half a dozen jumping jacks to circulate blood through my dormant brain.

I made my way across the front of the chapel, starting a second loop of the interior, and stared out the first window on that side once more. Soldiers were watching the darkness. Several of the guards were looking through their new starlight scopes. I was comfortably certain that no one could sneak up on us during the night.

Hand over hand in the darkness, I felt my way to the next window, I paused as distant AK-47 and answering M-16 shots broke the stillness of the night. Nothing to worry about, I thought to myself; the firefight was more than a klick away, toward Phong Dien. Then several grenades and four or five claymore mines detonated. The fight was escalating. Hurrying back to my radio in the darkness, I accidentally kicked my helmet, which skidded across the floor, making those chalk-on-blackboard screeching noises. It then slammed with a *thunk* into the wall. Everyone in the church was now awake and asking me what was going on. I didn't know. Lieutenant DeWitt, Wardle, Doc Bayne, and I gathered around the radio. Soon Alpha

Company's RTO reported that sappers, enemy commandos, had hit and were attempting to blow the Phong Dien bridge.

Our platoon was one of five ambushes set up on possible enemy retreat routes from the bridge. We instinctively went on 100 percent alert. At the lieutenant's command, I visited each of the positions outside the church and told the guys what we had learned from the radio. Soon we could hear the helicopter gunships "working out" at the bridge, and after that the sappers' small-arms fire ceased.

At 0105 hours, Doc Bayne heard Minnie coming through the front doorway and guided him over to us.

"We can see them in the starlight scopes!" he said. "They're coming up the road. Looks like about thirty of 'em!"

"Is everyone ready?" the lieutenant asked Minnie.

"I don't know, man. All I know is I'm scared shitless!"

"Look, Minnie," the platoon leader's excited voice quickly raised above a whisper. "tell everyone on the left side to wait until the gooks are in claymore range, then give them hell! I'll go tell everyone on the right."

He continued with his instructions: "Wardle, get out the back door and tell rear security to cover our asses. Rock, get on the radio and tell command what's going on, and Doc, stay here until you're needed!" With the plan of attack—or maybe defense—decided upon, the lieutenant and Minnie disappeared through the open doorway.

"Ambrose, Ambrose, this is Blade, over." Captain Becker answered my whispered call immediately.

"Roger Blade, this is Ambrose Actual; what is your sit rep, over?"

"We have thirty of the bad guys three hundred meters north of our tiger. I say again, we have three zero Victor Charlies, three zero zero meters on the November side of our tiger. Request air support, over."

"Roger Blade, we will have birds above you shortly. Inform your Actual that artillery will begin ASAP, over."

"Negative Ambrose, the bad guys are running up the road right into our tiger, they will be on top of us at any second. Just get the gunships here ASAP, over!"

Before another word was spoken, two claymores detonated, quickly followed by a third. A '60 singing solo was soon joined by a chorus of '16s and '79s. The weapons choir was singing the sappers' swan song.

Lying on the floor of the chapel with the radio handset still to my ear, I realized that rear security had initiated the ambush. That was not the way it was supposed to happen. Evidently the sappers had changed directions. Instead of staying on the road and coming through the center of the deserted *ville*, they had decided to go around it. I explained in a burst of words to the lieutenant, who had quickly returned from outside. I paused once as AK-47 fire hit the window frame just above me, peppering me with concrete chips.

My work on the radio accomplished, I rose to my knees and took a quick look over the window sill at the ongoing firefight. Green and red tracer bullets raced in opposite directions, passing each other in the night. The fire-breathing lead identified both the source and the destination of the deadly projectiles. That was the trouble and benefit with tracers—they worked both ways.

I saw a flash of green coming at me but could not react before it passed through my window and splattered against the far wall. I pivoted away from the window, placing my back against the safety of the wall, but it was all after the fact. Had the gook been a little luckier, he would have blown my head off. I rotated the fire selector switch on my M-16 to rock and roll and waited a second before joining the firefight. I guessed that the gooks' shots were random; I had not yet fired and I didn't think he could see me in the darkness.

John Wayne style, I stood up and pivoted into the window frame. In one quick burst I fired my entire twenty-round magazine at the spot the green tracers had come from. Back safely against the wall, I relived the vision of seconds earlier. Hand grenades, Claymores and rocket propelled grenades (RPGs) ended their existence in glorious flashes of blinding white light. It was like lightning during a thunderstorm, except counting the seconds between the flash and its ominous thunder was impossible. Television and motion pictures could not come close to capturing the ear-splitting crack of high-power automatic rifle fire and the mind-numbing sounds of ordnance exploding "up close and personal." In my enclosed concrete environment the reverberating concussions rang giant warning bells in my head.

I smacked the palm of my left hand against the M-16's release button, and the empty magazine clattered onto the floor. I then slammed a loaded magazine into the void and chambered the first round. Doc, at the window next to me, was expertly sending three-round bursts from his weapon toward unseen targets. Unlike some other medics, our pill pusher had no conscientious objection to protecting his life or mine.

An enemy mortar shell exploded in a treetop high overhead, tearing loose a large branch that came crashing to the ground in front of Doc's window. Another shell detonated next to the wall, causing the old building to shudder.

Screaming to be heard above the deafening blasts of the high explosives, Doc yelled, "They're walking the mortars up to the church!"

Before I could verbally confirm his assessment of the situation, something caught my attention. A figure darted through the rear door and disappeared into a corner of the church. Quickly dropping to one knee, I planted the butt of my rifle firmly against my right shoulder and stared over the barrel into the darkness. I waited for a sound to fire at. When the noise came, it was not what I had expected. Crying. Someone was crying. Doc, thinking one of our guys must be hit (gooks never made a sound even with the most painful of wounds) silently advanced. My twitching trigger finger caressed the M-16's firing mechanism. The medic briefly flipped on his red filtered flashlight and found Sergeant Taylor, the new squad leader, rolled up in a ball in the corner of the room. Trembling like a little pup that had just been kicked, the sergeant pleaded with the medic between sobs.

"Please don't make me go out there" he bawled. "I'm going to die!"

Doc grabbed the crying sergeant by his shirt collar and roughly dragged him out of the corner. His cursory examination revealed no wounds. Taylor was untouched. The dust cover on his weapon was still closed; he had not fired a shot. Doc shoved him back into the corner to cry alone while he returned to his window and the firefight.

Every few seconds a tracer would burst into the room, ricochet off a wall or two and then die on the floor. Since the majority of the gooks' rounds were not tracers, I knew a great deal of unseen hostile lead must be entering our sanctuary. In the confusion of the battle, the gooks seemed to think the church was the cause of their destruction, and they concentrated their fire on the old structure. As Doc had predicted, the next mortar shell hit the center of the roof. It blew a big hole in the tiles, scattering the broken fragments over us and the floor. The wooden beam that ran the length of the building made a loud CRACK! and the roof began to cave in. A jagged one-pound fragment of red-hot shrapnel slammed into the floor after first piercing my poncho liner; the intense heat caused the nylon blanket to shrivel up until it was the size of a small pillow.

"Let's get out of here, the roof's caving in!" Doc shouted.

He spun and headed for a window on the opposite side of the room. I started to follow him but then stopped. I had not seen the lieutenant for a while; evidently he had gone back out the door in the excitement. I grabbed the radio and bee-lined for the same window Doc had just jumped through. I tried to high jump the three-and-a-half-foot windowsill, but the radio and the rifle had changed my center of gravity. My foot caught the sill and I tumbled out, six feet to the ground, landing on my back. As I made my graceful exit, an RPG slammed into the wall next to the window I had been fighting from. A five-foot section of the concrete wall, including my window, disappeared in the ensuing blast.

Outside the church someone began to call me on the radio; it took a few seconds for me to catch my breath before I could answer. Two helicopter gunships gave me an ETA of 60 seconds and requested that we mark our perimeter with strobe lights. I yelled the instructions to the guys closest to my corners of our formation and told them to pass the word to the other side. By crawling to the northeast corner of the building I could hear the rhythmic *whop whop whop* of the inbound choppers. Charlie could also hear them, and his hostile fire died quickly. While lying on the ground, peering around the corner, I grabbed the radio headset and directed several rocket and machine-gun runs at the sappers' last known positions. It was critical that the gunship pilots knew exactly where we were; this was no time for "about" or "approximately" or "close to." My instructions and the following adjusted fire had to be exact. During my strafing directions the lieutenant ran up and dove to the ground next to me.

"Good work, Rock," he whispered. "How did it go back here? Anybody hurt?"

I told him I hadn't talked to anyone except Doc, and we were OK. He picked up the radio handset, called Ambrose and gave a glowing report of the platoon's heroic firefight. Listening to Lieutenant DeWitt describe it, one would think we should all receive Medals of Honor.

After the gunships had retired to the quiet of Camp Evans, each of the squad leaders crawled in to meet with the lieutenant. He instructed them to hold their positions until dawn. The three reported that Sir Charles had been unable to inflict a single wound on anyone in the platoon.

We anxiously waited for the rest of the night to pass so we could get an enemy body count at first light. Morning stars were still visible when Lieutenant DeWitt declared it was light enough, and we began the search. Carefully watching for booby-traps, we expanded the perimeter around the church. Zorn and West, standing fifty meters beyond their foxhole on the side of the church, began shouting that they had a body. The lieutenant and I walked over to them and the gook who lay facedown in the dirt. Two fist-sized bloody holes in the back of his green shirt easily identified where Zorn's 7.62 mm M-60 bullets had exited the body.

Zorn completed his probing underneath the body for booby-traps, stood up, put his foot on the shoulder of the corpse, and kicked. The body flopped over, revealing several things that we found very interesting. First, we noticed a tin whistle on a leather string around his neck. We had discovered back on Hill 51 that enemy officers often directed assaulting units by giving short blasts on whistles, much like the buglers did during our own bygone cavalry days. Our guess that he was a Viet Cong officer was substantially confirmed by our second discovery. In the soldier's left breast pocket were several dozen regimental identification pins. We guessed that he had stripped his men of their identification pins prior to the attack on the Phong Dien bridge. He had been unfortunate enough to get blown away during their retreat, just when he thought he was out of danger. We left the body to rot in the hot sun.

The guys in the squads continued their searching but with limited success. Members of Sergeant Tew's squad did find three RPG-2s and 400 rounds of machine-gun ammo, but the most important indicators of success, bodies and weapons, had all been removed. Four different spots where substantial blood had soaked into the earth were proof enough for the lieutenant to call in a body count of five. One squad made a half-hearted effort at following one of the blood trails. No one was anxious to get ambushed, so when the blood quit, so did they.

When the resupply chopper landed later in the morning, three more FNGs climbed off and Sergeant Taylor climbed on. The lieutenant told everyone that the Sarge was going to the rear temporarily for "medical reasons." If cowardice was suddenly a reason for sending a soldier to the rear, the lieutenant was sure there would be others who would suddenly develop "who gives a damn" attitudes and become cowards.

The drudgery of filling sandbags and spit-shining boots, the harassment of senior NCOs and officers, and even the hated "shit burning" detail were acceptable for some in exchange for the safety of the base camp. The only danger REMFs generally had to deal with was eating too much steak at the mess hall or drinking too much beer at one of the clubs. Maybe an occasional ankle was sprained as a half-drunk clerk walked home from a movie, or a USO or Red Cross show. Worst of all, one of them may have gotten a sore back from sleeping all night on a bed that was too soft.

Lieutenant DeWitt knew that some grunts would gladly endure the REMF dangers versus the lousy living conditions and the perils of dismemberment and death we were being subjected to. To some, being identified as a coward was only a temporary brand they would have to live with. The key word was—live.

The lieutenant could not trust Taylor any longer. Hostile fire will always separate the real soldiers from the pretenders, and Lieutenant DeWitt was certain that Taylor was a genuine tough-guy pretender. He was a hazard to us all. No tears of brotherly love were shed when he boarded the bird and was carried off.

Zorn strutted around all day with a "swelled head" the size of a basketball. He was given credit for the dead gook and was taking laurels for most of the ambush. Within seconds of finding the body, the machine gunner had ripped off his colorful Screaming Eagle patch and stuck it in the mouth of the corpse.

We were proud of the fact that the 101st Airborne was the only division in Nam that did not wear a subdued (camouflaged) emblem on the shoulder. Within our own ranks, stories were plentiful of Charlie's fear of those wearing the colorful eagle-head patches. We had psyched ourselves into believing Charlie would rather run than ruffle our feathers. The patch in the mouth was a symbol of a Screaming Eagle kill to anyone finding the body, be they villagers or Vietnamese Communists.

In his usual bullying and bragging manner, Zorn told us his story as he pulled a cigar butt from his pocket and lit it.

"I spotted them f---ers through the starlight scope about 400 meters down the road. They were all bunched up and double-timin' it toward us. I knew what had to be done, so I told Minnie to go tell the lieutenant and get us some air cover. The lucky f---ers would have run into the main part of the tiger, in front of the church, if they hadn't stopped fifty meters short of claymore range and changed directions." He blew a grey smoke ring into the air.

"One of them gooks pointed to the others showing which way to go, so I figured he was their officer. I kept ol' Betsy here pointed in his direction. The dumb idiots in rear security with Sergeant Wardle blew the frigging claymores way too early or we'd've blown them all away. I made sure I got the officer first, and then blew away two more before a friggin RPG hit a tree by me and I had to go for cover. I know I got at least three of 'em, and I saw three or four others go down before the explosions blanked out my starlight scope. Ain't nobody gettin by me!"

Zorn spent a lot of time blowing his own horn, but unlike Sergeant Taylor's war stories of a few days earlier, everything Zorn said was probably true.

## CHAPTER 11

# LIFESTYLE

Most of the month of January and the first half of February we spent in and around Camp Evans and Phong Dien. For a bunch of infantry dudes this was good duty. There were many long boring days but no one died. We ambushed a road or river two or three nights a week, but most of the time our patrols and defensive positions were within a klick of the quiet little Vietnamese village. Chances of our meeting Sir Charles were minimal. Our favorite hangouts for night defensive positions were an abandoned gravel pit and an old French fortification. Both were on Route 1, less than a klick from Phong Dien, so access to the *ville* was convenient.

We established friendly speaking relationships with several locals, mostly because they were trying to do some business with us. The guys spent many hot afternoon hours drinking iced American beer or soda water from rusty tin cans at one of the many roadside shops. We had to pay five times the price charged on base for the black market drinks, but our only other choice was hot canteen water. When not selling local food items or begging C-rations from us, the children entertained us with questions about everything from the price of rice to how many VC we had killed. Sometimes on school days they would stop on the way home and tell us what they had learned in class.

The goal for these children was to get an elementary education. Children began school at age six, starting with grade five. By their fifth year, at age 11, they hopefully would have advanced to the first grade (the grade numbering system was opposite of the American system.) School was compulsory for only the first three grades (five, four, and three), but the authorities did not enforce the law. If the kids graduated before being forced to work with their families in the rice fields, they qualified to take a higher-education test. Few of these poor village children would make it through the five years and have a chance at additional schooling.

Traditional clothing worn by these children and their parents consisted of loose-fitting trousers and long-sleeved collarless shirts. Black was the most common color for the light cotton basic outer garment. Most of the villagers went barefoot or wore Ho Chi Minh sandals made from discarded automobile tires.

The villagers' dwellings were small. If they were owned by merchants, the little residences usually had some kind of shop in the front. The hootches were generally made of bamboo and thatch with compacted dirt floors. They were simply furnished. A table with several simple chairs, large bowls for storing food and water, and hardwood planks which served as beds comprised the main household goods. The focal point of the main room—usually the only room—was a simple ancestral altar where fragrant punks were lit and prayers were said to departed relatives. The smell of the burning incense made the *ville* always smell sweet.

There were a few solidly built homes made of concrete or cinderblocks, but these belonged to the rare well-to-do. What really impressed (or should I say, depressed) me were the homes of the very poor. Sometimes families lived in houses with walls made of flattened cardboard boxes, with split-open beer and pop cans for roof shingles. The average Vietnamese civilian lived at a level far below even the most impoverished Westerner. The poor in America lived in comfort of which these peasants could only dream. Telephones, washing machines, feather pillows, and eyeglasses were just pictures in old magazines.

During the Vietnam orientation classes my first week in-country, Army instructors taught me many health-related things that only much later did I begin to understand. Malaria, tuberculosis, intestinal diseases, and parasitic infections were the main causes of illness and death among the civilians, and bubonic plague was well established in much of the country. Diseases such as these were rare or nonexistent back in the world. Even U.S. soldiers taking daily or weekly doses of anti-malarial drugs, notably Chloroquine and Primaquine, were not immune.

Instructors warned me that in the area to which I was going, a drug-resistant malarial parasite (Plasmodium Falciparum) had become a big concern. These were some big words that did not find a place to rest in my brain. The odds, however, of U.S. soldiers spending time in a military hospital for these Vietnamese illnesses were good. Besides all the diseases, they warned me repeatedly about internal lead poisoning—the kind that comes from an AK-47 bullet.

I watched the mama sans as they went about their morning household duties before going into the fields. At first light, when civilians could leave their homes without having to fear being shot at, mama san went for water. Some families lived more than a klick away from the nearest well or river. Mama san balanced large cans, maybe three gallons apiece, on each side of her head using a wooden yoke placed across her shoulders. With a smooth, steady gait, these small women carried the heavy loads for long distances without spilling any of the precious liquid.

Most of the river water available to the civilians and us was polluted. Not even the larger cities had safe drinking water and, due to pollution seepage, underground wells were also contaminated. The discolored and defiled water that we drank almost every day was an ideal breeding ground for many waterborne diseases. Some soldiers in the company had become ill multiple times. Sometimes they were sick enough to require hospitalization at Camp Evans.

The Army tried to supply us with fresh water when possible, but it was not always feasible. We were issued water purification pills, but they took 30 minutes to become effective, and sometimes we couldn't wait that long. Besides, purification pills made the water taste like iodine. An alternative to the situation, one that we "wealthy" Americans could afford, was the black market beer and soda water. The Vietnamese, who had built up a certain resistance to the contamination, were still not completely immune, and occasionally they paid the price.

Many common unsanitary practices were also contributors to the poor health of the people. They commonly used open ditches as communal toilets. Mamma san often washed the family eating utensils in sand or stagnant water. Food was generally stored, prepared, and served among swarms of flies.

I complained often about eating the same 12 C-rat meals day after day, but these poor peasants mostly just ate some variation of rice and vegetables at every meal, every day. Sometimes small portions of pork, fish, chicken or shrimp were available to supplement the rice, but not often. *Nuoc-maum*, a sauce made from rotten fish, could always be found among the basic household food supplies. The fermented flavoring was a required ingredient in many Vietnamese dishes, or it could just be added to plain rice. It smelled terrible. American soldiers derogatively called it armpit sauce.

Families ate their food from individual bowls, and even the small children handled chopsticks adeptly (fingers were never used.) My attempts to use the sticks always brought giggles from the children. Family groups, including second and third generations, who would generally gather in a circle, squat down on floor mats covering the compacted earth, and eat their meal.

Family cohesiveness and parental respect were the most important elements of the Vietnamese way of life. Hot tea brewed in a large earthen pot over a small wood fire followed the meal; usually this was accompanied by foul-smelling handmade cigarettes. Perhaps some future civilization will look at the present American lifestyle and marvel at our primitive ways, much as I marveled at the poor Vietnamese.

## CHAPTER 12

# MUSKRAT GETS LOST

Someone once defined a combat infantryman's life as follows: "Day after day of boredom interjected with moments of pure terror." Our visits to Phong Dien were the highlights of these days of drudgery. We did not complain, however, because the assignment was generally safe. Whenever we operated back in the jungles of the mountains, or even near them, the "moments of pure terror" were much more frequent.

On one of our daytime patrols investigating possible tiger sites, we found and searched an old masonry farmhouse. For years, soldiers like us had visited the abandoned house, evidenced by the graffiti inside. Names of warriors and their thoughts about the war, women, Nam, or the number of days to DEROS (date of estimated release from overseas) covered the inside walls. The house provided a good daytime sanctuary, and we visited it often. The roof kept us out of the rain or sun, whichever plagued us that day. Up on a slight rise, the structure provided a commanding view of the surrounding rice paddies and fields.

One afternoon after everyone in the platoon had awakened from midday siestas and the boredom had become almost intolerable, “Major” Poulson excitedly entered the house. Lieutenant DeWitt and I were sitting on the hard, debris-littered floor, leaning against a cool interior concrete wall.

He spat on his glasses and rubbed the lenses with his fingers while exclaiming, "I heard a noise in the well! I think there's a VC tunnel down there!"

Lieutenant DeWitt turned his head and gave me the "Is he nuts?" look. Twenty-five meters east of the house stood an old circular concrete well. The well had been dry for many years, and for that same amount of time American soldiers had used it as a trash dump. I looked down the 25-foot shaft each time I tossed in half-eaten food or empty cans—it was easier than digging a hole for disposal. There were tunnels down there all right, but they were rat tunnels.

Answering the lieutenant's nonverbal question, I raised my eyebrows and shrugged my shoulders as if to reply, "Don't ask me if he's crazy." We didn't know if Major really believed what he had said, or if he was just trying to suck us into some self-generated excitement.

"What do you propose we do about it?" asked the lieutenant.

"W-e-l-l . . ."

He pushed his heavy plastic-framed glasses up his sweating nose and thought it over.

"The way I see it, if I were to drop a frag down the hole, I could save the platoon from an ambush."

Lieutenant DeWitt said, "What you have requested to do is above and beyond the call of duty, soldier. God be with you on this dangerous mission."

The smile the lieutenant was desperately trying to hold back appeared briefly at the corners of his mouth.

I put down the can of warm peaches I was eating and followed the lieutenant out the front door. While exiting the house, I warned everyone that "Major" Poulson was about to trigger a "fire in the hole," so they had better pay attention. A small crowd soon filled the windows and doorway of the old building. Everyone wanted to see what was going on out by the well, but since "Major screw-up" was in charge, it was safer to be inside the house. Only Lieutenant DeWitt and I ventured beyond the concrete walls with Poulson. We felt kind of responsible for what was happening.

Major pulled a frag from his shirt pocket and held it close to his chest as he struggled to pull the pin. After he had successfully removed the safety, he leaned over the hole and dropped the grenade. The spoon flipped off as it fell, allowing the grenade to arm itself and start the four-second fuse to self-destruction. We stepped back from the opening in the ground and heard a clink, clink, as the frag landed in a decade's worth of old empty cans.

The explosion deep in the well was normal, but the resulting echo and unusual visual effect was not. A gray smoke ring burst from the oval opening, seeming to pulsate as it rushed into the sky. With each smoke ring pulse came a rapid high-pitched *whoop-whoop-whoop* sound. About 100 meters into the sky the ring and the accompanying noise finally dissipated. The peeling whitewashed farmhouse reverberated with the thunder of cheers and a few clenched fists, all salutes to the Major.

The lieutenant winked and declared that we had now

eliminated the threatening hordes of enemy soldiers. We should pop a couple of smoke grenades into the well and see where the smoke filtered up.

"It might lead to something."

Within ten seconds, a dozen members of the platoon had quickly tossed smokes from the house to our feet. The opportunity to lighten a ruck by the weight of a smoke grenade was tempting. I selected two yellow smokes and tossed the rest back to their owners.

*Smoke grenades do not detonate like fragmentation grenades do. When the safety pin is pulled and the handle released, fire and very dense smoke are forced out of the bottom of the can for about 30 seconds. Among other things, smoke grenades identify us to friendly aircraft.*

With a smoke in each hand, their pins pulled, I leaned over the hole and dropped the grenades. Each of them popped as they fell, and the thick yellow smoke soon began to fill the concrete enclosure. After 15 seconds, when the smoke began to spill over the top of the well, the lieutenant pulled the pin out of a frag and threw it to the bottom of the shaft. Four seconds later, the same thing happened as before, except that accompanying the *whoop-whoop-whoop* was a perfect bright yellow four-foot smoke ring floating high into the afternoon sky. Other platoon members experimented with the well, using a variety of colors, and each time the results were the same.

Later that afternoon, Ambrose Actual called on the radio with some hot information. Twenty VC soldiers were in a tiny farm hamlet just 13 klicks to our west. A farmer passed the information to a South Vietnamese unit, which notified U.S. intelligence, who in turn ordered Alpha Company to check out the report. There was a possibility that we could be entering an ambush, so Captain Becker decided we would hump into the area long after dark. An o-dark-thirty surprise gave us the best chance of catching Sir Charles unaware.

After sundown, first and third platoons rendezvoused with us at the house. The captain and the three platoon leaders spread their maps out on the concrete floor. The soft glow of the red filtered flashlights lit the interior of the command post room like the coals of a dying campfire.

Captain Becker took the position of head chief. The little band of platoon-leading warriors sat cross-legged around him. We four RTOs, one belonging to each sub-chief, hovered like squaws around the edges of the pow-wow monitoring our radios. From our unique vantage point, we could pass on little scraps of information to the guys that never made it through the chain of command.

We learned from the 45 minute pow-wow that the 20 VC, mostly local yokels, had been recruited as early as 1962 into the People's Liberation Armed Forces, (called Viet Cong by South Vietnamese and American soldiers) to fight against the "Imperialist Americans" and their southern anti-communist brothers. At night, villagers in Phong Dien and other nearby *villes* often saw them. They visited "girlfriends," resupplied themselves with rice, and maybe collected some taxes. Most of the villagers did not like the communists. They were afraid that the VC would forcefully recruit and re-educate more of their sons. A disgruntled farmer had compromised the mid-sized *ville* where these soldiers were hiding.

Alpha, our sister company Delta, and one ARVN company all had parts to play in the unfolding scenario. The captain's plan called for the three companies to set up ambushes and blow away the VC as they return to the mountains.

If there was anything difficult about the captain's plan, it was the ARVNs. The South Vietnamese made our job harder rather than easier. The unreliable ARVNs seldom carried more than a handful of bullets each. When fighting broke out they ran. Maybe South Vietnamese Rangers and Airborne units elsewhere could hold their own in a firefight, but I never saw any that could.

Sometimes when we were trying hard to keep our presence unknown, South Vietnamese soldiers would betray us by cooking over a bonfire. Other times one of them would "accidentally" fire his rifle. It was obvious to us that Marvin the ARVN didn't want to get into a firefight. He hoped the enemy would run when alerted to our presence. The strategy may have worked sometimes, but mostly it just caused us to get ambushed and killed.

The ARVNs I worked with were poorly disciplined, poorly trained, poorly equipped, and more than willing to let the gung-ho Americans do all the fighting. Why were the NVA and most of the VC such formidable fighters while their ARVN brothers were so incompetent? I knew the ARVNs and their thought processes. They could just dump all the fighting on us, and we would do it for them.

American soldiers had yet to lose a major battle in the country. We knew that if the politicians left us alone we could win this war. We also knew that if the newly elected president, Richard Nixon, ever pulled us out, the country would fold to the communists in a heartbeat.

At 2400 hours the officers called the squad leaders into the house and briefed them on the mission. The lieutenants took ten minutes to explain their plans. Deliberately withholding information from the troops was common among many officers. It seemed they felt more important if they knew more than the men they commanded. I'm sure the rationale was that we were being told everything we needed to know to get the job done. That way if any of us were captured we would have very little hush-hush "intelligence" to give up.

At the end of Lieutenant DeWitt's briefing he told us that Zorn was officially the new leader of the third squad, and that he had requested Zorn's promotion to sergeant. Zorn's elation at the good news was evident as he dug into his shirt pocket for the ever-present partially smoked cigar. His cocky attitude had just received a shot of adrenaline.

The squad leaders dispersed to the perimeter surrounding the house. They advised each of their squads of the situation and told them to pack up because the company would be moving out in one-five minutes.

When everyone was saddled up in their heavy rucksacks, Captain Becker gave the command for second platoon to take the lead. Lieutenant DeWitt gave the command for second squad to be the first in line, and soon-to-be Sergeant Zorn in turn told West to take the point. Everything was accomplished in an orderly manner, following the chain of command. Minnie fell in behind West. The lieutenant stepped in third. He had the map, compass, and the responsibility to get us to our destination, thirteen klicks away. Since I had the radio and needed to stay with the platoon leader, I was next. Fifth, stumbling after me, came Muskrat.

The first few klicks were easy and we quietly slipped through the night. The ground was dry, and the quarter moon provided enough light to see up and down the column with little difficultly. Six klicks and two hours later we entered ankle to knee-deep rice paddies. The map told us the paddies would continue to obstruct us until we reached our targeted *ville*.

We could have followed the main dirt road all the way to the *ville*, but that would have compromised our position. The gooks would be watching the road, and we would likely be the ones getting ambushed. Coming in the back way through the rice paddies, we hoped, would spoil any pre-made plans to catch us by surprise. Any RPGs or claymore-type weapons the VC soldiers had would not be aimed toward the vast expanse of rice paddies to their rear.

As soon as we entered the water the clouds began to move in and hide the moon. Closing the five-meter intervals that separated each of us was dangerous, but necessary. Each man had to keep physical contact with the soldier ahead or he could become separated in the darkness. As soldiers in the front of the column increased or slowed the pace, the accordion effect was greatly exaggerated by the time it reached the end of the column. The guys who were required to run to maintain contact one second were forced to stop when they suddenly and unexpectedly ran into the rucksack of the soldier in front of them. Frustrated, they quietly swore at each other as they collided up and down the long line.

Periodically, Lieutenant DeWitt called for ten-minute breaks so the column could tighten up. He also needed the time to reorient himself with the map. Most of us were not near a dike during those breaks, so we just sat where we were, sometimes in water several feet deep. The waterlogged packs on our backs acted as anchors, preventing our exhausted bodies from floating off into the darkness.

The mud and water were difficult to move through. It took every bit of energy and concentration I had to hold my place in the line. Occasionally Muskrat violated the rule of silence by whispering to me to slow down. I wished I could slow down, but I knew I would lose contact with the lieutenant if I did. The hump exhausted us all, but the pace had to be fast or we'd never reach the *ville* on time. With each step my heavy rucksack shifted, threatening to pull me sideways into the water. Left foot, right foot, left foot . . . come on Rock, keep on going, right foot, left foot . . . is DeWitt still there . . . yes . . . right foot . . . I can't make it much farther.

I stopped to catch my breath and redistribute the weight on my back when I realized that I couldn't hear anyone sloshing in the water behind me. The ruck straps digging into my shoulders were causing my neck to go stiff, so I swiveled my body to see behind me. There was nothing: no noise, no movement, nobody. Where was Muskrat? Where was the rest of the company?

I turned back around as quickly as I dared and took four fast steps forward. I grabbed the back of Lieutenant DeWitt's ruck to get his attention. He was in no mood to have someone hanging on him. When he spun around and knocked my hand away with his elbow, I lost my balance and fell face-first into the paddy. My pack fell forward onto the back of my head and mashed my face into the warm mud.

Air, I needed air! Pushing my hands into the slimy muck to roll over proved useless. They just sank deeper and deeper. Desperately, I spread my legs as wide as possible. I twisted my shoulders enough to allow the ruck to slip off my back. With that weight gone, my body floated up enough so I could pull my knees back under me. Finally I shoved my still-helmeted head to the surface. Kneeling there in the water, gasping for air, I thought of Muskrat at the Rao Cao River. Suddenly that incident wasn't so funny anymore.

Lieutenant DeWitt, West, Minnie, and I were all alone; the rest of the company had disappeared. The four of us stumbled to a nearby dike where we could drop our rucks and wait. I suggested using the radio to contact one of the other RTOs. DeWitt thought the column may be close to the ambush site, and he didn't want our voices on the radio blowing their surprise.

We talked about humping to the target *ville* ourselves, but decided it would be just our luck to run onto the 20 retreating VC. Even worse, we might get ambushed by our own guys. The lieutenant decided we should stay put. If we heard any movement nearby, we could slip down into the water and hide. The four of us were certainly unable to challenge a platoon of VC soldiers.

For three long hours we sat on the dike, back to back, listening and waiting for the sun. When it finally got light enough to see, it was Minnie who spotted them first. Almost a klick away, across the flat of the rice paddies, was good ol' Alpha Company. We could see they were in a defensive perimeter, nowhere near where the ambush was to have taken place. I called Ambrose Actual on the radio and handed the handset to the lieutenant. If the company commander wanted to chew some butt, it wasn't going to be mine.

Contrary to my fears, Captain Becker was relieved to hear from us. He told Lieutenant DeWitt that Muskrat had lost contact with me during the hump (that much we already knew.) Rather than admit he was lost in the strange mucky terrain, Muskrat had led 107 dead-tired soldiers around and around in a big circle as he looked for us. For several hours the company had sloshed in the gooey mud, following their self-appointed and lost leader. Everyone thought they were still humping to the target; only Muskrat knew that they were hopelessly lost. I heard later that the captain personally delivered a proper "attitude adjustment" to poor Muskrat.

After rejoining the company 45 minutes later, Doc told me everyone was so mad at Muskrat they would have hanged him, had a tree been handy. Several minutes after our arrival, word came over the radio from battalion that Delta's ambush had been successful. They caught five gooks in the open and in a brief firefight they blew them all away. One Delta rifleman was hit in the hand by a VC bullet.

Surveying the company perimeter, I could see soldiers in various states of exhaustion. Some troops were sitting on their rucks in the water, staring expressionlessly at distant horizons. Others found high ground on the dikes and were lying back in the slimy black mud. A few of the ground-pounders did little more than lay their helmeted heads on a dike. They slept there while their bodies floated in the paddy.

Although we were all anxious to get out of the muck, the captain's directive to move out provoked loud groans and bitches. They accused Captain Becker of being sexually active with his mother, of being the son of a female dog, and they compared him to the posterior opening of the alimentary canal. They even condemned the Creator in his behalf. Of course nothing was said to his face, which would be tantamount to military suicide.

Nam was a breeding ground for the four-letter-word language. One may have suspected that many of the soldiers were victims of Tourette's Syndrome. That grizzled old drill sergeant back at Fort Ord could have honed his sharp tongue to a razor's edge with a few months of "education" in Vietnam. Only the Vietnamese children could out-expletive a grunt. Then again, they had many years of practice.

As the days, weeks, and months passed, my reaction to hearing certain profanities numbed. Familiarity bred acceptance to the extent that I noticed a sentence without a curse, instead of the other way around. It was all just war-talk. No offence was meant and none was taken. Our profession was a dirty rotten job by nature, and the language most employed reflected everyday life. The war-talk was cliquish in nature and thus allowed that certain feeling of belonging, no matter how crass it may have seemed to me at first.

It didn't take very long to realize that the hump back would be hot and miserable. Periodically a soldier would scoop up a helmet full of warm water and pour it over his head, trying to cool down.

"Damn, it's going to be another hot day. Can't wait to get on that Freedom Bird bound for Chi Town, "Major said loudly to himself. "Only nine more months to go, and I swear I'll never complain about the Chicago wind or the cold winters again."

Several of the short-timers took the opportunity to harass

Major about his having a lifetime to go. Zorn said he'd slit his wrists if he had nine more months "in the Nam." I'd learned long ago never to compare DEROS dates or even talk about it when a short- timer was around.

We managed to stay on the checkerboard dikes most of the time, but occasionally someone would slip in the mud and fall into the water. The plunge would be temporarily refreshing, but exhausted rucksack-burdened bodies sometimes did not cooperate in our attempts to climb back up onto the slippery dike path.

Captain Becker passed the word up through the column to Lieutenant DeWitt to find some high ground where we could take an extended break. I hoped that was what he really said; sometimes other interpretations got mingled with the facts as they passed from man to man.

I was slowly moving forward, my head down, watching every step and trying to forget how tired I was, when a thought stuck in my mind. For some reason, I remembered a quotation I'd read on a bulletin board—or was it on a latrine wall? No, nothing intelligent was ever written on latrine walls. The quotation was from Thomas Payne, back in the 1700s sometime: "Those who expect to reap the blessings of freedom must, like men, undergo the fatigue of supporting it." If fatigue was the criterion for reaping blessings, I thought we certainly had earned our share during the previous 12 hours.

One hour before the sun would be straight up in the sky, one of Sergeant Martindale's men on point found an island in the rice paddies. It was about the size of a football field. Lieutenant DeWitt thought the high ground could easily accommodate the company, so he led us toward it. Each squad in the company grabbed some dry real estate around the perimeter of the island and quickly searched their areas for booby-traps.

When the captain finally made it to the high ground, he called in our map coordinates. He then radioed the Alpha REMFs and ordered them to get fresh water and hot chow to us, ASAP.

We collapsed back against our rucks and napped for the first half hour, at last out of the slimy muck. DeWitt called for a meeting with the squad leaders. Captain Becker told the three platoon leaders that he wanted the island "gone over with a fine-toothed comb." Lieutenant DeWitt and the squad leaders began to organize a more thorough search of our area. I was halfway to dream world when the lieutenant called my name.

"Sergeant Rock, get around to each of the positions. Tell the men to stay put until the entire island has been cleared of booby-traps."

I dragged myself to my feet and visited each of the seven positions. I passed on the platoon leader's order and my knowledge of the soon-to-arrive hot chow. Everyone was tired, hungry, and thirsty.

The squad leaders were just beginning to organize the men for a sweep toward the center of the perimeter when the food chopper landed. Even before the rotor wash sandstorm had settled, several men broke ranks. Thirst sometimes overwhelms discipline. The guys ran toward the white plastic water jugs that were the first to be off-loaded. Sergeant Wardle and the lieutenant began shouting at the men to get back, but the chopper noise drowned out the warnings to the impatient soldiers.

Twenty-five meters from the settled bird, the unmistakable *Ka-whump!* of a detonating hand grenade drove us all to the ground. In the center of the grey smoke I saw Spec. 4 Paul Hamada, one of the new guys that had just arrived in the platoon. He was on the ground, screaming in pain. Everyone froze in their tracks except Doc Bayne, who, like a magnet, was always the first on the scene of an explosion.

I yanked the radio from my ruck and called in a medevac. It looked, however, like I might already be too late. Even from 50 meters away I could see that most of Hamada's left leg was gone. Doc began yelling instructions to the group of guys who had come to help the fallen soldier. He applied a tourniquet up next to the soldier's groin and twisted it tight with a piece of bamboo. Doc then shoved a morphine needle into Hamada's hip and began screaming for the damn medevac. I got on the radio again, only to hear that the first chopper had been diverted to another emergency. A second bird was just lifting off from Camp Evans to come to our aid. Doc was really frantic when I told him the news.

He threw his helmet to the ground and yelled, "The guy may not live long enough for a second medevac!"

Having accomplished everything he knew or was trained to do, the frustrated medic squatted back on his heels. For a long time he looked up into the sky. If a prayer is what he offered, the sounds of an inbound chopper 30 minutes later at least partially answered it. The bird with the big red cross painted on its tail settled to the ground. Four grim-faced guys from Hamada's squad carried the FNG's lifeless-looking body aboard. Two hours later we got word from Alpha

Co. HQ that Paul Hamada had died at the 18th Surgical Hospital at Camp Evans. Damn! I'm sure Hamada had thought he was immortal; we all felt that way. The other guy maybe, but not me. We kind of expected that one day we'd get wounded—hopefully what the old soldiers called a "million-dollar wound"—but get killed? No way that would happen.

Fighting the North Vietnamese or the Viet Cong man to man, or even getting ambushed with the odds against us, was acceptable. Firefights were an expected part of the deadly game we played. What I could not tolerate was the booby-trap. It was just not fair. Booby-traps never allowed us to fight back. We just had to watch our friends get mutilated or killed, and we could inflict no punishment in return.

We felt that booby-traps were a coward's way to fight. Then again, the British thought the Americans were cowards during the Revolutionary War because we hid behind trees and stone walls when fighting, while the redcoats bravely (stupidly) stood in the open, in formation. Every war teaches new tactics, and maybe we were just slow in learning these.

In fighting this war, the only reference point was the enemy himself. An area of operation deemed safe may have been a VC/NVA stronghold a month later. When there was no enemy for us to fight, our frustrations built. They did not dissipate easily. There were times when these frustrations were released, to an extent, on prisoners or VC- sympathizing civilians. While I cannot condone such action by the American fighting man, I do understand how it could happen.

Since the biblical account of Cain killing Abel, innocent people have been involved in the quest for domination. I wish that everyone could understand, however, that sometimes the innocent are not always as guiltless as they seem. War is supposed to be their best against our best, fought by gladiators, according to the rules. Often the deadly booby-traps that killed our best were set by "noncombatant" women and children. For us to kill a woman or child during a battle, however, would label us as baby killers; such incidents poured fuel on the fire of the war protest movement and gave the newspapers great headlines. We were in a no-win situation.

U.S. soldiers and their Allies during World Wars I and II destroyed great cities in Europe. They killed thousands upon thousands of civilians during famous battles which we praised them for winning. How is it those G.I.s escaped the labels the returning Vietnam soldiers had to wear? Our predecessors dropped atomic bombs on Hiroshima and Nagasaki in August 1945, killing many more thousands of civilians. The newspapers saluted the returning airmen as heroes.

The old-timers in the company told me about the atrocities the VC and NVA committed during the Tet (Vietnamese Lunar New Year) Offensive beginning on January 30, 1968. The communist soldiers tortured and murdered religious leaders, politicians, and schoolteachers. They had bayoneted or hacked to death the village chiefs and those sympathetic to the South. The bodies of 2,800 civilians, some buried alive, were found in mass graves. The Tet Offensive turned out to be an overwhelming military victory or the South Vietnamese and ourselves. The news media portrayed it to the American people as a defeat. Why is it that the headlines failed to tell of the courageous victory? Why did we who accepted the call of our country, instead of running off and hiding in Canada or Europe, become the villains?

I prayed that the parents of Spec. 4 Paul Hamada would remember their son as a hero, because we did.

## CHAPTER 13

# THE FEARED A SHAU VALLEY

"Pack it up! Choppers are inbound, ETA is one-five. We're going to the A Shau Valley!"

The shocking announcement by Lieutenant DeWitt sent us scurrying around the gravel pit we had called home during the last week. I shoved the radio and the extra battery in my ruck and walked over to my rifle and frags. I was suddenly wishing I had a few more M-16 rounds and maybe an extra frag or two. And I wasn't the only one wanting more ammo—someone had stolen two of my three grenades.

Just the name A Shau struck fear into the hearts of even the bravest of the Screaming Eagles. The "valley" was really a 50-kilometer-long mountainous jungle region that hugged the Laotian border. Extreme geography and miserable weather tended to isolate the place from U.S. troops. The area was a cobweb of enemy supply routes originating in North Vietnam. Hundreds of wide dirt roads and narrow trails crisscrossed the region. We often referred to these well-used trails as red ball expresses.

The valley was a stronghold for both the VC and the NVA; thousands of enemy soldiers lived in the tropical rain forest hideaway, and they were continually attacking and sometimes overrunning firebases in the region. The NVA had recently mauled several of our sister companies during their brief assignments in the enemy hellhole. This was not a good place.

American commanders were so anxious to take the fight to the enemy that we were about to patrol in their own jungle house, and goad them into attacking us. I could appreciate the "master" plan of going on the offensive, but the soldier tasked to go agitate Sir Charles was me. It was me who would be offering to take the first punch, not the commander secure in his bunker back at Camp Evans. I did not like the plan.

For 45 minutes Alpha Company flew over the triple-canopy jungle toward an unknown LZ. Nothing was visible from the air but the thick green foliage, mostly the tops of immense teak trees. The tropical hardwood trees were over 40 meters tall, supported by wide trunks. Outdoor-furniture makers loved them for their ability to withstand the elements, and American infantry soldiers hated them for the protection they gave to the enemy living under them. We knew that the area contained many enemy base camps, hospitals, and war-making factories. That was precisely why we were going there—to find and destroy them. Accompanying us on the flight were two of the sleek new fire-support Cobra gunships, which we had frequently seen in the skies above us. The Cobras had much more firepower than the older Huey gunships, so we felt much more secure knowing they would support our assault into the A Shau.

Several times in the previous month, Cobra pilots had jokingly dived on our positions, pulling out at the last second. I'm sure the hot-shot pilots had plenty of humorous stories to tell on those evenings, back at the officers' club. The slim, dark green airframes had shark's teeth painted across their fronts—a terrifying sight as they dove toward us. We were never sure if the pilots were just playing or if they really had mistaken us for bad guys. We prudently dispersed, just in case. I guess the joke was on us, but we never found it very funny.

To be on the receiving end of their weapons meant sure destruction, and running would not have helped, but we always ran anyway. The gunship's fuselage was only three feet wide. The two crewmen, one seated above and behind the other, were all the manpower necessary to control the awesome weapon-systems platform. Cobras were armed with four pods that carried seventy-six 2.75-inch rockets. Under the nose of each ship was a revolving turret containing a 40 mm grenade launcher. The weapon fired M-79 fragmentation grenades at a machine-gun-like pace. To me, the most fearsome weapon on the Cobra was the 7.62 mm six-barreled mini-gun. We were told that this single gun could fire 6,000 rounds per minute. (I guess that was true. I never tried to count them.) The chopper jockeys harassed us, but at least they were Americans and not North Vietnamese.

The small mountaintop was smoking, and the smell of expended explosives was evident as we made our quick approach. Big artillery guns from fire support bases many miles away had devastated the peak just before our arrival. The gunships then began their turn working out, first with rockets and, as we got closer, with their mini-guns and grenade launchers.

From my vantage point in the fourth chopper I watched the

first three birds go in without receiving incoming fire. It was most likely going to be a cold landing zone. An ambushing enemy would normally have fired up the second or third chopper as it landed, stranding those soldiers already on the ground while their buddies helplessly flew around in circles high above them. When our turn came, the eight of us jumped to the ground before the skids even hit the earth. Every one of us was anxious to get away from the hovering helicopter because it presented such a tempting target for hostile mortars rounds and RPGs. The lieutenant and I ran out of the small landing zone that had been blown into the jungle. We became part of the quickly expanding perimeter defense forming in the dense undergrowth.

When the company was safely on the A Shau soil—an oxymoron if I ever heard one—third platoon took the point. Swinging their machetes in the thick undergrowth, the first three soldiers cut a trail for the rest of us. We were eager to find an enemy footpath or streambed to follow, since cutting our own trail through the rich green jungle was noisy and exhausting. Tall hardwood trees spread their branches wide, sucking up the sunlight at the expense of their smaller neighbors, including us.

After several hours of slipping in the mud down a long, steep ridge, the point men found a small stream about four feet wide. It must also have filled the needs of the North Vietnamese Army as they occasionally meandered down to the Gulf of Tonkin flatlands where everyone else lived.

The map showed that the stream flowed in our direction of travel, so we decided to follow the path of least resistance. It was the easiest and safest thing we could do. From the view of a buzzard high above us we must have looked like a long, very slow green caterpillar with 200 legs.

We were in a vulnerable position. Steep mountains rose on each side of the stream, so we were particularly quiet and attentive. We took our time traversing the slippery, moss-covered boulders. After two hours of slip-sliding down the rocky streambed, several soldiers in the front raised their hands, signaling the column to stop. I passed the hand signals on to the guys behind me. The lead RTO told me via the radio that the point men had spotted several bunkers and they were going to investigate.

The cool water swirled around my knees as I intently watched the ridge on my left. I was thinking that this was a perfect spot for an ambush. There would be nowhere to go except toward the enemy in a long single column. Not good. My right thumb slipped the fire selector switch two clicks to "AUTO." I nervously waited and watched up the steep mountainside. My breathing and heart rates increased, even though I was just standing in the water doing nothing.

DeWitt still behind me whispered, "Freeze, Rock!"

Though barely audible, I knew that he meant business. Out of the corner of my eye, I watched as he reached back and pulled a razor-sharp machete from his ruck. At first I thought he must also be sensing danger and was preparing for hand-to-hand combat. Then he raised the long knife over his head and grunted as he swung at my neck.

"Duck!" he hissed.

I instantly obeyed his command. The steel blade swooshed overhead as I fell to my knees in the streambed. Before I could even look up to assess the danger the head of a Bamboo Viper, one of the most poisonous snakes in the world, dropped onto my shoulder. Then the fanged head fell into the water. The writhing 16-inch body unwrapped itself from a long jungle vine and fell onto the back of my neck. I frantically clawed at the headless wriggling creature until I finally flipped it into the stream. In my panic, I did an overemphasized Mexican hat dance on it with my hard jungle boots. This 160-pound soldier came within inches of being killed by a tiny, almost florescent green snake weighing no more than a few ounces.

Third platoon's search of the bunkers proved that they had been unused for a long time. We did the best we could to destroy them, short of using explosives, and then moved on. This time we carefully followed a small trail that led from the little bunker complex down the hillside.

Night overtook us before we could find a suitable NDP, so the captain organized us into a small perimeter right on the steep slope of the mountain. A pounding rain suddenly began. Over my first twenty-one years of life, I had developed the very demanding habit of eating regularly. Periodically this new environment, especially the rain, caused me to miss some of those necessary food fixes. On those occasions I went "cold turkey"—pun intended. Other times, to satisfy the cravings, I had to shield the little heat tablet and the C-ration can of "something" with my hunched-over body. This position semi-prevented the can from collecting and then overflowing with rainwater before the "whatever it was" was sufficiently burned on the bottom. The rain and the necessity for noise and light discipline made this a no-food night. Maybe in the morning I could get that fix and ease the noisy cravings of my stomach.

The cold rain continued and the slippery mud became even slipperier. Every time I pulled my helmet over my face and lay back to get some sleep, I lost my footholds in the muck and slid a few feet down the steep hill. To remedy the situation, I removed my belt, looped it around a heavy vine and put it back on. I was gambling that the gooks were smart enough not to be out in miserable weather like this, because I was now firmly secured to Mother Earth. I did however, practice speed-grabbing the bayonet on my hip in case I had to cut the vine quickly.

The sound of the rain beating against our ponchos would have given our position away, so we left them in our rucksacks. Cascading down the mountain, cold rivers of mud and water gushed over and around us human leeches. Desperately we clung onto any deep-rooted vegetation that would hold our weight and waited for the sun to smile at us.

An hour after dawn the rain finally subsided enough to allow us to clean our rifles and pants of the gooey mud. We warmed C-ration cans full of cocoa and coffee over heat tabs and got feeling almost human again. I even got a can of burnt Turkey Loaf in me before it was time to move out.

It was second platoon's turn for point, and Muskrat volunteered to lead us. No one argued. After unscrewing his face from his last sip of C-ration instant coffee, Lieutenant DeWitt took his customary fourth place in the column, which meant I would be fifth. Though danger lay ahead, it felt good to have blood circulating and be on the move again.

About noon, our little-used trail intersected a well-worn red ball express, but the mud from the night's rain showed no fresh sandal prints. DeWitt quietly sent scouts up and down the trail for several hundred meters to look for enemy signs. The scouts walked in the grass just off the wide path, careful to leave no footprints of their own. They reported back 30 minutes later that they had found no signs. I called their negative reports back to the old man; he then called for a short lunch break.

The captain ordered two squads to act as lookouts up and down the main trail during the break. I volunteered to be the communications link for one of the squads. I grabbed the bulky radio and walked 50 meters up the trail with Sergeant Martindale's squad. We dropped our heavy rucks in the wet bushes off the red ball trail, sat down on them, and began opening C-rat cans of chow.

I searched my pockets for my little P-38 can opener but could not find it. Polansky, sitting in some thick ferns across the trail from me, offered me his, after he was finished opening his tin of peanut butter. I picked my ‘16 up by its pistol grip and then paused. I looked up the trail, then walked across the path and waited for Polansky to lick his lid clean. Polansky handed me the P-38, and I started back to my ruck. Glancing up the trail again as I broke out of the thick ferns, I saw three NVA soldiers! They had packs on their backs and AK-47 rifles slung muzzle-down on their shoulders, casually ditty-boppin down the path toward me, only 30 meters away. Before I could react, they saw me and began to swing their weapons off their shoulders. I brought my M-16 up to my hip. By the time my weapon was pointed in their direction, my thumb had already rotated the fire selector switch to SEMI.

*Per our training, we never carried our weapons on our shoulders, ever. Many hours of repetition had also taught us to place the index finger of our left hand alongside the rifle barrel handguard and point it at the target whenever we shot at night, or from the hip. Finger pointing seemed to improve our accuracy.*

I began firing single rounds as quickly as I could pull the trigger. Although they outnumbered me, they were still fumbling with their rifles and at a huge disadvantage, so instead of returning fire they instinctively dove into the thick jungle. In just a second or two Polansky joined me in the center of the trail and also opened fire, but Charlie had already disappeared. I did not want a “return to sender” frag—in the grenade toss business it is much better to give than to receive—so I pulled the pin of a frag and held the live egg for two seconds before throwing it into the jungle where I saw them last. After the detonation and a shower of water from the leafy vegetation above us, Polansky, Salvetti, and I charged the position. There was no such thing as fire discipline or conservation of ammo; we fired at least one long burst at anything that could hide a North Vietnamese Army soldier. We shredded the jungle with several hundred bullets but never received a single round of opposing fire from the vanished NVA.

Our quick search of the area was successful. Polansky found an AK-47 assault rifle lying in the middle of the trail, and a short distance away Salvetti found two backpacks full of rice. There were no blood trails or bodies, so I guessed that in my excitement I had missed. My first several shots were not very accurate, granted, but I had been anxious to make the gooks go for cover rather than fire at me. There were three of them, remember. Taking the time to aim could have cost me my life. I ejected the round that was chambered in the AK-47 and put it in my pants pocket. Superstitiously, I hoped "the bullet with my name on it" could now never be fired.

*It was said that if an American soldier was killed by enemy gunfire it was because he was hit by a bullet with his name on it. There was nothing he could have done to prevent it. The two were destined to meet. It was just fate.*

To keep the NVA guessing at the company's location and prevent the ambush that would now be waiting ahead, we quickly backtracked a klick and then climbed the escarpment on the west side of the trail. I use the term "climbed" loosely. A true climber or even a good hiker would be embarrassed at our lack of artistic technique.

The triple canopy vegetation prevented any breeze from disturbing the hot humid air, making our cross-country trek even more difficult. One would think humping through the shade of the tall jungle trees would bring a respite from the stifling rays of sun, but that was not true. The thick upper growth of vegetation trapped the hot air like an enclosed steam room, sapping our strength. During breaks I could see vapor rising from my sweat-soaked uniform.

We clambered down the steep wet mountainside, sliding almost as much as we had when climbing up. Progress was slow. On one occasion, as our long column traversed a particularly steep muddy slope, I lost my balance and mud-surfed ten feet. I stopped by wrapping myself around a sturdy cactus plant. My shirt was open and its sleeves rolled up due to the heat; consequently, several hundred quarter-inch needles embedded themselves in my arms and chest. They stung like an army of ornery red ants. I very carefully pulled myself away from the large plant, not knowing what to do next. Any movement at all caused intense pain.

I couldn't expect the entire column to wait for me to solve my personal problem. I did the best I could to remove the tiny hair-like needles one at a time as we moved forward. If life hadn't been miserable enough already, that #*=+&% cactus plant had saved me and really screwed me up at the same time.

Our attempts to cover our trail proved impossible. A small recon squad could maybe slip undetected through the jungle mire, but not one hundred heavily loaded grunts. A blindfolded Boy Scout could have followed our trail. Undoubtedly, North Vietnamese or Viet Cong trail watchers were keeping track of our movements and radioing them ahead. It felt good to be accompanied by a company of infantrymen everywhere I went. The awkward movement, however, of the large force of soldiers in Charlie's own backyard announced, "Come and get me, I dare ya!" It was a challenge that no self-respecting gook could pass up, I was sure.

About 1800 hours, the last squad in the column dropped off to ambush anyone following us. The main body of the company continued another half klick to a high plateau, where we organized ourselves into a defensive perimeter. I hurriedly cut some bamboo with my bayonet and built a poncho tent. There is no sunset in the jungle; the dark shades of green just turn black. I needed the last bit of sunlight to work on the cactus needles. I didn't have a radio watch until midnight, which was good.

At sundown, just as the ambush squad was returning, I crawled into the poncho tent. The ground was soaked. Even during the "dry" months the jungle floor remained spongy, so we always just searched for less-wet sleeping accommodations. This time a three-inch layer of vines, leaves, and moss kept me out of the mud. I used my helmet as a pillow, and my tired, sore body accepted sleep quickly.

At 2400 hours (midnight), when Doc Bayne awakened me for radio watch, I thought I was still dreaming. The ground around me was glowing. It was as if someone had thrown millions of luminous watch dials onto the jungle floor. Against the glowing background I could see black figures moving around the NDP. Guards were rotating into and out of their lookout positions. Probing the wet earth with my fingers, I discovered that the jungle's decaying organic matter was responsible for this unusual effect.

I began to crawl on my hands and knees out of my little tent when something beneath me moved. A soft, slimy mass under my left hand suddenly grew firm and large. Thinking of the Bamboo Viper from the day before, I yanked my hand away and instinctively rolled to my right. The bamboo center pole of my tent snapped against my weight, and the poncho collapsed on me. In my panic to get away from the snake, I rolled again. That accomplished little more than to wrap my body in a wet poncho cocoon. Thrashing around, I finally rid myself of it. I found myself sitting up, leaning against the lieutenant's rucksack. I pushed the ruck up on its side and grabbed the flashlight that he kept next to his two-quart collapsible water bladder. I jerked the light off the pack, spun around and illuminated the area I had just rolled through. There it was! . . . a worm? It was a giant earthworm.

When my breathing eased a bit, I crawled over to get a closer look. The worm was three feet long and as big around as my little finger. When I touched it with the flashlight it recoiled, just like it had under my hand. Lieutenant DeWitt crawled over to see what all the excitement was about. When he saw the worm, he kidded me about a Utah country boy being afraid of a little ol' earthworm. Gently grasping the slimy creature, I tossed it on the lieutenant's legs. The lieutenant jumped up, stepped on his ruck, and fell backward. He came to rest in a sitting position, squashing the worm with his butt. I laughed as quietly as I could until my sides ached. It was the funniest thing I'd ever seen.

We rested until about noon the next day. I used part of the time to scrub my chest with mud and jungle leaves, trying to remove very small cactus needles. It hurt like crazy.

We needed to stay put to give Delta company time to hump into the area. They were going to act as a blocking force about six klicks up the trail from where I had fired up the three NVA soldiers. Using another route, we were going to go back to that area and start pushing up the trail again. Hopefully we could squeeze some NVA between us.

It was first platoon's turn to walk point, which meant I would be in the middle of the 100-man column, as safe as I could be under the circumstances. Upon reaching our destination, first platoon's point men found a pair of Ho Chi Minh sandals that we had missed in our earlier search. A thousand meters up the trail they found a spot where a soldier had lain and bled, but he was no longer around. Maybe my shooting hadn't been so haphazard after all.

While we were searching for a body, I told the lieutenant that I thought I could smell smoke. He stopped, confirmed the smell, and called the old man. The captain sent patrols in several directions to recon the area, and within 15 minutes a first platoon squad reported they'd found a small base camp with two cooking fires still burning. They told us where to find the trail that hid the camp's secret entrance. The path began in large moss-covered rocks just off to our right. Company strength, we crept into the enemy camp just 100 meters off the main trail. Most of us had never been inside an enemy base camp, let alone one that was alive.

Five grass hootches, several bunkers, and a large vegetable

garden made up the little community. Everything was well camouflaged. The enemy's base camp would be invisible from the air. Even we on the ground could not see the camp until we were actually in it; the jungle provided great natural concealment. Evidently the gooks had heard us on the trail and *didi maued* from the area, leaving behind their meager treasures.

Each thatched hootch contained several hammocks, with mosquito netting made from American white nylon parachutes. The inventive enemy had also fashioned kerosene lanterns from our discarded C-ration cans. Their garden was next to the platoon-sized little community. The plot had several strange vegetables growing and 25 or 30 ripening red pepper plants. We gathered almost 50 pounds of rice from the two cooking areas, and dumped two gallons of a stinky fermenting liquid; perhaps it was rice wine.

We found six empty M-16 magazines and two AK-47 banana clips full of shells. First platoon soldiers also found nineteen 60 mm and twelve 81 mm mortar rounds, plus 10 RPG-2 grenades. They stacked it all on the ever growing pile of bounty. The biggest ordnance find turned up when Martindale's squad found and explored a nearby cave; it contained 103 SKS bolt-action sniper rifles.

Upon closer examination we discovered that each of the AK-47 shells we recovered actually contained two copper jacketed bullets; the second round was coned inside the tail of the first. When fired, the bullets would separate, doubling their lethality. Although we found these unique shells from time to time, I suspected that accuracy was a problem, and that was the reason they were not standard issue.

The captain called in the report of our discovery and requested a Huey to haul out the loot. We used one-pound blocks of C4 to blow down the surrounding trees. We then cleared the undergrowth with our machetes so the chopper could land. An hour later, Sergeant Wardle popped a purple smoke grenade to give the Huey our exact location and show wind direction, but the smoke just lazily swirled on the ground. When the bird finally found our purple hole, it hovered momentarily as Sergeant Wardle ran into the new clearing. Holding his rifle with both hands high overhead, the platoon sergeant slowly guided the hovering airship to the ground.

First we off-loaded a case of TNT to blow the cave. We then unloaded a dozen five-gallon jugs of drinking water, followed by ammunition. The last thing to come off the Huey, but the most important to our sagging morale, was the big orange bag that held mail from the world.

It only took a few minutes to fill the chopper with the weapons we had captured. We divided the rice and peppers among ourselves. I filled one of the stinking wool socks I had received in the mail a few months earlier with my share.

Before we abandoned the site, we burned down and blew up anything that could possibly be used again by the enemy.

## CHAPTER 14

# MISERY IN THE A SHAU VALLEY

After almost three weeks in the forsaken A Shau Valley the company was still finding it difficult to move around. The rain that had begun in earnest two weeks earlier had not stopped. I didn't think the monsoons were due until around June, so each day I hoped for the tempest to quit, but no such luck. The mud we walked in and slept on was like peanut butter, sticking to everything. As we moved down a trail, the sucking noises from 200 boots entering and exiting the ankle-deep mire echoed down the ravines for half a klick. Sir Charles must have had problems of his own, because he left us alone.

Keeping us supplied with food was difficult. Air controllers grounded our resupply birds most of the time, leaving us to fend for ourselves. During one of those bleak periods, two choppers found us in the heavy jungle, hovered, and kicked out 30 cases—370 meals—of C-rations. Before the kick-out, we had been without food for three days. During a break on one of the hungry days, Muskrat had found a teaspoon-sized packet of sugar down deep in one of his rucksack pockets. He shared it with Lieutenant DeWitt, West, and me. We were so hungry that we had begun chewing on roots and jungle leaves. We hoped that if they didn't taste bitter they would be OK. We were wrong.

The lieutenant, lying next to me in our two-man poncho tent, was extremely sick and had the dry heaves. Whatever he had eaten the night before he had already vomited onto the mud on the floor of our tent. I scooped up the foul-smelling puddle with my entrenching tool and threw it far into the jungle, but the place still smelled really bad. I swallowed often to keep my own stomach contents where they belonged, but I knew they might explode at any moment.

The temperature had dropped substantially over the previous two weeks. Nights probably reached a low of 70 or 75 degrees, but because we were soaked it felt really cold. My first real warmth on one of those cool nights came when I peed my rain-soaked pants. Boy, it felt good. Due to the lieutenant's sickness and the difficulty of getting out of our little tent, I just said, 'What the heck,' and let 'er go. The rain flooding under our ponchos quickly washed the welcomed warmth away, however. About the same time that Mother Nature was making her call, the deluge of rain and wind slowed a little. I tried to count the splats as the raindrops hit our poncho tent, along the same lines as counting sheep, but it was impossible. Sleep was not going to happen.

Our two ponchos were snapped together at the peak of the tent, which allowed some rain to drip down the center of our living space. To remedy the problem, I tied some strings around each of the snaps and ran them down to rocks outside our cover. The drops of water then followed the string down to the ground. If the lieutenant and I were careful not to disturb my cobwebs, we avoided the famous Chinese water torture.

Along with the rain, the vampire mosquitoes began to swarm us by the thousands. They flew into my ears, nose, and eyes, searching for a warm place to get a meal. They seemed to come at me in swarms, as if their sheer numbers alone could overwhelm me. With a swat of my hand against my neck, or any other exposed area, I often killed ten or fifteen of the little tormentors. The smell of the squashed ones seemed to drive the new arrivals crazy. Their steady hum audibly increased every time I defended myself.

Just for the heck of it, I once allowed half a dozen of the winged bloodsuckers to attach themselves to the back of my right hand. When they had almost filled their transparent bodies, I stretched the skin tight. Unable to remove their beaks, they danced around in circles and attempted to fly away, but all was in vain. When I had satisfied my curiosity, I slapped the back of my hand, leaving six dime-sized red splats, each with a ragged black dot in the center. I had virtually bathed in the Army-issued insect repellant about an hour before my little experiment. As always, the mosquitoes just ignored it.

Out the downhill end of our tent, I saw that Tew and Wilson had built a small, smoky fire of little pieces of C-4 and wet leaves under their tent in an attempt to drive the mosquitoes out. We were not fooling anybody concerning our whereabouts, so a little daytime smoke did not matter.

I reached down into one of my leg pockets and retrieved a foil-wrapped heat tab. I removed the outer aluminum package and put a match to the tab. The piercing ammonia-like odor stirred up the grey swarm that had settled on the underside of our wet ponchos but, as far as I could tell, none of them left.

Staff Sergeant Wardle, who had gone to the platoon leader's briefing in place of the sick lieutenant, suddenly appeared at the foot of our tent. He spilled the bad news.

"We're gonna be movin outta here in a coupla hours, so don't let your stuff get scattered around. The cap'n knows everybody's sick, so we ain't movin far."

Lieutenant DeWitt sat up, avoiding my cobwebs, and after several tries asked Wardle, who was on his second tour in Nam, when the rain was going to stop.

"Beg'n your pardon, sir, but these sprinkles don't mean nothin'. When the monsoons come you'll know it, and that's when we start sufferin."

Everybody liked the platoon sergeant; he could get a little bit cantankerous at times, but it was kind of his job to be that way. He was responsible for the lives of a bunch of crazy teenagers with guns. Most of us were away from home for the first time. Sarge was of average height, average build, average looks, and nothing really made him stand out. When the Lord created the "good ol' boy" assembly line, the prototype had been the Sarge.

As Wardle had told us, an hour before dark the company packed up and we moved 200 meters down the trail—a wise move, as it turned out. At 0230 hours, metallic clinking noises outside of our perimeter alerted everyone on my side of the defensive position. No more than 40 meters away, we could hear a mortar being set up by the gooks. We couldn't identify their exact location in the thick jungle darkness. Lieutenant DeWitt decided we should just stay quiet and not give our new positions away. Sir Charles was most likely crawling around in the mud, probing our old day defensive positions, trying to get a fix for their mortar.

Laying low meant that another team of very lucky gooks was going to escape the talons of the Screaming Eagles. Had they come a little closer, we would have blown them away with claymores and rifle fire. A little farther away, and we would have called prearranged arty in on them. Either way, they would no longer have borne the burden of breathing.

Before dawn, our visitors packed up and moved out, never having fired a single mortar shell at us. They couldn't find us. The gook mortar team never knew how lucky they were to have made it through the night alive.

When it got light enough to see, two squads from first platoon reconnoitered the area. In the muddy bottom of a small ravine, just 40 meters from our position, the men found imprints of two 81 mm mortar base plates. They also found tire-tread sandal footprints from the six or seven bad guys.

During the next week, on three separate occasions, long-range snipers engaged us, but that was our only contact with Charlie. The sun was out most of the time, making the humidity skyrocket, but at least the red mud on my uniform dried enough to peel off. Kick-outs of food and mail also arrived regularly, so our spirits picked up a little.

During one of my forays into the thick rain forest, while assigned to a squad-sized recon patrol, we heard noise on the trail ahead. All ten of us dove into the brush off the trail. I pulled the pin on a frag and we waited. . . . Thirty seconds later, three noisy monkeys, oblivious to our presence, swung overhead. I re-pinned the grenade and we climbed back onto the trail. Suddenly discovering strangers in their neighborhood, the long-armed primates began screaming with excitement while they circled overhead. They tempted us to shoot them, but we just threw a few rocks into the treetops to get them to move on.

Later that day, one of the other recon squads killed a six-foot python with a machete and brought it back to camp. The jungle was full of wildlife, from red ants to striped tigers and leathery elephants. The animal we feared most, however, was the one that carried an AK-47. We surprised some of them a few days later.

We were on a routine company-sized patrol following a narrow trail up the side of a heavily vegetated hill. Huge twisted trees, more than 125 feet high, merged over the path, forming an umbrella which no sun could penetrate. Sergeant Martindale's guys were on point; I was with the lieutenant in the middle of the squad. At noon Captain Becker called on the radio and told me to start the word back down the company column to take a half-hour break for lunch.

Sweat had completely saturated my fatigues and dripped steadily from my nose and chin. It looked as though I had been in a rainstorm. I collapsed off the side of the trail and rested a few minutes before digging into my ruck for some food. I was halfway through a custom-made treat of Tropical Chocolate Bars, peanut butter and crackers, when DeWitt looked at me.

"Are you responsible for that putrid fart?" he asked, holding a hand over his nose.

I hadn't noticed the stench until about the same time he did.

"Noooo sir, that's not me!" I answered.

Under similar circumstances back in the world, my dad would always use the old line that "A skunk smells his own stink first." I tried it on the lieutenant, but he pleaded innocent.

The slight breeze wafting through the deep jungle shifted again, and suddenly it smelled like I was sitting in a multi-seat outhouse. I looked around and accounted for everyone. No one was fertilizing the terra firma, as often happened during long breaks. Lieutenant DeWitt looked at me again, this time looking concerned. A quick sideways tilt of his head gave me my instructions. We grabbed our rifles and carefully started searching the area.

I quickly found it: just ten feet behind our rucksacks was a gook facility. The lieutenant and I quickly examined the hole. The builders had laid a support network of one-inch bamboo poles over the top. They then covered the bamboo lattice with dirt and other jungle debris. It was camouflaged to look just like the surrounding area. In the center of the lattice work was a four-by-four-inch hole through which waste material passed on its way to the pit. It was a clever contraption and almost undetectable.

Lieutenant DeWitt and I began conversing in hushed voices, but it was too late. The enemy base camp that we knew must be nearby was already well aware of our presence. The platoon leader quickly called the captain on my radio while I ran down the column, warning the guys of a possible ambush. I met the captain and his small entourage coming up the trail and escorted them to the point.

After a brief whispered consultation with Lieutenant DeWitt, Captain Becker told him to send squads in four directions to find the elusive enemy. Sergeant Martindale's squad made contact with the enemy about five minutes after leaving us.

The distinctive AK-47 cracks that filled the air were soon countered by half a dozen M-16s on rock and roll. Most of the company was dispersed in the jungle. Without command, however, we all began to advance, almost running toward the firefight. By the time we had traveled the 100 meters to the source of the action, only a few random M-16 shots were still being fired. We had discovered another base camp, this time a rather large one.

As I topped a small rise, I saw a well-maintained village down in the small mountain draw. There were at least fifteen hootches, equipped with large bunkers under each. Some of the guys had already passed down through the camp by the time the lieutenant and I got there and were carefully working their way up the hill on the far side. I stopped to help Doc and several others with a downed soldier. It was Sergeant Martindale. He had been hit by rifle fire four times, twice in the upper thigh of each leg. Bright red blood covered the ground and vegetation around him. Both of the sergeant's legs had been laid wide open, exposing serious compound fractures.

The blue-eyed freckle-faced squad leader was conscious, but Doc had him so doped up he didn't care about his wounds. Speaking quickly but distinctly into the radio handset, I requested a medevac and gave battalion HQ our map coordinates. It would take three or four hours for us to blow a hole large enough for the medevac to land, so Captain Becker decided we should carry Martindale back to a mountaintop clearing we had passed earlier in the day. Going back meant a tough two-hour uphill climb, carrying the Sarge on a makeshift poncho litter, but we really had no other choice. Since he was the only casualty, Martindale's squad volunteered to carry their leader to the pick-up point. Our commander suggested they take a radio along, so I agreed to accompany them.

It took all six soldiers to carry the 220-pound squad leader. He writhed in pain a bit when the guys grasped the rolled sides of the improvised poncho stretcher and lifted. Salvetti walked point, ten meters ahead of the tight cluster of men, and carried four of the soldiers' weapons. I brought up the rear, carrying the communications radio and the three extra M-16s.

For two long hours the tired squad side-stepped their way up the steep, hot mountain. Several times the litter carriers stumbled over obstacles on the boulder and vine-strewn trail, accidentally dumping their wounded squad leader onto the ground. Everyone begged forgiveness each time he fell, but Martindale knew his men were doing their best and never complained. The guys needed to stop and rest often. At each rest stop, the sergeant was laid on the jungle floor as gently as possible and the soldiers stretched their sore, aching muscles. Relieved of the weight, the litter bearers' arms felt as if they wanted to float.

Since only Salvetti and I carried weapons, we were very concerned about the possibility of getting ambushed. Charlie may have still been watching our every move, and we were not in any position to beat back a quick assault. It was a great relief to everyone to find a medevac waiting at the clearing with gunships circling overhead, providing cover for the extraction.

The litter bearers lifted Sergeant Martindale aboard the chopper, and the medics quickly began working on his bullet-shattered legs. The squad tried to yell get-even pledges to their leader; no one was sure if Martindale could hear anything over the noise of the rotor blades, but they yelled anyway. I knew the pain these guys were suffering. The loss of Sergeant Pearson, my old squad leader, still weighed heavily on my mind.

Within 45 minutes of standing in the medevac's turbulence, the eight of us had made our way back to the Viet Cong base camp. Most of the captured food and equipment had already been inventoried, and it was stacked next to a landing pad that was finally being blown open.

A large 50-gallon drum was filled with bullets recovered from the site, mostly M-16 rounds. The VC had probably captured them after quick ambushes or while overrunning firebase's somewhere in the valley. We captured six type-56-1 assault rifles (cheap Chinese copies of the Soviet AK-47) and a stack of several hundred 60 mm and 81 mm medium-weight mortar shells. We stacked forty RPG-7 rockets and their two launchers next to the mortar shells.

*The Rocket Propelled Grenade -7 was a cheap weapon to manufacture but the shaped charge projectile was very lethal. It was replacing the older RPG-2. The weapon could penetrate 11 inches of steel, thus disabling or even destroying a multi-million dollar armored tank. The RPGs made a loud pushhhhh sound, like the opening of a soda can, when fired, and left a trail of fire and sparks until detonation.*

An assortment of other weapons, explosives, medical supplies, bicycles, and gas masks were also among the spoils. The guys ripped down several hundred meters of commo wire that the enemy had strung through the tops of the tall hardwood trees. It now lay rolled up on the jungle floor.

We string-tied several bundles of VC documents together and waited for it all to be airlifted out. Upon later examination, translators and document evaluators could tell us the significance of the base camp.

The two things that impressed me the most were the way the VC had piped water into the camp, and the smoke dispersal system for the kitchen cooking fire. Beginning a klick away in a small stream, the innovative gooks had built a gravity-fed pipeline made of bamboo poles. The bamboo had been hollowed and then mated by inserting the small end of one pole into the large end of another. They sealed the connections with tar and then buried the pipeline several inches under the earth. Only at the camp was the pipeline above ground and visible. At the camp end of the line, next to the cooking hootch, the VC had created a homemade on-and-off valve. The cleverly constructed pipeline could fill a gallon bucket in less than five minutes.

Equally impressive was the way the gooks made smoke disappear from the cooking fire. Because this base camp had housed eighty to one hundred Vietnamese Communist soldiers, substantial cooking over a wood-burning fire was required. We discovered that the fire area inside the cooking hootch had been dug several feet below ground level and recessed another two feet into clay-lined dirt walls. A hand-fashioned clay box above the fireplace caught the rising smoke and separated it into vents running several hundred meters up the slope in four different directions. The earthen vents created a draft that vacuumed the hot smoke off the fire and pulled it through the tunnels. Little wisps of smoke escaped here and there along the way. The smoke was dissipated over 1,600 hundred square meters, so seeing it from the air was impossible. Very clever.

During the next hour, as I helped with the camp's destruction, I learned about the firefight Sergeant Martindale's squad had walked into. Salvetti said that while carefully searching the jungle close to the gook outhouse, the guys discovered the cleverly camouflaged hideaway. The alert soldiers cautiously entered what appeared to be a deserted camp. Suddenly, automatic AK fire hit them from a hillside above. Evidently the occupants of the camp had grabbed everything they could carry and *didi maued* while we were sitting eating our lunch just one hundred meters away.

The few remaining VC camp watchers fired up Martindale and his people before escaping over the hill. The squad's immediate reaction was to attack and crush the defenders left behind. Their quick reaction prevented the enemy from getting organized and causing us a much greater loss. The only casualty was Sergeant Martindale. I guess we were all lucky. The nearly 100 VC soldiers could have blown us all away had they taken the time early in their evacuation to set up a proper ambush.

U.S. soldiers all over South Vietnam were successfully destroying remnants of the Viet Cong Army since the enemy's crushing defeat in their Tet Offensive. The communists had betrayed their cease-fire truce by infiltrating and attacking cities and allied camps all over South Vietnam. Now, the newer and more formidable North Vietnamese Army was taking over the battle responsibilities, and they were more often willing to stand and give a traditional fight.

Communist soldiers were famous for following strict protocols concerning battlefield tactics and movement. Junior officers were not given the liberty to be inventive like ours were. If a North Vietnamese lieutenant, for instance, failed to follow orders exactly as he received them, he would be severely disciplined. Had the commander of this camp taken some initiative and decided to fight rather than run and await further orders, he may have been the victor of this little engagement. But he didn't, and he didn't. He failed twice.

American officers, conversely, are given a great deal of latitude concerning the what, when, and how of combat tactics. "The book" is routinely deviated from as the on-site officer evaluates each immediate situation. In a captured document from another war, American tacticians learned a valuable lesson from a Soviet junior lieutenant's notebook: "One of the serious problems in planning the fight against American doctrine is that the Americans do not read their manuals, nor do they feel any obligation to follow their doctrine…"

Toward the end of the day, Lieutenant DeWitt came over to shoot the breeze with Doc and me as we lay against the cool moist hillside, resting.

"I've got some good news and some bad news," he said. "The good news is we're being rewarded for the capture of this base camp with a two-day stand-down at Camp Evans. We fly out of here tomorrow."

He followed with the bad news: "We just received word that the doctors will most likely have to amputate both of Sergeant Martindale's legs. What's even worse, he was scheduled to rotate back to the world tomorrow. He was going to be picked up by chopper this evening to start out-processing. This was going to be his last day in the jungle."

# CHAPTER 15

# FIRE!

The two-day stand-down at Camp Evans was great. As a consequence of our Christmas fiasco, when celebrating potheads and juicers had fired their weapons and thrown frags, on the morning we arrived Captain Becker ordered us to strip ourselves of all weapons. A rotund PFC supply REMF parked a small trailer on the helicopter landing pad. The captain stood with his hands on his hips as we filed past, filling the trailer with the ordnance we each carried. We dropped off all our machine gun and M-16 ammo, M-79 and hand grenades, claymores, LAW rockets, TNT, C4, and whatever else we carried. The same PFC then pulled the heavy trailer away with an old Army Jeep and secured it in a warehouse.

The first day back at Camp Evans, Army Rangers taught us how to rappel from hovering Huey choppers. They made us practice the technique repeatedly. Captain Becker told the men that if one of our sister companies needed immediate support, we would be their rescuers. Rather than humping into the firefight and maybe arriving too late, they would expect us to rappel down ropes through the thick jungle. We were going to be a quick response team. Dangerous. We were also trained to descend chain ladders that hung from the rear of hovering Chinook helicopters. Holding on to the bottom end of the ladder, so others could climb down was extremely difficult—it was like schoolchildren holding hands to form a long line and playing whip. As the leader of the whip ran figure S's around the playground, the snap end did just that. Holding on was impossible. I was not sure the prestige accompanying these new skills was worth the risks involved.

That night, the next day, and the second night, most of the guys passed their time by playing poker and getting drunk or high. They also plugged nickels into the slot machines at the various clubs or caught up on sleep.

At the PX I bought my third little Instamatic camera since my arrival in-country six months earlier. Usually I carried the cameras wrapped in several plastic bags and then stuffed into a canvas ammo pouch hooked onto my web belt. Even with all my precautions, Nam's rain, mud, rivers, sand, heat, and humidity took their toll on the camera's delicate parts. Paying $19.95 every few months for a camera was a little expensive for my Spec. 4 wages. Still, I was determined to record a photographic history of my year in Vietnam.

At 0430 of the third day, the officers rousted us from our cots, the floor, or wherever else partying soldiers had slept the last few hours of the night. Captain Becker told us they had scheduled choppers to arrive at 0900, and that the mess hall would be open for our early breakfast.

As we slid our grey plastic trays down the serving line, we passed the same old belligerent, antagonistic mess sergeant that someone had fragged on Christmas. He was back on duty, and his disposition had not changed one bit. He watched us very closely, trying to imagine who it was who had rolled the frag into his room. We gorged ourselves on so many steaks and eggs that I doubted we'd ever be hungry again. The Sarge had a lousy bedside manner, but he sure could cook.

*Condemned prison inmates sometimes got this same pre-dawn "last meal." Maybe the captain knew something that he was not telling us.*

At 0800 another REMF supply clerk pulled the trailer laden with our weapons to the rear of the supply hootch. Sixty of us, anxious to get our basic loads packed up, crowded around the small explosives-packed vehicle. We pushed and shoved each other in competition for the newer and prettier equipment. New explosives were rumored to be more reliable, but in all reality the beat-up frags and bullets worked just fine.

In the hustle and bustle of filling our rucksacks, someone grabbed a yellow smoke grenade from the pile. The arming safety pin on the smoke happened to snag on other ordinance, and it accidentally pulled out. This allowed the safety spoon to flip off and the percussion cap to "pop," igniting the smoke-producing powder. With smoke and fire spewing from the bottom of the can, the surprised soldier quickly dropped the hot device back into the pile of ammunition.

If the flaming smoke grenade had stayed outside the trailer, everything would have been OK, but as it was we were in instant danger. As if by command and in unison we all did an about face and ran for our lives. Most of us were still within a few meters of the trailer when hot bullets began to cook off. Shortly thereafter the trailer was violently blown apart in a quick series of tremendous blasts.

We ran to a small hill 300 meters away and watched as the company area went up in smoke. The explosions and the resulting inferno destroyed the headquarters, supply, and three platoon hootches. A few soldiers made brief attempts to salvage personal equipment from the burning plywood structures, but it was impossible. Many of the soldiers on the hill with me leisurely smoked a joint or two as they "grooved" on the spectacular 4th-of-July like fireworks.

Rockets launched themselves at indiscriminate targets, detonating upon impact. Small parachutes with flares hanging beneath their nylon canopies gently floated through the bright red, green, yellow, and purple psychedelic smoke. Colored "star cluster" flares ignited as they blasted into nearby buildings or skittered along the ground. Mines either blew up or fiercely burned. Thousands of bullets cooked off in rapid succession, as if they were long strings of giant firecrackers. Explosives, which had been blown to the far corners of our compound, continued to detonate randomly, igniting more fires.

Only one soldier was brave enough to challenge the exploding ordnance. A colonel that I had never seen in the field before dashed from burning hootch to burning hootch, looking for casualties. He found none and somehow did not become one himself. The officer had gone "above and beyond the call of duty." He deserved a medal for risking life and limb, and I hope he got it. As much as we bad-mouthed officers in general, this one valiantly demonstrated that he could do more than drive a desk.

We watched the show until the fires finally burned themselves out several hours later. Expressions like "outta sight," "far out," and "groovy" floated from the lips of those enveloped in the pungent marijuana smoke. Those of us not involved in the smoke's artificially induced euphoria described the display in more traditional terms, but it meant the same thing. Our high came from the realization that the accident would mean at least another night in camp, and that was really worth celebrating.

When it was safe, we ventured back down into the fire-ravaged company area. The place had been completely destroyed. Many soldiers, especially those who had been on R & R (rest and relaxation leave), stored their personal treasures in Army-issued duffel bags in the supply hootch. The fire had been so intense in the area that much of the sandbag wall surrounding the building had melted. There was no chance that any of the canvas bags, or their contents, had survived.

One of the enormous explosions had completely blown the trailer's axle in half, smashing one end into and through both sides of the mess hall, 50 meters away. Many of our black plastic rifles had been abandoned in the excitement; they still lay on the ground where we had dropped them. Some of the weapons were split wide open by the fires intense heat or melted beyond recognition. After evaluating the damage that was done, we decided that we were lucky no one had been killed or seriously hurt.

As I had guessed, Alpha Company did in fact remain at Camp Evans. Our death-row sentence was delayed for another twenty-four hours. We spent our time cleaning up the burnt hootches and filling replacement sandbags. We complained a great deal about the duty and goofed off when possible, but somehow most of the mess got cleaned up.

The next morning, after chow—pancakes this time—and prior to getting new combat gear, officers ushered the entire company back into the mess hall. A pale-faced civilian was sitting in the corner of the room next to one of the large blown-open holes. He was dressed in a dark three-piece suit and really looked out of place. Once we were all seated he slowly stood up and introduced himself.

"My name is Mr. Janex. I am from the office of . . ."

I didn't catch what he said, something about the Department of Defense.

"I understand you gentlemen lost some personal belongings in the fire yesterday."

I thought to myself, did I hear him right? Did he call us gentlemen? What is this guy, a comedian?

He continued, "Because your losses were a result of combat—" (Oh boy, here we go again.) "—the United States Government will reimburse you for the full value of any personal items you had secured in the supply hootch. If you will please fill out this DD form 200-3 in triplicate, listing your losses and the price you paid for said articles, I will see that you are fully compensated."

When he finally passed around the white, yellow, and pink forms, with carbon paper inserted between each sheet, I took a stapled set and began to fill it out: "One each Instamatic camera, $19.95; three each rolls of 35 mm color slide film, $4.50; one each St. Louis Cardinal baseball cap, $.95." My mind was really busy: I didn't want to lie, but if the government was really going to pay me for the stuff I had in my duffel bag, I surely didn't want to miss a thing.

"Major" Poulson was sitting next to me in thinking mode as he smeared the dirt on his thick glasses with a mess hall paper napkin. The "cleaning" didn't do much for his glasses, but it did give him time to think creatively. I looked on his paper as a source of inspiration. The very first thing on his list was, "1 each 1969 Cadillac."

# CHAPTER 16

# NUMBA ONE HONCHO

We uncrated the many cases of ammo, explosives, and C-rats we needed for our new departure to the boonies. Everyone got new rucksacks, ponchos, and other equipment due to the fire. We reorganized everything into individual piles in front of the burnt-down supply shack. The challenge was to stuff the 70-pound basic loads into rucksacks designed to carry 50 pounds. When everything was finally packed, we were ready to move out.

The entire company of soldiers climbed aboard four waiting deuce-and-a-halves. The 2 1/2 ton trucks transported us several klicks to the Phong Dien bridge. After we off-loaded, Lieutenant DeWitt and the other platoon leaders met with two captains who were waiting for us to arrive. They introduced the lieutenants to two former Viet Cong soldiers who had recently surrendered under the Chiu Hoi program. The American government now paid them to act as guides/interpreters in their old areas of operation. They called these indigenous soldiers Kit Carson scouts. Although not totally convinced of their new loyalty, in certain situations we knew they could be very helpful to us.

“Never let the scouts stand guard, and keep them short of food and ammo. They must be dependent on you.” That was the last advice the platoon leaders got before assuming responsibility for the Kit Carsons.

Captain Becker gave each lieutenant his individual recon orders, and Alpha Company’s three platoons went their separate ways. For three days our platoon humped at a nearly forced pace up the Song O Lau River. I wasn't sure what the hurry was, because when we arrived at the assigned map coordinates no further orders awaited us. We just lay around in the undergrowth and tried to stay out of sight. The army's oft-repeated adage of "hurry up and wait" again applied. We did absolutely nothing for the next week but leisurely wander back down the river.

Late on the eighth day of our lay-low assignment (I really think battalion just forgot us), we finally received ambush coordinates. After dark we packed up our belongings and began chopping a trail northward through the tall leafy vegetation and intertwined wait-a-minute vines. An hour later the lieutenant halted our movement. He requested a short meeting with Wardle and the squad leaders. Lieutenant DeWitt told the little group that we could not reach the tiger site in a reasonable time. He was also afraid that our noisy trail-cutting exposed us to unnecessary risks. He knew that calling the REMF command post would not get our assignment changed. It was time to improvise.

"Sergeant Tew, lead us back to the river. We'll set up our defensive position there. I'll call in a phony location showing us at the assigned tiger site."

His decision was contrary to orders, but our general consensus was that it was correct.

Calling in inaccurate coordinates was something we had done before, during my first five months in Nam. Sometimes the desk jockeys in the rear gave us really dumb or impossible tasks to accomplish. REMFs gave assignments where the necessity-versus-danger ratio was not reasonable. It was easy for them to do as they sat on their butts, staring at a map. We assumed some risks when we weren't where we were supposed to be, but in situations like this we were willing to take them.

Long after dark we had managed to cut our way back to the banks of the Song O Lau River and were safe. We organized our 30-man perimeter in the sand on the water's edge and set up guard schedules. The mist rising off the warm river created a light fog that hung close to the water. That, aided by the starless night, made it difficult for us to see. Our starlight scopes were useless because the winding river, with jungle almost to its banks, cut our field of vision to zero. We became listeners.

Forty-five minutes after everyone except the guards had gone to sleep, two VC soldiers came ditti-boppin up to our little circle in the sand. They were following the river out of the mountains and were completely unaware of our presence. Several of us heard them talking, but we all assumed the voices belonged to our new Kit Carson guides. We were so unaccustomed to hearing enemy soldiers casually conversing with each other that we completely ignored the possibility that they could be bad guys.

Polansky was the only guard who was aware that hostile forces had penetrated our perimeter. The catch-22 position he found himself in, however, made it impossible for him to do anything about it. When he discovered that the conversation was not coming from friendlies, the gooks were within 15 feet of his position and getting closer. Since the M-79 on his lap was loaded with a high-explosive grenade, he knew they were much to close to fire upon. Any movement or attempts to wake his sleeping companions would result in getting himself blown away, so he did nothing but pray that his slumbering buddies did not move. Polansky just sat as motionless as a tree stump with his hand squeezing the grip of the bayonet on his waist. The VC, oblivious of the danger, passed within five feet of the wide-eyed guard. They strolled unaware through the fog, as if magnetically drawn to the center of our defense.

In the center of the mostly sleeping GIs, one of the black pajama-dressed invaders unknowingly stepped on the back of our slumbering medic. Doc was suddenly awakened by a foot on his kidneys. He thought one of our guys was playing a practical joke, and he was not amused. Doc rolled over and trapped the enemy soldier's foot between his own body and the sand. The gook gave a little grunt as he yanked his foot free. While extricating himself, the soldier’s Ho Chi Minh sandal came off. I can't imagine what the guy was thinking. He actually bent over to retrieve his tire-tread footwear.

Suddenly the light bulb in the VCs’ mind turned on, and the soldier realized what was happening. He reached back and grabbed the AK-47 that was hanging muzzle-down over his right shoulder. Swinging the weapon up, the soldier cut loose with a long, poorly aimed burst of automatic fire. At exactly the same moment Sergeant Wardle, who was lying between Doc and me, also realized that something was wrong.

Maybe it was the platoon sergeant's years of experience, his training, or just instincts. In any case, Sarge knew that the two figures standing above us were unfriendly and certainly not our Kit Carsons. Wardle grasped his M-16 lying in the sand next to him and squeezed the trigger as he rolled toward the misty black silhouettes. The M-16 erupted, sending a handful of red tracers into the dark sky.

The sudden discharge of two automatic weapons from the center of our position, one of them an enemy AK, ripped the cobwebs from our sleepy brains, and we responded. One of the laws of combat I learned in my first months in Nam was, "When one soldier fires, everybody fires!" Returning fire when one thinks all of the Americans are shooting at him is difficult for any enemy soldier to do. Besides, with all of us shooting, someone might actually hit a bad guy.

*I learned many other life-saving combat principles that I logged into my jumbled brain under the heading: "Sgt. Rock's laws of combat." I will introduce some of them to you as this account progresses.*

In a quick succession of deafening blasts, guards around the parameter detonated all of our claymores, thinking sappers must have penetrated our defenses. Then with rifles, machine guns, and grenade launchers, we shredded the heavy jungle around us. For five minutes, the one-sided firefight was wild and fierce. When a grenade or bullet caused a tree branch to crash to earth, we instinctively turned and concentrated our aggressive firepower at the noise.

Finally, Lieutenant DeWitt yelled, "CEASE FIRE!"

We listened carefully for 35 seconds, but a long mournful groan coming from a short distance down stream turned us on again. At the lieutenant's second cease fire order we heard the "aaaaaaah" again, so for a third time, platoon strength, we cut loose with everything we had.

Twelve minutes after we had fired our first erratic shots, the groans from the gook had stopped. Since our ammo was running low, we obediently observed the final cease fire. Our hearts hammering, we all intently stared into the fog for the rest of the night. No one talked, smoked or slept.

The early sun wasn't strong enough to burn away the morning fog, but it was trying hard. A half hour was all we gave it before "ants in our pants" curiosity overcame our apprehensions and Lieutenant DeWitt ordered us to start the search. Beginning in the center of our NDP, we followed spilled rice that led us down toward the river. Hansel and Gretel couldn't have left a better trail.

Fifty meters away we found an enemy backpack that had been full of rice. Now the pack was mostly empty and torn open by rifle fire. Just twenty-five meters further down river, we found an AK-47 with its half-empty banana clip. We also found the first signs of blood.

West and Wilson soon found the Viet Cong soldier who belonged to the rifle and the blood; he was lying facedown in a small creek a short distance from his weapon. He was dead. Doc Bayne's examination of the VC's chalky-white corpse told him that someone had hit the soldier once, just once, above his left knee. The soldier must have died of blood loss (although we did not find much) or shock because the wound itself should not have been a fatal one.

"Sometimes," Doc said, "the kinetic energy of a round entering a body can cause such a concussion that it causes the human body to go into immediate shock, even if the bullet hits a normally non-lethal area of the human frame. If not treated quickly, the shock itself may cause the death."

With all our furious expenditure of ammunition and explosives, only one projectile had found its target, which made me think that there may be a third cause for the gook's untimely demise. Maybe we had just scared him to death.

I retrieved a worn brown leather wallet from the VC's pants pocket. The wallet contained a small stack of large-denomination piasters, equivalent to almost 50 American dollars. This large amount of money led us to believe that the soldier was someone important (small bills would have indicated that he was a tax collector.) Our suspicions were verified when our two Kit Carson scouts examined his identification papers. The scouts began jumping around and speaking very excitedly in their native tongue. After they had settled down, they explained in broken English that the soldier was a Viet Cong colonel. Since both of our scouts were former VC soldiers in this area, they recognized his name and kept telling us he was "Numba one honcho!"

The dead VC's comrade must have escaped our hail of bullets completely, which was unbelievable. We searched the area very carefully, the river's fog hindering us a bit, but never found a trace of him.

An hour after my radio report to Alpha's command post, in which I continued the fabrication about our exact location, military intelligence confirmed the importance of the body. The victim, Tran Dihn Nhu, had once been a local schoolteacher. He had risen to his powerful position in the full-time Main Force Vietnamese Communist Army over the previous ten years. This highly organized, trained, and supplied army was in sharp contrast to the local paramilitary, part-time troops who were also correctly called Viet Cong.

The American Intel community ranked Tran Dihn Nhu high on the "most wanted" list. They congratulated us for the one-man body count. The dwindling VC army was now one soldier smaller. Some U.S. Army colonel would now likely get a medal for planning the successful ambush—the one that we were supposed to be on.

We tied Tran Dihn Nhu's hands together in front of him and did the same with his feet. Sergeant Tew and Polansky slipped a thick bamboo pole through the dead soldier's arms and legs then picked up the corpse. We humped almost ten klicks with the body swaying to the rhythm of our steps. At Phong Dien we dumped the corpse in the center of town. Relatives could claim him if they wanted to. It was also a dramatic and physical warning to those with family who were fighting against the Screaming Eagles.

Before we departed Phong Dien, Lieutenant DeWitt ripped the 101st Airborne patch off his shoulder and stuffed it into the dead soldier's mouth.

## CHAPTER 17

# PHONG DIEN

Much to our satisfaction, it was around the middle of March before the company next contacted Sir Charles. Rumors had been circulating that the enemy was massing for another Tet-type offensive.

Alpha, Bravo, and Charlie Companies were assigned areas of operation (AOs) close to Camp Evans. Should the gooks choose to attack the base camp, the infantry grunts were going to come charging in and save the day. That way the cooks, clerks, truck drivers, and senior officers could get out of bed and leisurely find a place to hide. We ground-pounding grunts had a strained relationship with the REMFs. While I realized that each of us had important and necessary jobs to do, this business of guarding them so they could sleep really ticked us off.

On this particular night, half of Alpha's second platoon was tasked with ambushing Route 1. My half set up another tiger on the Song O Lau, watching for river traffic. A large influx of fresh targets for the gooks to shoot at had arrived over the previous month, which allowed us to organize a fourth platoon.

Although my second platoon was now split in half, our ambush strength was still good. First and third platoons were several klicks away on either side of us. The plan was for them to patrol toward us during the night. They hoped to stir some movement between them that would end in one of our ambushes. At 0215, M-16 fire several klicks away on first platoons side awakened me. Bob Thurmon, the captain's RTO, told me they had made contact with gooks right in the center of Phong Dien.

We normally did not patrol in the *ville* during the night because civilians might be harmed if a firefight were to erupt. We went to great effort not to harm or even involve the civilian population. Our strategy had always been to intercept the gooks as they entered or exited populated areas. This time first platoon was just trying to get from point A to point B. The easiest way was right down the *ville*'s main street, where they accidentally came face to face with Sir Charles. First platoon's RTO, Robert Pauli, said they had killed at least one and they were searching for other bodies. Captain Becker told everyone to stay put and try to catch the stragglers running around the area.

We heard or saw nothing more from Victor Charlie for the rest of the night. At 0630 we broke our tiger and joined the first platoon in the *ville*. The excitement of combat had evidently already worn off. Most of the tired soldiers already in the *ville* were sleeping. I leaned my rucksack and radio against the grass wall of a hootch and walked half a dozen steps to examine the enemy corpse.

The Viet Cong soldier was dressed in the usual black pajamas. He had a red bandanna tied around his neck, and a green canvas money belt around his waist. I took a picture. Later some villagers told us why the VC had been in the *ville*: the communist guerrillas had decided taxes were due, and the poor civilians, under the threat of decapitation, were going to pay them. The dead soldier's money belt told us that he was probably a VC paymaster.

Enemy soldiers were paid in cash, and this poor guy and his comrades were out to collect whatever taxes they needed to pay the troops. It was not uncommon for us to kill or capture soldiers like this one. They had to enter populated areas to collect the taxes. It was extremely dangerous work because that was the same place the Americans frequented. We always made every effort to get the money back to its rightful owners, or maybe to an orphanage somewhere nearby.

The small-denomination paper bills we found in the soldier's money belt did not seem like much to us—about 35 U.S. dollars. To the Vietnamese storekeepers and farmers, the 2,557 piasters (South Vietnamese dollars) was a considerable amount.

Within an hour of first light, the courtyard crowded with civilians. Everyone was claiming the money from the soldier's belt. The children were the only ones who seemed to notice the dead gook with the bullet holes in his gut. Older kids came first, then the baby sans followed. Watching each other for moral support, they cautiously approached. Braver children poked a finger or toe against the cold flesh. Once they had proven their bravery, they slipped back into the crowd where they felt safer.

Captain Becker turned the piasters over to the village authorities; the language barrier made it impossible for us to get the money back to those families from whom it had been taken. We hoped it would indeed get back to the proper owners and not end up in some corrupt official's pocket.

During the morning's activities, I overheard the captain tell Lieutenant DeWitt that he was recommending Specialist Carpenter for the Army Commendation Medal. It was Carpenter who had blown away the gook tax collector. He made the right decision at the right time and lived to tell about it.

The curfew imposed on the civilians of this *ville*, and most all others, was from sundown to sunup. Anything moving around after dark was assumed to be hostile. It was one of those simple rules of war. After close-in fighting like this, only the quick and the dead are left. To invite a shadow or noise to identify itself was like asking for a bullet. Those who shoot second die first.

That night, Carpenter had been the point man for the first platoon patrol. He saw movement in the street where there should be none. Reacting as he had been taught, he fired. The rustling of enemy soldiers scrambling for cover confirmed his suspicions and brought supporting fire from his squad. Behind their firepower, the platoon moved forward and found the body. The other VC soldiers, meanwhile, slipped between the grass hootches where the Americans were not likely to shoot at them. They quickly disappeared into the night.

Carpenter's quick thinking not only saved his own life but probably several others. Many villagers, who a few hours earlier had been under the threat of death, approached the shy Montana cowboy, now turned reluctant hero. The mama and papa sans displayed their betel nut-blackened teeth as they smiled and expressed friendly Vietnamese to the shy American. Translation to English was not necessary; all of us understood their thank yous.

At 0900 the company moved out of Phong Dien and into the abandoned old French fort next to the bridge just outside the *ville*. The structures had served as home for twenty-five or so French soldiers assigned to guard the bridge fifteen years before. After they vacated the fort, the locals stripped everything of value, including the iron bars in the parapet machine gun openings. Two concrete barracks and a fortified bunker, overlooking the river, were all that was left of the fort. We liked it because it offered plenty of room to lounge around, protected from the sun and rain. We were also safe from mortar attacks or daytime snipers. The Vietnamese civilians liked it because it served them as a giant latrine. Each time we moved in, we had to scoop out the stinking remains of the previous "temporary" tenants.

An hour after shoveling and sweeping our new living area, most of us were ready to start an afternoon siesta. Sergeant Tew suggested a swim in the river, and that idea restored our energy levels. The squad leader wanted to teach his FNGs how to catch water leeches, but he didn't tell them that in advance of the swim. We old-timers knew what he was up to and followed him down to the water's edge.

As I stripped down to my birthday suit I thought about my first experience with the slimy black creatures. I wondered if these first-timers would be as terrified as I had been. I was a new guy, in Nam just one hot dirty month. During a routine patrol in the middle of nowhere, the platoon stumbled across a small "fresh water" pond. A bomb had created a pock mark in the earth's crust where rain had accumulated. With security posted a hundred meters in each direction, I joined the first group of men to take baths. My body was going through the final stages of my first sunburn, so I appreciated the chance to wash off the dry, flaky skin. I found a spot in the pond next to a grassy bank where I could kneel and shave.

I propped a little two-by-three-inch mirror up in the mud and began to remove a week's worth of itchy stubble from my face. I rinsed the razor in the water by my left thigh, and that was when I noticed something on my leg just below my knee. I stood up for a better look and was terrified to discover that a long ugly water leech had attached itself to me. I had never seen one of the creatures before. Its flat slimy body hung all the way down to my ankle. Panicking at the sight of the black bloodsucking worm, and afraid to touch it, I kicked my leg back and forth trying desperately to flip it off. The momentum of each kick just caused the leech to wrap around my leg and then unwind and wrap around the other way.

I could not feel the three saw-like jaws which had clamped onto my knee. It was the mere thought of the slimy creature that drove me to panic. Bursting out of the water and onto the bank, I did another facsimile of the Mexican Hat Dance just as I'd done on that Bamboo Viper in the A Shau Valley. Other new guys like me quickly scrambled out of the water, but the old-timers just sat back and enjoyed my antics. Ten seconds out of the pond the leech fell to the ground, and I regained control of my racing heart.

Six months later, I was one of the old-timers ready to watch someone else put on the show. Most of the new guys suspected that something was just not right and that maybe they were being set up. They refused to enter the water. No threat of violence or taunts of 'chicken' could make them submerge even a toe into the murky Song O Lau.

"C'mon Wilson and Sergeant Rock; let's show these cowards what it's all about."

We accepted Sergeant Tew's invitation. The three of us waded naked into the warm current until it gently lapped at our chins.

It was just a matter of seconds before the first bloodsucker sensed my presence and began its graceful, undulating swim to my shoulder. Its sucker firmly attached, the leech began to cut in and gorge itself on my warm blood. Uninterrupted, the segmented parasite could eat eight times its weight, but I had no intention of letting things progress that far.

Within minutes, I could see half a dozen of the creatures busily eating lunch at my expense. Tew announced it was time to get out of the water and all three of us proudly waded back onto the river's sandy beach. We slowly rotated, displaying our trophies—the leeches, I mean. The chickens on the beach made a quick count, not daring to touch. Wilson had nine leeches hanging from his body. They ranged from one to about eight inches in length. He won our little contest.

Water leeches did not like to be out of the river very long, especially if they were not firmly attached. After 60 seconds most of my leeches had dropped off. We liberally soaked any of the critters that had not fallen with the Army's oily mosquito repellant. They fell to the sand, convulsing like freshly unearthed night crawlers. Wilson dropped to his knees and scooped the wiggling leeches into a pile. He soaked them again with repellant. Wilson then took an olive drab book of matches from a shirt pocket. With the dexterity of a seasoned smoker, he opened the cover with one hand, bent a single match over and slid it along the striking surface. With great flair he applied the burning match to the leeches and lit them on fire.

A small Vietnamese boy paraded a dozen water buffalo through our leech beach several times, disrupting our show. While the little herder could crawl between the water buffalo's legs, we big tough soldiers gave them a wide berth. They would charge us for just looking at them wrong.

For some reason neither the land nor the water leeches carried any of the diseases commonly spread by Vietnam's other tormentors, mosquitoes and ticks. If we removed the leeches quickly enough, the anticoagulant they produced would shortly bleed out, leaving us with only a tiny red hickey where they had been attached. Their antiseptic saliva allowed no real harm done. The men gained confidence from our little demonstration, and the water soon teemed with man-hunting leeches and leech-hunting men.

# CHAPTER 18

# MALARIA

"You're sick all right, Sergeant Rock; temp's at 103 degrees. Pack your gear up and I'll have a jeep here in 45 minutes to take you to the hospital."

Doc's decision to send me to the rear was based on the thin red line inside the tiny glass tube he had just removed from my mouth. At 102 degrees I stayed in the field, but if the thermometer read one degree higher I qualified for hospitalization. It did, and I did.

For two miserable days I had been getting progressively worse. The diarrhea was uncontrollable. When on patrol, I tried to anticipate Mother Nature's sudden calls. I would dash to the point of the column and do my duty as the guys filed past. Most of the time my insides just exploded with no advance notice, and the warm olive colored liquid would run down my legs. Within a few hours of my first "accident," both pant legs were soaked and acted like magnets to the swarming flies.

I tried to keep myself clean, but it was impossible. Soon I was so sick that I didn't care how I looked or smelled. In fact, it didn't matter to me if I lived or died; the latter choice seemed more desirable as time went on. Doc's allowing me to go to the hospital meant I could lie down instead of continuing to hump the boonies with the platoon; that was good. I was getting too weak to keep up and really didn't care if I did.

For several hours, it seemed, I lay in the dirt just off Route 1 waiting for the 45 minute ETA of the medic's promised transportation. Doc sat with me, but most of the time he kept his distance. I didn't hear the jeep when it finally arrived, but the dust it stirred up was the feather that broke the camel's back. As a thank-you for their help, I threw up half a quart of partly processed fruit cocktail, spaghetti, and stomach acid all over Doc and the jeep driver. Had I been in their shoes, I might have just left me on the road to fend for myself, but the good Samaritans stayed.

I must have passed out because I don't remember any of the

ride back to Camp Evans. I do remember the driver and Doc helping me into the battalion aid station and the fuss it caused. Most of the half dozen staff on duty wanted me left in the nylon lounge chair outside the building. Doc Bayne would have no part of it. The REMF medics complained that I would contaminate their working area, but my friend insisted. The young soldiers had seen a great deal of blood and guts, but I guess I presented a different challenge that no one was eager to accept.

Once I was inside the aid station and lying on a stained canvas cot, Doc listened to my heart one last time and said, “Well, your heart is still beating, that’s always a good sign.” The humor didn’t work. Doc then explained that he had to get back to the company. I tried to properly thank him but my speech was mostly incoherent; I wasn't sure he understood. My entire body ached something terrible, so I tried not to move around very much. I did, however, discover that the pain diminished somewhat when I stopped breathing. But I guess that wasn’t such a practical discovery.

Very tired and weak, I quickly fell asleep. When I awakened it was dark outside. It felt like someone had put me in a hot cement mixer with a pallet of bricks. The one bare light bulb in the center of the room seemed to be focusing all of its brilliance right into my eyes. It was as if the goal was to bore a large hole right through my brain. I turned my head to look around the enclosure, causing a bag of ice to fall to the floor.

The creaky sounds of footsteps coming across the plywood floor told me I was not alone. The noise of the steps stopped as a young PFC medic, no more than 18 years old, appeared at my side. I guessed everyone else outranked him, so he had drawn the task of caring for me. His clean blond hair, soft blue eyes, and freshly scrubbed face gave him a heavenly choirboy appearance. Maybe I was dead and he was an angel? It had been so long since I had seen anyone so innocent looking that I wasn't sure.

The medic bent over, retrieved the ice bag off the floor, and carefully placed it back on my brow. He said something to me about keeping still, but it didn't register in my near-comatose brain. The bag was uncomfortably cold against my fevered head, so I reached up to rearrange it a little. The choirboy shouted several unholy words at me and quickly walked back to my cot. He started playing with a bandage around my arm; it was then that I noticed the IV bottle hanging overhead.

"Pull this needle out again, soldier," he threatened, "and I'll let ya lay here and dry up. This ain't no picnic being in here with ya, so hold still!"

The tone of his voice shattered any delusions I had about his being a compassionate angel.

The throbbing headache, which seemed to be centered just behind my forehead, pounded against the back of my eyeballs, matching each beat of my heart. The thousand-watt (it seemed) light bulb continued to stare only at me, further aggravating my miserable condition. I wanted to tell the medic to turn the light out and bring me a drink of cold water, but I couldn't think of the words.

I remembered thermometers being slipped into my mouth often during the night, and the blood pressure sleeve making my arm go numb. I awoke sometime in the morning to voices around my cot. Gradually I opened my tired eyes and tried to focus on the figure bending over me.

"Good morning, son; how do you feel?" said the blurry green shape.

My answer was short and to the point. I didn't feel like giving a long explanation.

The questions he continued to fire at me were normal medical questions, but I got tired and just stopped answering. When I opened my heavy eyelids again, he was still standing there, but this time I could identify him. The silver oak leaf cluster of a lieutenant colonel was on one collar and a medical insignia on the other. This grey-haired officer was obviously a doctor.

"Son," he again called me, "your temperature has risen to 104 degrees. That's hotter than a cheap pistol. Let's get you transferred to the 326th Medical Hospital up the road a bit; do you think you feel up to it?"

Without answering, I sat up in the cot and asked where the latrine was. The doctor, being very patient with me, pointed outside and to the rear of the building.

"We think you have some kind of jungle dysentery, so we're requesting some tests to help in our evaluation. There is a shower 200 meters up the hill. Do you think you can make it that far?"

Finally I told him that I thought I could, and the young medic at his side began to unhook me from the . . . water bottle, or whatever it was. As we parted, he told me that a jeep would be waiting in 15 minutes, about the time I should be finished with my shower. He seemed to emphasize 'shower' each time he said the word. I took the hint.

From the time I was barely old enough to remember until late in my teenage years, my dad took me fishing every summer in Wyoming. In the west central part of the state is a rural farming community called Star Valley. My father grew up there, so en route to the Snake River we always stopped to visit my cousins. They lived on the same farm that Dad had plowed and worked as a boy. Dad wanted me to appreciate "how easy my generation had it," I think. During each visit, he would show me the old wooden outhouse, still in use, and still standing behind the milking barn.

The latrine I occupied behind the aid station was much like that old outhouse behind the barn, except the military version was a two-holer. The distinct odor was exactly the same, and it made me feel like vomiting. I guess my insides were already empty, because nothing much came out of either end, except little bubbles of foul air. Hurrying the process was necessary as I suddenly got very dizzy and had to lie down.

Stretching out across the raised wooden platform with my shoulders and rear-end each covering a hole, I tried to pacify my demanding body. A few minutes in the putrid environment, with its flies and heat, were claustrophobic, and it was all I could take. I rolled to my side and kicked the wooden door open, allowing the even hotter but fresher air in. As I slowly sat up again, the throbbing in my head became almost unbearable.

If an enemy soldier had slipped into the latrine and shot me, I would have patted him on the back for the merciful relief. I sat for a few minutes with my elbows on my knees and head in my hands. I stared at my feces-covered fatigues, still around my ankles, until I thought I was ready to make a try for the showers.

Up the hill, 200 meters away, was an Army shower. It was built of plywood and screen, and it was gravity-fed. Its old faded green color pleaded for a REMF detail to cover it with new paint. On a wooden two-by-four platform above the roof of the shower were two rusty red 55-gallon drums soaking up heat from the sun to warm the water inside. Head bowed, I concentrated on taking one step at a time toward the structure. Halfway through the very long trek, I spotted another almost identical shower facility just twenty-five meters to my left. The paint was much fresher on this little structure. In black letters on a white background, the sign above the screened door entrance said: OFFICERS ONLY. The entire hill looked deserted to me, so I made a sloppy left-hand pivot and trudged down the hill to that shower door.

Making sure the coast was clear, I looked around once again. No activity. I pulled the squeaky screen door open and staggered inside. The floor was slippery from soap residue and water. Moss or mold grew in the corners of the room and between the cracks of the painted plywood walls. Three shower heads had been piped down into the center of the 10-foot cubicle.

My hard jungle boots made wet sticky sounds as I approached the center showerhead. Without removing my fatigues, I grasped the chain and pulled. A sprinkle of sun-warmed water wet my head and filtered down through my clothes. Soon a small stream of green-brown water ran from my boots to the drain in the center of the stained concrete floor.

The slam of a thin wooden door 50 meters up the hill refocused my attention toward the officer's barracks. A baldheaded gentleman (by act of Congress) cleared the two wooden steps to the ground with a quick hop. He had a white towel tucked in around his waist and swiftly walked through the hot sun toward me.

The officer's flip-flops slapped against the bottoms of his feet as he marched toward the shower door. I could almost hear his mind singing, "Godia-lep, godia-lep, godia-lep-rat-lep, hup-tup-thrip-fowa." Grasping the handle, he paused and looked around. The beginnings of his beer belly swelled as he took a deep breath. The gentleman wrinkled his forehead and slowly pulled the squeaking screen door open and peered through the six-inch crack. His darting eyes searched the darkened interior until he saw me. He immediately released the door, allowing the rusty spring to yank it shut. Standing in the bright sunshine outside the structure, the officer glanced both ways as if he were about to cross a busy street. He then did an about face and quickly marched back up the hill, flip-flop, flip-flop, flip-flop.

I knew there were military consequences for an enlisted man caught using the officer's shower, especially someone who was fouling it up as badly as I obviously was. Thoughts of getting away before old baldy could get reinforcements were beaten back by my sickness-inspired, "Who gives a damn?" attitude. What was the worst thing they could do, send me to Nam?

I never did remove my fatigues or use any soap. I had so little energy; I wasn't about to expend it on excess movement. When the water running off my boots appeared to be roughly the same brackish brown as that sprinkling over my head, I released the chain. The shower was over.

Walking back down to the aid station was much easier than the trek up the hill ten minutes earlier, but it still exhausted me. Upon reaching the rear of the medical building, I collapsed on its two wooden steps, unable to go any further. Three medics, who were watching me through the screened windows, came to my assistance. They carried my limp body all the way through the plywood building and gently placed me in the passenger side of the waiting jeep.

The trip to the 326th Medical Hospital only lasted ten minutes, during which the hot wind whipped my clothes dry. The hospital looked much like the aid station had; certainly not what I had expected. The floor and the four-foot-high walls were constructed of weathered plywood. Above the wall was another four feet of fly screen that met the corrugated steel roof. Like most military buildings in South Vietnam's tropical climate, ventilation was not a problem.

I had nothing more than a cot to lie on, again. While re-envisioning some of the places I had slept during the previous months, the cot looked quite good. Within an hour of my arrival at the hospital, my temperature had risen to 105 degrees. Orderlies stripped me of my clothes and covered my naked body with a blanket of wet towels. The cool towels turned cooler when the orderlies placed a large fan by my cot, pointed it at me, and turned it on. The warm air blowing across the wet towels worked on the same principle as an evaporative cooler. An hour and a half later my temperature was back to 103 degrees and under control.

One of the orderlies gave me a clean set of jungle fatigues. They were several sizes too large, but considering my trade-in, I was happy. A male nurse, who was obviously not very familiar with the procedure, broke two needles and punctured me nine times while trying to get IVs started in my arms. Finally succeeding, he fished catheters up my veins about six inches. The saline bottles dripped their fluid into my desiccated body at two drops a second. Liter bottles of the liquid hung on either side of my cot. They were my constant companions during my stay there.

The 326th was a hospital for patients with minor medical problems. They took the soldiers with serious combat wounds or life-threatening illnesses to the 18th Surgical Hospital. I couldn't imagine how anyone could have an illness more serious than mine, and that proved accurate.

Two weeks to the day of my entering the first aid station, the 326th Medical Hospital transferred me to the 18th Surgical Hospital, also at Camp Evans. The M.U.S.T. (Medical Unit, Self-contained, Transportable) hospital was a successor to the M.A.S.H. (Mobile Army Surgical Hospital) of the Korean War. The facility was the northernmost hospital in South Vietnam designed specifically to treat serious combat casualties.

While I was being admitted into to one of the strange round-top structures, blue-shirted male nurses rushed out to the helipad. They unloaded the newly arrived medevac's mostly lifeless cargo. Although I was seriously ill, I was much better than the dying soldiers they rushed past me into the waiting operating room, so I just patiently waited my turn. The first infantryman they carried in was missing a foot. It was obvious to me that he had tripped a mine.

The outside look of the Quonset-like operating unit was identical to the five wards and the administration buildings nearby. The giant inner tube halves, glued together and lined up in a row, were really heavy rubberized fabric cells inflated with air. Each time a nurse opened a door, a gush of air-conditioned, dentist-office-smelling air rushed out, and the rubber building temporarily deflated a bit. The hospital beds, with real “back in the world”- type mattresses, made my illness almost bearable.

The same nurse who had helped me out of the jeep upon my arrival now assigned me to a bed. He handed me a paper cup and asked for a "sample" next time nature called. It wasn't urine but a stool sample he was after. Every day I was in the hospital, I had to give the same orderly another filled cup. I felt sorry for anyone who had to examine excrement for a living.

As modern as the 18th Surgical Hospital was, one fixture remained the same: the outhouse. The big three-holer beyond the 10-foot-high sandbag wall was, however, equipped with white horseshoe-style toilet seats— a real touch of class.

During my first day in the hospital ward, the nurses admitted another soldier who, like me, was suffering from fever and diarrhea. He was assigned to the bed next to mine. The very first time they measured my new companion’s temperature it was 105 degrees. The thermometers I sucked on hourly fluctuated up and down but generally only read 103 or 104 degrees. Within minutes of his arrival, orderlies carried a portable stainless steel body-length tub to his bedside and filled it with ice and water. They lowered the fevered patient into the bath. He stayed in the freezing water for fifteen minutes until his fever broke. The orderlies or nurses had to repeat this procedure on him six times over the next three days.

I thought it was just sympathy for the guy's ice-water treatments that caused severe chills to start alternating with my fever, but I was wrong. On the fourth day, Doctor Goldberg told me I had malaria. I had faithfully taken the little white pills each day, and the big orange ones each Monday, to prevent this very thing from happening. The chemicals didn't always work, I guessed. The doctor said the pills had filled me with anti-malarial drugs, making it difficult for them to diagnose my condition. The news didn't make me feel any better, but finally I knew one of the reasons I felt so bad.

Lieutenant DeWitt and Doc Bayne came to visit me on my seventh day in the rubber hospital. For the first time in three weeks I was feeling almost well, and I really welcomed their visit. The lieutenant was the one to give me the good/bad news concerning Doc and himself. I knew that an officer or medic's duty as a "front line" soldier was limited to six months. Still, when he told me they were rotating to the rear it seemed much too soon. I was extremely happy that these jungle caterpillars had emerged from their invisible protective cocoons alive and were turning into REMFs. It meant, however, that I would be losing my two best boonie-rat friends. And I'd now have to speak with a little reverence when bad-mouthing the rear echelon guys.

Doc had been assigned to the same battalion aid station I had processed through at the beginning of my medical facilities tour. I knew personally that any soldier under his care would receive the best the Army could offer. Doc Bayne was a superb medic and friend.

Lieutenant DeWitt said that he was going to be working out of the battalion's command center. His primary job would be supervising a dozen clerks and radio operators. It would be a waste of his talented leadership, I thought. But at least he wouldn't be getting killed out in the jungle somewhere. Outstanding boonie-rat officers were few. Everyone in the field would miss him. I would not be surprised to see a star on his shoulder some day—he was that good.

During our conversation, we exchanged home addresses, which we later lost. I accepted promises of visits from them whenever the company came in for stand-downs in exchange for my promises to keep my head down. I realized, however, that we would soon be wrapped up in our own little worlds and promises would be forgotten, except for mine. Doc would go home to Fargo, North Dakota, and Lieutenant DeWitt to Portland, Oregon. We would likely never see each other again.

So many of my good friends in this miserable country were either dead or wounded that it was with happy but tear-filled eyes that I said my last goodbyes. I totally respected these two soldiers. They had worn the title of boonie rat well. They were brave men and like brothers to me.

The day after their visit, tragedy struck. I was sitting in my soft hospital bed, writing a letter home, when the compound's speaker system summoned all medical personnel. Doctors, nurses, and orderlies were ordered to the HQ bubble. After the 60-second briefing was over, everyone quickly went about their individual responsibilities, preparing for a large influx of combat wounded. Spec. 5 Galbraithe, who had watched over me since my arrival at the hospital, told me that a large firefight had just concluded. The American infantry unit had suffered enough casualties to fill five medevacs, and they were flying in to the $18^{th}$ Surg. fast.

I crawled out of bed and exited my air-conditioned inner-tube building. I walked to the edge of the landing pad and leaned against a thick sandbag wall for support. Far away I spotted some dark dots high in the afternoon sky; they looked like black pepper specks floating among the white clouds. I patiently stood there watching as the black dots silently approached, gradually turning into thundering medevac helicopters.

The medical staff efficiently put stretchers, IV bags, and other first-aid equipment to use as the first two choppers landed on large red crosses painted on the PSP (interlocking Perforated Steel Planking.) They quickly unloaded unconscious patients from both sides of the Huey. The other three birds impatiently hovered overhead, awaiting their turns to land and unload.

*The word "medevac" has ambiguity written all over it. To the recipient of its services it is a godsend, while to the rest of us the very word conjures* negative *thoughts of violence and death. We never hope to see one.*

Several of the casualties on the first medevac were heavily wrapped with pale green gauze and compresses. The bandages were now saturated with drying blood. Even before the staff could carry their burdens to the operating bubble, quick-acting nurses had shoved

IV needles into the arms of each patient and had evaluated the severity of each soldier's wounds. Other medical technicians took blood samples, which they would type and compare to the victims' dog tags.

When they ushered the first unconscious soldier past me, I quickly stood up and ran after him. Catching up as the orderly waited for the double doors of the operating room to swing open, I took a second look at the silent victim. It was . . . it was Bob!

Bob Thurmon, Captain Becker's radio operator, was lying in a pile of saturated green bandages turned red and brown. Someone had tied several large compresses around his head, which were now all stiffened with blood. Bob's left arm lay beside him on the stretcher, unattached. It had been ripped apart at the elbow.

I ran back to the sandbag wall just as Lieutenant Jeffries, from the fourth platoon, was being carried off the pad. Thick drops of red life splattered down onto the PSP as the orderlies rushed him past me. Next was my buddy Bennett from St. Louis. A guttural moan came from deep inside his throat when he saw me. It looked like he had been hit badly in the left hip. In horror, I then watched as the litter bearers carried Captain Becker's lifeless-looking body past me into surgery. His guts were spilling out through the temporary dam of field dressings held in place by empty M-79 bandoleers. I KNEW ALL THESE MEN: THEY WERE MY BROTHERS! It was MY COMPANY that had been blown away!

Within five minutes, orderlies and nurses had rushed fourteen of my best friends past me. They were now in the sanctuary of the three 12-by-15-foot surgical rooms or other triage areas. Four other soldiers remained lifeless on the helipad. Their body parts were wrapped in bloody ponchos. I did not know who they were, nor did I have the courage to dig for dog tags. I guess I really didn't want to know. For them, there was no hurry: the war was over forever.

While I watched the doctors' feverish attempts to save the living, a deuce-and-a-half from the Camp Evans morgue, Graves Registration, silently pulled up. The soldiers quickly put the body parts, ponchos and all, into black rubber body bags, careful not to slip as they worked on the bloody PSP. Everything would be sorted later. They zipped up their cargo and hauled it away.

Large oval windows in the operating room doors allowed me a bird's-eye view of all the action under the bright operating lights. I was only able to watch for maybe ten minutes before the gore forced me back to my bed, where I buried my face in the foam pillow. In agony, I pounded the side of my mattress. How could this have happened? How could an ordinary firefight do so much brutal physical damage?

Bob Thurman died on the table. All the others, though very seriously wounded, were still alive the next morning. The 18th Surg. doctors immediately sent most of them to more permanent hospitals in Vietnam or Japan.

It was obvious that our earlier promises to finish each other off had been forgotten. None of us wanted to return home grotesquely maimed, or missing body parts. Yet putting a close friend out of his misery, while he still had a chance to live, was easier said than done.

Billy "The Kid" Barret was an 18-year-old PFC from the fourth platoon. He had just joined the company while we were at the costal sand dunes. He carefully told me the story of what had really happened. Through a bandage wrapped around his head, patching a five-inch tear in his cheek, came the straight scoop.

The company had just made an uneventful chopper air assault to the foot of the mountains, west of Camp Evans. After the troops had humped their rucks up to the top of a small hill, the captain called for an extended break. From the hill they could see for miles; there was no danger anywhere close. The guys dumped their heavy packs in a clearing at the peak of the hill. They peeled off their shirts and crawled under small bushes, seeking refuge from the hot sun. Later, upon hearing Sergeant Wardle's command to "Saddle up!" the clearing filled with sweaty ground-pounders sorting through the pile of rucks.

Billy said a familiar *thump-thump* came from a nearby ARVN camp. They were lofting artillery shells high in the sky toward some faraway target. After listening for a second, the artillery forward observer (FO) crouched and dashed for his radio. Many of the guys, even though they couldn't hear the whine of the shells that the FO did, still took his hint and dived to the ground. Most of them didn't make it. For some it would not have mattered. Two huge 155 mm howitzer projoes (projectiles) weighing more than a hundred pounds each smashed into the top of the hill. They landed in just the right place at the totally wrong time.

Billy said that bodies flew everywhere. The tremendous explosions dug two large craters in the soft earth and mangled all the human flesh caught in their blasts. The hill instantly became a scene of mass confusion as the dead, dying, and incapacitated littered the area. Medics rushed around, liberally injecting morphine and caring for the most seriously injured. RTOs screamed into their radio handsets for dust-off choppers.

Billy cried as he relived the story to me. "The officers and NCOs began yelling for everyone to get off the hill. They anticipated more shells would follow. Thank God, they never did!"

What occurred on that hot afternoon, at grid coordinates 734 771, was an accident. It had been the South Vietnamese—our allies—who had fired on the hill by mistake. It was a very costly mistake that ended the lives of five soldiers. In varying degrees it mangled the bodies of 13 other friends. These battle-hardened Screaming Eagles were among the best soldiers the United States of America could produce. They had been blasted to bits by the very soldiers they had come to support. South Vietnamese "friendly fire" (the worst-named phenomenon in war) had proved to be quite the opposite. "True" friendly fire always lands on the bad guy.

I felt guilty because I was lucky enough to be in the hospital when the tragedy struck. Fate can sometimes be a soldier's friend; sometimes not so friendly. My presence on top of the hill would not have made any difference, except possibly by adding to the body count. While I was enjoying the benefits of the hospital—air-conditioning, clean sheets, three hot meals each day, television, and round-eyed female nurses—my brothers were dying in the dirt. I had always thought that Captain Becker was just too tough to die in Vietnam. He, however, who was responsible for all of us, had probably lost himself.

*We talked with each other about these men for as long as any of us were left in that sorry country. We never found, however, whether the captain or any of the others wounded that day had made it home to their families alive.* Sorry to end their stories, and lives, so abruptly, but that is what war does.

Thoughts of my going back to all that pain and suffering were repulsive to me, but I knew I had to do it. I was getting soft while enjoying this rear echelon life. Maybe my mental and physical edge would be gone if I lay around the hospital much longer. I was tired of sleeping and sick of fevers. The worst of the sickness had mostly passed. It was time to go back.

Thirty-one days after malaria first introduced itself to me, Doctor Goldberg released me to return to the company. Everything I ate still passed like soft mud, but the fever, chills, and headaches were gone. Even the worms that the doctor discovered infesting my lungs had been medicated to death.

Back at Alpha Co. HQ, the staff sergeant who ran the place put me in charge of a half dozen of the new guys. He tasked me to dirty up their crisp new uniforms with a sandbag-filling detail. The next logistics bird that was scheduled to fly supplies and reinforcements into the field would relieve me of the "make work" assignment, but it was not due to fly out for two days.

I met "Major" Poulson the first evening back in the company area. He told me he was cremating human remains again (shit-burning detail.) His explanation was not necessary; it was evident to me by the way he smelled. I was sure Major Poulson would never survive his last six months if he stayed in the jungle: obviously others had the same idea. His new assignment, to keep the battalion area free of human waste, could be done in relative safety. It would greatly increase the odds of his returning to Chicago alive. I hoped he appreciated that his guardian angel wore olive-drab combat fatigues with captain's bars.

Many REMFs were recycled combat infantry soldiers who were not suitable to the ground-pounding life. Some were on physical or emotional medical waivers. Some were cowards and others, like Major, were a danger to themselves and to those around them. Most REMFs had an M.O.S. (Military Occupation Specialty) that required them to be far from the suffering and killing, e.g., cooks and clerks. That didn't dissuade infantry grunts from speaking negatively of them, in colorful language, most of the time. The acronym REMF had a descriptively negative connotation, but everyone, including the REMFs themselves, used the word.

Enlisted soldiers and even many of the lifer NCOs disliked officers most of the time; it wasn't personal. To be a REMF officer was especially bad, in our eyes. While everyone recognized that war zone officers were responsible to get the job done, the actual doing the job usually fell on the lowest ranks. Army casualty lists, whether on paper or granite walls, were weighted heavily with the infantry ranks of PFC, Specialist, and Sergeant. It was easy to blame a REMF officer for that inequity, and we did it with much enthusiasm.

On my final day in camp, the 0900 mail call brought me a letter from home. My parents were frantic that I might be near death due to combat wounds. Putting their recently received clues together, I guess I would have come to the same conclusion. Normally I wrote one or two letters home each week; however, once I fell victim to that tiny little disease-carrying anopheles mosquito, my writing had abruptly ceased. Realizing a change in my writing pattern would cause concern, I had in fact made an attempt to call home toward the end of my stay at the 18th Surg.

A MARS (Military Affiliate Radio System) station was located just 300 meters from the hospital. On one of the rare days when I was feeling a little better, I yanked my IV needles out of my arms and staggered over to the communications building. Several other GIs were ahead of me in the line, waiting their chance to make a free five-minute call. I filled out a sheet of required information (everything had to be complicated or it wasn't the Army way), found a bench in the hall and sat to await my turn.

It was necessary for the Army radio operators to make links with other MARS stations. The shortwave signal had to travel halfway around the world, ending at Hill Air Force Base in Utah. From there, operators could make a landline connection to my parents' home. One of the operators at the MARS station told me that the entire procedure could take an hour, *if* it got through at all.

The bench in the hall did not offer enough room for me to lie down, which I desperately needed to do. After ten minutes of sitting in the hallway, I told the Army operator that I would wait outside. I found a rock-free place to lie in the dirt on the shady side of the building and started counting the minutes. When the count reached 90, my hopes of getting sympathy from home vanished.

I took frequent rest stops but finally made it back to the hospital and my bed. Unknown to me, the connection with my parents was made just five minutes after I gave up and abandoned my post outside the little communications station.

Back in Utah, my parents were awakened by the persistent ringing of the telephone in the middle of the night. When my father sleepily made it to the kitchen where the phone hung on the wall, he answered. The operator told him a call was being patched through from South Vietnam.

"Sir, Specialist 4, Rocky Olson, who is presently hospitalized at the 18th Surgical Hospital, will be on the line shortly, sir. Hold one moment, sir."

The letter from home explained that shortly thereafter the operator advised my father that I could not be located, and he canceled the call. Since the mailbox at home had remained empty for two weeks, and the middle-of- the-night MARS call, my parents were frantically imagining the worst.

To correct the misconception, I hurriedly explained my situation on a piece of sweat-stained stationery and dropped it in the mailbox in the orderly room. For the next few days, or maybe a week or more until my parents got the letter, I expected a Red Cross telegram seeking the details of my wounds.

## CHAPTER 19

# COASTAL SAND DUNES

Two log birds carrying me, six new troops, and supplies for the company flew north. With mixed feelings, I was rejoining Alpha Company after a month in the hospital. New-guy butterflies all over again. Eighteen klicks from Camp Evans, near the Gulf of Tonkin, the choppers settled in a rotor-whipped self-perpetuated sandstorm. I covered my exposed skin as best I could and led the squinty-eyed fresh young warriors on a 35-meter dash out of the rotor wash.

I looked around for the command post. Much of Alpha's leadership had either been rotated out of the field or been blown away since I left them last. I knew I could find the new company commander, however; he'd be the guy surrounded by all the lieutenants.

Without much difficulty, I found the company headquarters situated in the center of a small patch of banana trees. The trees provided the only shade on the otherwise vast expanse of hot white sand. The coastal sand dunes gave no mercy to the uninitiated, and the sun was relentless. Shady terrain was worth fighting for.

Platoon guard positions, established in a large circle outside of the shade, were abandoned to the sun. Violating one of the cardinal rules for self-preservation, all of the grunts were tightly packed under the small, broad-leafed trees. It was under conditions such as this that a single exploding mortar round would be devastating.

I turned a slow 360 degrees as I dug embedded sand from my scalp and ears. I surveyed the low rolling sand dunes around me. There was no place for an enemy mortar team to hide within two klicks of our position. A mortar attack was highly unlikely. Beads of sweat began dripping from my eyebrows to my cheeks. I wiped the sweat-dampened sleeve of my new uniform shirt across my forehead and undid its first two buttons. Maybe the clustered men were not so dumb after all. It was hot!

Several of my old friends sprang up to greet me as I worked my way into the banana grove; many of the faces, however, were new to me.

"Sergeant Rock, welcome back to Alpha."

The voice was unfamiliar, and I quickly decided the face was strange also.

"I'm Captain Knight," he said, thrusting his right hand toward me.

I replaced my steel pot (my brain needed more baking.) We then did the formal grip-and-grin routine. Handshaking was rarely the formality between an officer and an enlisted man, but I obliged. I wondered how he knew who I was and if he understood about the nickname.

"Staff Sergeant Wardle here has been briefing me on the second platoon. He gave me a good report on ya."

Glancing down, I spotted Wardle sitting against the base of one of the banana trees, trying to stay out of the sun. That answered both of the questions I had just asked myself.

"Thank you, sir," I answered. "I'm glad to be back."

That was a partial lie, but making a good first impression would have been impossible had I told the truth.

"Sergeant Wardle has been running the show since your old platoon leader rotated back to the rear. He'll continue to do so until the new lieutenant arrives. He's processing right now into the company.

"Yes, sir." I replied.

"The sergeant has requested that you be assigned to the second platoon in your old position as RTO. I've decided to do it. Any problems with that, soldier?"

"No sir, thank you."

I thought I was good at the job, and to tell the truth, I enjoyed the special responsibility. There, contained within that 25-pound radio, were Cobra gunships, artillery shells, Phantom jets, and squads of combat-ready soldiers. The power it provided me to defend American lives was substantially greater than that of an ordinary rifleman. Because I carried the radio on my back, I also had considerable influence with the decision makers, influence that even some squad leaders never acquired.

Sometimes new enlisted troops, fresh from the training environment back in the world, were intimidated by the gold or black bar on a platoon leader's collar. Often they came to me looking for an intermediary: Sergeant Rock, would you ask the lieutenant . . . ? and I was able to help.

Later in the afternoon, Wardle and I had a chance to chew the fat. I found that my first impression of the new company commander was essentially correct. He was a good officer and genuinely concerned for his men. Several times he had even gone so far as asking advice from old-timers before making difficult decisions, the sarge said. Sergeant Wardle then told me that because the company was so short on experienced officers, Captain Knight was reassigned from another infantry company within the 101st Airborne family. He had been with Alpha for about two weeks.

Our new leader had been in-country for eight months. The last month and a half the captain had spent in the bush doing infantry stuff. He was not exactly a new guy. That was good; we wouldn't have to train him. "True" field experience is something no one gets until just after he needs it.

It is imperative that infantry soldiers be given the best, most experienced leadership available. Combat is no place to train a second-rate officer how to lead men. It seemed like every time a new leader arrived, we had to go through the same training cycle. The greater the rank these first-time combat leaders had on their collars, the more there was to teach them. Much of the old stateside tactics they had been taught needed to be forgotten. Many times, ground-pounders paid for ineptness or learning mistakes. Quite often by the time an officer got himself squared away and earned his Combat Infantry Badge, his six months were up. He then rotated to an assignment in the rear, and we started all over again.

Career officers needed combat command experience in their personnel file; it added important points and kept them competitive for promotion. I didn't blame the individual officers, except those who had their own private, damn the cost, career-building agendas. It was the system that kept front-line infantry companies perpetually short of trained leaders. This war, while providing the command combat "experience" for young officers, was also sacrificing many of my friends. For the first time, I began to have second thoughts about the politics behind it all.

As if my concerns for lack of competent leadership were an omen, early the next morning I met Lieutenant Mackelroy. Like a magician's trick, from the swirling cloud of the just-arrived supply chopper there appeared a pale-faced boy in a man's freshly starched combat uniform. Marching through the sand as though he were on a manicured military parade field back in the world, the lieutenant approached the waiting commander. Five feet from his new leader he planted both feet firmly in the sand and threw up a salute that would have made a drill instructor proud.

Wardle and I were 50 meters away and we could not hear the conversation, but the lieutenant's quick censure by the captain was obvious. The formality they demanded at Camp Evans was frowned upon, even dangerous, here in the boonies. The new lieutenant had much to learn.

From attention, Mackelroy went to parade rest and then, within seconds, an exaggerated slouch as he desperately tried to please his new captain. Staff Sergeant Wardle, a 16-year veteran of the Army, put a hand on my shoulder and mumbled a prayer intended for my ears only.

"Lard, if he's assigned anywhere else 'cept the second platoon, I promise I'll faithfully go ta church fer the next two years!"

Jokingly I looked up toward the cloudless sky.

"Sarge, your prayer is too late. We're all going to pay for your sins. I feel a plague coming."

Staff Sergeant Wardle was a good man, an Army man through and through. He had been married to civilians three times, but the Army was a jealous mistress and he had returned to her each time the civilian stuff failed. The Army was his home, all he really had.

Fifteen minutes later, Captain Knight brought the new lieutenant over for an introduction to the men. The plague was here. I started off on the wrong foot when I broke into laughter at what happened next.

As the two officers approached Wardle and me, we struggled to our feet from our nests burrowed deep in the cool shady sand.

"Sergeant Wardle, "I'd like you to meet your new platoon leader, Lieutenant Mackelroy."

Wardle quickly brought his hand up, as if to salute. He abruptly stopped short and began scratching his chin. The lieutenant, still primed for stateside garrison military etiquette, threw his right hand up to return the anticipated salute. He realized his error too late. Trying to hide the embarrassment of making the same mistake twice in just 15 minutes, the red-faced officer wiped sweat from his forehead with the back of his hand. To me it was obvious that Wardle had bluffed the salute on purpose. He held a straight face; I could not.

When I was a young boy sitting in Sunday school with some of my friends, occasionally one of them would do something funny and we would all break out in contagious snickers. Soul-piercing glares from the pious teacher sometimes corrected our impoliteness. Invariably, however, our glances at each other would turn us back on again, rude as it may have been. I was a kid then, but I had no excuses now. I was trying as hard as I could, but my broad grin and involuntary chuckling could not be suppressed. Finally I just walked off, hoping my disrespect would not result in six months of make-work projects or an assignment as permanent point man.

Sheepishly, I returned ten minutes later, after the two officers had departed to another location and approached Wardle. He looked up at me from his seclusion under a tree, and we both burst into subdued laughter.

Lieutenant Mackelroy appeared to be no more than 17 years old, although he must have been at least twenty-two. His curly dishwater-blond hair was cut perfectly, "high and tight." His complexion was pale, almost transparent. There was a hint of cultivated blond fuzz above his lipless mouth from which, we were to soon learn, stupidity spewed forth. The lieutenant's tailored jungle fatigues and highly polished boots just didn't fit into our rude and unrefined environment. This was to be Mackelroy's first command assignment out of Officers Candidate School. Lucky us!

At noon, when most of us were lounging in the shade or eating our Cs out of tin cans, the new lieutenant made his first decision.

"Sergeant Wardle, I don't like the men all clustered together here in the trees. Have them move out to their guard positions."

I normally would have agreed, but this particular situation was different. Wardle tried to explain that the enemy could not sneak across the blinding white sand surrounding us. He pointed out that from two klicks away we could hardly even be seen, let alone accurately fired upon. Wardle then explained the tiring and dangerous effects of the hot sun, but it was all to no avail. The new lieutenant gave the order again, and the now-angry men moved. The platoon HQ, composed of Mackelroy, Wardle, Czech (the new medic), and I remained in the comfort of the shade.

The lieutenant's next order, later in the evening, caused another stir.

"How can we expect to win the respect of the Vietnamese people when we have no respect for ourselves? By tomorrow morning, all of the men WILL have polished boots and WILL have clean-shaven faces!"

Beating the platoon sergeant to the punch, I tried to explain.

"Sir, that can't be done. The closest can of boot polish is 18 klicks away back at Camp Evans. As to shaving, we barely have enough water to drink. Shaving is a luxury we can't afford."

Raising his voice to remind me of his authority, the officer looked directly at me.

"You don't seem to understand, soldier. I-AM-IN-CHARGE-AROUND-HERE. The men WILL have clean-shaven faces by tomorrow morning, and at the next stand-down at Evans, you all WILL procure proper boot dressing! I do not know what was wrong with your previous platoon leader, maybe he was lazy, but you are now in MY platoon, I am not in yours. In MY platoon we WILL go by the book. All proper military dress, rank respect, appearance standards, and professional military benchmarks will be strictly adhered to. We will be exemplary in everything we do."

I had intended to develop a little sensible dialog with the young officer—a teaching moment, if you will. Another option available to me was a simple "Yes, sir!" It probably would have been much better. Or I could have argued until I got myself into trouble, like I just had. Of my options available at the time, maybe I had not made the wisest choice.

While I passed his new order around the platoon, the men gave me a laundry basket full of four-letter words to deliver back to the lieutenant. Most of their descriptive obscenities I tried to keep out of my vocabulary, and since other more proper words just didn't carry the same impact, I decided not to say anything. Only Zorn's declaration, which he yelled as I walked back to the radio, reached Mackelroy's ears.

"Tell that friggin' A-hole he can push me, but he'd better not bend me out of shape!"

Pretending not to hear was the first wise thing the "butter bar" (gold bar of a second lieutenant) had done since his arrival.

At 0800 hours the next morning, after the guys had finished their painful dry-shaving, the entire company moved out of the position they had settled in four days earlier. We humped in a southwesterly direction for about four klicks to an area containing several large Vietnamese cemeteries. We assembled our rifle-cleaning rods and used them to probe the sand and brush, searching for caches of weapons or supplies we had been told might be there. The probing was successful. We found more than 50 sandbags filled with rice. We also uncovered two U.S. Army ammo cans that were packed with hundreds of linked Chinese 7.92 mm machine gun rounds.

Learning from the success of others, I began probing under low-lying vegetation and around the circular grave mounds. About 1400 hours, I made a small but very significant find. Between two willow-type bushes, six inches below the surface of the sand, my cleaning rod struck what felt like soft plastic. Carefully, I uncovered a three-by-four-foot sheet of grey polyethylene, which was wrapped around an oiled canvas document pouch. The pouch had been buried along side an olive-drab American .50 caliber ammo can. The document pouch produced two diaries or log books, handwritten in Vietnamese. They contained lists of VC names and supply records. The ammo can was filled with hundreds of electrical blasting caps.

Later, I learned that much valuable information was revealed from the translated log books. A regional Viet Cong command infrastructure of as many as 500 soldiers was eventually disabled by the arrest of many of its leaders whose names appeared on those documents.

The blasting caps were sent to the United States for military evaluation. They turned out to be of Soviet origin. It was an important find—the first discovery of this particular blasting cap in Vietnam. Our military was aided greatly in determining the source and types of explosives being employed against us.

The second day of the search-and-clear mission commenced with a bang, literally. Members of first platoon tripped a wire, which launched a Bouncing Betty. The high-explosive mine popped up out of the ground and detonated waist high. Two of the guys were cut in half by the intense concussion and deadly flying steel. The scene of the blast was sickening to see.

The violent death of the two first-platooners had a big emotional impact on some of the new guys, but I managed to remain emotionally detached. It helped that I didn't know them. The sudden and dramatic termination of life was becoming commonplace to me, and I was learning to be tough when facing it. I'd learned to deal with the sight and smell of death by just hanging around long enough to get used to it.

Sergeant Pearson told me once, "Just tag 'em and bag 'em and get on with your job."

No sooner had the victims been body-bagged and chopperd out than one of the FNGs, who had just arrived with me two days earlier, found a booby-trapped frag the hard way. The unfortunate grunt lost his left foot in the blast. In less than a week in Vietnam the soldier had a Purple Heart medal in exchange for his mangled leg. Suddenly it became evident that the area which was safe the day before had become deadly during the dark of night.

Mackelroy passed the word around to watch for booby-traps, "Because there might be more of them."

“Brilliant deduction!” I said under my breath.

Trying to decide where I would hide my loot if I were a VC, I saw a grave site that was slightly larger than the rest. Surrounding the rounded mound of sand containing the "bed of eternal rest" was a two-foot ornamental concrete wall. Thinking it would be a good reference point in a graveyard full of identical mounds, I decided to start my search there. The opening in the low circular wall was also an obvious place for a booby-trap. I visually examined the area before moving toward it but saw nothing abnormal. I should have paid better attention to what was directly at my feet.

While taking my first step toward the sandy mound, my right foot snagged a vine that lay curlicued across the path. The area was full of woody, dead vines, so catching my foot was not unusual. I yanked my size-10 boot free of the vine, as I had done so many times before. This vine was different from the others, however; there was an American hand grenade tied to one end. The rusty green sphere rolled from under a bush right between my legs. I now had less than four seconds to live.

My first reaction was to scream a warning, "Frag!"

Men all around me dived to the ground in attempts to avoid the thousands of tiny jagged steel projectiles about to rip through the area. My second thought was to snatch and heave the explosive device somewhere far away from me before it could detonate. The white sand and small shrubbery around me, however, was by then spotted with prone soldiers. Saving myself would likely result in the death of some of my best friends. Even if I dived to the ground, I would still catch enough steel to kill me. I elected to do nothing. I guess I could have dived on the grenade and become a hero, but I happened to be terrified about my life ending at that exact moment and I didn’t think of doing anything heroic.

Thoughts of home and family were what raced through my mind at lightning speed. I wondered if my parents knew I was about to die? I’ve heard that mothers sometimes get premonitions when tragic things happen to their children. Did Mom know she was about to lose her firstborn? All of these thoughts and decisions were made in those first four seconds.

My eyes were still transfixed on the object. The seconds ticked away . . . five . . . six . . . seven. Something was wrong. I was still alive. The fragmentation grenade had not detonated. My body parts were not spread all over creation. Fuse time had expired and I was not dead. It was then that I noticed the rusty safety spoon. It had not separated from the frag; the grenade was not yet armed. I dropped to my knees and grasped the frag in a two-handed eagle-talon grip. I held the spoon tight against the frag's steel case, preventing any further possibility that it could arm itself.

The oblong sphere felt as though it were alive. The metal jacket covering the explosive pulsated as though a goose egg were hatching in my hands. I could feel it breathe. Holding it tightly, I discovered the throbbing of the grenade exactly matched the beat of my pounding heart. It was my rapidly palpitating ticker that seemed to give life to the device.

Carefully, and in slow motion, I turned the frag over. The arming pin had not been completely extracted by the momentum of my swinging boot. A small kink in the pin was caught in the rusty casing hole, preventing the spoon from releasing and igniting the fuse. The vine, which was still tied to a bush on the side of the trail, was also still tied to the ring on the safety pin. I had actually yanked the frag free from the bush it had been tied to without removing the arming pin. Dumb luck.

The grenade may yet have been booby-trapped (short fused), so I treated it like any other suspicious explosive device. Jim Wilson and I embedded the dangerous ball in a one-pound block of high explosive C4 while Doc Czech watched us. From a safe distance, we blew it all to bits. I was getting good at avoiding the best Sir Charles had to offer, but this mistake had nearly cost me my life. It was another mistake I swore I would never make again. If intelligence didn't replace luck, I would soon be cocooned in a cold rubberized body bag. My heart and breathing continued to race for some time after the successful detonation. I could have used a paper bag over my mouth most of the time.

Doc Czech called me a "dumbass," and walked off. I wasn't sure whether he was kidding or serious. Doc's personality was a little different, maybe strange was a better description. He generally kept to himself, unless he was bad-mouthing me or one of the other guys, I guess. He certainly was no Doc Bayne!

The "how-to-find-it" lesson in the Advanced Infantry Training Manual was woefully short, and it was developed in an era long before the Vietnam War. Tactics had certainly changed; it was time to update the manual. The first chapter could be titled: Modern Booby Traps and the Proper Techniques to Find Them. Maybe the word Proper should be underlined.

Although we did find more rice, the two guys who had been killed and the one who was wounded during the second day of searching made our exploration decidedly slower and less than profitable. Seventeen potentially lethal booby-traps were either dismantled or blown in place by the observant searchers. Rumors that we were humping out of the deadly area before nightfall were met with much enthusiasm. This miserable place was just not worth it. Many of the guys had become so paranoid over the sudden infestation of the deadly entanglements that they had refused to continue the search. I think Captain Knight wisely decided that the best way to avoid possible insurrection was to get the heck out of the area.

The move proved to be a short one. Captain Knight organized our NDP just two klicks to the west. A small three-acre oasis of tall coconut trees that had been a half a klick to our west that morning was now that same distance to our east. While humping around the small oasis earlier in the afternoon, we saw seven or eight civilian hootches among the trees. I suspected that battalion's real reason for sending us to this gulf AO was to watch this little hamlet; we had in fact found a lot of rice and weaponry around it. It was another case of our not being told what was going on.

The third morning, we relaxed among the burial mounds of the well-manicured cemetery. It was an extension of where we had spent the night. *Burial mounds were extremely important to the Vietnamese; strong family ties continued beyond the grave. They believed that ancestral resting places must be well cared for, or their own spirits would be lost forever.*

Lieutenant Mackelroy strutted around the platoon positions, spreading the word that we would continue the search-and-clear mission "he" had started three days earlier. He stopped to watch Zorn and Muskrat clean their weapons and got into a heated argument over the amount of grease that should be used to coat the moving mechanical parts.

"The maintenance manual specifies that a thin coating should be applied." Mackelroy said.

"That's well and good, sir, for shooting 50 or 100 rounds of single-shot target practice. You'll find, sir, after you've had some combat experience sir, that your book learning was wrong, sir!"

I could see that the young officer was becoming greatly irritated. Zorn had verbally shot himself in the foot so many times it was amazing that he could still walk, but he just wouldn't let up on our new leader.

"When your life depends on your weapon firing on rock and roll for long periods of time, sir, a lightly coated bolt will soon seize up and leave you helpless, sir. Heavy grease takes longer to burn off, and thus you won't have to throw your weapon away in the middle of a firefight, sir."

The two opposing voices were raised high enough by then that most of the activity in the perimeter had slowed to a crawl. Everyone was watching Zorn as he verbally challenged the lieutenant.

"Look, Specialist, I happen to know that heavy grease can cause a weapon to clog, and it's just plain stupid!"

"Well, sir," came Zorn's counterargument, "if it's stupid but it works, it ain't stupid!"

The lieutenant could not believe that an enlisted man, far junior to him, would dare to defy him.

"As long as you work for me, soldier, YOU WILL DO IT MY WAY!"

Zorn, also losing control of the situation, yelled, "No cherry-ass FNG officer is going to get me killed! I'll care for MY weapon any way I please, SIR!"

He was smoking, even without the customary cigar butt between his teeth.

Had Zorn been having this confrontation with another enlisted man, the big Kansas farmer would have had the other guy's teeth prints on his right fist by now.

"That's it, Specialist! You and I are going to see the old man, RIGHT NOW, and along the way I'm going to decide what rank to bust you to, got it?"

"Lima Charlie, sir!" *L.C. in the military phonetic alphabet stood for "loud and clear."*

Both Zorn and 'Muck-it-up-roy' (the lieutenant's new nickname) stormed off through the sand heading for Captain Knight's command post. Two hundred eyes watched the journey of the "friendly" combatants.

I was in the unusual situation of not knowing which side of the dispute to cheer for. The only two soldiers in the U.S. Army whom I really disliked were embroiled in a quest for pecking-order status. I felt Zorn's side of the argument was correct, but losing his temper and swearing at the lieutenant was wrong. Zorn had less than 30 days left in the bush. If he had ever hoped to get those promised sergeant stripes, he had just blown it. I couldn't imagine the captain supporting that "little Hitler" of a leader we had, but to side with Zorn would destroy any semblance of authority the cocky little lieutenant possessed. The poor company commander had a tough decision to make.

Pretending to go about our own business, everyone in the company continued to watch and listen carefully. It was almost as exciting as a sniper attack, and no one would get killed . . . maybe. The captain locked both soldiers at attention and the hushed conversation began. The only sign of excitement came from Mackelroy as he continually waved his arms. He reminded me of the rear end of a cow during fly season.

Twenty minutes later, the captain made a brilliant decision. He requested two loaded magazines from every rifleman in the company and announced we were going to have a shoot-off. Captain Knight then assigned a third volunteer to shoot with Lieutenant Mackelroy and Zorn. The participants applied heavy, medium, and light applications of LSA (Lubricant, Small Arms) on the bolts of their three weapons.

The three men then began to fire the 20-round magazines as fast as they could load them into the M-16s. A small sand dune 20 meters away absorbed the hot lead. Handfuls of sand danced into the air each time rock and roll bullets impacted with the little hill. The dune seemed to erode away as hundreds of 5.56 mm bullets attacked it over the next five minutes.

At almost the same time, 20 or so magazines into the shoot-off, all three of the rifle barrel hand-guards became too hot to touch. After 30 magazines, the barrels visibly turned a dull red. Zorn wrapped his tee-shirt around his weapon's hand guard, and the shirt burst into flame. Soon rounds began cooking off as quickly as the M-16s automatically chambered them. A finger on the trigger mechanism was no longer necessary. To stop a runaway M-60 we simply twisted the ammo belt. That jammed the rounds and prevented them from entering the over-heated chamber. But this was an endurance test for both the shooters and their weapons, so they kept cramming new magazines into their M-16s and let them run free.

When the weapons became too hot to handle, all three soldiers laid their rifles on the ground. The shooters each kept one of their boots on the butt of their weapons, which kept the rifles from snaking around in the dirt and shooting one of us in the foot. When the captain called the test off, about 35 magazines into the experiment, all three weapons had been destroyed by the intense overheating. Although each weapon had continued to fire, the glowing red barrels of all three rifles drooped a half an inch as though they were made of rubber.

After the '16s cooled, our detailed examination failed to substantiate that the amount of lubricant made any difference what-so-ever. The captain wisely declared the test a draw. Playing King Solomon, Captain Knight gave a bit of credit to each of the soldiers. Both Zorn and Mackelroy were able to save face. The baby was not cut in half. Previous threats from each of the antagonists were forgotten . . . at least, they were temporarily shelved.

Following the morning's educational entertainment, we probed the surrounding area thoroughly and found several hundred more pounds of rice. We chopperd it to one of the several orphanages in the area, as we did each time we made substantial food cache discoveries. There were no booby-traps in the new area this time, but we did not relax our concentration at all.

The fourth day of the mission started much the same as the second. One of the guys from second platoon (again it was an FNG I didn't know) walked a hundred meters beyond the night's defensive position. He had an entrenching tool in hand and intended to visit with Mother Nature. As he followed a winding little trail through the bushes, he scraped against a sharpened bamboo pole that had been hidden in an overhanging bush. It had not been there the day before. The booby-trap was crude but effective. Doc Czech cleaned and patched the small cut in the soldier's side, but because the spear was probably poisoned, the unfortunate victim was quickly medevaced to the 18th Surgical Hospital for a more thorough examination. For the second time in four days, a docile area was rigged for violence overnight.

To perform the day's search-and-clear mission as expeditiously as possible, the platoon leader's organized squad-size scouting teams. Mackelroy and I accompanied Sergeant Tew's squad to a checkerboard of dry rice paddies separated by tall hedgerows where we probed the dense rows of vegetation all day long. Together we found several small rice caches and more homemade booby-traps.

About 1700 hours, just as the lieutenant was "teaching" me the proper procedures for calling in our coordinates on the squawk-box, Wilson sang out from across the field: "I've got something big over here!"

Eight soldiers, including Mackelroy, responded to the first real excitement of the day. I was the only one who continued my probing task instead of yielding to curiosity and investigating Wilson's find. Entrenching tools ready, the eager grunts began digging up a steel fifty-five-gallon drum full of rice.

Fifty meters away, I carefully advanced step by step, paralleling the hedgerow to my left. My head was bowed as my eyes raced over the terrain ahead and explored the vegetation by my side. I paid particular attention to curlicued vines.

The quiet hedgerow suddenly burst alive with motion and noise. A ghost jumping out at me in a haunted house could not have scared me more. I spun left toward the sudden activity and instinctively threw my rifle up across my chest for protection. I thought I was being attacked by a large animal. But I was wrong.

An NVA soldier, in a khaki combat uniform, was just 15 feet from me. The gook had spotted me first and crashed through the thick foliage as he tried to flee. Stealth and noise suppression were no longer his priorities. I swung the muzzle of my rifle toward the soldier and fired a chest-high 20-round rock and roll burst into the cover. But as suddenly as he had appeared, he was gone. I smashed my left palm against the magazine release button and the empty container fell to the ground. I ripped a full replacement magazine from the bandoleer around my waist and shoved it into the weapon's empty receptacle. With dispatch I chambered the first round. I then sprayed 10 more bullets into the general area. Suddenly, 30 meters to my rear, seven M-16s and a machine gun opened up. AMBUSH, we're being ambushed!

I did a 180-degree spin and over my sights looked for a target. The lieutenant and all of third squad were hugging the earth and shooting toward me. Their invisible lead mowed down the hedgerow to my rear like a wheat combine at harvest time.

We were not in the middle of an ambush at all. Sergeant Tew's squad was just busy supporting me with fire. As always, (remember Sergeant Rock's laws of combat) when one soldier shoots, everyone shoots. Again I turned to face the hedgerow. I raised my left arm to the square and gave the cease-fire hand signal. Waiting in the sudden stillness, my ears and eyes were alert for the slightest sound or movement. There was none. Nathaniel Victor was either dead or he had made it through the thick vegetation and was running to the safety of the next hedgerow. In either case he was no longer a threat.

I yelled out what had happened, and under the cover of a few random shots Sergeant Tew brought his men forward two at a time. Our fearless platoon leader was last; he was still trying to figure out what to do. The battle-wise boonie-rats spread themselves along the hedgerow without being told, but waited for the command to advance. The lieutenant, after regaining his composure, gave the signal, and we moved in. Slowly and carefully we searched as we worked our way through the 20 feet of dense hedgerow greenery.

*Kerr-Whump*! The explosion came from twenty-five meters to my left. Painful screams quickly followed. Americans were crying in burning torment. I could tell by the sound that the detonating fragmentation grenade was not one of our own.

Someone screamed, "Booby-trap!"

The next excited voice belonged to Sergeant Tew.

"Rock, get on the Prick-25 and get us a medevac! We've got three guys down!"

Reaching over my right shoulder, while still intently watching the area to my front, I turned the radio speaker volume knob all the way up. I used my code name for the month ("Lightfoot") and requested immediate medical assistance.

"Roger Lightfoot," came the reply.

"You have a dust-off inbound; ETA is seven minutes."

I yelled the information back to the sergeant and the lieutenant, who had just joined him.

There was nothing I could do to help, and a cluster of soldiers is a great target, so I deliberately stayed away and continued to search. By chance I found a concealed hole in the side of a small dirt bank in the hedgerow. Following my cry of "Fire in the hole!" I emptied the '16's remaining 10 shells into the blackness. Very cautiously, I then wedged myself, rifle and flashlight first, into the small opening. I found a 4 x 4 x 6-foot room. I also found a small sack of rice and a canvas backpack in the hole.

I dragged my find from the darkness into the sunlight for examination. The backpack contained a crude first-aid kit and peasant's clothing, including a bamboo conical hat. The NVA soldier I just met had undoubtedly been playing the part of a local villager in order to obtain supplies and intelligence information.

Tew's squad attended to their wounded while Mackelroy and I stood guard and completed the search of the hedgerow. We found no dead Nathaniel Victor, nor could we find his weapon. I couldn't understand how he had escaped the first hail of bullets I'd sent after him. It made me feel guilty about possessing the expert M-16 rifleman's badge, but then again on the rifle range there was no need to worry about the black cardboard silhouette shooting back.

After the medevac departed with our three wounded (none serious) we set fire to the hedgerow to expose any more booby-traps. We then searched it more thoroughly. I was quite sure the NVA soldier did not have a weapon when I fired him up—otherwise he would have killed me before he ran. Apparently I had surprised him while he was hiding in the bushes watching the squad dig up the rice barrel. The gook's frantic attempts to get away made such a startling racket that my initial fright may have been greater than his.

In the after-fire search, I found the green North Vietnamese Army pith helmet the soldier had been wearing as he disappeared from my view. The singed headgear had the customary small brass star on the front. I tied the helmet to the back of my ruck as a souvenir. It remained there until one of the guys safely hand-delivered the helmet to my new duffle bag in the brand-new supply hootch at Camp Evans. Many REMFs would love to have the enemy headgear, so the whole operation had to be done very covertly.

We continued to look for Charlie's weapon. Jim Wilson found an unusually large dirt mound beside a small pond in the corner of the field; we knew from experience that fighting bunkers and hideaways were often built next to water, so naturally we were suspicious.

The seven of us explored and probed around the edge of the pond looking for underwater entrances into the mound. The lieutenant found a dark spot in the pond under some overhanging willows, but no one was eager to go underwater to investigate. It was the kind of thing Minnie Martinez was good at, but unfortunately he was searching another area with Zorn's squad.

Wilson finally agreed that since he had found the mound, he would check it out. He borrowed the lieutenant's .45 pistol, removed his boots, and waded into the water. Upon taking his third step into the murky pond, Wilson did a little hop, as if his bare feet had suddenly touched sharp rocks. He bent over in the waist-deep water and reached to the bottom of the pond. Feeling around a little, he grasped an object and raised it triumphantly skyward. It was an AK-47.

Wilson shouted, "I've got the gooks rifle!"

The weapon was heavily greased to prevent corrosion, and it was in excellent condition. The soldier I accidentally encountered in the hedgerow was not only missing his food, clothing, and helmet but now his weapon was gone.

Wilson dove under the willows and probed along the entire bank with his hands but found no entrance. The pond search ended as the sun disappeared over the horizon. We ate our Cs in the dark, then humped to pre-designated coordinates where we joined the rest of the company. We recounted the day's events to anyone who would listen and showed off our souvenirs. At midnight, an ARVN company joined ours and together we moved out again. Three klicks to the east was the same little village (Thon Tan Hoi) that we had been patrolling around for several days. This time it was our destination. The moon was full and the evening's temperature began to cool. The monsoon season was approaching. Except for a little ankle-deep swamp water, the hump that night was almost enjoyable. Under the cover of darkness we quietly and professionally cordoned the *ville*.

At 0700 hours the next morning, the South Vietnamese troops began the search. Alpha's assignment was to act as the blocking force. Lieutenant Mackelroy briefed the platoon that a VC squad was using the pastoral little rice-farming community as a base camp, and to expect unfriendly inhabitants. The warning proved prophetic.

The advancing ARVNs were hit by a dozen rounds of sniper fire and tripped two booby-trapped frags as they entered the village. Their two dead and four wounded were quickly medevaced out. When the sweep of Thon Tan Hoi was completed, our ARVN allies had nothing to show for their efforts. The frustrated soldiers repeated their search but once more drew a blank. Someone from the *ville* had fired them up, but the ARVNs could find nothing. The locals were mute. They knew "nothing."

As part of the blocking force a hundred meters away, I watched as the infuriated South Vietnamese dragged the village chief into a small adjoining cemetery. The sun-leathered skin draped over the old man's bones was covered by shabby silk pajama clothing. His short black hair was clearly visible, but the very thin goatee—a symbol of power, respect and wisdom—customarily worn by most old men was too sparse for me to see. It was obvious however, that he was the *ville*'s numba one honcho. Mercifully, I was not close enough to see the details of what happened next. Distance undoubtedly saved me from adding more weights to my already capsizing bad-memory ship.

When screamed threats by the ARVNs produced no answers, the interrogators got rough. Several soldiers beat the old man with their fists. Multiple kicks to his groin still could not make Thon Tan Hoi's Chief talk. The old man fell to the ground and pleaded for mercy in a language I could not understand. But the South Vietnamese soldiers showed no mercy. They dragged his gaunt body over the top of a small concrete Buddhist shrine. The cruel inquisitors beat the chief mercilessly with their rifle butts until he was unconscious. Thoughts of their own dead and wounded earlier in the day inspired their merciless treatment. The chief gave up nothing.

No one in the little *ville* would disclose anything; it may have been fear, maybe loyalty; who knows. Questions by their countrymen about where the Vietnamese Communists were hiding, who had fired the shots, or who had been setting booby-traps were all met with naive stares. They just squatted on the ground acting oblivious that their country was even at war.

It was obvious to us that our movements were being closely monitored. The deadly unmanned booby-trap ambushes were being set each night by village inhabitants or the VC they were hiding. There was no doubt about that. No one confessed any knowledge of anything.

Four hours after the ARVNs entered the hamlet, we carefully went in. Except for a large amount of rice being stored there, we could find no evidence of Charlie's presence: no tunnels, no weapons, and no one willing to talk. We knew that these peasant farmers and the VC they hid were responsible for the week's casualties—four dead and nine wounded—but all traces of hostility had been hidden too cleverly for us to find.

Although it caused great emotional pain, we finally relented to the "I-know-nothing" villagers and prepared to move out. Our South Vietnamese counterparts took the lead. The lieutenant and I joined our platoon's first squad in rear security.

As we followed the little dirt cart path out of town, one of the ARVN point men stepped on a newly laid anti-personnel mine. The blast sent us all scurrying for cover. Radio traffic said the soldier had been killed. Only some slightly cooler American heads prevented the infuriated South Vietnamese soldiers from returning to the *ville* for revenge.

Normally rear security was considered good duty, but this assignment offered me no opportunity to relax. I was anxious for the situation ahead to get resolved so I could get my tail out of the village. I felt like a mouse crawling over the triggering mechanism of a mousetrap. At any second, my deceivingly peaceful environment could suddenly slap shut. Working around the *ville* seemed like an organized exercise of Russian roulette; it would eventually get us all.

Mackelroy whistled a sigh of relief when our turn to pass through the tree-lined perimeter proved uneventful. Again, feelings of security were premature. One hundred and fifty meters later, a burst of machine-gun fire from the same trees we had just passed through ripped Polansky's rucksack apart, knocking him to the ground, unhurt. With all the firepower the squad could muster, we plastered the treeline while the two companies quickly withdrew to safety. Two thousand meters away, they re-formed into defensive positions and waited for us to join them.

Now that the two companies were safe, the lieutenant wondered who would cover us as we retreated. His question was answered; the United States Navy, 20 miles offshore, could give us all the cover we could ever want. Captain Knight had spoken to "higher authorities" and got the radio frequency for the battleship New Jersey; she was eager to help.

Captain Knight was so frustrated and infuriated over losing his men day after day in the *ville* area that he finally decided to just eliminate the entire target. Little Thon Tan Hoi had pushed the big green machine one too many times. *Nemo me impune lacessit*: "No man provokes me with impunity." The hour of retribution had arrived.

As soon as the first white phosphorous marker shell was confirmed as zeroed, the captain gave the command to fire for effect. Giant artillery shells from the Navy's big guns, weighing up to 2,700 pounds, began falling like rain on the far side of the *ville*. The shells, capable of penetrating 30 feet of reinforced concrete, provided us with the signal to get out of the area fast. We ran as quickly as our bouncing rucksacks would allow, always keeping sand dunes between us and the violence.

Like the Old Testament story of Lot and his family fleeing the wicked cities of Sodom and Gomorrah, we dared not pause to watch the destruction. Finally, from a safe distance, we turned to see the carnage. The soft earth shuddered, then heaved as each high-explosive shell detonated. Brush, hootches, and the little cemetery were all being blown to bits and thrown high into the sky. Large clusters of coconut trees fell in a scattered array like pick-up sticks. Huge black clouds like giant bowling balls rolled skyward toward imaginary pins. The thunder of their meeting placed X's on the scorecard. I pressed my fingers to my ears to muffle the effects of the tremendous concussions. It was the greatest display of firepower I had ever seen. It even surpassed the excitement of the terribly destructive Camp Evans fire several months earlier.

Never forgotten in the overwhelming devastation was the death it caused. Not only were those guilty of killing our friends being repaid (and going to meet their Buddha in the sky), but so also were the women and children who may or may not have been innocent. This was not the first time poor rice farmers or fishermen peasants had been caught in the hostilities of war nor, sadly, would it be the last. American soldiers could display significant acts of human kindness and extreme violence in the same day.

The thundering bombardment of the ville lasted for 15 minutes; deathly silence followed. The idyllic little *ville* was a visual abomination, no longer serene and picturesque. Our memories now contained the vision of black acrid dust settling over the low sand dunes.

Although the shredded steel had settled, the death haze may have still contained the ghosts of the perished. We did not wish to survey the destruction of our Sodom and Gomorrah any closer, so we loaded up and humped out, never to return.

## CHAPTER 20

# COASTAL SAND DUNES (PART TWO)

Captain Knight organized the company on the beach. We were just a few klicks from Thon Tan Hoi, and most of us wished we were a little further away.

"We'll be here for several days, so keep your act in order," he said.

We were happy to dump our heavy gear onto the sand and set up a perimeter. The prospect of a little R & R in the ocean caused a buzz of enthusiasm, and it took our minds off the destroyed *ville* a little. We peeled off our filthy fatigues in preparation for a swim in the warm water of the gulf. The lieutenant said something about not being able to rinse the salt off after the swim, but his warning was given little consideration. Most of us had worn the same sweat-soaked fatigues for so long that they and we were saltier than the ocean anyway. After *tee tee* (very little) thought, we quickly splashed into the *boo coo* (very large) ocean.

I didn't realize how many sores and cuts I had on my battered body until the salty seawater made each of them scream in pain. The jungle-rot between my toes and under my arms, the chafing between my legs, the dry-shaving nicks, and the elephant grass cuts on my arms all proclaimed their instant displeasure.

We body-surfed naked in the breaking waves of the Gulf and lay on the beach soaking up the sun's rays. With the exception of the burning red on my posterior that evening, the day on the beach was relaxing and very enjoyable. For a short while, I almost forgot about the death and destruction I'd witnessed that very morning.

To make the day even more entertaining, the afternoon log bird brought each one of us a pair of Army-issue, bubble-eyed, wrap-around sunglasses. They were the rage back in the world. We strutted around the beach, wearing nothing more than smiles and high-fashioned eyewear. We were really cool dudes!

One of the "fresh meat" replacements, who arrived with the

supply chopper, told me that we were now in the first week of May. Each month, each day, each hour, brought me closer to my DEROS and a reserved seat on the freedom bird back to the world.

As darkness began to chase away the hot sun, Sergeant Wardle jogged through the sand up to the lieutenant.

"Sir, I just noticed that I ain't seen Doc Czech since this morning in the *ville*. D'ya have him somewhere on a detail?"

Mackelroy, lounging back against his rucksack in the sand, sat up. He glanced around the company perimeter, then jumped to his feet.

"Damn! Sergeant Rock, you and Sergeant Wardle get around to the positions and talk to the men. I'll go to the CP (command post) and report the situation to the old man."

Our questioning of each man proved fruitless. No one had seen our medic since the *ville* was blown away early that morning. The lieutenant reported the missing medic to Captain Knight and got his butt chewed real good, as only the military can do.

"The captain is sending us out to look for Czech. We're going back to the village tonight," he reported. "He contacted a cavalry unit just west of us. They are sending several Armored Personnel Carriers to give us a ride through the booby-trapped area and to provide security."

Interjecting a little concern for himself, the young officer confided, "If anything bad has happened to that pill-pusher, I'll face court-martial proceedings."

We climbed aboard the APCs when they arrived an hour later. The troopers on the tracks did not seem very excited with this new assignment. We grunts were happy for the ride, however. Everyone grabbed a few cans of Cs, some ammo, and frags and climbed aboard. Off toward the unknown we clanked.

There is a difference between being scared and being spooked. I had been scared many times during my first six months in Nam: during nighttime patrols, during ambushes, and always when watching a friend die. But this business of going into a ghostly *ville*, of sun-ripening corpses, was just plain spooky. Put an M-16 rifle in my hands and I was at least an equal to anyone trying to do me harm. Fighting the ghosts of women and children was something quite different, though. I kept telling myself that I wasn't responsible for what had occurred earlier in the day; what had happened to the *ville* was a result of war, brought on by its own inhabitants. Intellectually, I could justify the actions of the CO, and I knew that under similar pressures, in the heat of combat, I might have made the same decision. Morally, however, it was difficult; had we done the right thing? Killing civilians in order to kill the enemy was not new; it had been going on for many thousands of years.

"Lightfoot, Lightfoot, this is Dragonfly, over"

*To disrupt any listening enemy's ability to identify us, we changed radio frequencies and call signs often.* The radio's little speaker box sitting on top of my rucksack spoke into my right ear interrupting my thoughts. I reached around and turned the volume up as my call sign was repeated again. I depressed the small handset transmit bar and responded to the caller.

"Dragonfly this is Lightfoot; I hear you *(hear is the correct army radio terminology, "read" is Air Force pilot speak)* loud and clear, over."

*Since only one soldier can speak (transmit) at a time the word "over" signals the end of the speakers turn and allows the soldier on the other end an expected response. If the speaker is concluding the conversation he says the word "out", which ends all transmissions. Hence there is no such thing as "over and out," as is commonly said in the movies.*

The RTO requested that I put my Actual on the phone to speak to his Actual. I turned as far as the radio on my back would allow me from my sitting position on top of the APC and passed the handset back to Mackelroy. Everyone heard the lieutenant's conversation with Captain Knight, even above the rumble of the 400 horses powering our tracked chariot.

Doc Czech had been found, alive. He wandered into another Cav Troop camp, six klicks west of where we had seen him last. The troop commander said our medic was "higher than a kite" from drugs he had been using out of his medical bag. The Cav commander then reported that Doc claimed to be an escaping POW. He also said that the medic had fired up a little grass-hootch fishing *ville* near their location; luckily, no one had been hurt.

Later that night, I learned that Czech had been accused of using his own drugs before; consequently, he was transferred out of his company and to ours. "Long Binh jail, make room for another junkie," I thought to myself. The lifer NCOs and officers tended to look the other way at grunts smoking a little grass, but the medic had stepped way over the invisible line. I knew that Alpha Company would never see Doc Czech again.

Since Doc had now been located, there was no reason to proceed to Thon Tan Hoi. That was great as far as I was concerned. Rather than charging off through the dark and wasting another precious hour of sleep time by returning to the other two platoons, we stopped right where we were at and set up our NDP.

The lieutenant decided he wanted a squad to set up a tiger by the cemetery that we had previously found to be so heavily booby-trapped. After meeting with the squad leaders and announcing his plan, he selected Zorn's squad for the mission. Zorn, however, told Mackelroy that his ambush idea sucked, and he would not lead his men into the explosive-laden area in the dark. The platoon leader then gave him a direct order. Zorn calmly refused again.

"There ain't no friggin way you can make me do something so stupid!" he said.

Second to the expletive he had just used, the most commonly spoken words in Vietnam followed next.

“What are ya gonna do, send me to Nam?"

As a sign of disrespect to the young officer, Zorn then shoved his hands deep into his front pockets and waited for Mackelroy to say something.

Considering that Zorn's DEROS was only four weeks away and his Army separation date was just three days after that, threats of any punishment would be hollow. Other than a fine and a bust in rank, Lt Mackelroy could do nothing to the squad leader. It would be a waste of military time and money to file formal charges against the short-timer, and both Zorn and Mackelroy knew it.

Trying to intervene and negotiate a peaceful settlement to the situation, I stepped up and spoke up. (When was I going to learn to just shut up?)

"Sir, I think the odds of our ambushing Charlie in the booby-trapped area are just not worth the risk to the squad. If I may suggest—"

Halfway through my brilliant idea I knew I should have kept my mouth closed. Mackelroy's face reddened and purple veins stood out on his skinny neck. Everyone could tell that his blood pressure was skyrocketing.

"You *have* no opinion, Specialist; you are *just* a radio operator. If I want a comment out of you, I'll ask for it!"

Momentarily forgetting Zorn, the lieutenant continued his tirade at me.

"I'm sick of you, Olson, and all the other enlisted men who think they know so much about how to fight this war. I have a college degree and a commission in the United States Army. No soldier of inferior rank tells me what to do! I know you are all irritated with me because I'm an officer and make the decisions, but that doesn't affect me one bit. I'm in charge and you *will do exactly as I* say! You'll thank me for it later, trust me."

"Why, you self-serving, paranoid, little prima donna!"

The second half of my furious rebuttal would undoubtedly have contained things I would later be ashamed of, but I was stopped by Staff Sergeant Wardle's command: "Shut up, Olson!" He pointed an index finger directly at my face and without saying another word he rolled his hand over palm up and rapidly curled all four fingers several times telling me to follow him, immediately. One finger was a casual "Come over here." Four fingers meant "Get your butt over here, now!" Taking charge, as he knew he had to, to stop a mutiny and quell the insurrectionary language, the Sarge sent Zorn and me to the far side of the perimeter to cool off. As I walked past one of the APCs, its three-man crew stood up and applauded. I was too steamed to even acknowledge their presence. In the time the little walk offered me to think about what I had just done, I was pissed that I had gotten in trouble for defending Zorn. Of all the people to defend!

Forty-five minutes later, Wardle quietly approached. Speaking in mellow tones designed to smooth our ruffled feathers, he expressed sympathy for the positions we had taken. He then said he wanted to speak to each of us privately. Zorn departed to one of his squad's positions where he undoubtedly would be received like a conquering hero. I was left alone with the platoon sergeant.

"Sergeant Rock, I kinda expected more outta ya than that. A good time to keep yer mouth shut is when yer in deep water."

Thus began the official reprimand he'd negotiated with the pompous lieutenant. It was a substitute for my getting busted to PFC. He explained that I was being relieved of my responsibilities as RTO—that was good news to me. I could no longer stand being around the lieutenant. Also, Wardle explained that I was getting an Article 15 (a non-judicial punishment, for minor offenses, as identified in Article 15 of the Uniform Code of Military Justice). It would cost me $25. The Sarge said Zorn was being busted from Spec. 4 to PFC. There was nothing he could do about that. Zorn had just burned too many bridges with the lieutenant. He was also getting a $50 Article 15, but he would continue to serve as the squad leader.

The company was short on combat-experienced leaders, so the lieutenant elected (he really had no choice) to leave the "new PFC" in charge until he rotated back to the States. Then, Wardle asked me to help keep Zorn out of Mackelroy's way.

"I'm afear'n what the ol' boy might do to the butter bar if'n he gets fire in his eyes again."

The staff sergeant gave me one last bit of advice before looking for Zorn.

"Sergeant Rock, ya gotta remember that the 'Louie' has faults like everyone else, but because he's an officer, bein' wrong ain't one of 'em."

Spec. 4 Randy Karras was the leader of the first squad. He was a really good guy. Wardle told me to report to him, and that was just great with me.

An hour after sunup the next morning, just as I was polishing off a peanut butter, powdered cocoa, and cracker sandwich breakfast, a shot rang out. I shoved the remaining bite of the desiccated sandwich into my mouth and raised the '16 to my shoulder. I quickly glanced over my field of fire but saw nothing except white sand. I then looked over my right shoulder toward the origin of the shot. One of the newly arrived soldiers sat sheepishly staring at his weapon.

"Who fired that shot?!" screamed Mackelroy.

"Sorry, sir," came the soldier's embarrassed reply. "It was an accident."

The spit-shined toes of the platoon leader's boots gleamed as he stormed over to the red-faced grunt. The soldier had just finished cleaning his weapon. After locking a magazine in, he chambered the first round and visually checked the safety. He pointed the rifle into the air and pulled the trigger to make sure the safety worked. The M-16 fired.

Muck-it-up-roy flew off again on another tangent about poor safety habits. The rifleman was wrong and knew it. He made a stupid mistake by not first physically checking the fire selector switch to see that it was on safe, and by testing the weapon with a round in the chamber.

When the 10-minute verbal discipline was over, the young officer shouted another of his "brilliant" commands to everyone in the platoon.

"As of right now, no soldier in this platoon will carry his

weapon with a round chambered."

. . . After a long 15 seconds of silence, wherein we just looked incredulously at each other, a few of the newer guys felt the heat and expelled their chambered rounds.

"All right, ya'll heard the man, get them rounds out."

It was not until Staff Sergeant Wardle reinforced Mackelroy's command that most of us complied. It seemed the longer each ground-pounder had been in-country, the slower he was to eject the bullet. Several of the real old-timers, including Zorn, held their rifles high above their heads. They put on a show of protest by jacking the spinning rounds as high as possible into the air. We all watched as gravity pulled the shells down into self-created miniature craters in the sand.

I had seen many close calls where the clicks of a pulled charging handle and a sliding bolt would have made a critical difference in my, or others', health. Now the platoon leader was ordering me to violate a practice that I felt had helped keep me alive. I mulled over the pros and cons in my mind. Many more infantry men were going to go home in reusable metal containers, from just being too slow "on the draw," than would ever die of accidental rifle discharges. I agreed that a loaded weapon was dangerous, but then again, that was the nature of our profession. We were professionals at our work, and we were sent to this country for a specific purpose; this certainly was no Southeast Asian vacation. I thought that taking away whatever edge we had by making us carry unloaded weapons was stupid.

After I concluded the debate with myself, and the lieutenant's stare had become intolerable, I also complied with the order. I held the M-16 high over my head and yanked the bolt back. I felt like a chicken for not getting in the lieutenant's face, but it was too soon for another run-in with the wimp. I couldn't help but believe that a village somewhere in America had lost its idiot when Muck-it-up-roy joined the United States Army.

That night was uncomfortably cool. The poncho liners that could have been put to good use by us remained rolled up and stowed in our rucks back with the company. The advantage was that preparing to move out the next morning was "no big deal." I just took a big swig of iodine-tasting canteen water and climbed aboard a waiting APC. Above the idling of the big diesel engines, some of the men heard me yank on the charging handle and slam an M-16 round into the chamber of my rifle. Without looking for permission, most of the guys dropped the bolt on a round themselves.

The M-113 armored personnel carriers transported us about a klick. We dismounted and bid our tracked vehicle hosts farewell. We envied the guys in the cav. They got to ride everywhere they went and seldom had to go where a big tank couldn't—like the jungle of the A Shau Valley. I guess they had their disadvantages also, but we infantry guys wouldn't have listened to them.

At our new area of operation we performed the same well-rehearsed routines we'd practiced the previous week, probe and dig. The OJT paid off as almost immediately one of Sergeant Tew's men found a buried 250-pound bomb. It was booby-trapped. The "dud" had been "policed up" from an old U.S. Air Force target and transported to this site by resourceful and daring Viet Cong soldiers. Tew's squad placed a pound of fused C4 next to the detonator on the bomb and blew the rusty but still lethal military ordnance in place. The blast blew a crater five feet deep in the sand.

Tony Salvetti and I teamed up and decided to probe in a new area that was a hundred meters away from everyone else. We followed a little-used path through waist-high brush.

Suddenly Tony screamed, "Rock, don't move!"

I froze in my tracks and waited for Tony to make the next move. He carefully crawled the five paces between us on his hands and knees. Tony gently began brushing away my last footprint in the sand. The almost invisible black line in my boot indentation grew longer and longer as the fine-grained sand was brushed aside. What Tony found and carefully uncovered was a taut trip wire, hidden under the light skiff of sand. He then discovered an explosive device at the end of the wire, four feet off to the side of the trail. The U.S.-made 105 mm artillery projoe had been booby-trapped by the enemy and was designed to detonate with just the slightest tug on the wire. Luckily, I had uncovered the trip wire without disturbing it.

I yelled the traditional warning of "fire in the hole." Tony put his Zippo lighter to the three-foot fuse leading to the C4 explosive charge, and we ran for safety a hundred meters away. The smoldering crater we examined afterwards told us just how quickly I would have vanished had my boot pressed a little deeper in the sand.

The sand was temptingly easy for the enemy to dig into and plant another type of trap—sharpened bamboo stakes. After urinating or defecating on the stakes to maximize their potential danger, the pit could be carefully hidden with a camouflaged cover. The idea was for an American to inadvertently step into the hole and have a poisonous spear shoved into his leg or foot. While the concept of a "punji pit" was scary, and the commercial press loved to report great stories about them, they were very seldom effective against us. We found many of them here and in other areas like this, but the easy digging sand also allowed the sides of the holes to quickly cave in and expose the intended traps. The punji pit was a local VC, or VC sympathizers', weapon. Contrary to dramatic war stories, no one was ever killed by a bamboo stake in a punji pit.

At noon, while the squad guys were eating the few C-rations that had escaped breakfast, Staff Sergeant Wardle hurriedly visited each of the squad leaders. Karras crawled out of the shade of his improvised fatigue-shirt tent and was briefed about our next objective. During a routine flight, the crew of a resupply bird had spotted movement in an old and supposedly deserted village, and Alpha was ordered to investigate. The other two platoons, back at the defensive position, were also boarding choppers.

"Our air transportation will arrive shortly." Wardle said.

Tradition in the company dictated that the first man to identify the *whop-whop-whop* sounds of inbound choppers would bellow out the warning "C.A!" A combat assault by infantry carrying Hueys was always scary, even though nineteen times out of twenty they were uneventful. When airborne as often as we were, that "one" time came way too often, however. I looked forward to leaving this old booby-trapped area, and I always enjoyed the exhilaration of the open air rides. I hated the landing though, due to the danger it sometimes entailed.

From someone on the far side of the perimeter came the signal cry that we had been awaiting. Making one last check of my gear, I placed a black plastic cap over the muzzle of my M-16 to keep the swirling sand out. I then ran to my assigned boarding position. Once the birds had landed, we scurried into the five choppers. We were soon flying safely above the dangerous booby-traps, gooks, and sweltering heat.

Within five minutes, our platoon joined the tail of a 12-bird formation carrying the rest of the company. The jet helicopters flew eastward at a thousand feet for 15 minutes, then quickly dropped out of the sky like an eagle after a rabbit.

The old village rested in the center of a small island

surrounded by marshy flatland. There were too many trees on the island to allow a dry combat assault. We were going to be inserted in the water. Captain Knight designated third platoon as the searching element. First and second would block possible escape routes from the small island. We had played this game many times, and everyone knew exactly what to do.

As soon as the skids had lightly settled in the mire, I jumped from my sitting position in the Huey's doorway and immediately sank to my knees in the stinky swamp muck. That same instant, two automatic weapons from the island 200 meters away randomly raked the mud around my legs. Little fountains of brown water spurted 13 or 14 inches skyward in reaction to the violent impact of the steel-jacketed projectiles. The pilot was anxious to get away, to *didi mau* the area, to protect his bird, so as the rotor speed increased the remaining grunts hurriedly bailed out both sides of the rising bird. *Thunk, thunk, thunk*—the helicopter got hit three times but seemed to fly away with no trouble. The last thing I wanted was for that egg-beater to come down on top of us.

My new environment of stagnant leech-infested water and rotting vegetation was so disgusting that I hesitated momentarily before finally diving headlong into the sticky bog. I held my rifle above the muck and randomly emptied the magazine at the unseen enemy. The second magazine I pulled from the bandoleer was coated with gooey black mud. I slithered forward about ten feet to a small puddle of surface water and rinsed the magazine until it was reasonably clean. I slammed the magazine home, chambered its first round, and joined several others providing cover fire for guys who found themselves in muddy pockets of even deeper water.

The two weapons that had begun shooting at us increased to four or five over the next few minutes, but we were spread out and gave more that we got. The gooks were probably disorganized and surprised by our helicopter assault. Six of my 20-round magazines later we had not made an inch of progress. The defenders on the island continued to pin us down in the bog. Joe Romero, the lieutenant's new RTO, stayed busy yelling coordinates into the radio handset.

Within five minutes of touchdown, artillery began prepping the dry ground for our assault. Enemy rifle fire stopped. When the three-minute barrage was over we moved forward. We were immediately met with heavy automatic AK and SKS sniper fire again. It was obvious that the gooks were in heavily fortified positions and probably impervious to all but a direct artillery hit. I wished the New Jersey were still within range, but unfortunately she was not. The job of routing out the enemy would fall on us.

First and third squads took turns laying down a heavy base of small-arms fire. Zorn, leading the second squad, crawled along the far side of the raised trail leading into the *ville*. He was attempting to flank the island bunker which had the rest of us pinned in the mud. His squad slithered through the water to within 50 feet of the mound. It was as close as they could get and remain undetected. From my vantage point I watched Zorn take one quick look up over the raised dike trail and scream “Fire!” The squad suddenly popped up and opened fire on the bunker. The surprised gooks, not prepared for the close-in automatic weapon and grenade attack, quickly fell silent.

A PSYOPS (psychological operations) team arrived on the scene and began broadcasting from helicopter loudspeakers high above the firefight. In Vietnamese they called for the VC to surrender, telling them they were hopelessly surrounded and outnumbered. We did have them outnumbered about a dozen to one, but we certainly did not have them surrounded.

No longer attracting hostile fire, Karras clenched a fist and pumped his arm up and down several times. We recognized our squad leader’s double-time signal and charged, as best we could, the treeline. All of us were anxious to get out of the open and the rotten-egg-smelling muck. Also, we thought the sun at our backs made us stand out like black silhouettes on a rifle range. We had to quickly find cover in the trees, and then we could accurately apply our superior firepower.

Half crawling, half slogging, we finally reached the dry higher ground just short of the bunker. Karras led us right up and over the bunker, which five minutes earlier had been so hot. Buckets of adrenaline pumped into my system as I burst through the earthen entryway and into the heart of the heavily fortified fighting position. I quickly looked for a target. There was none. The interior of the mound was lifeless and quiet. The sun found a hole in the thick trees overhead and reflected off a brand new AK-47 assault rifle. It was laying in one of the firing ports. The weapon was the first thing I saw; it caught my attention before the bodies did.

"What have ya got in there, Rock? Do ya need any help?"

I hollered back to Karras that I had three Viet Cong KIA and a small storeroom full of supplies.

"Make sure they're dead, then get out here! Second squad is taking heavy sniper fire; it's our turn to bail them out of trouble!"

From inside the "new" underground coffin, I could hear the *crack*s, *pow*s, and *ka-whump*s of the war going on outside around me. Occasionally a ricocheting bullet whined nearby.

I looked around the dim room once more. All three VC were, in fact dead—as dead as they could ever be. Each pajama-clothed soldier had been shot through the head, probably as they stood aiming rifles through the bunker firing ports. Hair, blood, and brains were splattered against the back side of the bunker. Two bolt-action SKS sniper rifles, with their high-power scopes, lay on the dirt floor next to the mostly decapitated bodies.

I pulled the AK out of the bamboo window casing that served as the fighting station. I squinted through the portal at the brilliant sunshine outside. The setting sun, which I had guessed was silhouetting us against the water, was doing quite the opposite. The reflected glare off the smooth stagnant marsh had made it almost impossible for the enemy to see us. The gooks could have looked in our direction no more than a fraction of a second before being overwhelmed by the brilliance of the solar disk at our backs. Thus the scoped rifles, which should have been ideal for picking us off, proved almost useless. Our random firing was not much more inaccurate than theirs had been.

When we charged (actually, it was more like slogged) out of the sun, the protected and concealed enemy hadn't stood a chance. That brilliantly shining object in the sky, our nemesis on so many other days, saved all our lives this time. We were all very lucky.

Not only was I safe down inside the bunker, but I also observed how much cooler it was. I wasn't eager to join the "kill and be killed" going on above. Sharing close quarters with the headless, however, was not a reasonable alternative. The AK had a full banana clip, so I kept the weapon with me.

I exited the tomb and found that Karras had gone already. He'd probably taken the squad and moved forward into the island's vegetation. I did a quick survey of the area the shooting was now coming from and spotted Salvetti and Polansky. The duo were busily feeding the machine gun as it spat fire and lead toward a small cluster of banana trees. I sprinted the thirty meters between us in record time, firing a few shots as I ran. Momentum caused me to slide head first up against the mostly broken concrete wall the two were shooting over.

Without taking his eyes off the target, Tony released the trigger on his gun. He spread his arms wide like a baseball umpire and shouted, "Safe!" I could hear bullets impacting the other side of the wall, so I did not feel very safe. Polansky's pant leg showed a hand-sized stain of shiny bright red.

"What . . . have ya got out . . . there?" I stammered, gasping for air. *Sometimes the sudden need of oxygen can be caused by intense excitement and have nothing whatsoever to do with energy expended.*

"We need some more ammo!" yelled Polansky above the renewed short bursts from the '60.

"Home boy and I were running through the same clearing you just crossed, and we got fired on from the trees. I got hit in the calf. It stings like hell, but I don't think it's too bad. Get us some ammo!"

We normally carried a hundred-round belt for the gunner, but we packed it in our rucks, and we hadn't seen those in the past 24 hours.

"Have you seen Mackelroy?" I asked, before shoving my rifle over the wall and sending three rounds into the trees.

"He's with Tew over there."

The Pennsylvania Pollock pointed toward a burning hootch seventy-five meters to our right, while still eyeballing the trees.

I leaned the newly acquired AK with its 30-round banana clip up against the concrete wall as an emergency back-up for the two men. I then crawled to the far end of the barrier. Through the smoke of the burning hootch, I could see two GIs lying in a shallow, dry ditch, thirty-five meters from the fire. One of the guys was lying on his side. He held his rifle up and fired the entire magazine indiscriminately at the roaring blaze. Sprinting most of the way to their location, I jumped into the same ditch they occupied and crawled the remaining few meters that separated us. Sure enough, the guy doing the shooting was Lieutenant Mackelroy.

"Rock, you gotta help us!" screamed the terrified platoon leader.

Blood patches on the back of his fatigue shirt matched almost perfectly with its shrapnel holes.

"One of 'ems in the hootch! I threw a frag at 'em through the door, but I think he threw it back! Please help us!"

Joe Romero lay next to the babbling officer; his eyes were partly open but he was unconscious. Bright blood was leaking from the left side of Joe's head and shoulder area. The Prick-25 radio was still on his back and it had several small holes in it.

"They're going to kill us, Rock, they're going to kill us! Please help us!"

The roar of the intensely burning thatched grass made the ground around us almost rumble.

"Cease fire, cease fire!" I yelled. "If there's anyone in the hootch now, he won't bother ya!"

I plucked the radio handset off the shoulder of the uncaring RTO. It had been broken by shrapnel, but it worked fine when I depressed the squelch button. I turned the volume on max. Before reaching for the handset, I pressed my fingertips on the side of Romero's bloody neck; his pulse was still strong.

My urgent radio demands had already been anticipated by Captain Knight. Two squads from third platoon were already double-timing it toward the smoke. Heavily loaded with the ammo we needed, they were also escorting two medics. I quickly gave our situation report, exact location, and signed off. Neither of these soldiers seemed to have life-threatening wounds, so I told the lieutenant to stay with Romero. I then stripped the communications box from the RTO's back, climbed into its tacky-wet harness, and ran forward in search of Staff Sergeant Wardle.

The firefight died to sporadic bursts of small-arms fire, except on my far left, where the cracks of weapons I did not recognize were intermingled with the familiar M-16 sounds. Figuring Sarge would be where the action was; I turned and headed toward some thicker cover in that direction.

Swiftly but carefully moving between some dilapidated old grass hootches, I picked up two stragglers from first squad who had become separated like me. We were relieved to be in each other's company. The greater our numbers, the more secure we felt.

As we got close to the strange-sounding rifle fire, we bent low as if leaning into a strong headwind and quietly picked our way along a narrow dirt trail through thick ground cover. The three of us managed to sneak to within 30 meters of the VC position; that's where the trail took us. We could see where gooks were, but we could not see them. Their rifle muzzle-blasts caused the elephant grass around their well-hidden hideout to shudder; it was a dead giveaway. As a result of our circuitous route we had quite accidentally managed to flank the gooks. I led the other two soldiers forward another 5 meters, until our cover ran out. Then on my signal we cut loose with our three '16s. An old infantry axiom demanded that when in doubt, empty the magazine. Dead Vietnamese Communists do not return fire.

"*Chu hoi, chu hoi*!" screamed the VC from within the grass, "*Chu hoi, chu hoi*!"

We ceased fire, but our itchy index fingers continued to caress the little black levers inside the protective trigger guards. Stinging sweat dripped into our eyes, but none of us dared blink. We each slammed fresh magazines into our weapons as we eagle-eyed the green grass.

Using our best Vietnamese, the three of us accepted their pleas to surrender by ordering them to come forward. "*Lai day, lai day*!" With their hands stretched high overhead, the universal sign of capitulation, two young Viet Cong soldiers slowly emerged from their concealment. Their bodies quivered from head to foot, but they followed our instructions. Half bowing, they slowly walked toward us. Neither of them was more than four foot eight inches tall. Together they could not have weighed more than 160 pounds. It was hard to believe that these little boys were the same enemy who seemed so much larger behind their weapons.

Halfway across the small clearing that separated us, our shouted "*Lai day*!" commands turned to "*Dung lai*!" The wide-eyed American-killers stopped as we had ordered. They did several deep bows of capitulation and then squatted on their heels. Their arms fell slightly as if their hands may have to fend off our bullets.

Thirty seconds earlier, killing the two VC would have been considered heroic by our comrades. We would have been congratulated for the enemy body count. Maybe a medal would have been in order. Now, however, the rules had changed. We had taken prisoners, and I wondered if it was a mistake.

I desperately wanted to squeeze that right trigger finger; just an eighth of an inch. Resentment, even hatred, had built over the previous few months of watching my brothers get mangled and destroyed. A great deal of satisfying revenge could be realized with just a little flex of the finger. If the situation were reversed, would they let me live, or would they kill me and run? It was a stupid question; I knew exactly what they would do. These soldiers didn't have any "rules of engagement;" instead they would receive congratulations for heroically executing the big bad Americans. Since I would get no mercy, why should I cede any?

My mind was heavily influenced by my emotions, and it

continued to debate with itself. Yes, I knew all about the Geneva Convention and "the rules of war," but the communists did not recognize or abide by the rules, so why did we have to wear those handcuffs? As far as the communists were concerned, if I was captured I would be treated as a war criminal and they could do anything they wanted to me. Please do not talk to me about being humane; this was a war of survival. I was just a poor drafted grunt schmuck, but I did know that only the fast, the strong, and those willing to kill survived. Nice guys didn't.

I had been sworn to defend my country and its interests, but if I did it too vigorously (in the eyes of some politician, or even worse, the liberal press) I could be charged with a war crime. The media and the war protestors would love that. I had never seen a reporter heroically stop a bullet or even fire one to save an American's life. They were just there to take pictures and tell of our dying.

The battlefield ethics we lived by stated that I could kill a VC or NVA soldier even if he were unarmed, so long as I did it at long range. Snipers operate that way. If the enemy soldier is near me and unarmed, shooting is a no-no. What kind of logic is that? It was acceptable for Navy gunner's mates to shoot shells weighing as much as a Volkswagen, totally obliterating villages full of people. Air Force pilots were customarily commended for dropping huge bombs that destroyed *villes* full of civilians. But the same rules of engagement said it was morally wrong for me to shoot these two enemy combatants, even though a minute earlier they had been trying their best to kill me.

I was trained to kill, pure and simple. All the little marching jingles I learned in basic training taught me to kill, kill, kill. That skill would keep me and my buddies alive. If we could capture an enemy soldier, that was just a secondary option. Our mission was to kill the enemy without regret.

The revenge-seeking animal inside me seemed to control my brain and win the argument. But the civilized Christian in me controlled the death-dispensing trigger finger. For the moment they lived. The scales were so finely balanced, however, that a sudden move or an attempt to run would have easily reversed my decision.

Once our shooting had stopped, Sergeant Wardle and Spec. 4 Karras brought the rest of the men forward and relieved us of our tempting targets. Our search of the half-finished bunker that these VC had fought from netted us their old M-1 rifles and a handful of ammunition. The strange-sounding weapons we had heard were American but from another era.

The results of the day's firefight were decidedly in our favor—that is, if killing people can ever be a way of measuring man's success. The platoon's first squad had sustained four wounded (all would return to fight another day) but no deaths. The Viet Cong army suffered seven KIA, and we had captured four others. These soldiers were all poorly equipped local VC, but this was one enemy force we would never have to face again. We'd done well.

Weapons and supplies we captured included two AK-47s, two SKS sniper rifles, two M-1s, three .30 caliber carbines, and a single .45 caliber pistol. In addition to the weapons, we found over five thousand rounds of assorted ammunition, 25 anti-personnel mines, and several Chicom claymores. Small amounts of rice, dried peppers, and half a dozen unserviceable gas masks were also among our booty. In the first bunker that Zorn's squad knocked out, we found several shoe-sized wooden boxes that were packed with thousands of anti-American propaganda leaflets. I pulled one of the papers from the box and read its comical contents to everyone.

**GI's!**

**What has Jonson said to you ? and What have happened (taken place) before your eyes in Vietnam ?**

**It is massacre no spare old folks, children and pregnant women.**

**It is flattening villages, consuming tens of thousands of houses, digging out graves and destroying crops, pagodas and churches.**

**Is it the " help " to the Vietnamese against communists and preserving "the Free world" ?**

**No ! It is action of**

> **aggression, of barbarity, of immorality.**
> **It is action of cornered wild beast flinging himself about frantically.**
> **It is action contrasting with the will and traditions of civilization, freedom and Democracy of the United States.**
> **For your individual interest, conscience and honor of the Americans, you should :**
> **-Oppose to orders of mopping -up operations, reinforcement!**
> **- Don't commit crimes against the Vietnamese people !**
> **- Press for you repatriation! Don't get killed for the cannon - dealers!**
> **- Cross over to the side of the NFL, you will receive humanitarian treatment and help to go home!**
>
> **The National Front for Liberation.**

The next propaganda leaflet I pulled from the box had undoubtedly been edited by someone having a little better command of the English language. Word usage and punctuation were greatly improved.

> **1. Demand that the U.S. government put an immediate end to the war against the**

South Vietnamese people, restore peace in Vietnam and bring U.S. troops home!
2. Vietnam to the Vietnamese--The internal affairs of the South Vietnamese people must be settled by the South Vietnamese people themselves!
3. Hands off the lives and property of the South Vietnamese people!
4. At any time and in any place, American troops may be hit harder and harder. The U.S. war of aggression will certainly be defeated! The South Vietnamese people will certainly win victory!
5. American soldiers! Rise up and struggle together with the American people against the U.S. government's war in South Vietnam! Rather be jailed (but sent home) than die in vain in South Vietnam!
6. Refuse to fight! Refuse to be stationed in advanced posts! Deman to be sent to the rear, to the cities and be repatried, alive!
7. In battle, surrender quickly to the Liberation Armed Forces! You will receive humanitarian treatment, pending release and repatriation!
8. Cross over to the

**Liberation Army! You will be welcomed and will receive help to go home or wherever you wish!**

**9. Negro G.I.'s won't fight against the South Vietnamese people struggling for their freedom. For American Negroes, the battlefield is right in the United States.**

**South Vietnam NFL**

There were seven different leaflets, each basically telling the same story: American soldiers, you are good men. It is your capitalistic war-mongering government that is conspiring to have you all killed. Surrender to the Liberation Armed Forces. You will be treated well, given housing, food, and medical attention. As soon as arrangements can be made, you will be sent home to your families and loved ones.

Some of the propaganda papers were downright stupid. The guys in the platoon competed with each other to see who could find the biggest lie, the most incomprehensible sentence, or the most humorous leaflet. How the communists expected any American to believe the idiotic claims and turn traitor was beyond our wildest imaginations.

Not so funny was a little booklet containing 27 newspaper editorial-page cartoons. The parodies came from papers around the world. The little blue book was appropriately titled "The not so Comic book." What we found so offensive was that some of the cartoons came from American newspapers. The editorial cartoonists may have brought a snicker to the lips of the antiwar protestors in those cities, but to those of us who were dying in the unpopular war it was like a stab in the back.

One drawing showed the "Grim Reaper" stacking coffins that formed a stairway to heaven. The caption below the artist's rendering simply read: "Escalator." Hugh Haynie of the Courier-Journal, Louisville, was the cartoonist.

Another cartoon depicted a white man in a business suit

carrying a briefcase. He was crawling up to a black soldier as bullets flew overhead. The caption, spoken by the white guy, read: "The U.S. government regrets to inform you that your parents were injured in hostile action by whites while trying to move into a segregated neighborhood." According to the booklet, the cartoon came from "Fischetti in the Times, Los Angeles."

It is guys like me, American combat soldiers, who protected the rights of a free press, not the brave reporter who sat behind that rata-tat-tat typewriter and attacked us. Sometimes that order got a little perverted. Indirectly, I guess, we fight for the rights of anyone to speak, or draw on a piece of paper, anything they care to think about. Killing invading communists and providing an Asian foothold for democracy is not enough for some of them.

We often found propaganda sheets like these lying on the ground around our large military facilities. The papers would quote negative comments by prominent politicians, movie stars, or war protestors back in the U.S., and it drove us nuts! We were being stabbed in the back because we were following the orders of the president of the United States, our commander in chief, whom all soldiers were sworn to serve, regardless of personal politics.

People who knew nothing of combat, or physical danger, or even sleeping with the bugs in the jungle, could stand in front of a microphone next to our nation's capital and accuse us of violating Charlie's rights. It was a long succession of American soldiers that gave them the freedom to assemble next to that historic building, not the self-aggrandizing anti-war agitators.

Because of the American citizen's Constitutional right to speak his piece and the newspapers' freedom of the press, every time Jane Fonda, Abbie Hoffman, Dr. Timothy Leary, or Joan Baez spoke against the United States government or for the communist cause, the North Vietnamese used it to maximum benefit. None of these "characters" had even so much as had a cup of coffee with a U.S. soldier in a combat zone, yet they told the world what ruthless, savage killers we all were. It was soldiers just like us that gave them that freedom of spotlight seeking speech, not their glib-tongued notoriety. Try demanding these rights in North Vietnam and watch the excitement. Pack a big lunch, buddy; years of maggot and rice soup is what the communists serve their own prison-guest antiwar protesters.

We loaded the leaflets, weapons, VC POW and KIA on choppers. All our wounded, including Lieutenant Mackelroy and Joe

Romero, were flown to the 18th Surg. Polansky asked to stay with us in the field, but Doc wanted him checked by a doctor, even though his leg wound was only superficial. After dark we placed shaped charges (directional high-explosive devices) on the bunkers and blew them into oblivion. Our rucksacks arrived later that night on a log bird. Sergeant Wardle and I sat against a squatty little banana tree and ate hot canned peaches, and then prepared for our own airlift. Before we left, the Sarge told Karras that he was going to "borrow me back" from the squad for a while.

Since I still had the radio on my back, I was the first to know that we were heading west to the gulf. Our new AO was near the fishing village of Phuong Gaip Dong. The area was sparsely populated: great news for us all.

## CHAPTER 21

# HAMBURGER HILL

The first morning at Phuong Gaip Dong, a resupply chopper replenished our depleted C-rations and ammo. It also delivered new weapons that we'd never seen before. We had been selected to do a trial test and evaluation of some new equipment. The M-203 ("funny guns," as we called them) fired regular M-16 bullets from the top barrel while the large bottom barrel launched M-79 grenades. In the heat of combat, grenadiers found themselves nearly defenseless much of the time. The single-shot launcher, with a grenade in the chamber, was ineffective at point-blank range or in thick vegetation. Also, most soldiers carrying this weapon did not have a supporting sidearm—pistols were bulky and hard to get. Consequently, between launches, the grenadier had little more to offer than himself as a diversionary target.

Polanski would've loved to have this over & under when Numba One Honcho came walking through his position on the Song O Lau. He'd probably have dropped his companion, Numba Two Honcho, at the same time. We thought the combo was a great idea. Initially, everyone was excited about the funny gun concept and wanted one. But only those with a '79 to trade in were issued the new weapon.

Mark Twain once said, "Thunder is grand; thunder is impressive; but it's lightning that does the work." The appearance and concept of this new weapon thundered with possibilities. It soon became apparent, however, that along with a basic complement of M-79 grenades (30 ea.), the grenadier would also have to carry 10 magazines of M-16 rounds. The new ammo's additional bulk and weight caused problems. And because the funny gun's 12-inch tube added three pounds under the barrel of an M-16, it quickly lost its popularity and lightning appeal.

Most of the weapons were recalled from our unit within six months and transferred to soldiers at base camps or firebases. The larger basic M-79 loads that may include high-explosive, smoke, illumination, CS (tear gas) and buckshot rounds would not be such a burden to those infantrymen. The poor M-79'er in the field soon found himself back in the same one-shot situation again.

In the afternoon of that same day, Staff Sergeant Wardle returned from a meeting with the captain. He crawled under my poncho-rigged sunshade and wriggled his body into the cool sand.

"Got some good news fer ya, Sergeant Rock. The COs decided ta cancel the Article 15 action against ya. I know that breaks yer heart. Now that the Louie's gone, there ain't no reason ta pursue somethin' he wasn't comfortable with in the first place. He wouldn't budge on Zorn's disciplinary action, however, so ya better keep this here conversation under yer hat fer a while."

The sarge slid a little closer to me and glanced around the area. Finally, with my curiosity piqued, he whispered some even better news.

"Cap'n has requested that Lieutenant Muck-it-up-roy be reassigned to some other company when he gets released from the hospital. He says the Louie's 'poor relationship' with the men was the reason. Ain't that an understatement! But," Sarge continued, "the Louie's now got sumthin' you and me ain't—a Purple Heart to show off back home."

Without waiting for a comment from me, he went on with more news.

"We got a brand-new butter-bar a comin' inta the platoon either tomorrow or the next day. Hope this one's squared away."

Just as the sarge had foretold, early the next morning a Huey landed and off- loaded its human cargo of FNGs. One of the shiny-booted soldiers led the other five to the CP. He was obviously the lieutenant.

The company commander did the same hand-shaking routine with all the new men that he had done with me. Perhaps he was not as pleased to have me return as I had earlier imagined. Maybe he was just a "my men come first"-type officer. This was in great contrast to Mackelroy, who was the epitome of one hundred years of Army tradition, unencumbered by common sense.

A few minutes after being introduced to our new platoon leader, Lieutenant Egginton, it was obvious to me that he possessed many of the same likeable qualities as Captain Knight. Maybe the new leader will be OK, I thought to myself. Lieutenant Egginton had piercing green eyes and he was very tall for an infantry soldier, standing at six-foot five. He towered above all of us, and his deep commanding voice made him stand out among the other lieutenants. I had been wrong about Sergeant Taylor, so I restrained my impulse to like him, just a little bit.

Also arriving with the new contingent of grunts was a new medic, Spec. 5 Allan Wursten. The Doc was not quite as tall as the new lieutenant, and he was very skinny. The 24-year-old wore military-issue heavy-framed eyeglasses. He looked like the studious type.

"I'll bet he carries a dozen pens in a pocket protector and fluently rattles off words with more than three syllables," I said to Wardle.

Our new medic had been in the Air Force for four years. At the end of his first enlistment, he enlisted in the Army for the next go-around.

"Wanted to see some action," he later told me.

He qualified for the title of "Lifer," but somehow it didn't seem to fit him. Besides filling the medic's vacancy, his arrival meant that I was no longer the oldest (age-wise) enlisted grunt in the platoon. He had me by a year.

I felt sorry, and very concerned, for guys like Doc Wursten and Muskrat. Glasses were a definite disadvantage in combat. The darn things were heavy, and they were always slipping down the noses of the soldiers during hot, sweaty humps or the stress of fighting. They also tended to get dirty very easily, and on humid days, especially in the breezeless jungle, they fogged up. If a sniper takes a pot-shot, or the side of a hill suddenly comes alive with people wanting to kill you, it is a lousy time to have poor vision.

Mickey Mantle of the New York Yankees was famous for his ability to read the bottom line on the eye chart. Consequently, Mickey could see the rotation of the baseball as soon as it left the pitcher's hand. Superb vision was a great advantage he had over other ball players, and it allowed him to become a great hitter. He could see what most others could not and then react correctly. Like Mickey Mantle, I was blessed with that same great vision and often thanked God that I was not cleaning glasses when bullets were flying toward me. There was only one thing worse than having to wear eyeglasses, and that was not having a pair when you really needed them. I never saw an enemy soldier with glasses; maybe all of them had 20/20 vision. Ya think?

On our platoon hump, later in the day, I was impressed with

the way the new lieutenant took charge without making a big deal of it. He organized the order of march and announced that he would be the fifth man in the column, right in front of the radio (me.) After watching several other grunts saddle up in their 75-pound rucks, Lieutenant Egginton sat on the ground, leaned back against the ruck's frame and cinched up the shoulder straps. He rolled over onto his hands and knees and involuntarily grunted (Maybe that's where we got the nickname?) under the heavy load as he stood. Awkwardly, he assumed the infantry stoop. He did it just the way we old-timers did it. Physically I was impressed with Lieutenant Egginton, and I almost hoped for an easy little skirmish with Luke the gook so the new officer could get some combat experience. We could then evaluate his mental toughness.

Rumors about the possibility of our returning to the A Shau Valley were becoming rampant. Everyone who joined the company, after spending time in the rear, had a different story to tell. Billy "The Kid" Barret, upon his return from the 18th Surg., announced that a firebase had been overrun and we would rebuild and occupy it. "Major" Poulsen, who had helped deliver supplies on a log bird, told us that he had spoken with a radio operator at battalion. The RTO told him the entire battalion was going to leave within a few days for a "secret" A Shau location. Even Lieutenant Egginton "confidentially" told me what he had heard as we traded radio watch during the night.

"The day before I reported to the company, I attended a command briefing at Battalion HQ. I learned that several companies of grunts near the Laotian border are getting their butts kicked real hard. There is a good chance someone else will be involved shortly. As soon as battalion can resolve the logistics problems, somebody is going after those gooks in 'The Valley.' We may be the lucky ones."

The rumors were of great concern to us. During our previous visit, we had experienced nothing but misery in the A Shau Valley. Some new guys, like the new lieutenant, had never been on the receiving end of a real butt-kicking. They spoke to each other in machismo terms reserved for the uninitiated. They were eager to bring the military might of the indomitable U.S. Army down on the poor ill-prepared gooks. The smell of gun gas was something they looked forward to. The FNGs were too young and inexperienced to appreciate the devastation of hard-fought combat. They still had that "John Wayne" hero fascination with war, and they couldn't comprehend its consequences.

Old-timers, who had grown to respect the power and intelligence of the hidden enemy, knew better than to play around with the Vietcong or North Vietnamese Army. Even the smallest of animals will fight fiercely when forced. The animals we pursued had proven, on occasion, to be more than we could handle. We were hunting the smartest animals of them all—humans.

The North Vietnamese Army was home for the most experienced soldiers on mainland Asia. Their fathers and their fathers' fathers apprenticed them in guerrilla warfare. The Vietnamese people had been fighting each other, or foreigners, for many hundreds of years. Now we, the new kids on the block, were learning the lessons of hit-and-run warfare. We were doing a lousy job of learning overnight what our opposition was born to.

A third group of men, besides the fearless new guys and the respectful old-timers, were the scared-to-death short-timers. These guys were close to the end of their tours in Vietnam. Shortly they would be going back to the world and their wives or girlfriends. They wanted nothing to do with the war and its hazards.

"I'm too friggin' short to walk point," were common words among the group. During times when quick action was required, we learned to expect an anchor of short-timers dragging behind. Realizing that in six months I would be wearing those short-timer boots, I kept the criticism to myself. Besides, I couldn't blame them for not wanting to catch a round after having successfully evading them for nearly a year. Sergeant Martindale got his legs blown away on his last day in the field. I didn't want to see another friend go through that.

Speaking of Sergeant Martindale, the platoon got a letter from him the second day after our arrival at Phuong Gaip Dong. Teary-eyed buddies passed the correspondence around. No one could fight back emotions long enough to read it out loud. When my turn came, I read what the courageous Screaming Eagle had written to us:

*Hi Gang!*

*I am not much of a letter writer, but I'll try my best because I think you all deserve a word of thanks from me.*

*First I'll tell you where I am and how I am getting along. I am at Camp Drake, Japan and arrived on the 19th of March (24 hours after I was hit.) The first few days they tried to save my legs knowing that it would be pretty hard. Then they told me they both had infection and there was no way they could be saved and that both would have to come off. Well now instead of legs, I'm left with two stumps. It will be about seven weeks of treatment here before I'll be able to go stateside and be fitted with artificial legs. I have a lot of pain, but I think of my buddies--YOU GUYS--out there in the middle of nowhere humping your heavy packs and believe me it makes my pain disappear.*

*I want all you guys to know I pray for you every day and night and hope to God that you'll all make it safe and sound. See, I'm finished with it and I don't have to worry, because thanks to you guys you got me out of there in a real hurry. I know I was all doped up, but I still remember the hills and the faces of the guys carrying that jungle litter up that hill. Thanks!*

*There are a few people I do remember that did something a little special for me and I'd like to thank them personally with a few words.*

*SSgt Wardle—Right there after I got hit giving me water and words of encouragement. Thank you. You're a great guy.*

*Eddie Zorn—Up there talking and giving the medics a hand. He collected all my personal stuff and promised to get them all home for me. He was the one who kept pushing the guys on the litter to hurry up. He never dropped his side. Eddie, you know I think you're tops. Thanks again.*

*The medics—I had two arteries hit and lost a lot of blood but they (3rd platoon and 2nd platoon) both worked on me and pulled me through.*

*Lt. DeWitt—He always does a number one job. He made sure I had cover and that he got enough men to carry me up the hill.*

*I could put everybody's name down but I don't have the time. I just want to give a few more people some thanks.*

*"Mo Town" Harris—Carried me*

*Capt. Becker—Having a medevac ship right there when I got to the top and a little extra for the favor he did for me.*

*Lt. Balken, Woody, Chad, and all the guys who came to see me at the 18th Surg. I really appreciate it. Thanks. I know I wasn't much to talk to, but I knew you were there and I'm grateful.*

*There's probably a lot of other guys I left out that did a lot, but I was doped up and forgot. I know anyone of you guys would have helped me because as a team you were great.*

*Thanks*
*A-Co-2/506*
*101st Airborne*

*Sergeant Martindale*

***PROUD I SERVED WITH THE BEST GROUP IN NAM!***

The rumors about the A Shau proved true. Each warning we got contained a fragment of truth. About noon the next day, Captain Knight gave each of the platoon leaders and squad leaders a contour map of our new AO. Circled in red was the most prominent mountain in that area of the A Shau, Hill 937. It was high enough that the map even gave it a name, Dong Ap Bia. That was our ultimate destination. 'Come into my parlor,' said the spider to the fly.

Lieutenant Egginton and Staff Sergeant Wardle briefed the platoon about the impending firefight. The 937-meter mountaintop fortress was just two klicks west of the Trung Pham River and the rugged Laotian frontier border. On the north side was the Dong So Ridge and to the south was the Rao Lao River. Seven tough companies of Screaming Eagles from the 3/187th and 1/501th battalions had already assaulted the steep mountain for more than a week. The heavily entrenched enemy stronghold, however, had not fallen.

The U.S. military as a whole experienced a great deal of frustration trying to find the enemy. Since we were fighting a war on a battlefield with no front and not much of a rear, extended contact generally came at a time and place chosen by Sir Charles. Which brings us to Sgt. Rock's laws of combat: The closer two armies get, the more likely combat will happen.

It was the hope of senior officers, all the way back to that big Pentagon-shaped building, that this might be the chance for a decisive victory over the usually elusive communist army. Since the North Vietnamese troops had not chosen to abandon the fight and flee to the safety of "neutral" Laos, our job now was to prevent them from doing so by destroying them in place. So far, we had been reacting to events, rather than initiating them, and that was about to change. The "secret" allied master-plan that was hurriedly developed called for a final overwhelming airborne assault, aided by additional infantry soldiers from three battalions of the U.S. and South Vietnamese armies. This was a big deal, too great an opportunity to fail. They would totally dominate the battlefield. The plan did not allow for this to be a fair fight. Now that the enemy had been found, they would be crushed. Within a few hours companies from the American 2/501st, along with the 4/1 and 2/1 ARVN battalions, would be flown to the mountain to begin the final assault. They would surround Dong Ap Bia and trap the 27th North Vietnamese Army Regiment on top.

When I was a small boy and my mother decided it was time for me to take that dreaded bath, sometimes she let me play with a bar of Ivory soap to entertain myself. When I pushed the bar under the navel-deep water, the soap always popped back up somewhere else in the tub. Likewise, every time we encircled Sir Charles, he seemed to disappear and pop up elsewhere. We were never able to keep Luke the gook confined. Maybe this time, I thought, it will be different.

Lieutenant Egginton and Wardle told us that the one thousand infantrymen from the 101st, supported by the 400 troops from the

Vietnamese divisions, would now reinforce the survivors of the first seven days of fighting and fully cordon the large jungle-covered mountain. That was a great deal of man- and fire-power.

What they did not tell us was that our company, the single representative of the 2/506th, would spearhead the final assault. Under the command of Major General Zais (commander of the 101st Airborne Division) we were going to be attached to the 3/187th. The battalion commander, known only to us by his call-sign Blackjack, would personally take operational control of our company during the attack. Of the four companies in Blackjack's battalion, two of them had already been reduced by almost 80 percent due to the fierce fighting. The NVA had eliminated 50 percent of the other two. Of course, we were not very excited about joining them.

Sixty howitzers from the nearby firebases Airborne, Bradley, Cannon, Currahee, and Berchtesgaden were providing artillery support for the fight. Army helicopter gunships and Air Force fighter-bombers were also heavily involved in the action. The man- and fire-power dedicated to this operation only emphasized to us how dangerous leading the confrontation was going to be.

Captain Knight told the platoon leaders and the platoon sergeants, "Potentially, this could be one of the biggest battles of the long Vietnam War, a defining moment that turns this thing around for the positive. The good news," he told them, "is that Alpha Company has been chosen to be the first up the mountain."

We learned a short time later that we were going to be the first up the mountain on the ninth day of unsuccessful attempts. There is an old Army saying: “If at first you don’t succeed, call for artillery. When that doesn’t work, air strikes. When all fails, send the infantry back in.”

"Big Red" Redmonds, a short-timer from first squad, stood in the back of the crowd of attentive grunts while the news was being relayed to us. He was not impressed with the enthusiastic lieutenant's rehearsal of the battle plan. Along with constantly shaking his head negatively, he kept repeating, "Never happen GI, never happen. You're all *boo coo dinky dao*" (Americanized from *dien cai dao*, meaning very crazy.) Zorn, of all people, came to Lieutenant Egginton's assistance. A long string of many-times-spoken clichés flowed from his sneering lips, and they were all directed at Redmonds.

"Hey man, if your time is up, your time is up. So your bullets out there, what the f---, it don't mean nothin' anyway. In the whole

Army scheme of things, you ain't shit, so don't sweat the small stuff. Ya gotta die sometime and someplace anyway, might as well go down a hero in Vietnam, Republic of. You'd probably just die on the streets back home, a nobody, anyway!"

Big Red, taking offense at the last sentence from Zorn, shoved several nearby soldiers aside and buffaloed his way toward the PFC. Showing no signs of intimidation, Zorn put one foot forward and clenched both fists at his sides. The thick red hair on his bare chest and arms could not hide his tensed sweat-glistened muscles. Redmonds threw his boonie hat to the ground and, nose-to-nose the squad leader issued a definitive challenge.

"This nigger is going to bust your honky ass!"

Screaming at the top of his lungs to "KNOCK IT OFF!" Lieutenant Egginton wedged his tall frame between the two combatants. Neither soldier voluntarily gave up an inch of ground, however. Like a pair of young bulls with nostrils flared, they continued to defiantly eyeball each other.

"I said to KNOCK IT OFF. I don't want any flack about it either, THAT'S AN ORDER!"

The officer's direct order seemed to ease the tension just a bit.

"Save your energy for Luke the gook. You'll have plenty of opportunity to expend it in a couple of hours."

The young officer then turned to face Zorn and gently began backing him up. Sergeant Wardle and several other "soul brothers" stepped into the newly-created space and began backing Redmonds off.

Pressure and strain, built up over the previous weeks, was ignited by the news of our impending operation. Zorn had violated Big Red's high ground of status among his peers. The soul brother's well-known courage had begun to suffer recently. His DEROS date was nearing, and with time finally on his side, he had become cautious about what he did and where he went. When Zorn, another short-timer, confronted him in front of the men, his facade crumbled. Big Red was also a bit sensitive about the riots in his hometown of Detroit. Zorn's accusation that he was a nobody there had pushed him too far.

There was much to do before the choppers arrived, so the two bulls finally allowed themselves to be separated. Our internal problem now solved, Lieutenant Egginton continued with his briefing about our external problem, and it was a huge one. I wished that he could solve it as quickly.

"This operation has been code-named APACHE SNOW. It began on May the 10th and it will continue until we disrupt this enemy staging area in Thua Thien Province. Don't ask me how long that will take; it'll be over when it's over. Remember, a dead gook is a peaceful gook. Blessed be the peacemakers.

"I want everyone packing *boo coo* ammo. Empty your rucks. We won't be humping them. Get all the claymores, frags, and machine gun shells you can carry. We'll also want to carry any LAWs we can scrounge up from other units we meet along the way. Oh yeah, one smoke grenade each will be enough, but make sure we have plenty of red (red smoke signified contact with Charlie)."

I wanted to procrastinate . . . immediately. This was deep serious (worst possible position to be in) stuff.

"Choppers will be here in three-zero, so squad leaders, get the men divided up into eight-man chocks, and DON'T FORGET THE AMMO!"

When the briefing was over the squads hustled back to their own areas of responsibility and began preparing for the CA into Charlie's back yard. Conversation was short and subdued. Everyone's mind was on our task. Benjamin Franklin once said, "There never was a good war or a bad peace." I had been in Nam long enough to appreciate that.

We sat on the ground, strapped into our aluminum and nylon rucks for sixty empty, boring, minutes of waiting. Adrenalin no longer propped us up. I thought it was a lousy way to spend the last minutes of one's life.

A group of soldiers in first platoon finally began the familiar cry of "CA!" Immediately the eyes of all 125 of us turned skyward. We searched the gray-blue for the sixteen pepper-like specks that could, within seconds, be transformed into rotor-winged hearses. Not only could these multifunctional vehicles deliver us to our deaths, they would also perform the double duty of delivering our bodies to the safety of the morgue after it was too late to be saved.

Tightly holding on to our steel headgear, each of us turned our back to the violent downdrafts of the arriving slicks. Amid miniature hurricanes of swirling debris we dashed for the interior safety of the birds. We tried to minimize the sandblasting that rapidly removed layers of our exposed skin.

During liftoff, I flashed and received the split-fingered peace sign from third platoon's second squad. They were being left behind with our mostly emptied rucksacks. They would throw them onto trailing Hueys and follow us.

Each meter of altitude we gained enhanced our panoramic view of the Vietnamese countryside. Small clusters of tan, frail-looking dried grass hovels with their supporting frameworks of bamboo rushed by our noisy platforms in the sky.

Farmers, who several months earlier would have been thigh-deep in rice paddy water, were conspicuously absent from the water-starved fields. The peasants and their land were both waiting for the life-giving rains of the monsoon season. Family vehicles (water buffalo) were parked along the remaining waterways, refueling after a long season of carrying passengers and pulling plows. The bulky, horned creatures were oblivious to the choppers or anything else around them.

As our birds climbed higher along a southern route, the terrain changed from coastal sand to inland swamps and grass. The choppers continued to rise as the rotor blades beat the air into temporary submission. Not a word was spoken; each man was deeply engulfed in thoughts of his own. The "big picture" was left to those high-ranking officers who flew around in little observation helicopters. It didn't take an officer in starched underwear, however, to tell us that this was going to be bad.

Twenty-six klicks inland from the Gulf of Tonkin, massive jungle-covered mountains suddenly replaced the flatland. The uneven shag carpet of multicolored green was deceptively peaceful. We knew that underneath its facade of beauty lay the ugliness of the North Vietnamese and Viet Cong armies. Our chameleon opposition, hidden in green, was biding its time before displaying its true communist red colors.

Unlike the Rocky Mountains above my Utah home, lakes in the many little valleys below were not visible from the air; maybe there weren't any. There were, however, many winding rivers darting in and out of the heavy foliage far below us. From my vantage point, it looked as though someone had opened a stereo cassette and thrown its silver-brown tape onto a carpet of green and mashed it in.

Another long line of slicks joined our formation and flew parallel with us for several minutes. Screaming Eagle colleagues signaled us with peace signs or clenched fists raised high overhead. Our two "follow-the-leader" formations separated as we neared Dong

Ap Bia. Suddenly the air was filled with a dozen helicopter formations like ours. It was an air traffic controller's nightmare. When a lead chopper turned left or right, gained or lost altitude, trailing birds did likewise. The man-made snakes slithered through the air trying to avoid not only each other but also the deadly .51 caliber ground fire.

From our holding pattern high above Hill 937, I watched F-4 Phantom jets scream out of the sun. They slammed their deadly eggs onto the reddish-brown mountain top. Huge balls of fire and smoke identified each aircraft's target as it roared skyward again. Between each run, supporting field artillery blasted smoking craters into the soil. I wondered how anyone or anything could possibly survive the devastation. But they were still there, and they kept sending green machine gun tracers skyward, trying blow us out of the air. Guts!

The decreased whine of the Huey's turbine engine was my first indication that we were beginning our controlled drop out of the sky. The pilot wanted to get on and off the LZ as fast as possible. Rolling left and right to avoid the ground fire, the chopper fell like a rock. Door gunners, who had sat quietly and patiently in their webbed nylon seats, began to work out whenever the mountain peak appeared on their side, pumping M-60 bullets into the mass of green and red below. The machine gun provided accuracy by volume.

Prior to touchdown, one of the flack-vested gunners yelled to us. A Huey in the rear of our formation had been hit and might crash. Our pilot wanted us to know, said the gunner, that the eight of us had three seconds to off-load after the skids hit the dirt.

The landing zone was atop a neighboring mountain peak half a klick from Dong Ap Bia. When our turn came the helicopter fell out of formation. The chopper hit the LZ hard and the skids bowed, causing the ship to bounce a foot back into the air. The chopper's bounce was exaggerated because it was instantly eight hundred pounds lighter—the four of us sitting in the doorways had bailed out. I quickly got out of the way of Doc Wursten and the lieutenant, who were right on my tail. All of us scurried for cover outside the LZ. Hueys were coming in quickly, and we were anxious to be away from the deadly rotor blades.

The NCO directing the logistics of the LZ efficiently guided us through a maze of filled body bags, stacked C-ration cases, and piles of abandoned rucksacks. He gave us several cases of C's and pointed toward Alpha Company's rally point a hundred meters down the hill.

Lieutenant Egginton spent the next half hour guiding the platoon's fire-teams into their positions. He then ran back up to the crest of the hill for a strategy briefing. During his absence, I "scarfed down" a can of beans and franks and some pimento cheese on crackers. Who knew when my next chance to eat would come? I then leaned back against the Prick-25 and stretched my tired legs. After following the hyper lieutenant up and down and around the hill, I needed the rest. The radio weighed a ton.

For 50 minutes I listened to bombs, artillery, and mortar explosions on the mountain above me. During the entire time RTOs and officers up on the mountain called for more and more of the same. This was getting to be less and less fun. The few jungle birds not scared away by the previous week's bombardment chirped in without much enthusiasm.

Captain Knight and the lieutenants returned from their briefing near our off-loading site. They, in turn, called for a meeting with the platoon sergeants and the squad leaders. The officers drew the battle plans on their maps and gave each of us specific responsibilities for our upcoming attack.

Alpha Co. would begin the assault of Hill 937 after an intense air and artillery prep above our positions early the next morning. That news inspired prayers, even from unbelievers. We could expect heavy defense of the high ground by the NVA. Captain Knight told the NCOs that during the previous week 600 bombs and 7,000 artillery shells had been launched to soften up the hill.

*I later learned that, in all, more than 250 U.S. Air Force attack sorties had been flown against Dong Ap Bia. They unloaded more than a million pounds of bombs (15 percent of them were napalm.) Almost 22,000 artillery shells screamed into the target area during the ten-day assault.*

At 1400 hours, amid the deafening roar of exploding ordnance, we began to move down off our hill toward the pass separating the two mountains. The triple-layered jungle was topped with 200-foot teak trees. Their huge trunks and twisted hanging vines, some as large as baseball bats, allowed little sunlight to illuminate our route. The huge umbrella boughs and broad leaves on the trees shaded every living thing under them, including Sir Charles.

Our need to see was critical, as we anticipated that at any moment we could be hit by NVA soldiers attempting to escape the soon-to-be encircled mountain. Our rucksacks, stripped of our weaponry, remained at the landing pad with several hundred others. The less weight we carried the better. Slowly and oh so cautiously we crept toward our unknown fate.

The ambient heat, high humidity, and thick jungle permitting no breeze, was stifling. That, coupled with my own physical stress, caused sweat to flow profusely from every pore of my body. Heavy breathing through my nose echoed inside my helmet and made it even more difficult to hear. I risked swallowing swarms of buzzing mosquitoes as I sucked air through my mouth. The sound of spitting, I feared, would bring down the ire of my companions. Every noise seemed amplified. Snapping twigs underfoot sounded like firecrackers. I was as alert as I had ever been in my life.

As silently as we could, we worked our way through the thick palm fronds and vines toward the base of Dong Ap Bia. We humped several hundred meters without drawing a single hostile shot. Could it be that our air and artillery support had silenced the 27th North Vietnamese Regiment? Or, after more than a week of intense fighting, had they anticipated our strategy and slipped into neighboring Laos already? I wondered if all the hype and drama we had been subjected to would end in some anticlimactic cake walk.

We made contact with B/2/501st to our left and C/3/187th to our right; thus, our section of the mountain cordon was now secure. The captain sent several three-man teams twenty meters ahead, up the hill. They were to act as our forward OPs (observation posts) until ordered to pull back at dusk. Meanwhile, the rest of us attempted to quietly dig fighting positions in the hard ground. It was impossible. I guess it was no secret where we were anyway.

Under a two-inch layer of wet leaves and other jungle compost lay half an inch of super slick clay-like red mud. Within seconds, our entrenching tools passed through that easy digging and entered a very difficult layer of rocks and roots. Using the pick ends of our sturdy little shovels, we dug, pried, and wedged out the softball-sized boulders.

Defiant roots needed to be pried up and then hacked in half with our quickly dulling machetes. After several hours of intense digging, I managed to excavate a 6x2-foot hole 15 inches into the ornery red ground. I practiced resting the muzzle of my weapon on the dirt berm I had created in front of me while I scanned the mountainside above. It was important to memorize every detail in my field of fire. When darkness came it would be too late to see the many hiding places.

According to American combat strategy, unit integrity is

always maintained for purposes of strength; the gook war-fighting game plan was quite the opposite. After a firefight, an enemy unit (especially the VC) typically dissolved into two- or three-man teams. They often changed into civilian clothes, then melted into the surrounding countryside or jungle. Each man was responsible for himself until he rejoined his unit at a prearranged rendezvous point. Knowing of this dissipation strategy, Egginton visited each of the men in our platoon just before dark. He reminded them to be especially alert as they stood guard during the long night.

We would very likely make contact with probing enemy after sundown. That normally mandated a 100 percent watch, but action the next day was expected to be exhausting; we each really needed a good night of rest. Lieutenant Egginton attempted to compromise the sleep situation. He left the decision to the men at each individual guard position, with the caveat that at least a 50 percent alert must be maintained.

Doc Wursten had scraped a small cavity in the jungle floor 15 feet to the right of mine by smashing his half-extended entrenching tool again and again into the rocks and clay. He then dragged the little chips of material, and large rocks, from the shallow hole and created a berm several inches high around his new residence. He agreed to pass the vital communications box back and forth with me as the night wore on. That way we could stay in our fighting holes most of the time, below potential flying lead and steel.

During my first turn at watch, I stared up into the big black jungle-filled ravine directly ahead of my fighting hole. Artillerymen fired several dozen 155 mm illumination rounds high over the enemy. The bright white flares floated down under their little nylon parachutes and extinguished in the jungle above me much too quickly. The smoke from the swinging flare's burning phosphorus left a spiraling tail all the way to the momentarily lighted mountain. While lit, the illumination rounds destroyed my night vision. I tried keeping one eye closed during those times, but it didn't work very well. The flares also caused black apparitions to noiselessly chase each other through the thick undergrowth.

The devastating commotion that continued nonstop on top of the mountain made it impossible to hear any enemy activity. And we knew that it was most certainly happening out there in the blackness. The pyrotechnic effects of the bomb and napalm bursts, several thousand feet above me, eased my feelings of insecurity and entertained me during the first two hours that I sat alone.

At 0100 hours I called in a negative sit rep, then crawled over to Doc's shallow hole and gently awakened him. He stood up, stretched, did a few body twists, and yawned silently. After brushing some dirt and twigs from his hair, Doc sat on the edge of his excavation and watched the lights.

“Have ya seen anything?” he quietly asked.

“Not a thing, but you’ll enjoy the light show.” I replied.

We whispered in hushed tones for a few minutes more. I then crawled on my hands and knees back to the safety of my own shallow hole. I was exhausted after coming down from the all-day adrenaline high. Hugging the rifle close to my chest like a teddy bear, I found a semi-comfortable position on my back in the fresh moist soil and slept.

It only seemed an instant later that a tremendous blast immediately brought my senses to full alert. Simultaneous with the explosion, a heavy concussion swept over me, blowing my weapon from my sleeping fingers. Feeling helpless, I groped in the darkness to retrieve my rifle and found it lying across my ankles. Another blast, 20 meters up the hill—by sound and position, I recognized it as Doc's claymore. He immediately followed up with a long burst of rifle fire. I could tell by the ricocheting tracer rounds that his target was just a few feet from my sleeping place. I promptly rolled over onto my stomach and shoved my weapon uphill into the blackness. I squashed the trigger mechanism and blasted ten bullets toward the emptiness of one of my prearranged targets. The tracer rounds impacted with the steep mountain slope 30 meters away and ricocheted off to unknown destinations.

Lieutenant Egginton and several other nearby soldiers joined me in the assault on the night. Someone fired a hand-held star cluster illumination tube. The brightly burning flare momentarily lit up the area. That's when I saw him. Just feet from my hole lay a green uniformed NVA soldier! His motionless body was covered with fresh blood but thankfully, it was not mine. My rifle barrel instantaneously swung in his direction, and I waited for movement . . . none came.

Another star cluster flare raced up through the trees, and we quickly scanned the rest of the area.

"Has anyone seen anything besides the gook Rock got?" whispered the lieutenant.

When no reply came, he jumped from his hiding place in the dirt and dashed over to mine. Lieutenant Egginton’s rifle butt bashed into my ribs as he slid in next to me. Like sardines packed in a tin, we lay side by side in my little hole listening and watching. After 30 seconds of quiet he turned to me.

"Why didn't ya just shoot him? He was really close for a frag, wasn't he?"

I was still trying to catch my breath from the blow to my side but managed to explain that I hadn't done it. The platoon leader then asked Doc if he had thrown the grenade.

Wursten whispered back "No!"

Lieutenant Egginton wiggled around, trying to get his feet into my little hole, but his long body would not fit. He stared for a few seconds into the blackness ahead and announced that we were going to take a little look-see.

The platoon leader told Sergeant Wardle and Doc to cover us; he and I then crawled the five feet separating us from the gook. The NVA soldier's right arm had been ripped off and the right side of his head was partially blown away, but he was still alive. Head wounds always bled profusely. This time it was splattered all around us.

I rummaged through the pack still on the soldier's back and pulled out two Chi-com grenades. Evidence suggested that the gook must have been tossing or dropping a grenade into my hole when it malfunctioned and blew up in his hand. The NVA soldier lying before us was a victim of his own frag.

*The short-fused grenade may not have been accidental. Stories abounded of special 101st Airborne Long Range Reconnaissance Patrols that snuck into the enemy's munitions storage areas. Rather than destroying the ammo dump, they would sabotage it, doctoring much of it to malfunction or blow prematurely. AK-47 7.62 mm rounds, 81 mm mortar and 130 mm artillery shells were emptied of their gunpowder and filled with C-4. Critical parts were removed from RPG launchers and the LRRPs (pronounced Lurps) carefully short-fused frags.*

*Everything looked normal, but it had devastating effects on the users. Rounds exploded in rifle chambers. Mortar shells detonated in their tubes. And grenades blew up inches from the thrower's hand. Not only were the users maimed or killed, but their 'faulty' equipment must have crushed the morale of the enemy soldiers. Fighting an American was dangerous enough. The additional hazard of using the same equipment that just killed your comrade would make anyone apprehensive.*

We were not in a position to take prisoners, nor could we afford to leave medical personnel behind to look after the dying man. The lieutenant solved the problem by placing the barrel of his M-16 against the already mortally wounded soldier's head and mercifully blowing it off. All of the Screaming Eagles in the area maintained a 100 percent watch the rest of the night.

*Several days after the incident, Wursten asked if he could speak with me for a moment. He wanted me to know that he had not been sleeping on guard while the gook slithered down the mountain ravine. Doc was afraid that I may not have trusted him anymore, and he wanted to clear the air. I did not blame the medic, and I told him so. His quick claymore blast and rifle fire in response to the grenade explosion was proof enough for me that he was doing his job as best he could. Wursten was a good soldier.*

Once in a while I came across a soldier who claimed to be anti-war. This was particularly true for the medical staff, it seemed. While it was true that the Army could not make a soldier fight, Uncle Sam could make sure he ended up in an infantry company heavily involved with Charlie in the daily exchange of bullets. There he could re-evaluate his pacifist commitment.

Half an hour before daybreak, I heard the radio squelch break three times. It was the prearranged signal in case Charlie had compromised our frequency. The keying of the handset meant the assault would begin in exactly 15 minutes. We collected up all of the claymores and threw them onto a pile of unused C-rations. Captain Knight ordered us to travel as lightly as possible. Any unnecessary equipment was going to be blown shortly after we moved out.

*I heard later that Blackjack had actually communicated with a North Vietnamese commander during the night. Over a captured American radio, the Dong Ap Bia defender told the colonel, "Blackjack, we are going to kill all of your men tomorrow. When you come up the mountain in the morning, Blackjack, we will be waiting for you. All of your men are going to die. Can you hear me, Blackjack? All will die!" Blackjack reportedly replied, "We'll see who dies tomorrow, asshole!"*

Had I known about the colonel's brave challenge, at the time, I may have dialed up his radio frequency myself and personally "thanked" him for pissing off the gooks and then sending my buddies and me to do the actual fighting. I did not need an agent to pick my fights; I could do that very well myself, thank you.

I said a quick, silent prayer, thanking God for my surviving the night and for the captain's decision to have second platoon bring up the rear. We were going to be last, in order of attack up the mountain. Knowing what was about to happen, I included a sincere plea for protection for those who would be exposed to the hostilities ahead. Other soldiers around me, with heads bowed, privately petitioned for the same thing.

I could already hear small-arms fire 500 meters to our left when the lieutenant dropped his hand and we began to climb the steep ridge. Soldiers in first and third platoons were supposed to stay "on line" about five meters apart as they attacked, but that proved impossible very quickly. Besides not being able to see each other, there was a small ridge between the two platoons' first objective. The rock formation had slippery cliff faces. No one was going up there. The rugged A Shau terrain told us where we could go and where we couldn't, that changed our prescheduled game plan. Soldiers seeking easier climbing began following each other "in columns" up two small canyons.

We had climbed 500 feet up the 3,000 foot Dong Ap Bia when our point element made their first contact with Sir Charles. I listened to the first platoon RTO call for artillery fire on the cliffs above them. Enemy soldiers concealed in the rocks were lobbing stick-handled grenades down the craggy vertical ledges. Most of the explosive devices got caught in the undergrowth on the way down and exploded harmlessly, too far away to be effective. The source of the problem had to be eliminated, however, before we could move on. The captain thought this first resistance probably came from a small early warning observation post of two or three NVA. They would have been posted there to discover where our assault was to be spearheaded. We had to get through them quickly. Reinforcements would be on the way.

The first white phosphorous artillery marker round exploded in the treetops a short distance above the first platoon's own position. A jagged piece of the shattered shell casing crashed through the trees. Cory Tyler, the point man for the platoon, was unlucky and took the fragment in his left knee, smashing it open like a crushed pomegranate. The soldier grasped his leg and began yelling "Medic, Medic!" The pill pusher was only a few feet away and rushed to his side. After calming the panicked man down a bit with morphine, he applied bandages and a tourniquet above the bloody wound and left him in the care of a buddy. They would have to hobble back to the

NDP somehow, alone. The medic then hurried to catch the guys in his platoon as they had moved on. He knew the big test of his training and talents was yet to come.

Meanwhile, the screams of "Short round!" had come from nearly everyone in the platoon. The first platoon RTO, fully aware of the situation, was already adjusting fire coordinates. Soon a barrage of deafening 105 mm and 155 mm artillery shells began obliterating the cliffs above us. When the shelling stopped five minutes later, it had silenced Charlie's little observation post.

Except for isolated sniper fire, we advanced two-thirds of the way to the top of the mountain before we met any more of the bad guys. This time, however, our artillery support-fire could not budge them. Heavy AK and RPG fire had the third platoon pinned to the earth. Fortified bunkers and deep trenches had to be overrun before we could move up any further. This was a job that only the infantry grunts could do.

A squad from first platoon managed to flank one of the bunkers on the trench line. They eliminated it with a well-placed LAW rocket right into the aperture. Once the enemy line had been breached, Screaming Eagles aggressively poured through the opening. A dozen North Vietnamese regulars fought desperately, but they could not control both sides of their trench. We soon "wasted" them.

By the time I reached the scene, 20 NVA bodies lay in grotesque disarray up and down the long excavation. They were all dressed in brand-new green combat uniforms and pith helmets, indicating to us that they were recently out of the north. One American with a Screaming Eagle on his shoulder lay in two pieces next to a collapsed bunker. Three other "good guys" were being wrapped in green field dressings by their buddies while they waited for medics to arrive.

The double- and triple-canopy jungle that had proven a curse during the first two-thirds of the climb was suddenly gone: blown to pieces by the powerful ordnance that had rained on it for more that a week. We had to climb over the twisted mass of trees and vines that should have been above us. I realized how important the jungle cover had been to us as we started to receive long-range rifle and mortar fire. Long-range fighting was something we were not accustomed to. The reddish-brown clearing I saw from the air was really the top of Dong Ap Bia mountain, completely denuded of its lush green cover. We suddenly had very few places to hide.

"Redberry, Redberry, this is the Gardener, over."

Oh no—this is a bad omen, I thought to myself as I handed the radio handset up to Lieutenant Egginton. Okra and Jalapeno were the other two platoon call-signs. We frequently heard them over the radio as we climbed. Now the company commander wanted to speak to our leader.

The news was short but not so sweet. Using coded words and call-signs, Captain Knight excitedly told us that Lieutenant Kunz, from the third herd, had been hit. He then ordered Lieutenant Egginton to move forward so he could assume command of both platoons. The lieutenant's move up the hill to the point of the combat meant that I would be up there also! The platoon leader turned toward me, looked seriously deep into my eyes, and without a second's thought said, "Hey diddle diddle, let's charge up the middle!" It was not a joke, it was our plan of attack.

Like a puppy, my job was to follow the fearless platoon leader wherever he went and to keep second platoon's vital communications link open. Hell had come to the mountaintop, and our orders were to charge into it. I was scared to death, but Lieutenant Egginton seemed to take everything in stride.

We fixed the newly sharpened black bayonets onto our rifles as we ran the 200 meters separating the rear from the front. We discovered that in the hundred-plus degree sun, the men up front were exhausted. Many sought rest and cover. Lieutenant Egginton screamed and threatened as he prodded each of the reluctant grunts out of their protective bomb craters and from behind fallen trees. Maintaining our forward thrust, not giving the enemy a chance to regroup and repel our attack, was critical.

Dashing from one crater, rock, or tree stump to another, like a tray of Chinese Checker marbles rolling around, trying to find holes to drop in, upward we charged, firing as we ran, attacking up the mountain. Rocket propelled grenades, stick-handled frags, and machine-gun fire, much of it from point-blank range, tore into our ranks. The killing on both sides was fast and furious. Gigantic concussions from our own exploding artillery shells bounced us from our temporary hiding places, and the skin-blistering fireballs from detonating napalm sucked the air from our lungs.

*The NVA's Rocket Propelled Grenades were particularly difficult weapons to counter. The American Light Anti-tank Weapon was our comparable weapon to the enemy's shoulder fired rocket, but we used our weapons more selectively and at a different target set. In a squad of 10 VC, or NVA, several soldiers may carry RPG launchers with multiple cone-shaped grenades each. It was a primary offensive tool and they used them as first-contact personal weapons. An individual American soldier could draw the attention of an RPG. In an American infantry squad, LAWs were not frequently carried. Since we normally only fired them at enemy tanks or trucks (I never saw either of them) or fortified bunkers, we generally chose not to lug the awkward, shoot-once-and-throw-away weapons around in normal patrolling situations. In preparing for this assault, however, each squad did carry five or six of the weapons, but we only fired them at active bunkers.*

The noise of combat was so intense that I had difficulty hearing the radio, even at full volume. We had to give hand-signal instructions to soldiers just a few feet away. Periodically, above the base sounds of the combat, we heard high-pitched whistles as NVA commanders maneuvered their troops on the hill above us.

Along with the horrendous battle noises was the stench of rotting and burning human carcasses from the previous week's unsuccessful assaults on the mountain. Sun-blackened and bloating corpses were stacked two deep in some of the trenches we overran. The more freshly killed gooks lay in puddles of their own blood and urine. The rain-saturated clay could not readily absorb the fluids. Words on paper cannot describe the overpowering stench of old decomposing human bodies. I suddenly wished I had not complained the day before about those empty, boring minutes of waiting; I needed a whole bunch of them right then.

Blackjack, leading the charge from his observation helicopter high overhead, broke into our radio net periodically with instructions to "maneuver aggressively!" I got the distinct impression that he wouldn't be happy until we were all dead. His altitude deprived him of the personal relationship with the NVA that our horizontal separation did not. A rumor circulated around the mountain that there was a $10,000 reward for any American who shot down his little C&C ship.

Commanding the battle for Hill 937 may have been the colonel’s dream, or his worst nightmare. In either case, the American grunts on the ground hated him, and the enemy soldiers from the North were doing their best to kill him. Putting soldiers in harm’s way will not win popularity votes (by those being harmed) at any level of command, whether by mighty general or lowly squad leader.

Lieutenant Egginton continually acted 'above and beyond the call of duty.' Every time the men began to hug the ground, the young officer ran over, kicked a few butts, and got them going again. I knew he was scared, but he did his job over and over. The lieutenant was determined that his portion of the tightening circle would not lag behind. More than a few expressions of disapproval were targeted at the platoon leader, but his orders were obeyed. His gallantry scared me to death. Never charge up a mountain with someone braver than yourself. Sergeant Pearson had told me a lifetime ago—his lifetime—that true courage is not betrayed by fear. "What courage does it take to act, if there is no fear?"

By late morning the blazing sun was beating down on us at full strength. We were on the northern side of the mountain (finger 2.) The early morning shade had completely disappeared, and the sun was now bearing down on our backs. When I felt it was safe, I allowed myself a little sip of water from my canteen. Most of the guys had, by this time, consumed all of their precious liquid. They were forced to search the American and North Vietnamese dead for more.

Medical personnel were at a premium: if we had had four times the number, it wouldn't have been enough. Medevacs would not, or could not, get high up on the mountain where the wounded were bleeding. The second bad thing about getting zapped on Dong Ap Bia was that sometimes your buddies got zapped hauling your sorry butt back down the mountain.

Several times the lieutenant and I medically assisted each other on wounded soldiers who were hurt far beyond our ability to help them. We did what we could, even if it was only to gnash our teeth and involuntarily file away another unrelenting memory. On one of those occasions we jumped into a bomb crater to avoid a hail of machine gun bullets that had zeroed in on us. We found Kazuya Sakamoto, a third herd grenadier. He was all shot up. He was bleeding badly from the chest and stomach and mumbling through shock-whitened lips. Blood bubbling from his open mouth revealed that his lungs were filling with the red liquid.

"We-gotta-ventilate-him!" I yelled as if it were all one word.

I clamped my mouth over his cold bloody lips and felt my air bubbles going down his throat. Lieutenant Egginton meanwhile used his bayonet to cut the soldier's shirt away and expose the wounds. Thirty seconds later he put his hand on my shoulder.

"He's gone."

I tried one more time . . . but the lieutenant was right.

I was wiping Sakamoto's blood from my mouth when another soldier fell in the hole on top of us. It was Minnie Martinez. He began cursing and thrashing around, trying to remove the flack vest he was wearing. There was a small bullet hole, right through the U.S. ARMY stamped on the left breast of the vest. I grabbed at the zipper he was fumbling with. Minnie's dark brown eyes did not show fear, only anger. The bulky vest did not cooperate quickly, but once we got it off we saw another hole through the center of his shirt pocket. Lieutenant Egginton grabbed Minnie's shirt by the lapels and ripped it open while I blasted 20 rounds up the mountain. A flattened steel-jacketed AK-47 bullet fell out onto the red dirt. Just below Minnie's left breast was a large red mark (soon to turn black and blue.) The bullet had finally spent itself without even breaking Minnie's skin.

Lieutenant Egginton fastened the few remaining buttons on Minnie's shirt so friendlies wouldn't mistake him for a dark-skinned gook. Minnie then quickly scrambled out of the hole and rolled to the safety of a large boulder that had been blown from the crater. Since Minnie had not drawn any hostile fire, the lieutenant looked at me.

"Let's get out of here!" he yelled.

He ran to the same rock where Minnie was hiding and waited for me. As soon as my helmet cleared the lip of the crater, however, five machine-gun bullets kissed the dirt next to my head. They whined off into the distance. The shots came from behind a splintered tree stump, 30 meters up the hill. It was probably the same guy that hit Minnie and killed Sakamoto. The lieutenant and Minnie each emptied half a magazine at the tree stump and dropped back down behind their rock.

"C'mon Rock, ya wanna live forever?" Egginton yelled.

I crawled to the lip of the hole again and was about to shove my M-16 out and fire when another burst from the gook gunner raked across the crater's rim. It changed my mind. The only time the gunner shot was when I attempted to escape. Why was he waiting for me? Suddenly I realized that the radio antenna was making me a prime target. Every time I neared the top of the crater, the three-foot antenna waving above my head gave my intentions away. Charlie was trying to knock out our radio communications; it was nothing personal.

I realized it was too late to help this time, but I bent the flexible antenna down anyway and tucked it under a shoulder strap. When Wardle had asked me to take the radio again after Joe Romero got hit, he gave me some good advice. “Try ta look unimportant, because Charlie may be low on ammo.” I maybe should have remembered that a little earlier.

Trying to fool the machine gunner and possibly get some shots off first, I rolled to the far side of the hole. I pushed my weapon ahead of me as I crawled up the embankment. Just as I was about to pop up and fire, the distinct *thwump* of a detonating M-79 grenade came from the gook’s position. Gaining sudden confidence, my blood-shot eyes and rifle barrel simultaneously rose above the safety of the crater. Over the sights of my weapon I searched for my opponent, but it was too late. The gray cloud of an expended grenade hung over the area. I never found out who had wasted him, but I'll always be grateful for it.

Our well-planned attack was falling into disarray. No plan survives combat intact. Getting shot at changes a lot of things. Some groups of attacking allied soldiers were well ahead. Others had been pinned down or were in rough terrain and unable to advance as quickly. I listened to the radio traffic as an officer, somewhere on the mountain, complained about being pinned down by intense enemy fire. His men were unable to move. Blackjack cut into the communication with an order.

"Move out! You're being paid to fight, not for debating your damn situation on the radio!"

Many soldiers shot at anything that moved. That resulted in friendlies getting hit by each other. I saw several grunts hold live frags for a second or two, so they could not be returned, then throw them up over the crest of a small ridge before they attempted to leapfrog up. The problem was that some South Vietnamese coming up the other side had already captured it. Red ribbons were tied around the helmets of Marvin the ARVN to distinguish them from the gooks. In this case however, the Americans could not see the South Vietnamese. The ARVNs, knowing or unknowingly, answered with grenades of their own back over the hill. The lieutenant and I watched the action from a hundred meters away, helpless to do anything about it.

Unlike other times, when we estimated kills because the dead could not be found, on Hill 937 bodies were too numerous to count. Much of the time we had difficulty determining if the body parts represented four soldiers or six, or if they were gooks or Americans. RPGs, LAWs, mines, artillery, and napalm had done a good job of making the human shape unrecognizable. Human bodies do not come apart very cleanly, certainly not at prearranged seams.

The Gardener, after a very brief situation report from Lieutenant Egginton, ordered him to retreat several hundred meters down the hill. “Drag up the stragglers who have fallen behind!” he ordered. The lieutenant told me the big man in the sky (Blackjack) wanted our attack to be more "unified." That was very easy for the colonel to say as he sat on his butt in a bullet-free chopper. Perhaps all fourteen hundred of us should have lined up in a big rectangular formation like Revolutionary War British soldiers and marched up the mountain. Our casualty rate would have been astronomical, but unified.

Since Blackjack was not on the ground where he could personally participate in the festivities, he had not gained the support or respect of the soldiers actually doing the fighting and dying. From his altitude and attitude it was evident that he could not feel the high-explosive concussions, bullet impacts, exhaustion, or the terror of the close order combat. He could not see the blood-soaked dirt, hear the cries of pain, or carry the dead. A true commander should be on the ground to direct the battle, not isolated thousands of feet above the carnage.

As the lieutenant and I retreated down the blood-bathed mountain, and had more time to really look around, the impact of the warfare became very apparent. Bodies were strewn everywhere. We saw medics here and there desperately caring for the wounded. I, however, saw no living NVA. Another of Sgt. Rock’s laws of combat—the more numerous the casualties, the fewer the prisoners—and that is a hard law that applies to any war. Further down, where it was safer, we could see that medevacs were busy hauling away those patients who were not ambulatory.

We found Doc Wursten busily tending three casualties. It looked like a mortar shell had exploded between them. The soldier Doc was working on stopped gasping and just stared off into space. Wursten beat on the dead infantryman's chest with his doubled-up fist and gave him a few breaths of mouth-to-mouth. When he got no reaction, he mumbled to himself, "It don't mean nothin' " and moved on to the living. His next patient had been screaming with pain the whole time. The young PFC’s right leg had been savagely blown off just below the knee. Blood was beginning to puddle under his thrashing body. The medic grabbed the hysterical GI by the collar and violently shook him several times.

"Shut up!" he yelled. "Shut up and take it!"

A day in hell had destroyed Doc's bedside manner. The soldier stopped his screaming but continued to cry through clenched teeth.

Lieutenant Egginton and I ripped the blood-soaked shirt off the third unconscious soldier. The grunt's left arm was spouting a fountain of blood from a torn main artery. I applied pressure over the shrapnel hole with the palm of my hand to slow the hemorrhaging. The lieutenant then rigged up a tourniquet using an empty bandoleer and tree splinter. After stopping the blood, we wished the frustrated medic good luck and moved on.

It took us half an hour to get the men on our section of the mountain organized and moving again. During that time, I searched several dead gooks for papers, water, or anything else of military value. In one of the NVA backpacks, I made a startling discovery: a fully operational U.S.-made mini-starlight scope. The mini-scopes were so new that they had not even been issued to American units, yet I'd found one in the hands of the enemy. The mini-starlight scope was about a third the size of the "top secret" night-viewing devices they had issued our squad leaders just four months earlier.

We were ordered to guard our starlights with our lives, so my finding an even newer model in the hands of the gooks was a shock. Rather than destroying the device, I put it in a leg pocket of my jungle fatigues and took it with me.

*I continued to carry and use the mini-starlight scope for about a month. I was the envy of every squad leader in the company until a major from back at Battalion HQ confiscated it. He said it was too secret for me to be carrying around. The sorry REMF did not need it and could not put it to practical use, but I guess he enjoyed the prestige of owning it, just like I did. And it certainly was much safer, locked up all the time, in a steel military CONEX (Container Express) shipping box next to his hootch. Rank has its privileges.*

Pulling the stragglers along with us, the platoon leader and I shortly rejoined the bunker-to-bunker fighting. The lieutenant continually exposed himself—and me—to hostile small-arms and mortar fire as he fearlessly led the charge. I had earlier wished for a little skirmish with the enemy to test the new officer's mental toughness, and boy, was that lousy desire being answered in spades.

*For his bravery, the Army later awarded Lieutenant Egginton the Silver Star for his valor. For an FNG, he was one hell of a leader. There were many brave NCO and enlisted soldiers in Alpha Company that day, but if their individual heroics were ever recognized the Army kept it low profile. As it later turned out, the battle was getting a great deal of bad publicity back in the world. Too many American soldiers were dying, and very little land was being captured. The combat politics was all wrong.*

The assault on the mountain was costing us dearly in terms of manpower, which is a nice way of saying many Americans were being turned into casualties. But in fact, we were taking the hill. Nearing the top of Dong Ap Bia seemed to give the sweat- and blood-soaked guys new energy. The bullets that splashed mud and jungle debris into our faces did not matter any longer. Almost mechanically, Alpha Co. survivors continued the charge. The end was in sight. For the first time I began to believe I would survive the ordeal.

Climbing the last ridge before reaching the relative flat of the top, we received intense AK-47 fire from three very large and mostly underground bunkers. Bullets smashed into the fallen tree the lieutenant and I hid behind, showering us with bark and splinters. Artillery and gunships each took their turns trying to knock out the miniature fortresses, but they were unsuccessful. Five or six strategically placed gun ports in each of the clay mounds criss-crossed our path with deadly fire.

We were close enough to hear the gooks scream warnings every time we lifted our heads. Lieutenant Egginton decided that an old-fashioned frontal charge was the only way we could take out the bunkers. He coordinated the plan with the remnants of first platoon on our right. The gunners in the bunkers could easily handle us a few at a time. Attacking together, we could overwhelm them. Teamwork was essential; it gave the enemy other people to shoot at besides me.

On the lieutenant's signal I set the attack in motion.

I grabbed the radio handset and cleverly said, "Ready . . . Get set . . . Go!"

I then shoved the handset into a shirt pocket and joined 45 or 50 screaming boonie-rats who suddenly began swarming the 20 meters between us and them. The NVA met us with withering automatic fire from three or four AK- 47s.

Spec. 4 Dale Kelvin and PFC "Whitey" Whitemueller, from Austin's squad, immediately spun around and dropped in their tracks. Steel-jacketed bullets tore open their legs. Tony Salvetti's M-60 took three hits and was blown from his hands. A fragment of one round pierced the fleshy skin between his right thumb and index finger. Amazingly, he was otherwise unhurt. Billy "The Kid" Barret earned his second Purple Heart in two months when a frag rolled down from a gun port. In the ensuing explosion, he was hit nine times between the ankles and waist, but his manhood remained untouched.

Our suppression fire, aimed directly at the gun apertures, was enormous. It was likely the reason for the low number of casualties during this last advance. Leading the screaming horde, Egginton and I threw our bodies up against the safety of one of the earthen mounds. During our last few steps, the black barrel of an AK appeared from a hole in the mound and put a four round burst between us. The platoon leader shoved his black barrel back into the same opening and quickly fired the remaining six bullets in the magazine.

The few seconds that he kept the port quiet allowed me enough time to pull a frag from my leg pocket. In the excitement, the arming pin offered no resistance when I yanked it out. The spring-loaded spoon flipped end over end several times before landing with a splat in the red mud a couple of feet away. I held the live frag for two seconds then slam-dunked it into the six by six-inch hole. With just two seconds of fuse remaining, I knew the gooks inside the bunker could not return it to me. Right on schedule, dirt and smoke belched from the five firing positions. I was disappointed in the blast and concussion and suspected the grenade may have been a partial dud. On the count of three, the lieutenant and I each released the spoons on another two frags. We looked at each other for a moment and then crammed them simultaneously into the bunker. Two muffled explosions, like the first one, told us the room inside must have been large and well fortified.

We tried to avoid the intense rifle fire that occasionally peppered the ground near us by crawling through the mud to the back side of the bunker. Incoming fire always has the right of way. (That is another, in the growing library, of Sgt. Rock's laws of combat.) The rear opening had either been buried with explosion debris or there were tunnels leading into the earthen mound. Underground passages were a favorite and usually safe way for the Northern soldiers to elude Americans. Down there they lived, on the surface they died. We could find no way to access this bunker, but the important thing was we had killed it.

We raised ourselves to kneeling positions for a quick look around. There would be no more climbing. We were on the top. Alpha, 2/506 Infantry, 101st Airborne, was the first to reach the top. Second platoon had captured the summit. Within minutes others came into view from other sides of the mountain. I'm sure we would all claim the glory of capturing Dong Ap Bia.

Lieutenant Egginton was a little frustrated at not being able to get a body count from the bunker. He didn't have time to moan however, as we spotted three NVA soldiers about 30 meters away running across the bomb-cratered peak. At that range, they didn't stand a chance. A dozen M-16s, besides our own, cut them to pieces. The high-velocity bullets struck with tremendous impact, causing the bodies to jump with every hit. Long after they were lifeless, the jumping corpses continued to draw fire.

Even though we had begun the assault that morning at a terrible disadvantage, the combined American fire power had been devastating. Whenever and wherever we found the enemy, he was eliminated.

I was ever so pleased that we on the ground did not have to contend with enemy aircraft bombing and strafing us. The U.S.A.F. aircraft drivers enjoyed air superiority over North Vietnam and complete air supremacy over all of South Vietnam. I had never so much as even heard a rumor of anyone but us in the sky above. Luke the gook may attack us at ground level, or even come from below the earth's surface, but thankfully we never had to look skyward.

Individual credit for kills could not be given nearly as often as enemy wasted from our combined fire. Although death had become routine, the last thing any battle-hardened grunt needed to remember was the expression on a defender's face as his life was ripped away. Mercifully, what groups of soldiers did was much less memorable to us individually.

The little communist warriors deserved a good deal of respect and honor for their part in the battle. They were professionals, just as we were. Some had tied themselves into trees; others fought from spider holes from which there was no possible escape. Each man must have known he would die within hours, but he stayed and protected his territory courageously. Courage is not the absence of fear; it is acting in spite of it. Charlie had fought and died all in the line of duty, as he saw it. I began to realize that it was not the individual North Vietnamese soldier that I hated so much. It was the communist philosophy of conquest and dominance that had ultimately caused so many of my friends to die. Whether or not we should have been in Vietnam would never have been debated had the communist northerners stayed out of the south.

We considered ourselves the *corps d' elite*. Most of us had been drafted and did not choose to be there; the fact that we were, however, meant extreme danger for anyone who physically opposed us. On a helmet, back at Camp Evans, I read two sentences that seemed to illustrate my feelings about an infantryman's life and he who fought us: "A grunt has the second hardest job in the world. The hardest job in the world belongs to the man on the other side who has to face us."

In our last tactical offensive frenzy, we physically overran the last of the machine gun nests that would have prevented our victory. Nothing could have stopped us, as we had slipped into a realm beyond fear. The gooks that had not retreated were fragged or shot to death in their spider holes, bunkers, or wherever else they chose to die.

Stumbling from fatigue, we merged with other friendlies on the top of the mountain. Down a ridge, 300 meters to the west, action was still hot and heavy. Someone was destroying what was left of the 27th NVA Regiment. The "Pride of Ho Chi Minh," one of the crack regiments of the North Vietnamese Army, had just gotten its butt kicked.

Mopping-up operations continued for another hour, but essentially the battle was over. The costly triumph was ours. We were the kings of Bunker Hill. Joining with the other units as they made their way to the top from other sides of the mountain, we hastily set up a perimeter. For the first time that day, we began to receive direct support from the medevac and resupply birds as they began to do their thing in relative safety.

I slipped the radio off my sweaty back and collapsed on the ground next to it. Lying on my backside, totally exhausted, I stared up into the sky and made my peace with God. I was so thankful to be alive that I made impossible-to-keep promises. I intended to live such a saintly life that another book would have to be added to the Bible, chronicling my "After Hill 937" life.

When the few spare seconds that I had allotted to God were over, I laboriously sat up and glanced around my new environment. Suddenly, all of the blood seemed to drain from my head and the mountain began turning. The sweat on my face felt cold and clammy. I recognized the symptoms of heat exhaustion, so I lay back against the mountain again. In a few seconds, the spinning world settled down, and I regained enough coordination to unscrew the cap on my canteen and take a swig of the hot water.

Feeling a little better, I looked over at Egginton lying on his side next to me. He looked dead. His face was as white as a slice of Wonder (builds strong bodies twelve ways) Bread. The lieutenant's eyes had rolled back into his head and from his open mouth; a little string of saliva was suspended between his lower lip and the dirt.

"Egg, Egg!" I shouted as I rolled him over onto his back and violently shook his shoulder.

The body, inside the officer's sweat-soaked uniform, did not respond. Each shake seemed to flow down the length of his frame as though it were made of whale blubber.

I saw Wardle, a few steps away from us. He was sitting on the ground with his head resting on his elevated knees. I hurriedly explained that the lieutenant was sick or something.

"The guys are passin' out all over the mountain, Rock. Get his feet uphill and do whatcha can fer 'em. Doc will get here when he can."

Just as Sarge said, I could see small groups of bare-chested men at a dozen locations fanning their shirts over prostrate comrades. I filled my cupped right hand with precious water and let it drip onto the officer's face. Then, following the example of others, I stripped off my shirt and waved it over him. After several minutes, he blinked a dozen times and his glassy eyes returned to normal. The lieutenant mumbled a few slurred words to me. I couldn't understand what he was saying, but I knew he was thirsty, so I propped him up in my lap and gave him several swallows of water.

We would be in serious trouble if the vanquished Northerners chose to counterattack. After the intense combat subsided and our battle-fatigued bodies had stopped creating adrenaline energy, there was nothing left to sustain us. Soldiers were dropping so rapidly, it was as if poisonous gas had suddenly been released. A "fannee" on the ground one moment often found himself a "fanner" five minutes later.

Rationing water to myself, as if it were the last liquid on earth, I reached the summit with less than a quarter of a canteen left. Because I had been such a miser, I found myself between a rock and a hard place. It was my water. I carried it, I saved it, and I should be the one to drink it. On the other hand, if I did not share it, it could be the last water I'd ever drink. Sparingly, I sprinkled little drops of the hot liquid onto the faces of three of my friends nearby. When they were able to drink, I gave them each one swallow. Much too soon the water was gone.

In the late afternoon, about an hour after we had captured the mountain, and just as I had feared, we were briefly counterattacked. Twelve 81 mm mortar rounds landed on a ridge slightly lower than mine. I was so tired of dodging death that I didn't even bother to lie down. I just sat next to the radio and watched several ARVNs get blown away. One soldier was blasted several feet into the air. He did a complete somersault before returning to the earth, dead.

*Contrary to the dramatics of television, exploding mortar shells do not produce large balls of fire. Immediately after detonation the dirt, rocks, and other jungle debris settles back to the ground, then the grey smoke gradually dissipates. If you are able to watch this scenario of events, chances are you are not dead.*

Fifty to seventy-five NVA regulars, weapons blazing, moved up from a semi-intact treeline on the western side of the mountain far below us. They were courageous but foolish. It was suicide. I guess they knew it. They were no match for the 500-plus American and South Vietnamese troops above them. The assault was quickly repulsed; more NVA bodies to litter Dong Ap Bia. Except for scattered sniper fire, we heard nothing more from Sir Charles.

When no one volunteered, Captain Knight assigned a squad to gather all of our canteens and fill them in a muddy, tainted creek we had crossed 500 meters down the mountain. Resupply choppers were steadily dropping off the weapons and ammo we so desperately needed. But the small amounts of water and Cs they delivered could not satisfy the mass of parched throats on top.

Our next task was a grim one: we had to clear the mountain top of enemy bodies before it got dark. Some of the remains were intact, but most were not. The stench of some week-old decomposing corpses and other, fresher ones that had been badly napalmed was beyond description.

None of us wanted to sleep with the dead enemy. When possible, we dragged the remains by their blood-soaked clothing over to a nearby cliff and dropped them over. Some of the smaller odds and ends (i.e., hands, feet, heads or internal organs) we threw into bunkers and blew them shut. During this whole procedure, grey clouds of flies hummed their disapproval. Most of us, if not bloodied during the climb up, were completely saturated with the smell of death.

During one of my trips over to the cliff I passed a splintered four-foot tree stump—all that remained of a giant hardwood tree. Two weeks earlier it had stood proudly in a dense South Vietnamese rain forest. Someone had used a black grease pen to scrawl a message on C-ration cardboard and leaned the homemade sign against the tree stump. Satirically, the one-sentence message read: "WELCOME TO HAMBURGER HILL."

*The United Stated military had just fought the last major offensive battle of the Vietnam War.*

***Authors note**: Many years after I had written this chapter for the book, I came across a piece of information that I had long wondered about. Who was it that scribbled that famous and poignant sign atop Hamburger Hill? While I was doing some Internet research to determine how many kilometers it was from this point to that one, I found a very interesting article written by Greg Taylor entitled Hamburger Hill Revisited. According to Mr. Taylor, he visited the famous landmark twice in the mid 1990s. As part of his research on Hamburger Hill he found a website (that no longer exists) which credits Edward J. Henry with the signs authorship. That is entirely possible as Sgt. Henry was a squad leader in my company (Alpha 2/506 Infantry 101st Airborne Division) and he was one of the hills attackers.*

## CHAPTER 22

# AFTERMATH

Just before dark someone found an entrance to a large underground tunnel complex full of rooms. The ceilings of these huge bunkers were 10 feet or more below ground level. During heavy bomb or artillery attacks, the enemy simply retreated into the safety of the almost impenetrable rooms and waited. Unless one of these shelters took a direct bomb hit, the gooks simply rode out the storm of flying metal above. When the air sorties ended, the NVA quickly reappeared back in the trenches at their firing positions.

Even the sun had to close its eyes on the day's sickening adventure. Ashamed of what it had seen, it slipped over the horizon. I was summoned to the battalion command post that evening to begin a night of listening to radio traffic. The senior RTO gave me an assignment to monitor the transmissions of four command radios from 0100 to 0300 hours. Except for that two-hour watch, I could sleep all night. I really looked forward to the sleeping part. Every muscle in my body cried for rest.

I was able to kick a six-inch indention into the middle of some loose jungle debris using the toe of my jungle boot. I was much too tired to dig. This, I hoped, would offer some protection in case of another mortar attack. Exhausted, I lay down in the depression. Before I could even relax, I was startled to hear digging sounds below me. At first I thought it was rats, but suddenly a Vietnamese voice pleaded, "*Chieu hoi, chieu hoi.*" The voice scared me half to death. I jumped out of my hole as if it were full of snakes.

A hand holding a bloodstained white bandage broke through the surface of the jungle wreckage next to where I had been lying. I pointed my rifle barrel at the hand and pulled some debris away so the gook could free himself. He slowly crawled out of a bunker entrance buried by our explosives. Climbing from his would-be tomb, the soldier rolled over onto his back and cowered on the ground. The little guy, powered in better days by a gut full of rice, now empty, lay petrified with fear at my feet. He was face-to-face with his worst nightmare, a giant American.

The soldier's entire body shook in uncontrollable spasms as he pleaded for his life in words I did not understand. Dried blood had coagulated in both ears and his nose, a result of up-close and personal explosive concussions. The guy had been through a day of hell, maybe a week's worth of it. I put my size-10 jungle boot on his chest and the muzzle of my M-16 in his mouth, unconcerned for his black-stained teeth, then called for help.

There must have been 30 soldiers who came to my aid, and to see a live NVA soldier. Everybody understood the significance of the capture. Whatever his status was in the North Vietnamese Army, this soldier had a lot of valuable information. During the assault of the mountain I would have thrown a frag into his hole at the first indication of life and moved on. Now, with more time, professional interrogators could strip his mind of Who, What, When, Where, and Why.

I tied his hands behind his back so tightly with an empty bandoleer that they must have been turning blue. It was an act of extreme kindness on my part; it kept me, and others, from blowing his head off. Two ARVN officers began the interrogation process almost immediately. With permission from the battalion commander, the ARVNs took him back to their camp. I thought that that might have been the end of him.

*The next day the ARVNs put the captive, still alive, aboard a just-emptied log bird. Egginton said the gook was going to a POW camp somewhere near Quang Tri.*

The four Prick-25s I monitored during my shift were each set on a different radio frequency. I knew most of the code words and quickly discovered from the radio chitchat that other 101st Airborne infantry companies had been dropped into the surrounding jungle. As I understood it, they were forming a horseshoe-shaped cordon open only on the lazy broad (Laotian border) side. The plan seemed flawed to me, because the lazy broad was the obvious direction the escaping NVA Regiment would head. Why were we allowing the gooks freedom?

Toward the end of my watch, a little FAC spotter plane signed off the air. The pilot had had a long conversation with ground troops somewhere below him. In his last sentence, he said there was a "little surprise coming up," and he had to *didi mau*. I had no idea what he was talking about. Within five minutes a tremendous jet engine roar suddenly engulfed the mountain top. I thought several F-4 Phantoms were about to embed themselves into our position.

Before my Pavlovian-disciplined mind could order my body to hit the ground, the seismic activity of the mountain did it for me. Concurrent with the violently quaking earth that rocked my feet from beneath me was the brilliant flash. I threw my hands up to protect my night-dilated eyes from the sudden illumination. It was as bright as mid-day. I could see clearly for miles around from the vantage point at the summit of the mountain. I quickly scanned the mountains and valleys surrounding Hamburger Hill to find the source of the phenomenon. The audible answer followed the flash of light and rumbling earth by no more than a second.

*Kaa-blammm! . . . Kaa-blammm! . . . Kaa-blammm!* From the Laotian boarder to our west came massive reverberant explosions. Huge bombs were detonating; probably 10,000 pounders, many of them. The roar was a 'Strike Package' (most likely three) of B-52 bombers. They had already passed over us and dropped their deadly ordnance before we even heard them. The open end of the horseshoe was their target. Although the bombs had made their very impressive and violent impact almost two klicks away, I bounced around in the dirt like a water droplet on a hot skillet.

When the deafening concussions of the exploding bombs had ceased and the echoes inside my head subsided, I began to understand why the NVA had been permitted that avenue of "escape." The effect of the B-52 strike was undoubtedly a devastating final smash to the ragtag remnants of the 27th North Vietnamese Army. And the strike didn't cost a single American ground-pounder his life. Every conqueror on Hamburger Hill was by this time awake, on his feet, and cheering. We may have been depressed when the night began, but the United States Air Force lifted our spirits in an instant. Maybe a little late, but the 'cavalry' had arrived.

The roar of another wave of B-52s subdued our enthusiastic response. We looked skyward but were too late. Again the dazzling light accompanied the earth's rocking and shattering thunder. *Kaa-blammm! . . . Kaa-blammm!*
*. . . Kaa-blammm!* Everyone was prepared for it this time, and we readily absorbed the full effect. No sooner had the quiet of the night returned than the third of the triad of aircraft unloaded on the jungle between us and the lazy broad.

*Kaa-blammm! . . . Kaa-blammm! . . . Kaa-blammm!* echoed off the canyon walls and up the valleys. All of us on the mountaintop were ecstatic that the monsters in the sky were American. B-52s are the ultimate close support weapons.

First thing the next morning, choppers ferried our rucksacks to us from the LZ. It wasn't until after most of the soldiers had reclaimed their packs that I finally concluded that mine was missing. Brian "Beetle" Bailey, the company RTO, told me why. One of the birds carrying our rucks to Hamburger Hill took several .51 cal machine gun rounds in its tail. During the pilot's evasive maneuvers several of the packs fell overboard.

There was nothing much of military value in my ruck, but it did contain my little camera *(thus no pictures of Dong Ap Bia)* and a small 9-volt transistor radio. A gook somewhere in the valley was probably trying to understand what the heck Johnny Cash was talking about when he heard 'A Boy Named Sue' on his new American radio.

At noon, I hand-carried second platoon's official casualty report back to Battalion HQ. Luckily, we had somehow completed the assault on Dong Ap Bia without taking a single KIA. The platoon did, however, suffer eight WIA: that was almost a third of us. Spec. 4 Ben "Gentle Ben" Taylor, Jefferson City, Missouri, had multiple mortar wounds. Spec. 4 Dallas "Tex" Zack, from Dallas, had a bad bullet wound in his neck. Spec. 4 Tony Salvetti, Binghamton, New York, got a fragment wound in his hand. The remaining wounded included Spec. 4 Terrence Bullock, Waycross, Georgia, who got multiple mortar shrapnel wounds. PFC Kevin Jackson, Chattanooga, Tennessee had multiple head and arm grenade wounds. Spec. 4 Dale Kelvin from Overland, Missouri, had been shot in both legs. PFC Jimmy "Richman" Richie, Azusa, CA, was hit in the leg by our own artillery. Spec. 4 Ricky Ryan, Granite City, Illinois, had bullet wounds in a leg and his chest and wasn't expected to live.

Several of the guys, including Salvetti, would spend a little time in the rear recovering and then rejoin us. Most, however, were going back to the world for good. We had indeed captured bloody Dong Ap Bia, but the hail of victory did not pass the lips of any of us lucky enough to survive.

At the time we did not know the full details of the battle or the enemy body count. We received more "information" within a week or so from the Armed Forces newspaper, STARS AND STRIPES. The May 21 and 22, 1969 editions of the paper contained descriptive front page articles about Hamburger Hill. I quote a little from each:

*May 22*

*'HAMBURGER HILL' TAKEN*

*Saigon- American paratroopers and South Vietnamese infantrymen, in a four-pronged assault, Tuesday seized "Hamburger Hill," a 3,000-foot North Vietnamese mountaintop fortress along the rugged Laotian frontier. It was the 10th day of heavy fighting for the position.*

*May 21*

*Hundreds of fresh Allied troops Monday joined the week-long fight for a Communist-held mountain overlooking the A Shau Valley, a fight described by one U.S. paratroop officer as the worst he had seen since World War II.*

*About 600 troops from the 101st Airborne Div. and government 1st Inf. Div. were dropped by helicopter around 3,000-foot-high Dong Ap Bia mountain to reinforce other Allied units attempting to seize the peak 375 miles north-northeast of Saigon from a North Vietnamese regiment estimated at about 600 men.*

*"This is my third war and I haven't bumped into a fight like this since World War II in Europe," declared Col. J.B. Conmy Jr., 50. "The enemy has stood up and fought and refused to retreat."*

*May 22*

*Military spokesmen said the Communists lost 426 men killed in the battle for the mountain, while U.S. casualties were put at 39 killed and 273 wounded.*

*Figures published sometime later put the count at 56 American dead and 420 wounded. Enemy loses raised to 505 killed. The casualties were incurred over a grueling 10-day period, culminating with our final day-long assault.*

Why were ground-pounding soldiers pressed into service when a few B-52 strikes in the first week of the battle could have accomplished the same thing? Maybe only the brass at Div. HQ, or above, knew the answer to that question. Possibly they thought the prestige of a major infantry victory would raise the morale of all allied soldiers in Vietnam. The protesting, back in the States, may have also diminished if they perceived us as winning the war. Perhaps getting a body count was just easier if the grunts were physically there to do the killing and counting.

The 101st Airborne Division cut its teeth and gained much notoriety while fighting in the big one, WWII. Names like Bastogne, Normandy, Utah Beach, and Hitler's own Eagles' Nest were held in reverence by we who succeeded those valiant soldiers. Several well deserved Presidential Unit Citations for extraordinary heroism and gallantry were earned by those 101st Airborne, 506th Infantry, paratroopers.

*In March of 1992, we "Currahee" (a Cherokee Indian word meaning "stands alone") veterans of Hamburger Hill were also recognized for extraordinary heroism, even if it had been years earlier. The Department of the Army General Orders 16, 31 awarded us a third Presidential Unit Citation for action at Dong Ap Bia.*

Other than it being the tallest peak in the surrounding area, the newly captured terrain had no tactical significance for the U.S. Army. They (the war planners) didn't intend for us to keep or occupy it. Like other famous mountain climbers have often stated: "We climbed the mountain because it was there." And I should add; "Because that's where the enemy was." Our real mission was not to capture and secure the mountain, but to kill all the communists on it.

Many gallant men suffered, bled, and died on a piece of real estate we didn't even want. Remember, one of the goals of this engagement was to provide a positive turning point in the war's direction. Based on the sensational notoriety the battle received back in the States, the turn was anything but positive. Editorialists from around America banged on their typewriters with graphic accounts of each day's losses. To an American public, already tired of the Vietnam War, and for the antiwar politicians looking for headlines, Hamburger Hill was just too much to ignore.

At the 1400 hours platoon briefing, the captain gave us the details on our next objective, Firebase Airborne. East about six klicks and visible to us from Hamburger Hill was a small artillery support base. The North Vietnamese Army attacked it during the early morning hours of May 13. Under the cover of darkness the 6th North Vietnamese Army Regiment assaulted the base in human waves. They overran two-thirds of the firebase in the fierce two-hour firefight. Finally, morning light and the courageous defenders (Alpha/2/501st) forced the bad guys back into the jungle. We were ordered to re-secure and occupy the much-needed fire-support fortress.

The move to a new area of operation meant that I was going to sit in an open-air Huey during the transfer. Cool air was welcome. I guessed that the firebase might even have enough water to shave and bathe in. The clothes we had worn for months were now as stiff as canvas with blood and crusty salt formations. Weeks of continuous perspiration had caused large white salt crystals to grow on the fronts and backs of our shirts. The underarm area of the jungle blouses felt like sandpaper. Pouring a helmet-full of clean water over our heads would do us no harm at all.

All day long choppers plucked weary soldiers from atop Hamburger Hill and delivered them to new areas of operation. Our perimeter kept getting smaller and smaller. Finally, Alpha Company's turn came. By nightfall we had completely vacated Hill 937. Within several days all American and South Vietnamese troops would be gone from Hamburger Hill.

We gave it back to the NVA.

## CHAPTER 23

# FIREBASE AIRBORNE

Firebase Airborne was about what I expected. It was 200 meters long and about 50 meters wide. The firebase was shaped like an elongated chicken egg, with the southern end being a little wider. It was on one of the small tentacle ridges coming off a large Octopus-like mountain identified on the map as Co Pong. There were steep down slopes on two sides, north and west, of our new 'unfortified' fortification. Twenty-five meters outside the eastern perimeter and through a shallow ravine was a small knoll. The little hill was independent from, but part of, the main firebase area. An 81 mm mortar platoon occupied the knoll. The fourth side, to the south, was a gradually climbing continuation of the ridge.

The helicopter landing pad was just outside the razor-sharp concertina wire on the flat fourth side. Beyond the perforated steel planking, laid to keep the choppers out of the Monsoon mud, the mountain's finger climbed steadily. By following the finger across the landing pad and out the southern end of the firebase, a soldier could eventually climb to the crest of Co Pong, north of Airborne. The ridge circled halfway around the small base. The peak was just two klicks away, as the crow flies. Co Pong and its long circular downhill ridge to Firebase Airborne offered a great vantage point for the NVA to monitor everything we did and to pop off a sniper shot occasionally. The mountaintop was about five klicks away if we followed the winding trail up the ridge. Fear of getting killed prevented Americans from trying to navigate the entire roundabout trail. Co Pong's massive and dense green jungle-covered ridges towered over our diminutive firebase. These difficult-to-understand details were important to us during the next few months.

On the western side of the base, 1500 feet below us, lay one of the main arteries of the Ho Chi Minh Trail (highway 584); thus the significance of Airborne's position. Another reason for the base's location was a mountain pass, seven klicks away, through which highway 584 passed.

The name Ho Chi Minh Trail is a bit deceiving. Hundreds of clandestine trails originating in North Vietnam fanned through the A Shau Valley. All of the trails were part of the same network and carried the same name. Periodically, these trails were forced to merge as they funneled through large difficult-to-go-around mountains. One of those merge points was the canyon that Firebase Airborne's artillery was tasked with keeping closed. The pass's dirt highway allowed much foot, bicycle, and even truck traffic access to northern South Vietnam. At the slightest hint that the VC or NVA might be using the canyon, Airborne's FAGs (field artillery guys) manned the two 105 mm and the single 155 mm howitzer batteries and very effectively plastered the area. The firebase was a thorn—more like a thorn bush—in the side of the communist's resupply route. Charlie took every opportunity to try and knock it out, or at least diminish its effectiveness.

The enemy assault, several days before our arrival, began at 0330 hours with a heavy mortar attack. With the element of surprise on their side and their own exploding 81 mm shells, the sappers from the K12 Sapper Battalion crawled across the landing pad. They began by cutting or blowing holes in the outer defensive concertina wire. When they had sufficiently weakened the perimeter, hordes of screaming North Vietnamese poured off the hill overlooking Airborne's southern end and fought through the American defenses.

The scattering gooks threw their satchel charges (bags or packs filled with explosives) into bunkers, mortar pits, and artillery stockpiles. Resistance by the Screaming Eagles manning the base was ferocious, greater than the gooks had expected, and with daylight approaching they were forced to withdraw. But not before they had killed 26 Americans and wounded 62.

During the next 17 daylight hours, the brave defenders policed up the enemy dead. The NVA bodies had been healthy, mostly young men, who sported fresh haircuts. The surviving Americans stacked the bodies of 39 dead attackers into piles. They soaked the human mounds and other debris with diesel fuel and set it all ablaze. Fire was the most sanitary way to dispose of the large number of corpses. Digging a mass grave by hand in the hard ground was impractical.

*The two fire-blackened scars on the ground survived most of the monsoon rains before Mother Nature's tears and her cosmetic foliage could finally hide it.*

Most of the attackers wore nothing but simple loincloths. Some of the North Vietnamese were entirely naked, allowing them to crawl through the defensive wire more easily. Several shirtless GIs were mistaken for NVA during the excitement of the predawn surprise assault and were shot by fellow Americans. Consequently, the first order we were given upon our arrival at Airborne was that under no circumstance were we to remove our shirts after dark.

We spent the first day at our new location stringing more coils of concertina wire and digging temporary foxholes. In a combat zone, home is where you dig it. To set a proper example, the lieutenant chose to defend Airborne's perimeter overlooking the chopper pad. It was right smack dab in the center of the previous path of attack. Since this was still Charlie's obvious avenue of approach, Wardle, Lieutenant Egginton, Doc, and I made our first night's position as invincible as possible. We strung 20 claymores out, and filled an empty artillery shell box in our hole with 45 hand grenades. Doc scrounged up a 90 mm recoilless rifle—an over-the-shoulder bazooka-type launcher—along with seven H.E. (high explosive) and three Flechette (thousands of inch-long, arrow-shaped projectiles filling the warhead) shells. He also found eight antitank and ten shotgun rounds for us to fire through the recoilless weapon.

On the far side of the landing pad, we half-buried two 55-gallon drums of jellied gasoline called Foo gas. Under each drum we placed several blocks of TNT. We could detonate the TNT from our hole with a hand-held clacker. It would throw flaming gasoline all over the ridge above us. The burning gas would improve our vision at night and also encourage the enemy to attack elsewhere.

We scrounged up an M-60 with 5,000 rounds of ammunition. During stressful conditions, happiness is a belt-fed weapon. When the enemy have targeted you, even if it's with just one bullet, it's a high intensity conflict. Prepared as we were, we still felt naked when the sun disappeared and the jungle's tropical darkness took control.

Shortly after midnight, rain began to pour from the sky. It quickly became evident that our foxhole was the low point in the surrounding area. That was poor preparation on our part. Civil Engineers we were not. Through most of the night's remaining black hours, we bailed water and dug long diversion trenches. Our only rest came at 0435, when a seven-round mortar attack caused us to jump into the waist-deep water. We finally got the baths we'd really needed. The rounds exploded harmlessly over the embankment on the far side of the base. No one was hurt. A ground attack did not follow.

Over the next three days we filled sandbags and started building more permanent bunkers. They were fronted with chain-link fences on which RPG and satchel charges would detonate before rearranging our carefully regimented sandbags. We salvaged some of our building materials from old fortifications that had previously been blown flat. Nobody complained about the hard work. We were surrounded by an enemy who intended to destroy us—that may have had something to do with the cooperative work effort.

Alpha was so under-strength that half of Bravo Company was assigned to beef up our sparse numbers while we provided security to the firebase. The other two Bravo platoons had the unenviable job of patrolling outside the wire, which was the northern armies' domain.

The third night at Firebase Airborne an AC-47 (Spooky) fixed-wing aircraft flew a large racetrack pattern, at an altitude of about 3,000 feet, over Hamburger Hill. The two, 6,000-bullets-per-minute, Gatling-type guns protruding from the right side of the aircraft created an elongated red cone as the highly visible tracer rounds targeted the mountaintop far below them. Just as we had predicted, it had only taken a day or two for the NVA to remount the mountain and begin new fortifications. Over the next few days artillery guns from nearby firebases periodically blasted Dong Ap Bia.

During our fourth morning, Bravo's patrolling soldiers discovered a "just-vacated" platoon-sized enemy camp. It was only 400 meters down the hill from my almost completed bunker. Later in the day they got involved in a quick firefight. Five of their men got hit. That engagement was within a rock's throw of our perimeter. Enemy losses were unknown. The beat-up and outnumbered Bravo guys had to withdraw inside the safety of the wire.

In the days that followed, my body never had a chance to get rested. We dug holes and filled sandbags all day and stood guard every other hour all night. Charlie harassed us with sniper fire while it was light. They often mortared us after dark.

We got hit by four fast mortar rounds during the early morning hours of our seventh day at Airborne. Considering their number, the shells caused an incredible amount of damage. The first projectile landed next to a four-man early warning LP (listening post) 20 meters outside the wire. Another round landed among four soldiers on the top of a bunker. They were sleeping there to avoid the hot humid air inside. Among the two groups, four soldiers were killed; the other four were seriously wounded.

A medevac helicopter made a daring pickup of the wounded, while Airborne was still under nighttime blackout conditions. The dead however, were left by the landing pad for a safer daytime extraction. The vision of four more friends lying next to the helipad, covered with ponchos, would take a long time to "mellow out" in my memory.

Their boots . . . it was seeing their boots (with the little yellow DD Form 1380, identification tag securely tied to a bootlace) that burned like a branding-iron image into my brain. No matter how the dead were enshrouded, their boots always protruded. It was a stark reminder that the bumps under the rubberized blankets were some mother's little boy. Our ponchos were long enough to be stretched over the head of each corpse down to his ankles. With the poor soldiers head protected—and hidden from our view—we had covered the bodies in the most dignified manner possible. American soldiers were never left uncovered and exposed to the elements for very long. I tried to resist looking in their direction. Maybe I could pretend that it hadn't happened. The bodies were like a magnet, however. I found my tear-filled eyes continually pulled in that direction. Each time a chopper landed or departed part of a poncho would blow free and flap noisily in the wind. Someone standing nearby would quickly redistribute the rock weights and hope the peace of the dead would not be broken again until their turn came to go home.

Along with the bad news came some good news. Good and bad news always seemed to be linked. The date everyone looked forward to the most, DEROS, finally arrived for two of our best. Big Red Redmonds and Eddie Zorn got orders recalling them back to the world. Captain Knight arranged for a dozen cases of beer and soda water to be sent to us in the field. When it was delivered, we found that "Major" Poulsen had also managed to smuggle several fifths of whiskey, especially for those two, in the big orange mail bag.

Some of the men were not big fans of Zorn, and Big Red never did mix well with anybody but Soul Brothers. The celebration of their "getting out alive," however, was enjoyed by everyone. It gave us all hope. We grabbed the rusty tin cans of warm beer and soda and broke into small groups to "party." In my bunker no one could find a "church key" so we opened the cans with the tip my bayonet. The pressurized containers blew their foam all over us but we didn't care, this was a good day. The "heads" managed to segregate themselves into several large bunkers. They smoked grass through the barrel of a shotgun and passed homemade joints around. When a reefer got too short to be held, the last head popped the still-burning roach into his mouth. He then swallowed it. It was a sign of masculinity.

At mid-afternoon a 40-foot Chinook, with rotors front and rear, arrived to bring us supplies and to take out the two homeward-bound GIs. It created large patterns of swirling red dust as it awkwardly lifted off the landing pad's steel interlocking PSP. In its belly were two "sloshed" and "stoned" grunts. One would think they were best friends the way they hung around together the last few days on Airborne. Long forgotten was the posturing toward each other the morning we left for Hamburger Hill. They were now beginning the magic transformation that would have them looking like civilians in less than a week (except for the last mandatory military haircut.)

I sat on the top of my bunker and gave the peace sign salute until the chopper was almost out of sight. The loss of Zorn and Big Red dropped the company's strength to 47, much less than half of what it should be. Lieutenant Egginton now commanded a platoon of just 13 men.

In an attempt to distribute leadership, the platoon leader reorganized the three squads into two. Karras kept Polansky and a new arrival named Peterson. He got Minnie and Muskrat from the old second squad. He got me again too. Sergeant Tew kept his guys, Wilson and Blackwell, and picked up West from Zorn's old squad. The remaining members of the platoon, the lieutenant, Wardle, and Doc, temporarily attached themselves to Tew's undermanned squad. Sergeant Wardle took provisional custody of the radio.

At the first squad meeting, Spec. 4 Karras gave us the usual pitch about how he thought his squad was the best in the company. Our new squad leader then shared a "care package" his mother had just sent him. The package mostly consisted of some broken and dry homemade Greek cookies; I didn't know what they were called. We even drew straws for the crumbs in the bottom of the can. Karras won; I guess that was only fair.

Karras next announced that Minnie and I were going to be his "Fire-team" leaders. We were each going to be responsible for half of the small squad. My half consisted of Polansky and Muskrat. Normally an infantry fire-team consists of five or six grunts, one of which usually carried a '60 and another a '79. Since the three of us all carried rifles, Karras told Polanski to trade his in for a funny gun to give us a little more firepower.

The rains came more frequently as the days passed. It seemed like it poured every night, especially during my hours of guard duty. The gooey, sticky, clay-mud made very little effort to dry out during the hot and humid days. Conditions just got worse and worse. We rebuilt Karras's bunker top and placed plastic sheeting between each of the four layers of sandbags. The heavy waterlogged sand caused the perforated steel planking to sag in the middle. Somehow, the pool of water that formed on top of the shelter found its way through the plastic. It trickled into our living area from a dozen locations and it didn't take long for a 6X8-foot lake to cover the bunker's dirt floor.

The lake problem had to be solved. Bailing water out of the gun port didn't work. The solution, we decided, was an artificial floor, made of empty wooden artillery boxes. Once the crates were in place we were able to lie down on our new floor and stay out of the six inches of mud and water. The uneven bed of sharp-cornered wet ammo boxes left much to be desired as far as comfort went, however.

The first few weeks at Airborne we performed the same tasks day after day. Bunkers could never be fortified enough. There was always room for another roll of concertina wire to be strung, and trees had to be felled to expand our fields of vision and fire.

To prevent the same kind of sneak attack that had been so disastrous three weeks earlier, Observation Posts (OPs) were assigned during the day and Listening Posts (LPs) went out at night. Both jobs were dangerous. Should the enemy attack, these three- or four-man teams would most likely be eliminated unless they could quickly reach the safety of the perimeter. The process of killing the lookouts, however, would provide enough warning to alert the firebase occupants that all was not well. Hopefully the warning, or sacrifice, would save many other lives. Each squad inside the perimeter took its turn sending men outside the wire.

It was June, the unlucky day of Friday the 13th, exactly one month from the attack on Airborne. In the middle of a monotonous early-morning sandbagging detail Lieutenant Egginton approached me. He was walking back from a company briefing at the command bunker.

"Sergeant Rock, I got a detail for ya," he said.

He pointed over my left shoulder, toward a high point on the ridge overlooking Airborne's southern end.

"Take your fire-team about a hundred meters up the hill and set up an OP. You shouldn't have any trouble, but stay alert. If you see anything at all, fire a few warning shots and get your butts inside the wire. Let the artillery guys be the heroes."

Karras explained that the rest of the platoon was going on a patrol. They would end their recon on the trail about 500 meters up the mountain's finger from us. He said they would pick the three of us up on their return to the firebase.

Polansky, Muskrat and I each took light loads of ammo—we were supposed to warn of enemy activity, not engage them. I strapped a Prick-25 to my back. We then moved out through the wire. Within ten minutes of selecting a spot on the ridge, we were all set up. A small tree stump acted as a single backrest for the three of us. We sat back to back, facing away from each other, allowing us a constant 360-degree view. The tree stump was just off the main trail that followed the ridge up toward Co Pong.

We were fairly well hidden in the jungle undergrowth, so after an hour of staring at the trail, I slowly took a rolled-up writing tablet from my leg pocket. My steel pot provided a firm but awkward platform for me to write a letter to my parents. While gathering my thoughts before beginning the letter, I surveyed the 120 degrees of terrain that was my responsibility to watch (including the 100 meters of trail that was visible to me.) Within my view down the hill were the many rings of curled razor-edged concertina wire surrounding the place we all called home. Even as I watched, the wire was parted and the two squads from good ol' second platoon disappeared into the thick green of the enemy domain. Off in the distance I could hear artillery shells detonating on Hamburger Hill.

*Dear Family,*

*I'm sitting on the top of a large mountain, like an eagle in its nest, watching the jungle and valleys below me for any sign of gook activity. There are three of us up here with a radio to warn the firebase if the gooks try to attack from this side.*

*Charles has pretty much left us alone the last couple of days although the firebases around us haven't been so lucky. I expect one day soon he'll try to mess with us and then I'll have something exciting to write home about again.*

*My platoon is out right now trying to find the gooks that have been firing on the choppers as they make their approach to land here. One of our sister companies, working just outside the firebase yesterday, found 150 80 mm mortar rounds and 450 . . . BREAK! . . . I just heard some explosions! My platoon has made contact! Now I can hear AKs firing! Over the radio, Wardle just said that they have wounded and they need help, ASAP! He said Charlie blew claymores on the guys. My squad was on point. There are at least four wounded and maybe more up at the front. I've got to sign off for now. Another platoon is hurrying to assist my buddies and the three of us will join them.*

I hurriedly rolled the writing tablet back up and shoved it into the leg pocket. In less than 60 seconds, I could see 20 soldiers comprising first platoon hustling toward our position. Beyond our observation point was no-man's land, so we would need to be very cautious while moving up the trail. We joined the file as they hurried past us. Because these were our friends pleading for help, we all rushed toward the ambush site almost double-time. That was dangerous; the ambush may have been a diversion allowing the NVA to attack an even larger American force that would surely be following the trail, the shortest rescue route to the first ambush site.

Within five minutes of the initial claymore blasts, the gunfire on both sides had ceased; Sir Charles had vanished. It was a quick hit and run. The gook ambush had been successful. They had killed the lead American and wounded four others before artillery could counterattack, or before the rescue soldiers could arrive.

When we got to the ambush site, three-man security teams automatically flanked to the left and right. Most of first platoon moved on up the trail in pursuit of the gooks. That left Polansky, Muskrat, and me to assist the two medics we brought with us.

We found Peterson lying on the trail in a pool of his own blood. The gook claymore mine had riddled his face and chest like a point-blank shotgun blast. He had been killed instantly. I hadn't really gotten to know the guy because he was still quite new to the company. I did not know at the time that he left a wife, with two babies, in Carson City, Nevada. The other four casualties were good friends of mine. It was good/bad news when Doc Wursten told me they would all live to fight another day.

Wilson and West were second and third in the column when the two claymore mines detonated. Because Peterson's body absorbed the brunt of the flying steel, they were mostly spared. Several BB-sized bits of shrapnel hit Wilson in the face and neck, but none of his vital facial organs were seriously touched. West's left arm was twice violated by the foreign objects, both times just above the right elbow. He shrugged off the wounds so convincingly that no one realized how serious the injuries were until Doc cut his sleeve off. The two peanut-sized holes went clear through his biceps. The other two victims each had single bullet wounds. They claimed the wounds were from the same bullet. Karras said he was crawling forward when a single round passed through the fleshy skin on both cheeks of his posterior. The bullet continued on, grazing Wardle's left knee. Muskrat kidded the two about being blood brothers.

"Ain't nobody gonna catch this brother eat'n no Greek food," Wardle jokingly responded.

Karras, showing some humor through his pain, promised not to sit down on the job for at least a month. Karras's comment was a little corny, but considering the situation, it was funny. Guess you had to be there.

Wilson and West managed to walk back to the firebase. We used stretchers for the other three. While all this was going on, first platoon discovered two dead NVA soldiers a hundred meters up the trail. Charlie had evidently been trying to drag away his dead. The pursuing Americans were closing in too quickly, so they abandoned the bodies.

An hour later, after the remnants of our platoon were safely back "home," first platoon called in another interesting report. They had found six bunkers and a major supply depot cache of supplies. Included in the spoils were 600 mortar shells, 20,000 AK-47 rounds, 25 RPG rockets, and 17 hand grenades. Among other odds and ends were, interestingly enough, 100 fishing poles with 10,000 meters of line.

It took two months for each "People's Porter" to hand-carry his or her 55-pound load down the Ho Chi Minh trail. Many man-days of hard labor, between the newly discovered bunkers and the North Vietnamese munitions factories, had been for naught. No telling how many American lives would be spared as a result of the find.

The next morning Lieutenant Egginton sent word with Doc that he wanted to see me in his bunker. I finished the can of warmed beef and potatoes that had served as my breakfast and hoofed it over to his position. Since Wardle and I were now gone from the command post, only the lieutenant and the medic permanently lived in the sandbag structure. When I entered the platoon leader's tiny hole in the ground, it was mostly devoid of the normal clutter of military gear and suddenly seemed very spacious.

"Sergeant Rock, the squad is yours," he said.

I guess I could have acted surprised, but I didn't because I wasn't. Three weeks earlier, there were five or six soldiers in the platoon who had the seniority and leadership talent that may have qualified them to be selected over me. Wartime attrition tends to disrupt the normal progression of leadership, however, and I had been thrust into the forefront.

I was fully confident, considering the situation, and felt I had enough experience to be an effective squad leader. Filling the combat boots of my predecessor was going to be a big task, however. Randy Karras was well respected among the guys in the squad, and he was a good leader.

Responsibility that was earned by World War II "men" in their mid-twenties commonly came to the Vietnam War "boys" during their nineteenth or twentieth years. That was partially due to one-year tours in the combat zone. If I was going to be accepted as a leader among my peers, I had to be more than just a figurehead filling a slot. The days of blindly following someone into combat ended with the advent of the Vietnamese "conflict." Seven months in-country hardly qualified me as an old hand, but I was the best, I guess, of the few left.

At the conclusion of my little chat with the platoon leader, he assured me that he would make every effort to get me promoted. Remembering Zorn's experience, I took the promise with a grain of salt.

When Lieutenant Egginton explained my advancement to the squad, everyone gave me the traditional back-slap congratulations. Even Minnie, who was the senior Spec. 4 in the squad, expressed his compliments and confidence in me. I had been concerned that he might not accept my leadership, but he actually seemed relieved not to have the extra problems that came with the job.

The entire first squad by that time consisted of just four guys: Polansky, Minnie Martinez, Muskrat Brostrom, and me. Tew's squad included just Blackwell and himself, and the two-man command post of Doc and Egginton. We were in sad shape, numbers-wise. It did not look like our many empty slots were going to be filled any time soon, either. The captain said that he was not aware of any new soldiers, already in-country, who were slotted to us. With so few to take turns standing guard at our bunkers, I could see many sleepless nights in the near future.

The company, now critically under-strength, was "grounded" to Firebase Airborne. For the next three weeks we were not permitted to exit the protective concertina wire, which really broke our hearts. The only exception to the confinement came about five days into the quarantine.

Word spread like wildfire through the company that because of our “heroic” accomplishments on Hamburger Hill, we were being rewarded with a two-day stand-down at Eagle Beach. Eagle Beach was a recreation area belonging to the 101st Airborne Division. It was just south of Hue. Screaming Eagle units that had distinguished themselves in combat got first crack at the resort.

In preparation for leaving the next day, and to make us look as respectable as possible, the Army flew portable showers into our mountaintop location. Much of the tan I had grown so accustomed to disappeared as I applied the soap and water. My ‘new’ fatigues were used, but at least they were clean. I ripped off the cloth patch, stamped with the name "BRETTENGER." An infantryman's superstition demanded that used clothing be checked for bullet holes. I complied. No holes. To wear a dead man's uniform invited extreme bad luck.

As scheduled, even though rain clouds made it difficult, choppers rescued us from the widow-making A Shau Valley and delivered us to the safety of Camp Evans. From the base camp, we motored via armed truck convoy through the city of Hue to Eagle Beach. We passed scores of young Vietnamese city-women, each of them wearing the traditional embroidered silk *ao dai,* slit up to the waist. They putt-putted along on their little Honda scooters, dodging slower bicyclists but paying little attention to the big truck convoy full of screaming American GIs. They'd seen that all before.

The resort was located on a beautiful stretch of white sand on the Gulf of Tonkin. We body-surfed in the ocean and played volleyball on the beach. As soon as it was dark each evening, a small club opened its doors and the thirsty GIs flocked in. The fact that I was not a "juicer" did not excuse me from the responsibility of occasionally buying a round for the house. Soda didn't seem to pass as quickly as beer did. I always had several unopened cans on the bar in front of me. The plywood bar was warped and stained by years of spilt beer and soldiers' tears.

Nobody can drink beer quite like underage infantrymen fresh from combat. When someone else is buying they will drink especially long and hard. Each night I sat with my comrades-in-arms telling, and sometimes listening to, war stories and talking about home. Until the wee hours of the morning, long after I was starving for sleep, I tried to match can for can with my drunken buddies. Only after the storeroom's warm beer had been depleted was I allowed to look for a place in the cool sand and crash.

The Australian band, playing at the club each night, featured a pretty mini-skirted lead singer, and she drove the grunts wild. Beauty is in the eye of the beer holder. Half a dozen bouncers were necessary to keep the rowdy inebriates off the stage. During one of the performances, the band sang "a new one from the Beatles." I finally understood why so many of our new arrivals had begun kidding me about "Rocky Raccoon."

Many of the club's military employees seemed bored with their assignments, but to someone who had just gathered body parts, this was Nirvana. Each morning the sun rising over the South China Sea revealed American bodies scattered all over the beach. But these soldiers were just sleeping, thankfully.

The return convoy to Camp Evans two days later was truly depressing, but at the same time exhilarating. We knew our ultimate destination would again be the deadly A Shau Valley. The truck convoy did, however, provide two interesting highlights. One came when we passed an old Vietnamese farmer using a motorized tiller in his garden. All of us stood and applauded his huge advancement in farming. I swear it must have been the only gasoline-powered tiller in all of Vietnam. All the other "tillers" we'd ever seen were water buffalo powered.

The second highlight was when we sped past several mama-sans, in their sampans, herding a thousand mostly white ducks down one of the roadside canals. In a country full of ugliness, that was beautiful. The trip back to Camp Evans was really quite safe and enjoyable. We were making good time, with emphasis on the "good," and that was a remarkable change for us.

We didn't even get to stay overnight at the base camp. What a bummer that was. Immediately upon our arrival, we were shoved aboard waiting choppers and flown back to our jungle prison. It all happened so quickly that we never even got a chance to complain. I guess that was the idea.

Greeting the platoon upon our arrival back at Firebase Airborne was Tony Salvetti and a contingent of ten new human targets. My old buddy, Tony, in his brand new uniform, looked rested and freshly scrubbed. I was really happy the NVA soldier on Hamburger Hill had killed the machine gun and not Salvetti. It was a miracle. Only the bandage on his thumb, and the look in his eye, distinguished him as a combat vet.

Next morning we divided up the new arrivals. The platoon had a great need for grunt replacements, but these new targets had no idea why. They had no comprehension of what they would see and do. Their innocence would be gone shortly. Sergeant Tew and I drew straws for first choice. I won. As if I were filling out a roster for a professional basketball team, I made Salvetti the first draft pick of my new "franchise." I then had the advantage of his whispering in my ear, to advise me on each of the next choices. Since Tony had gotten to know most of the replacements, my selections got the best men available. The third herd had the greater need, so after my fourth pick, Lieutenant Egginton stopped the "choosing up sides." He gave the remaining four men to Tew. Second squad continued to exist in name only. We still did not have enough fresh meat to fill it out.

Besides Tony, I picked three 19-year-old PFCs. Bo Hansen was a tall soul brother from Austin, Texas. He said he had played defensive back on the Texas Longhorn football team before his grades slipped and he was drafted. My second pick was obviously on the chubby side, but very intelligent, or so said Tony. Thurmand Smith was from Mountain Home, Arkansas, and referred to himself as an "Ozark Mountain boy." The last member of our team was also physically big but rather quiet. Ed Mason was from Fairfield, California. All in all I was generally pleased with the quality of the new troops. The quantity, however, still left much to be desired. We were still decidedly shorthanded.

Although none of us were allowed outside the wire to chase or be chased by Sir Charles, we still managed to create our own excitement. To discourage the gooks from getting "too close" during the night, "mad-minutes" were instituted. Randomly, two or three times a night, for one minute, we were allowed to cut loose with all the small-arms ammo and grenades we could expend. I'm afraid the guys at my bunker played the game to the extreme. After it got dark each evening, we sent a scout up to a point overlooking the ammo dump. When the coast was clear, he would give us a quick flick with his cigarette lighter. Two of our team would then sneak into the repository and "midnight requisition" an extra case of 48 hand grenades. Back at our position, we straightened the safety pins and partially extracted them.

During the first mad-minute, the two soldiers who happened to be on guard duty would attempt to throw all 48 frags before the minute was up. It really was a great deal of fun. After a week or so of this, we were ready for new and more dangerous challenges. We began to have contests to see who dared hold an armed grenade the longest. The more daring (or brainless) among us generally held the high explosive for a count of three. He then quickly slam-dunked it over the sandbag wall, where it would immediately detonate, harmlessly.

Our adventurism escalated even further. Soon we were building small homemade bombs during the day, which we blew to smithereens during the night. For our purposes, quarter-pound blocks of TNT, and M-16 magazines filled with C4, worked the best. We usually wrapped the explosives with four or five layers of nails and nylon tape. We then hung the bombs in trees at the jungle's edge. The highly explosive charges were not intended to be antipersonnel type bombs, although they very well could have served that purpose. We told ourselves that we were shredding jungle cover thus improving our fields of fire. But the real reason was that it was fantastically fun to just blow things up. Just like young teenagers playing with firecrackers, except we bigger boys had bigger toys. Only after the order came from the command bunker to "cease and desist" did our pilfering of high explosives stop. It put an end to the dangerous adventures.

One of the disadvantages to being permanent bunker guards was the inherent responsibility to care for the physical needs of the firebase. Along with building bunkers, stringing wire, and policing up the endless numbers of cigarette butts, came the dreaded "shit-burning detail." The three-hole latrine was in almost constant use. Human waste needed to be burned daily. Obviously we had no flush facilities, and moving the outhouse every time a hole got filled was impractical. To keep the latrine area as sanitary as possible, someone was assigned to "burn until ash" the offending human excrement each day. These soldiers were called “honey-dippers.” Everyone hated the awful offal. Squad leaders and junior NCOs were not excused from the very undesirable duty.

Under each of the three outhouse seats was a 55-gallon drum half. When the steel drum was filled to a midway marker, it had to be dragged from the privy to the fire-point ten meters away. Diesel fuel was the combustible liquid of choice to sustain the fire in the otherwise inflammable material. Diesel did not explode like gasoline did when a match was applied. As a matter of fact, any remaining fire in a barrel could be extinguished by pouring diesel fuel over it.

Usually we soaked a wad of toilet paper in the diesel fuel as a fire starter. Once the barrel's contents were burning, it was necessary to stir the mixture to keep the fuel and feces from separating. If the diesel was allowed to float on top it simply burned away, leaving the heavier waste material untouched on the bottom. We used a six-foot-long 2 X 2-inch piece of lumber for the stirring procedure. Like a witch mixing a brew over her cauldron, the unlucky detailee stood amid the stinking oily black smoke and hovering flies while blending the contents.

During one of my turns at performing this unpleasant honey-dipping duty, the fire in one of the barrels had nearly gone out. The contents of the container had not yet been burned. I picked up the empty five-gallon army fuel can and trudged over to the fuel dump for a refill. Each of the different fuels at the dump were contained in identical looking olive-drab, 55-gallon drums. Although I should have taken the time to read the yellow stenciled lettering on the side of the drum, I didn't. I had been pumping out of this same barrel all day—I thought. To read the labeling again would surely be a waste of time.

Besides, the little hand pump was still resting on top of the drum right where I left it.

I spun the cap off my five-gallon can and inserted the long rubber hose that was attached to the pump. By pushing and pulling the pump handle 72 times (it took exactly that same number every time) I filled the can. Without bothering to look at or smell the contents, I spun the lid back on the can and lugged the container over to the fire-point.

Not suspecting that my can held anything except diesel fuel, I twisted the cap off and proceeded to pour five gallons of highly volatile gasoline on the small fire. Just a thimble full of gasoline will create an impressive explosive fireball. As one can imagine, my little barrel-fire didn't stay small very long. The highly combustible gasoline instantaneously exploded, sending a giant orange fireball rolling skyward.

The explosion blew me onto my back. I couldn’t see or feel anything but fire all around me. I knew that I had to get out of the blaze immediately or I would suck the fire into my lungs. Quickly squeezing my eyes shut, to protect them from the searing heat, I began rolling down the hillside, and hopefully, out of the blaze.

I could feel my hair burning, and I frantically flailed at my face and head with my bare hands. The smell—I could remember the same smell from Hamburger Hill, but this time it was me. Nearby soldiers began yelling as they ran to me. Soon other hands yanked at my clothing. Friends were rolling me in the dirt.

Doc Wursten at some point joined my rescuers. He placed his cool hands against my hot face and calmly asked me to open my eyes. I couldn't. The melted hair of my upper and lower eyelashes had fused together, and they required the medic's assistance to be parted. My entire body quivered uncontrollably, but I held back my screams of panic. Fear is a great painkiller; it subdued the painful sting as Doc's fingers gently began to separate the tender flesh.

"I can't see, Doc!"

My words caused the already rapidly palpitating heart muscle in my chest to increase its rhythm. Seeds of panic began to take root in my mind. My eyes felt dry, and the immediate area around them suddenly began to burn. The afternoon sunshine upon my face seemed unbearably hot.

I twisted my head away from Wursten's gentle hands several times as he attempted to raise my eyelids and assess the possible damage. He repeatedly pleaded with me to hold still, but pain and fear would not allow me, even for a moment, to simply lie motionless.

I'd told myself, long before, that I would never scream in pain or beg for medical attention if I were wounded, like most Americans did. Enemy soldiers seldom made more than groaning sounds even with the most painful of wounds. If they could take the pain, I told myself, so could I.

While lying in the dirt, I repeated the self-imposed promise to keep my mouth shut, keep calm, and let Doc do what he needed to do. Although the growing pain was extreme, it was bearable and certainly not as bad as being shot.

I was not totally sightless. I could see blurry, human shadows hovering above me. That was a good sign. I also knew I was getting all the medical attention available at the moment. Wursten soothingly reassured me that although my jungle fatigues had been burned away in several places, my body appeared to be OK.

"Your face and the back of your hands will be blistered as though they were badly sunburned," he calmly said.

He also told me that his biggest concern was for my eyes. For that reason he was sending me to the 18th Surg.

The pilot of an OH-6 light observation helicopter that landed about the time the ordeal began quickly fired it back up. Doc and the guys rushed me aboard. Fifteen minutes into the flight, I pulled loose one side of tape that held the gauze pads over my eyes. I hesitantly peered through the helicopter's side window at the luxuriant green jungle growth far below. In a few long seconds, I was able to bring the green blur into full focus. I was not blind.

A stretcher was waiting for me when I landed in the middle of the big red cross painted on the PSP pad at the 18th Surgical Hospital. I was fully capable of walking, but the two hospital orderlies firmly instructed me to lie on the canvas litter anyway. Once inside operating room number 2, they allowed me to sit in a straight hard-backed wooden chair. I smelled jasmine as the perfumed female nurse began to gently remove the bandage. She smelled great to me. Considering where I had come from and what I was doing when the accident happened, I imagine the nurse could smell me too. Maybe my "perfume" was not quite so pleasant.

A doctor, whom I remembered from my lengthy malaria visit several months earlier, gave my eyes a complete examination. He began by shining a small flashlight on the pupils of each eye. He ended with my reading the eye chart. The prognosis was good the doctor announced; the prospect of full recovery was better than 90 percent.

"As a matter of fact" he said, "after a night's observation here in the hospital, you should be able to return to your unit."

He managed to give me the good news and the bad news all in one breath. The nurse gave me some burn ointment for my face and hands; she then led me to the same rubber bubble I occupied on my previous stay. Before she left me, she placed a towel across my arm and a bar of disinfectant soap in my hands.

She said, "Do us all a favor; hit the shower!"

I got the first look at myself while standing in front of a full length mirror outside the shower building. My dark brown eyebrows and eyelashes were gone, burnt off. Only the patches of hair on my head that had been especially dirty and matted down had survived the fire. The rest, curlicued and crisp, looked like steel wool and hugged my reddened scalp. My eyes were bloodshot and swollen. The sickening smell of burnt hair seemed even stronger as I stood there trying to believe the guy in the glass was really me.

Tiny water blisters had sprung up all over my face and hands, giving me a ruddy red complexion. The damage was minor really, nothing that wouldn't heal in, say . . . THREE MONTHS. This sucked.

*A week later I was able to pull long strips of dead skin from the burned areas. I was not scarred, but it made me look like a red zebra.*

Although I reveled at the thought of sleeping all night on a soft mattress, between clean white sheets, the morning's sun found me tossing restlessly. Yes, my face and hands burned with pain, but the real culprit was the bed. I wondered how any healthy person could possibly sleep on such a soft and confining piece of furniture.

When the base barber shop opened at 0900, the four little Vietnamese barbers found me sitting at their front door. They were kind and didn't make fun of me, at least in English. For 65 cents, in Military Payment Certificates, I got a closely cropped, Marine-style haircut. I chose to skip the full scalp and body massage that customarily accompanied a haircut. My burnt body wasn't in the mood.

At noon, I reluctantly reported to the Alpha Company orderly room. A PFC clerk (sometimes called a Remington Raider) looked at me funny, but didn't ask. He assigned me space aboard a Chinook for its 1400 hours liftoff to Airborne. I ate a lunch of potato chips and ice cream at the mess hall and endured more looks. I then hightailed it up to the landing pad. For a full 45 minutes I stood on the heavily oiled landing pad, in an afternoon rain squall, waiting for the weather to break so the chopper could lift off. The REMFs flying the bird wouldn't even let me inside until we were cleared for takeoff. I think they were afraid of catching something from me.

I was greeted by my "unusually" friendly buddies upon my arrival back at the firebase. I soon found out why they were so happy to see me. The shit burning detail had not been completed. The guys were about to draw straws for the dubious honor of finishing it. Now that I was back, they were all breathing heavy sighs of relief. They didn’t care how I looked as long as I could stir.

Late that evening, after I’d completed the burning task, I got some more bad news. At the squad leaders briefing Captain Knight told us some Army engineers were going to build another three-hole privy in the morning. The location he selected was on the edge of the helicopter landing pad right next to my bunker. The good captain had made some really brilliant decisions during his time with us, but this was not one of them. On a warm day the stench from these contraptions was overwhelming. Now he planned to build one next to where I lived? No way! My devious mind began planning a counterattack before the holes had even been cut in the latrine bench.

Within a week of the new head's construction, my plans for its demise had not only been formulated, but the means for its annihilation had been assembled. I had removed the guts (spring assembly) of an M-16 magazine. Into the small void, I then crammed a quarter pound of C4 high explosive that I pilfered from the ammo dump. From previous experience I knew this would work very nicely.

Approaching zero hour on the target day, I made sure I was the last one to use the new structure before the concertina wire was pulled shut in preparation for the night. When everyone was occupied with other duties and paying no attention to me, I inserted an electrical blasting cap into my bomb. I dropped the explosive between my legs down into the center hole of the privy. It plopped into the lumpy, foul-smelling excrement. Casually strolling back to the bunker, I unraveled and kicked dirt over the wire that would carry the electrical charge to the detonator. I hid the firing device under a sandbag next to the bunker. My preparation was complete.

The night was very warm and cloudless. Everyone elected to either sleep on top of the bunker or on the ground next to the combat trench. I threw my rifle and helmet up on the bunker's top, near the edge, early in the evening, thereby reserving my sleeping spot. For my plan to successfully work, I had to get at the firing device during the noise and confusion of a mad-minute.

I generally slept so lightly that the squelch breaking on the bunker's radio would not escape my attention. So at 0343 I awakened as word came from the command bunker to begin the first mad-minute. I grabbed my rifle and jumped to the ground before the first shot was fired. The four of us, who had elected to participate in the mad-minute, chewed up the jungle as we randomly cut lose with our M-16s and M-79s. Fifteen seconds into the spectacle, I reached under the special sandbag and retrieved the handheld clacker. In my panic to get the deed over with before someone discovered what I was doing, I frantically squeezed the device several times, but nothing happened. Immediately I realized that I had not released the safety. I felt stupid for having forgotten something so basic.

While firing my third full magazine on rock and roll, my free thumb flipped the metal safety clasp off the device. That allowed the spring-loaded handle to extend. Deceptively covering my real intentions with the fire-spitting M-16, I mashed down the handle of the firing device. *KAA-WHAM!* Wow. I hadn't expected the enormity of the explosion. Submerged in the confined space of the can, the explosion seemed to intensify. The concussion of the bomb's blast was immediately followed by a heavy downpour of human waste. For a full 15 seconds, chunks of constipation and tiny droplets of diarrhea and urine rained from the sky.

At the first signs of the unexpected surprise, I dived head-first through the bunker entryway and was able to avoid most of the falling excrement. My sleeping buddies, completely unaware of what was happening, were not lucky enough to avoid the downfall. They were rudely awakened by a putrid blanket of sticky brown rain. It completely coated them and all of their equipment.

I never ever admitted any involvement with the incident. To do so would have invited "get even" reprisals from half a dozen enraged soldiers who "couldn't take a joke."

For the next week, every time it rained, everyone in my squad stripped and stood in the downpour. The men and the area around the bunker were eventually washed clean by the monsoon's long heavy rain. I am happy to report that when the latrine was later rebuilt, it was constructed in a more suitable and hospitable location. Mission accomplished.

# CHAPTER 24

# FNGS

By mid-July, we were again performing regular day and all-night patrols out of Firebase Airborne into the surrounding jungle. Thankfully, contact with Sir Charles rarely involved more than just calling in artillery on his occasional sniper fire. Our limited engagements with him were due primarily to the heavy rains which pounded us day and night. Neither we nor the gooks were anxious to get very far from the cover of our hootches and bunkers.

NVA resupplies coming down the muddy Ho Chi Minh trail slowed to a trickle. Luke the gook was not willing to expend his much needed reserves—especially food—unnecessarily. Our own supply system had also nearly stopped. Resupply helicopters did not fly much during the very heavy rains of the monsoon season. Consequently, we had to make do with what we had. Firebase Airborne made the monsoon much more survivable, however, than living among the green leaves.

The company grew back to nearly three-quarters strength due to the sudden influx of FNGs from back in the world. Captain Knight organized a new second squad in our platoon, and Lieutenant Egginton made Tony Salvetti the squad leader.

My squad increased to nine with the addition of two new bodies, Melaney and Valdez. Both of the new guys were "Instant NCOs." After basic and advanced specialty training were completed back in the states, they attended a special 19-week training course. It was supposed to prepare them for combat leadership in Vietnam. Upon graduation, the Army promoted them to Sergeants (E-5) and shipped them off to the war. Hard-core grunts did not automatically accept soldiers promoted due to a few weeks of stateside schooling. They had to prove they could do the job.

The vast majority of enlisted infantrymen earned their rank the hard way, gradual promotion from within the enlisted ranks. They disrespectfully called school NCOs "Instant NCOs," or "Shake-N-Bakes." The funny thing was, lieutenants earned their bars almost the same way, by attending Officer Candidate School. No one questioned their right to the rank. Most of the officers had four years of college before military service began; that was the difference in our respect for their authority, I suppose.

At first, I believed that the assignment of two sergeants to my squad would result in my demotion as its leader. Captain Knight quickly said otherwise. During a company leadership briefing, he told the squad leaders that the battalion commander had given him nine Shake-N-Bakes. Alpha's depleted noncommissioned ranks compared poorly to other fully staffed sister units. "Now at least," he said, "we look good on paper." The captain cited me "as an example" when he explained how he intended to use the new non-comms in the company.

"I realize it's a bit unusual, but Sergeant Rock will continue to lead the first squad in Lieutenant Egginton's platoon. Even though he is a Spec. 4, the new NCOs will be responsible to him. I would expect that he will assign them as fire-team leaders and give them the practical OJT (on the job) training necessary to make them good combat leaders. That way they can quickly assume leadership in other squads."

Tony asked how the addition of the new sergeants would affect our chances of getting promoted. Since he already had the squad leader job, he wanted the money also. So did I. The captain answered that he would continue to push for our advancement. I thought his reply was rather vague, and brief, but no one else pressed for details, so neither did I.

After the briefing, Staff Sergeant Wardle, who was just back to us after recuperating from his leg wound, pulled Tony and me aside during a sandbagging detail. He explained the facts. He made it perfectly clear that our chances of earning a sergeant's pay was almost nonexistent. With the company back at full strength E-5- wise, no promotion slots would be available.

"Sergeant Rock," Wardle said, "ya gotta think like the brass. Yer squad's already got more sergeants than is authorized. Ain't no way they're gonna promote ya and have three E-5s in one squad. Sorry, but that's the facts. We desperately need you and Salvetti as leaders. Just wish we could give ya the grade ta go along with the responsibility."

There was a tremendous temptation to blame the Shake-N-Bakes, Melaney and Valdez, for what was happening, but I knew it really wasn't their fault. They were just taking advantage of opportunities that came their way, just as I would have done. There was no master plan to give me the shaft. After thinking it over, my grand conclusion was, "What the heck." The Army was not going to be my career anyway. In fact, I had less than a year of my two-year draftee enlistment obligation left to serve. Most important of all, if I could survive the next four months in Nam, the last six months back in the States would be pure coasting time. If, after my two years was up and I got out of "this man's Army" as either an E-4 or E-5, it really made little difference to anyone. There would be no civilian job résumés requiring combat leadership skills as a priority.

On the 19th of July, Wilson and West arrived back in the field. It was good to see that they suffered no permanent damage from their encounter with the gook claymore. I talked Lieutenant Egginton into assigning them both to my squad. He also gave me two more brand new troops, Morris and Goldstien. Morris wore peace beads around his neck. From the way he spoke, my first impression was that he must have been a "flower child" back in the world. He was from Tulsa, Oklahoma—not your typical hippie city. Goldstien hailed from University City, Missouri. It was near Saint Louis, he told me. He appeared to be a straight arrow. My squad was now bulging with 13 soldiers, mostly new guys. It was the largest squad in the battalion.

No sooner had I assigned the new arrivals to bunkers, and they'd gotten their rucksacks unpacked, than Lieutenant Egginton sent word around: "Saddle up; the platoon is moving out." Doc was the bearer of the bad news. He said we were going to set up a tiger near where the gooks had ambushed our platoon a month earlier.

An hour before sundown we climbed off Airborne's hill and slipped through the razor wire. We were on the far side of the firebase from our intended ambush location. Hopefully it would confuse the gooks, who were undoubtedly watching us from somewhere up on the hillside. We deliberately and aimlessly wandered around the mountain until an hour after dark. Egginton then took us straight to our destination.

Goldstien was with me in rear security. He was having a hard time keeping up with the 39-man column. I had to prod him along or we would have lost contact and been left behind. And I wasn't about to be left behind, not in the A Shau Valley. The FNG was sweating profusely and wheezed noisily every time he tried to breathe through his nose. I feared that he might collapse from exhaustion. The ruck he was carrying looked very heavy for a simple overnight ambush. I realized that I should have inspected his load before we passed through the concertina. Luckily, this hump was not going to be a long one, and the temperature was a mild 85 degrees.

We set our tiger on the uphill side of the trail leading to the enemy-controlled Co Pong and backed into the jungle until we were well hidden. No Claymores—the jungle was too thick. Squad- or platoon-sized ambushes had been set up every night for the previous month somewhere on the mountain. They had made no contact with the enemy. I believed this night would be no different from the others, so I brought my new nine-volt pocket transistor radio along. This night was going to be special, and I did not want to miss the action 238,857 miles away. Astronauts from the U.S. were about to land on the moon for the first time. I wanted to hear their live transmissions from the lunar surface.

Right after my first turn at standing guard, before attempting to catch some Z's, I turned on the radio and listened through the earpiece. The Beatles were singing "Get Back." It was the number-one hit on the pop charts back in the world. When the song was over, the military disk jockey read a two-minute message on how to protect oneself from the invisible enemy, venereal disease. I then listened while Neil Armstrong walked and talked on the moon. Lying on my back in the mud of the A Shau Valley, I tried to imagine what it must be like walking on the lunar surface so far away from Vietnam.

It was Sir Winston Churchill who said, "Nothing in life is so exhilarating as to be shot at without results." Since I had experienced that feeling often, I'll vouch for the truth of his statement. Nevertheless, as I lay there, focused on the silver ball high above me, I decided that making the first footprints in moon dust must be a close second.

Just as I had suspected, there was no gook movement during the night. Swarming mosquitoes and mud, slicker than grease, kept Charles at home. At daybreak we reversed our order of march and headed straight back for Airborne. I took point because I could not rely on any of the new guys just yet. Anything they did, including nothing, could get me shot. I brought West up to walk slack and cover my tail.

All the way back to the firebase, I could hear Goldstien's labored breathing as he struggled with his heavy pack. When we were safely back at my bunker, and before any of the guys could drop their rucks, I called for a rucksack inspection. A couple of the new guys complained about stateside harassment, but I was in no mood to listen and they quickly complied.

Rucksacks belonging to the old timers were all "squared away." However, several of the new arrivals, it became obvious, had no idea how to pack for a tiger, or what to carry. For our one-night ambush, Goldstien had packed three paperback books, a heavy rubber rain suit, a toothbrush and paste, two extra pairs of socks, two C-ration meals and several Playboy magazines. All this "personal" baggage was in addition to the ordnance I assigned him to carry before our departure.

What more than compensated for Goldstien's overload was what Sergeant Valdez had not carried. Except for a fist-sized bag of marijuana, he carried almost nothing. To a few grunts, even old-timers, almost anything that was heavy, including ammunition and water, was "unnecessary." Sometimes on long boring patrols when weight became unbearable, they could easily toss a few feet of linked machine gun ammo into a stream. Maybe they would hide a smoke grenade under some brush. After this happened several times, their packs would be much lighter.

Before long or difficult humps, we always "cleaned house" of "expendables." If we were not coming back, we removed toothbrushes, combs, letters, excess toilet paper, and books from our rucks and destroyed them all. Food, water, and ammunition were the top three priorities. It always seemed like the light stuff was unnecessary while anything heavy was mandatory. The Shake-N-Bake Valdez had pushed the limit. I laid down the law, using some motivational language I had learned in Vietnam. There was no doubt about what would happen if ever again I discovered he had less than a basic load.

Another of the sergeant's screw-ups was carrying grass on an ambush. As had been common practice of the day, I told Valdez it was "no big deal" if he smoked a little marijuana inside the wire during the day. The reality was, I couldn't put my hand in the river and stop the surging flood of soldiers "escaping" the war. But, I warned him, if I ever caught him "getting mellow" on guard or on a tiger, I'd get him busted.

"I am not going to risk my neck or anybody else's so some FNG Head can groove; dig it?"

"Yeah," he responded in a smart-alecky drawl.

From the tone of his voice and the look in his eye, I concluded he was never going to be my best friend. I undoubtedly ticked him off. A lowlife Spec. 4 was raking him over the coals, and he could do nothing about it. At the time, I really didn't care what he thought. Each time I looked at the smirk on his face, I just got hotter.

## CHAPTER 25

# THE MISSION

"The lieutenant wants to see Sergeant Rock."

"The lieutenant wants to see Sergeant Rock."

"The lieutenant wants to see Sergeant Rock."

I heard my name and the message noisily repeated as they passed it man to man down the column. It was noon on the second day of a platoon-size three-day recon patrol. We were about four klicks northwest of Firebase Airborne. Our feet were soaked from following a small creek down a jungle-clogged mountain draw. Wet feet didn't matter—it was raining anyway. The creek provided the only passage through the chaos of vines, so we followed it.

"Hey Sergeant Rock: the lieutenant . . ."

"Yeah, yeah, I heard already."

I was abrupt with Muskrat, but I was annoyed at the noise the message was causing. After all, we were in the middle of "Indian territory," a long way from the protection of the Cavalry. It seemed to me that the guys were shouting as loudly as a ladies' temperance committee at the swinging door of a saloon. Maybe that's a bit of an exaggeration, but any sound at all was an announcement to the enemy: "Here we are, come and get us!"

Getting down to the lieutenant was difficult. Carefully holding on to vines and other undergrowth, I slipped as quickly and as quietly as possible the 35 meters down the rocky creek bed to Egginton.

"Sergeant Rock, I just got a call on the radio from the captain. Something big is up, and you're in the middle of it. Three Hueys are on their way to extract you and your squad. They wouldn't even wait long enough for us to find a clearing to land the birds. The old man gave me an ETA of zero-five. You are all going to be extracted by jungle penetrator. Hustle back and inform your men. When you hear the birds, pop a yellow smoke. The other two squads will provide security while you're extracted. Now get moving!"

I needed a million questions answered, but the urgency in the lieutenant's voice suggested I should move quickly. I did an about-face in the creek bottom and skedaddled back to my squad as fast as my heavy pack and the slippery footing would allow. Noise was no longer a consideration. The hovering helicopters would do an excellent job of pinpointing our exact location to Sir Charles. Every soldier I passed in the column asked, "What's up?"

No sooner had I relayed the meager instructions to my squad than the rhythmic beat of our transport's rotor blades echoed down the deep canyon. Sergeant Melaney threw a smoke into the thick foliage and we waited. Dense yellow gas discharged from the canister for about 30 seconds. In the jungle's still, humid air, the smoke just spread over the ground. I asked for another smoke. Three of my men chucked canisters into the jungle. All three grenades gushed out their bright yellow smoke, creating a dense cloud that completely engulfed us. I could see no farther than a few meters away. I hoped that enough of the yellow would filter up through the vegetation's heavy umbrella so the choppers could see us.

My mind was still racing in circles. What special assignment awaited us? Why the urgency? What was our destination? Choppers were pulling the entire squad out with me; maybe we screwed up somewhere. Where? What was going on? Several of the guys, including me, were coughing and gagging in the thick acrid smoke. A blast of fresh cool air rushed passed me. The smoke began to swirl and dissipate as the first of the three choppers hovered just above the jungle treetops. A penetrator device slowly descended through the labyrinth of tree branches and vines until it reached us on the ground. Bo Hansen and I unfolded the three seats, which gave the contraption the appearance of a large yellow boat anchor. Sergeant Valdez was the first to ascend. We laid his rucksack across two of the seats, and he straddled the third. The steel cable connecting the derriere-bruiser with the hovering aircraft suddenly went taut, and the sarge was on his way. The wide-eyed soldier swung and spun around as he brushed against the wet triple-canopy growth. After only a minute or so, the door gunner pulled him into the open stomach of the steel bird.

When all 12 of my men were safely aboard the three hovering choppers, I straddled the last sky hook. The steel cable hoisted me out of the muddy green jungle. Safely aboard, I leaned back against my wet rucksack and relaxed just a little. From my vantage point on the cool metal floor of the Huey, I looked down to where 22 other buddies were still earth-bound. Although I had just left them and knew they were there, I could see no trace of their existence from the air.

The trio of helicopters gained altitude and air speed. One of the curious door gunners leaned over and shouted at me above the whine of the engines.

"What's the big rush, Sarge? What's happening?"

I remembered asking myself those same questions a half hour earlier. I still had no answers. I hollered back that his guess was as good as mine. I'd been hoping to get some answers from the aircrew. After hearing the gunner's question, I knew it would be a waste of time to even ask.

We flew northeast, completely bypassing Firebase Airborne. That eliminated my first destination guess. Twenty-five klicks later, the flat brushy terrain began to look familiar. We were heading for Camp Evans.

High above the base camp's landing pad, I could see that the area was empty of soldiers, except for one lone jeep and its driver. Questions still swirled in my brain. I was relieved, however, to find that we would not be rappelling into the middle of a jungle firefight somewhere.

When the two lead choppers landed, the jeep driver ran to the unloading ground-pounders and briefly questioned each group. He then returned to his vehicle and waited for my bird to settle on the oiled dirt. As quickly as the skids had touched down, the driver was at my aircraft's open door yelling for "Spec. 4 Olson!"

After identifying myself to the starched and pressed REMF, he told me that I should send my squad to chow. He then asked me to come with him in the jeep. Like everyone else I had talked to in the previous hour, the urgency was obvious. I complied with his request without first insisting on answers.

As soon as I slid myself onto the wet canvas seat of the jeep, we roared off toward the interior of the large Army facility. For a little more than a mile we slipped and slid on the wet muddy road. The driver kept the throttle mashed to the floorboards.

I recognized the Camp Evans command post as our vehicle's squealing breaks announced the stop. Enlisted grunts stayed away from the huge sandbagged bunker complex. That was where many "big cheese" officers worked. When I saw two senior officers climbing the bunker's wooden steps, I quickly wiped the mud from the toes of my jungle boots by sliding them up and down the backs of my pant legs. Completely ignoring the drizzle that was beginning again, they quickly approached me. I recognized Lieutenant Colonel Thompson, my battalion commander, just before he turned and introduced me to the other officer.

"Colonel Zanone, this is Specialist Olson, the squad leader I told you about. He'll be one of the leads on this mission."

I snapped to attention and extended my sharpest Stateside salute. Here I was, fresh from the field, muddy from helmet to foot (except for the toes of my boots.) My uncut hair was touching my ears. I hadn't shaved in three days, and I was being presented to one of the highest ranking officers in the entire camp. I was greatly intimidated just being in their presence.

I had never been the attention of such high-powered officers. The 'system' intimidated us lowlife enlisted grunts into respecting senior officers as if they were gods. I wasn't sure what my next move should be. I held my salute until both of the meticulously dressed Army commanders had returned it, and then stood at attention. In an informal voice Colonel Zanone invited me to "Be at ease, son." Something big was going on; they had extracted me from my combat AO in the jungle and had given me the highest of priorities. I had even just heard my name mentioned in the same sentence with "the mission," and the colonel wanted me to be at ease? Who was he kidding! What was going on?

"Specialist," the colonel began, "you're probably wondering what's going on?"

"Yes, sir," I replied.

"Come into the Command Post. The briefing is in progress."

Down inside the massive steel and sand-bagged bunker, we passed through a room loaded with operational radios and other electronic gear unfamiliar to me. Even at only five foot ten I had to duck as we passed through the heavy wooden-beamed doorway that led into the conference room.

Eight, 4X4 foot acetate-covered terrain maps, all but one draped with black nylon, were tacked to portable easels in the center of the bunker's meeting room. Eighteen or twenty officers already occupied the room; one of them was a brigadier general. A captain, standing next to the uncovered map, continued with his briefing as if he wasn't aware of our entering.

Colonel Zanone ushered me into a back corner of the room and directed me toward a grey metal folding chair. He seated me next to another young GI who was dressed like me, in filthy jungle fatigues. The soldier looked up as I slid into the chair. We gave each other little nods of recognition, one enlisted man to another, in a room full of brass. I didn't see any of the newly issued rank pins on his collar, but I decided he was undoubtedly a squad leader like me. There was no air-conditioning in the room, but small oscillating fans mounted high in the four corners kept the blue cigarette smoke swirling.

Senior officers sat in the front chairs by order of their rank—the general first, of course. He was accompanied by a few colonels. The second row consisted of several majors and a few captains. Next in order sat a whole bunch of young lieutenants. They were constantly leaning forward and whispering little tidbits of wisdom into their superiors' ears. NCOs were a little less formal about where they sat; some stood around the bunker's sandbagged walls. Other odds and ends low-level personnel, like the other squad leader and me, sat in the very back.

For almost 45 minutes I listened as the captain, who turned out to be an intelligence officer, warned the general (who was about the only one who could see any details on the small maps) of an impending NVA ground attack against good ol' Camp Evans. Periodically he tapped the map with his wooden pointer. Jungles were colored in light and dark green. Lowlands and sand dunes were mostly white. The DMZ and the Laotian border were a bold pink. The map was covered with tightly packed contour lines wherever the terrain was steep. Around Camp Evans the contour lines were widely spaced. Black and red grease-pencil arrows were all over the place. The captain briefed us blandly that one thousand North Vietnamese Army regulars were massing in the mountains to attack us that night.

"We expect a fierce human siege, so the entire camp will be placed on one hundred percent alert from sundown to sun up" he said. "All cooks, clerks, and supply personnel will be issued weapons and sent to the perimeter bunker line." For some of these REMFs, it would be the first time they had laid hands on a weapon since arriving in Nam. They had never even heard an M-16 fired in anger.

The captain said (and this is where my part began) that they would position two reinforced infantry squads to ambush the advancing enemy's lead element. The exploding claymores would alert the base of the imminent attack. After the ambush had been initiated, we would rapidly retreat into the camp's wire and bunker defenses according to the plan. "Apple Pie" was the password we were supposed to yell as we ran toward the bunker line. If all went well, the inexperienced REMFs would not shoot us when we tried to enter.

Being a potential target for soldiers on both sides of the war gave me some ownership of the details. The plan seemed to me like it needed a little work.

After the briefing, the other squad leader, Sergeant Campos, and I accompanied our battalion commander to his waiting helicopter. We donned white communications helmets and plugged them into the intercom system. As we lifted off, the colonel adjusted the speaker on his helmet and told us that his boss, Colonel Zanone, had demanded the two best squads in the battalion for this special mission. In reality, most of the infantrymen on my team were so new that I couldn't believe we were the best. I nodded in appreciation of the compliment, however; so did Campos. What his boss most likely really said was, "Find me a couple of squads to sacrifice at the two oncoming NVA regiments."

Soon we were several klicks from Evans, flying along one of the two routes they expected the enemy would use. I was very familiar with the area, having worked in the Phong Dien AO so often. Pointing the way to the pilot, I guided us to a kilometer-long ravine that paralleled Route 1. If the gooks followed the Song O Lau River out of the mountains, I figured they would leave it at the ravine. They could then follow the gulch and be out of the defenders' line of sight most of the way to their objective, Camp Evans.

I selected a particular tree-covered slope that I had been on before. From the hillside we would have an elevated view of the enemy's path. The colonel agreed that the hundred-meter-wide gulch could easily conceal the advancing attackers. He readily seconded my ambush location. After asking several pointed questions about my shoot and scoot plan, he placed a black X on his map and assured me that he would coordinate our position with Camp Evans artillery.

"Good job, this plan is all set," he said.

Following my instructions, we then flew to a small water buffalo-cart road that was on the opposite side of Evans. It was generally quite impassable during the wet season. The map identified the muddy route as Communal Road 601. It began as a foot path in the same mountain canyon the Song O Lau emptied from, eight klicks away. Because the little road intersected Route 1, just a stone's throw from Camp Evans, I suggested that Campos should ambush it. We all concurred on that tiger site. The colonel put another grease pencil X on the map.

That evening at 2100 hours, my squad and six other ground-pounders who had been attached to us met a small convoy of vehicles. They were going to carry us part of the way to our destination. The three machine-gun-mounted jeeps and two three-quarter-ton trucks departed on schedule through the sandbagged front gates of the base. Ready or not, here we come.

The plan called for the convoy to quietly cruise up Route 1, without lights. At Colonel Thompson's signal from the lead gun-jeep, my squad would step off the moving vehicles and disappear into the night. Any advanced scouts watching the road would have no idea that we had separated from the trucks. The convoy would continue as if nothing had happened. I repeat, "That was the plan!"

When I was a small adventuresome child, I tried jumping from speeding bicycles, wagons pulled by bicycles, and once from the rear bumper of a moving car. All ended in catastrophe. The 10 MPH convoy was supposed to permit us a graceful exit; maybe this time would be different, I hoped.

The night was black and heavy with humidity, as they all were during the five rainiest months of the monsoons. The clouds were slowly rolling overhead but had not yet ruptured to allow the suspended torrents of water to spill out. After what seemed to be an infinitely long ride, I spotted the soft red glow of the colonel's pen light. It was our signal to disembark.

We stepped from the tailgates, bumpers, and running-boards into the blackness that awaited us. Our attempts to estimate vehicle speed based on the hum of their engines was a total failure. Almost instantly all 19 of us went sprawling all over the newly paved asphalt road. We rolled and slid on the hard pavement. Our road-rashed bodies created soft little speed bumps between the vehicles. To anyone close by it certainly was no secret where we had gotten off.

There were the reverberating *thunks* of our steel helmets as they bounced down the blacktop highway. There was rattling and screeching of M-60s as they slid down the road minus their operators. Our dropped plastic M-16s sounded as though someone had thrown a box of Tonka toys from a passing supply truck. Anyone within a klick could have easily heard our grunts, groans, and cursing. Only quick scrambling prevented any of us from being run over by the following vehicles in our little convoy. Goldstien's rifle did not survive the ordeal. One of the trucks smashed it before he could pull it out of the way. He had to continue the mission without a weapon. The first part of our tiger had proven to be a complete disaster. I wondered if that was an omen.

We gently caressed our skinned elbows and bleeding knees and began walking off the bruises. There was neither time nor light enough to give them proper medical attention. We had a long way to go, and we had to be in place before the North Vietnamese Army found us first. I took a few words of abuse for “my stupid plan,” but that came with the territory, I guess. More that once I had voiced the negative critiques of my dumb leaders, and would do it many more times, I was sure.

I reorganized everyone and we departed Route 1. Our first obstacle was some old, dry elephant grass. The tall, sharp-edged grass stood well over our heads. It created a hazardous and noisy barrier that we had to traverse. In the stillness of the night, any sound we made seemed amplified. The crackling of the dry grass, parched from past dry seasons, seemed to cry out into the night with each step we took. Muskrat was walking point; he had learned well the secret of walking in the noisy, dry environment. Each step he took in the thick vegetation was purposely twisted to the outside. That partially mashed the slender flat stems away from him. The men following then had a narrow path to follow. By not having to do what Muskrat did, the rest of us could avoid the painful grass cuts.

The next obstacle was the Song O Lau. We encountered it about a half an hour later. We crept parallel with its banks for several hundred meters until we found a place where we could safely cross. Although the river was smooth and gentle, generally only armpit deep, there were many deceptively deep holes. Even during daylight hours fording the river was tricky.

When Muskrat took his first step off the slippery grass bank into the warm black water, it completely and almost silently swallowed him. He just disappeared. We anxiously watched for about five seconds for his reappearance, but the river’s surface just grew calm.

”Nuts! Muskrat’s going to drown again!” I whispered to myself.

Sergeant Valdez, walking second, spun around and whispered, "I can't swim!" Hansen, behind him, exclaimed the same thing. Coincidentally, none of the first four soldiers knew how to swim. Since I was fifth in line and a competent swimmer, I dropped my rifle in the grass, threw off my steel pot, and quickly unslung the claymore bag from around my neck. I took a deep breath and jumped feet first into the watery unknown.

Rapidly sinking to the bottom of the deep hole, I found my struggling friend. Muskrat was thrashing around in panic. He grabbed onto one of my wrists and kicked me in the stomach with his knee. I knocked his hand free and wrapped my arms around his struggling body. I turned him so he faced away and couldn't kick me in the groin. When I could feel the river bottom, I shoved Muskrat up to the surface. I then tried to reach the fresh air myself. Alarm set in when I realized that my rapid swimming strokes were not moving me toward the surface.

In my haste to get into the water, I had forgotten to drop two M-16 bandoleers. The 14 heavy magazines were still tied around my waist. I also had six hand grenades still in my pockets. Although the military had designed the ordnance to save our lives, it was having the reverse effect on Muskrat and me. I, however, had the advantage of being partially prepared when I entered the water with lungs full of air.

Muskrat descended again after momentarily having his head above water. I placed my hands against his butt and pushed him up once again. Then, kicking my legs free of the muck, I swam as powerfully as I could in the direction I remembered as the surface.

My jungle boots and the heavy equipment I carried were just too much to overcome. I quickly settled to the bottom of the river, never having reached the surface. Again I stopped my thrashing associate's descent. I shoved him for a third time to the surface. My own lungs were at the point of collapse. They burned from lack of oxygen. Alarm turned to panic. Momentarily forgetting Muskrat, I instinctively turned my efforts to self-preservation. I yanked at the tied bandoleer strings and dropped the ammo. The frags I still forgot. Squatting like a frog in the mud, I put my hands above my head and sprang upward paddling and kicking desperately with the last of my energy.

My head finally broke the stillness of the surface three feet above, and I sucked in the sweet air. During my momentary visit at the Song O Lau's surface, I managed to orient myself again. Submerging a second time next to Muskrat, I pushed him toward some tree roots that reached out into the river. My lungs burned again, but this time I knew how to get to the surface. On my trip up, Valdez and one of the attached guys grabbed me by the shirt. They yanked me onto the grassy bank next to the exhausted Muskrat.

While we rested, Mason stripped and slid into the water to recover our point-man's M-16 and my ammo. We were already short one weapon, and we couldn't afford to lose another. Between coughs Muskrat thanked me repeatedly for saving him. He reminded me that it was the second time he had almost drowned, and both times I had been his rescuer. After Muskrat had cleaned the mud from his glasses and dried them with a filthy shirttail, we were finally ready to move out again. Valdez found a safe crossing just 50 meters further up the river. This time our crossing was successful. On the far bank, I took map and compass readings. We were almost at the tiger site. It was 2330 hours, and we should have already been there. I hoped our luck in not meeting Sir Charles along the trail would hold a little longer.

I repeatedly reminded the men to "spread it out." Darkness, and possibly meeting two regiments of North Vietnamese, fostered a sense of overwhelming isolation in each of us. Against good judgment, we tended to bunch up. Closeness gave us a deceptive feeling of security, but actually it has just the opposite effect. Enemy soldiers were more likely to shoot or throw a grenade at a cluster of men than they were at individual human targets. Keeping five-meter intervals between the team members was difficult, but it improved survival odds.

Two hours after leaving the protection of the jeep-mounted .50 caliber machine guns, our little band finally slipped into the hiding place I had identified from the air. In the little stand of trees, 19 of us prepared to ambush a thousand heavily armed North Vietnamese soldiers.

We placed 15 claymores strategically along a hundred meters of the ravine floor. The men expertly aimed each mine to blow its deadly shrapnel waist high across the gully. We then carefully positioned our electrical detonating devices at each of the six overlooks we occupied, 20 meters up the hillside. I had several of the men place another seven claymores down a small animal trail on which we planned a strategic retreat. If all went well we'd blow them all at once as we backed away from the carnage we were about to bring on the lead NVA element. Once settled in our ambush, we listened to Camp Evans artillery pound some distant target, and waited.

No one talked, stirred, or smoked. All eyes concentrated on the blackness ahead. Fearing the pungent smell might alert our prey, we dared not even use insect repellant. Consequently, mosquitoes buzzed in our ears and eyes, and land leeches crawled over us. Only the sporadic rains gave us any relief from the bugs. Before my Vietnam tour was over I was going to be a full-fledged blood-brother to every crawling, buzzing, or undulating creature in the country.

Occasionally during the first few hours, unusual sounds came from the ambush area. Each time we nervously caressed the claymore firing devices. My plan was to allow the kill zone to fill with NVA, blow all 15 claymores in quick succession, and then quickly *didi mau* down the trail before the gooks knew what hit them. If no one fired his personal weapon the enemy would never be able to locate us, and our escape would be clean. Each of these first alerts proved negative. There was never anyone in the ravine. It was just rodent sounds that kept us jumpy, not the gook army. We continued to wait.

Tropical Vietnamese nights could chill a soldier to the bone, especially after lying for long motionless hours in the rain, muck, and 50-degree temperatures. Hours of wet immobility turned tired muscles stiff and sore, dulling mental alertness and reaction time. The dormancy of a soldier's gray matter could also cause him to imagine things that he wanted to see.

When the horizon finally began to show signs of the breaking dawn, and I thought we may have survived the dangerous night, I saw movement. In the early morning's rising vapor, I could see the blurry forms of soldiers slowly creeping single file through our ambushed ravine. My pulse quickened. I blinked my eyes and shook my head, trying to bring the shapes into focus. Is this what we had been waiting for all night or was I seeing things?

I looked at Melaney, sitting five feet to my right. Droopy-eyed, he stared down into the gully, totally oblivious to what was happening. What was wrong with him? It was like the emptiness of the night had hypnotized him. I opened my eyes as wide as possible and shook my head again. Soldiers that had appeared one by one disappeared again into the fog. Still not entirely sure about what I had seen, I slowly waved my hand to get Melaney's attention. He saw the movement and looked in my direction. I touched my eyes and pointed toward the gully. Shrugging my shoulders, I silently mouthed the question, 'Have you seen anything?' He shook his head and looked away. Sergeant Melaney was a sharp soldier and would be a squad leader soon, but in this situation I wanted a second opinion. On my left were two of the "attached" grunts. They were also watching the ravine, but they also showed no signs of excitement. I finally concluded that my brain was as numb as my legs were. My exhausted grey matter must have created the rifle-toting aberrations. Nonetheless, the pulse in my neck continued to throb until the full light of morning, when I knew we were past the critical period.

We were all pleased to see another day and the sun periodically filtering through thick early-morning clouds. The fact that we were seeing the sun again had not been a given when this little adventure began. The gook army would have to postpone any planned attack on Camp Evans for at least another 16 hours. Light was a definite adversary of the communist cause.

I told the grunts to quickly roll their claymores back in and stow them in their bags before our hump back to camp. Before departing, I physically searched the little gully. The only footprints in the morning dew were my own. It's been said that if an ambush is properly set, the enemy will never walk into it. Opportunities only come when you are unprepared.

We leisurely traversed the four klicks back to Evans. We were so excited that Charlie hadn't shown that the morning stroll down Route 1 was like a walk in the park. We were lucky this time. The jungle penetrator ride, the command briefing, and the convoy had all been for naught. Maybe military intelligence had just blown it this time.

I stood at attention that morning in the command bunker and reported to Colonel Zanone. He listened to my recitation of the night's activities and expressed appreciation for the courageous manner in which we had carried out the mission.

"It may be of interest for you and your men to know that this was not a false alarm. At 2100 hours last night, Delta Company intercepted approximately 500 NVA regulars attempting to pass their position near the foot of the mountains. Yours was not the only ambush out there. With many more of the infiltrators still to come down off the hill, Delta blew their claymores and one hell of a firefight followed. We dropped artillery on the enemy positions all night. This morning Charlie and Echo companies have joined the fight. The insurgents advance would have been down the Song O Lau. Your prediction about their route out of the mountains was 100 percent correct, Specialist. It's a good thing we could locate and interdict them before they reached your position. Knowing what we know now, you and your men wouldn't have stood a chance in hell of getting out of there."

For our "positive commitment" to his ambush, the colonel gave us the next 24 hours off. We slept.

# CHAPTER 26

# CO PONG

Before the Army could get a final body count from Delta's firefight, my squad was airlifted back to Airborne. I never did get an accurate report of the damage done—Spec. 4 squad leaders rank toward the bottom of the "need to know" list. Rumors circulated that many scores of gooks had "bought the farm."

Back at the firebase, amid a barrage of outgoing artillery, fellow grunts swarmed us. Everyone wanted to know what all the excitement had been about. Sketchy information received at the jungle outpost had the company believing my squad had just ambushed two regiments of NVA. Rumors of our heroics abounded. We loved the attention, but when the truth came out, it quickly knocked us from our towering ivory pedestals. We were soon relegated back to ordinary grunts.

When our turn came to listen, the guys told us of a near-tragic incident for first platoon that very morning. A 35-man team had been loaded aboard Hueys and flown halfway up the finger between Airborne and the peak of Co Pong. Since there was no landing zone in the area, the soldiers prepared themselves to rappel onto the crest of the ridge.

The first load went in successfully, and the six men took up defensive positions. However, just as the first two men rappelled from the second helicopter, several AKs opened up on the hovering bird. The pilot of the Huey put the ship into a steep dive down over the ridge. He headed straight back to the firebase to assess damage. Unknown to anyone in the aircraft, one of the repelling ground-pounders had not completed his egress to the jungle floor. Forty feet below, at the end of the rope, the frightened soldier clung to the nylon "thread" separating him from death. He was in deep serious trouble. The Huey's half-klick dash back to the landing pad was done in seconds, before the troops at Airborne discovered and could warn the aircrew about their unknown passenger.

Coming in fast and low over the firebase, the helicopter slammed the helpless soldier into the side of a sandbagged bunker.

The jolt disengaged him from the lifeline. Medics rushed to his aid. The soldier had broken a leg and an arm during his violent return to earth but was otherwise OK. The lucky grunt would now spend several months convalescing in the rear. He'd undoubtedly spend the rest of his infantry career in Vietnam pecking at a typewriter. When he got home he would have one heck of a story to tell.

The seven soldiers stranded up on the mountain, meanwhile, fought back with everything they had until gunships and artillery came to their aid. Under cover of the Cobras' fire, the soldiers retreated down the mountain and out of danger. Except for the broken bones, the platoon and chopper crew had managed to escape the potentially disastrous ambush.

An hour after our squad's arrival back at the firebase, the captain told us to pack it up. Battalion was ordering Alpha to take Co Pong. I knew it would happen sooner or later. The mountain was just too ominous to be left alone by us or the gooks. After first platoon's ambush, the eventual attack was moved forward. Gooks were on Co Pong right now; what better time to go get 'em? An artillery barrage began leveling a LZ on the ridge. The entire company was going to make a helicopter combat assault back onto it.

The huge mountain towering over the tiny firebase seemed to be a source of North Vietnamese strength. It was time to find out exactly what was up there. I wondered if we were getting ourselves into another Hamburger Hill situation. Everyone shared the terrible thought, though no one dared say the words. In complete agreement with Adolf Hitler's declaration, "Strength lies not in defense but in attack," we hurriedly prepared ourselves for the CA.

As often happened, our rush to prepare for the arriving birds was wasted effort. A sudden fierce rainstorm, driven by high winds, hit our little fortification with all its strength and fury. For two days we could do almost nothing except bail water from our bunkers. Wardle was certainly correct when months earlier he had told Lieutenant DeWitt and me that "We ain't seen nothin' yet."

Finally, on the third day, at 1300 hours they came: 20 Hueys, escorted by half a dozen loaded Cobra gunships. Dropping through a small hole in the clouds, the birds settled one at a time onto the helipad. The PSP prevented the choppers from sinking into the deep red mud. We had to duck against the powerful down draft of the swirling blades and rush aboard the aircraft as they settled to the ground.

At the first sign of choppers, the artillery guys began to "work out" with their 105 mm and 155 mm howitzer medium-range guns. The landing zone was being prepped to neutralize gook defenders or booby-traps. The clearing was so close that the projoes were just lobbed up the hill; we watched them all the way to detonation. My bird was the fifth to assault the LZ. Strafing Cobras accompanied it on each side, as were the first 10 ships loaded with their human invasion cargos. None of us received any incoming fire from the ground. The LZ was cold. As each slick settled through the thick green jungle, the tips of the rotor blades made *thwack, thwack, thwack* sounds as they clipped the surrounding vegetation. I understood why everyone nicknamed them choppers.

I directed my squad to the whiskey (west) side of the developing perimeter. We stood guard until the remaining 15 choppers were safely down. The company then slowly began to move single file up the ridge, following the well-beaten trail. First platoon was on point, and the third herd was in rear security. We in second platoon enjoyed the relative safety of being in the middle of the long green line.

We humped no more than a hundred meters when the concussion of a mighty claymore explosion ripped over me. Outgoing M-16 fire quickly followed the tremendous blast, as did the screams of the wounded. All shooting came from the front of the column. I led my squad approximately 15 meters to the left of the trail, where we guarded against a flank attack and waited for instructions. Salvetti was on the right side of the path with his men in the heavy cover. He called over to me, wanting to know what had happened. I had no answers.

The jungle was thicker than quills on a porcupine and much more dangerous. Following Wardle's instructions, we stayed put as flank security until Lieutenant Egginton arrived 10 minutes later with the news.

"First platoon got hit by a large Chi-Com claymore mine," he excitedly said. "Two are dead so far, but there may be more before the medevacs arrive. Move your men out another 20 meters until the dust-offs are safely away. Now do what I say; I ain't talkin' just to move the air around." The lieutenant knew we were in deep serious.

While coordinating our positions with the troops in front of us, I watched as five messed-up grunts were carried back down the trail toward the LZ where we had started. Covered with fresh red blood, they all looked dead to me. First platoon's leader, Lieutenant Van

Haften, and his RTO were among the five.

After the departure of the two hovering medevacs, we assembled back on the trail and began slowly pressing up the hill again. Although it was extremely hazardous, the trail was the only route to the peak of Co Pong. Chopping a parallel route through the thick wet jungle with machetes would have been impossible. The downslopes on each side of the ridge were steep and covered with slick mud. Attempting to traverse them would have resulted in even more casualties. If we diverted our attention to fighting the mountain, gook ambushes would be just that much more effective. It was a horrible choice to make, but battalion ordered that we take Co Pong, and following the trail up the ridge was the only real choice we had.

Just before dark, Charlie's command-detonated claymore hit first platoon again. The gooks had filled the homemade high-explosive mine with nails and broken glass. Immediately after the explosion several machine guns fired up the platoon for about 10 seconds. After the area was finally secured, the guys watched their two wounded get winched up through the jungle canopy in litter baskets by the waiting dust-offs. They were quickly flown back to Camp Evans.

Although we returned fire in each ambush, none of us saw anything to shoot at. Consequently there was very little chance we hit anyone. In each case the elusive gooks had simply concealed their claymores in trees. When we were within range, they remotely detonated the mines and ran down the trail on the opposite side of the hill. Our return fire just wasted lead. By the time artillery or Cobras got cranked up, there wasn't an enemy troop within half a klick of the area. Getting any gook body count would have been sheer luck on our part.

The company managed to move just 800 meters up the steep mountain on the first day. We organized our NDP on the ridge and hoped for a peaceful night. Our wishing was all in vain. The gooks may have slept, but the hungry hoards of blood- sucking mosquitoes did not.

Hour after hour during the endless night I was in mortal combat with the thick swarms of attacking tormentors. Perhaps it was their appetite for warm human blood, or the cold monsoon night that drove them to suicide. Whatever, they were willing to risk their lives to get it. Hundreds of the little bloodsuckers paid the supreme price. Each time I slapped my arm or neck and tried to brush away the bloated little vampires, irregular lines of smeared blood remained on my bare skin.

I lay on my back in the mountain's mud and wrapped my wet green boonie towel around the back of my neck. I flapped the ends of the towel across my face and neck and then tucked my hands under the small of my back. The position was fairly effective at keeping the irritating pests off, but breathing through the rain drenched towel was like sucking air out of a soda bottle. Each time I lifted my face protector to get a deep breath of air, I inhaled a dozen of the hovering, probing insects. I then sneezed and coughed until I exhaled or ingested them. I wanted to yell at the top of my lungs, "STOP, I CAN'T TAKE IT ANYMORE!" Periodically I checked the hands on my watch, hoping that somehow, magically, I would find them reading 0600. That's when the sun awoke from its long overnight nap and the tormentors would begin to dissipate.

I got some relief (or maybe it was just the distraction) when just before 0530 the lieutenant crept over to my position.

"How ya doing, Sergeant Rock?" he said softly.

"Okey dokey" I lied.

"The cussed mosquitoes are as heavy here as they were at my position up the hill," he said. "How about coming with me to check the line?"

I picked my rifle up from where it rested against a tree and grabbed a bandoleer of ammo.

"Lead the way."

There were 10 guard positions manned by the platoon. One third of the small oblong company perimeter was ours to defend. The three-man posts were 12 meters apart in the thick wet undergrowth. The probable avenues of attack were from up or down the trail. We were not responsible for either of those areas.

Lieutenant Egginton and I checked six positions and got negative situation reports from the guards before we approached the seventh. The Shake-N-Bake, Sergeant Valdez, was in charge of that position. The lieutenant shined his red filtered flashlight around the position. All three soldiers were fast asleep. Two of them were lying together covered by a poncho, protecting themselves from the attacking mosquitoes. The third, Valdez, was sitting up with his back to a tree. His head was flopped over to one side. Obviously, he was supposed to be standing watch. The new NCO's face and neck were almost black with swarms of the bloodsucking pests, but he was oblivious. The towel he had draped over his face now hung loosely over one shoulder. The butt of his M-16 lay on his lap, the flash-suppressor resting in the mud.

"What do you think I should do?" the lieutenant quietly asked as he stood looking down at the slumbering solider.

I was embarrassed and angry that the grunt sleeping on guard belonged to my squad. I had already figured, however, that of everyone in the squad, Valdez was the most likely to screw things up. Just a few weeks earlier he and I had gone the rounds because he took some grass on an ambush. Sergeant stripes, earned in school, would never make this guy a leader.

I told Lieutenant Egginton not to do anything. I recommended that we wait until daylight, less than 30 minutes away.

"Let the mosquitoes continue to work on him, he deserves it," I whispered. "I'll wake one of the other two guys to finish the guard shift."

"No," he answered, "I just got a great idea that will teach him a lesson. I need to get back to my radio and call the captain at the command post. Stand guard. I'll be back in five minutes."

While the lieutenant was gone, I quietly awakened West and Smith, the two under the poncho. They told me that the Instant NCO was in fact supposed to be standing guard at the position.

It took Egginton 10 minutes to get back to me, but upon his return he explained the delay.

"After getting permission from Captain Knight, I spread the word through the chain of command to expect a fire in the hole. OK, Rock," he continued, "throw this frag 20 meters over the hill. I'll grab our sleeping beauty if he tries to come up shooting."

A big grin spread across my face and I thought to myself, I can dig it. I began to realize what he was up to.

There was a gap in the vegetation large enough for me to safely throw the grenade. When the lieutenant was ready, I let it fly. Four seconds later, and from 20 meters down the steep slope, we heard the frags familiar *Ka-Whump!* We were immediately showered with a downpour of rainwater that had collected in the jungle leaves above us. Sergeant Valdez, however, just continued his beauty rest.

Lieutenant Egginton was furious that the soldier could sleep through a grenade explosion just a few meters from his guard position. He raised his muddy jungle boot and kicked the Shake-N-Bake hard in the thigh. Valdez, abruptly awakened from dreamland, yelled a string of profanities before he discovered who had kicked him.

The enraged officer looked over at me and made a quick sideways motion with his head. I took the hint. The lieutenant didn't want us around. I told West and Smith to follow me and we *didi maued* the area. Fifteen meters away and out of sight, we waited and listened as the lieutenant descriptively reprimanded the sergeant. The platoon leader's graphic expletives rudely greeted the rising morning sun. His language reminded me of basic training days.

At 0700 we began our snail-like trek up the mountain again. This time our platoon rotated to the front. We were next in this dangerous game. First platoon, the first day's leader, fell in to the rear of the column. The platoon plan called for us to change the point man every hour. No one individual would assume all the risk. We knew there were ambushes waiting. Each of us prayed that when the inevitable happened, we would be safely back in the column.

We were, in fact, hit three times by explosions during that day. Walking point equals claymore bait. Three of the guys in the platoon were savagely blown away. None of them had been in-country more than a month. Charlie wounded half a dozen more of us. Luckily no one in my squad was on point when the trail erupted. Almost mechanically, we cleared the area and flew our casualties out after each ambush. We each had jobs to do, and we held our emotions for another time.

For five days we climbed and fought up that bloody ridge. Two or three times a day we got ambushed, and I watched my friends die. Each time the medevacs came and flew away with the dead and the dying. Our repeated frustration at not being able to get even resulted in a high revenge factor among we who survived. Repeated confrontations with blood and body parts were not as able to bruise our callused hearts as they had been several months earlier.

On the morning of the last day it was again our turn to lead out. I walked point for the first hour, watching every tree and bush as far as I could see up the trail, looking for anything unusual. Each of my body's senses was on full alert. I acted professional, but I was scared to death.

On schedule, when the company took its first break, I rotated back to fifth. Minnie Martinez moved up to become point man. While sitting along the trail resting, we watched a resupply chopper hover overhead. The door gunner, realizing our difficulty, removed his "chicken plate" and threw it down onto the trail.

*Door-gunners often wore the heavy bulletproof upper body*

*shields and sat on folded flack jackets when flying over hostile country.*

Minnie picked up the fiberglass breastplate and strapped it over his chest and stomach before we moved out again. The heavy chicken plate was big for the little point man, but he hoped it would save his life. When the lieutenant whispered the word up the column to move out, we climbed back into our heavy waterlogged rucksacks. Minnie slowly and carefully began leading the hump.

We were nearing the crest of Co Pong and hoping for an airlift back to Airborne's safety. Suddenly Sir Charles detonated another claymore that he had hidden about head high in the fork of a tree 20 meters up the trail! Accompanying the blast this time were half a dozen AK-47s and Chinese-built light machine guns. I dove into the mud on the right side of the trail and began random suppressive fire as I looked for a target.

While I was slamming home my second magazine, several bullets smashed through a small tree just a foot in front of me. The deflected projectiles ricocheted past my head with a whine disproportionate to their size. They impacted into another tree behind me. Twenty-five meters up the trail, where the bullets had originated, I saw a gook as he rolled over in the bushes and took aim again. I needed to stop his next burst, so I quickly put three three-round bursts into the undergrowth and waited for movement. The jungle was alive with flying lead, but my target remained silent. While searching for another mark, I spotted Minnie lying on the trail.

*It's amazing what soldiers will do for each other during perilous times. Allegiance to one another is measured in terms far beyond that of mere friendship. Where intelligence and common sense mandate hiding in the mud among the bushes, the sight or cries of wounded buddies make us attempt the impossible. Maverick ideas cause us to defy common sense, or even orders, and do the unexpected (even to oneself.) Sometimes our most decisive decisions in life come with little or no thoughtful preparation. It was just this kind of mysterious loyalty that precipitated my next action.*

No longer frightened, but confused enough to forget to drop my pack, I sprang to my feet and dashed up the trail toward Minnie. My helmet bounced around on my head; canteens sloshed on my pack; bandoleers of ammo banged against each other, and my frag and smoke grenades clanked back and forth. I felt and sounded like a door-to-door pot and pan salesman from days gone by.

When I reached my fallen comrade, I grabbed his arm and rolled him over onto his back. HIS FACE WAS MISSING. Everything below his eyes had been completely blown away. The bloody cavity where his mouth had been frothed with scarlet and clear body fluids. Jagged pieces of pink and pearl jaw bone and teeth lay scattered over his upper torso and on the ground around him. Minnie's body trembled and his exposed neck gurgled fresh blood from severed arteries. I quickly knelt by his side, oblivious to the war around me. With no time to explore for further signs of life, I grasped his shredded chicken plate with my left hand. In one adrenaline-aided effort I picked Minnie and his ruck up, dragged them off the path, and fell into a slight depression about four meters from where he had fallen.

"Minnie, Minnie, what did you do?" I pleaded.

I unsheathed my bayonet and cut the straps from the shield. Thanks to the chicken plate, Minnie's chest and stomach had been protected from the claymore's flying shrapnel.

Doc Wursten, firing his M-16 as he ran, slid in beside me.

"Hot damn," he yelled, "give me some fire-cover!"

Raising up, I mashed my right index finger against the trigger mechanism of my plastic rifle, but nothing happened. In my charge forward, I must have emptied the magazine into the maze of vines and trees. While Doc dug into his medical bag I reloaded and then rock and rolled 60 more rounds of suppressive fire into the greenery to my front. A grenade exploded 15 meters to our left, but we were too busy to even duck. This was "deep serious" for Minnie, and more of us could soon be in the same condition if we didn't quickly get more fire-power to support us up in the front.

*People often think that soldiers have a panoramic view of the battle going on around them, that they can adjust their attack or fire based on support or danger to their right and left. This is not generally true. In the mountainous jungle, and even on an open flat beach, the individual soldier is totally involved with the enemy directly ahead, those in whose cross-hairs he is centered. Sightseeing is discouraged. If the target ahead is not removed immediately, nothing else matters.*

Our new machine gunner, Bo Hansen, charged up the trail wielding his fire-spitting '60 like a toy and crashed in beside us. Smitty, his ammo bearer, immediately followed him. Although an almost fresh belt of 100 shiny new rounds hung from the receiver of the hot weapon, it jammed when Hansen hit the ground. The gun now refused to fire. I remembered a little trick I learned from Salvetti. He had carried this very same gun. I leaned over and smashed the top of the tray down with the palm of my hand. The cover that had popped open when Hansen so ungracefully joined us clicked shut. Hansen's big black right arm yanked the bolt back and let the spring action slide the new round home. I was relieved when the '60 again began spewing out the hot empty brass.

"OK, Rock," Doc almost screamed, "I need your help!"

He held a sterilized surgical scalpel in his filthy hands.

"Have you ever seen a tracheotomy before?"

"No," I answered.

"Well, looks like this will be a first time for us both," he replied.

In the middle of a fierce firefight, covered in mud, the 20-year-old medic was going to attempt a delicate life-dependent surgery.

Minnie was all but dead. He had no way to breathe, his face and throat were clogged with blood and shredded flesh. He was only seconds away from drowning in his own fluids. Doc's best chance to keep the little Puerto Rican alive was to cut a hole into his windpipe so he could breathe.

Working quickly, he cut an unprofessional but effective air hole through the trachea. When Doc was finished with the procedure, he looked me in the eye and said, "I hope it works."

A year earlier I probably would have passed out watching what the medic had done to my faceless friend. But after 10 months of exposure to the hideousness of war, my participation was almost routine. We did what had to be done.

The last thing Doc said to me before rushing off to help with Morris, who had also been hit, was "Hold your finger here."

He pointed to the open incision in the trachea. "Allow air in and out, but don't permit any more blood down his throat."

The firefight was subsiding to a few sporadic shots as I slid my already bloody little finger into the warm air hole. Gently lifting, I felt Minnie's breath spasmodically rush up and down my wet palm as he breathed through the hole in his neck. A dust-off was on its way. I prayed that my little buddy could hold on long enough for the doctors at the 18th Surg. to have a chance at saving his life. The time alone with Minnie also gave me time to blubber out a few words of comfort—mainly for me, I think.

The reality of the mess was that Minnie was going to die

shortly, and I was mad at the world. Minnie, the devout Catholic boy, lay by my side for the last time. The green knotted string of rosary beads was still around his neck. That was important to me because it was important to Minnie. Though our religious beliefs were different, I couldn't help but imagine Sergeant Pearson grabbing Minnie by the hand and dragging him through the pearly gates. Maybe he would do the same for me before the day was over.

Other guys in the company began rushing past me as they set up a temporary perimeter to protect us. Doc Horsley, from first platoon, replaced Hansen and Smitty in the jungle depression's muck. He also relieved me of the responsibility of caring for Minnie. Stretching my cramped legs, I glanced at my bloody hands and arms. Minnie's frothy red blood was now turning dark and sticky. The smell of death hung in the still air around me. I wiped my hands on nearby trees and brush. My water was much too valuable to wash with. I said goodbye to my friend and walked away, leaving him in better hands: God's.

Within 15 minutes of the gook claymore explosion, the dust-off medical evacuation chopper lowered its wire-mesh recovery litter. I returned and helped hoist Minnie's near-lifeless body aboard the hovering ships wire basket. The medevac medics valiantly continued our first aid. I said my goodbyes to my friend again, trying to sound optimistic as I spoke. I don't think he heard anything I said.

*Minnie Martinez died within an hour on an operating table at Camp Evans.*

The chopper medics pulled Morris, who had only been with us for a couple of weeks, through the jungle's umbrella next. Blood was dripping from the saturated six-inch compress wrapped around his decimated stomach. Another thick bandage, tied around his upper thigh, was already stiff with drying blood and mud. Morris' unruly blond hair was now pink.

*Paul Morris would also be dead within 12 hours.*

Sometimes we memorialize fallen soldiers with words like glorious, gallant, valiant, and dignified. Such eloquence may be appropriate back in the world, but everything I had seen was horrific, mind-numbing, sickening, and repulsive. The spilling of one's blood for his country is not a glorious thing to see.

We captured the summit of Co Pong at 1330 that afternoon after five days on the trail. Nothing was there. We found no heavily fortified regimental-type positions like we did on Hamburger Hill. The human price our company paid here, however, was even greater than what we had suffered on that other mountain. Charlie had killed nine Screaming Eagles. Fourteen others had earned Purple Hearts and scars.

We did not find any supply dumps, weapons caches, or gook bodies. The mountaintop was without the prey we sought. I hated the thought that the long, costly recon patrol had been for nothing, but. . . .

## CHAPTER 27

# TRAPPED ON TOP

We used machetes and blocks of C4 to clear a small landing area on Co Pong's summit. We also organized a temporary DDP, fully expecting that choppers would extract us before nightfall. The mountain had no value to the Army any longer. Like we did on Hamburger Hill, we were going to give it back to the enemy. We just did not have enough manpower to occupy every mountaintop in South Vietnam.

For the previous five days logistics birds had not resupplied us with food or water. Only daring medevac pilots braved the drenching rain to lift out our dead and wounded. Most important was the fact that we were critically short of ammunition. During Advanced Infantry Training at Fort Ord, a small sign hung at one end of the hallway in the old WW II-era wooden barracks I lived in. The sign read: 'If you are short of everything except enemy, you are in combat.'

Several times before dark we heard our olive-colored "liberators" hovering above us. The chopper pilots were making valiant attempts to rescue us from our precarious isolation. Soupy grey clouds rested on the mountain's peak, and the pilots could not see our smoke signals. The helicopters finally abandoned us to the night.

Captain Knight conceded victory to the elements at about 1800 hours; we weren't going anywhere. He passed word to the men through the chain of command to prepare a night defensive position. The captain also said there was to be no digging, no lights, and no smoking. Perhaps the high ground and the night's invisibility would guard us. Morning's light would surely bring us some luck, and relief.

Fog quickly came and went as though it were an eagle soaring through the deep valleys and over the tallest mountain peaks, leaving the hazy gloom in its wake. The bird finally sank its talons onto our defensive position, and the thick mist enveloped us for the night. Observation outside our surroundings was impossible, so we quietly listened for tell-tale sounds of the grim reaper climbing the hill as he searched for us. I'd made up my mind that if I died I didn't want my parents or anyone else to open the casket and have to remember me by the way I looked on the worst day of my life.

The slate-colored blackness of the night passed slowly. The greens of the jungle fought valiantly to maintain their vibrant colors but succumbed to the tired sun and turned dark. Claustrophobia wrapped its clammy arms around us. Sir Charles stayed in his hammock that night; he was probably as miserable as we were. The dense fog seemed to inhibit the usual swarms of buzzing mosquitoes, which was good. A sporadic drizzle about midnight was also welcome.

Some of the men caught the light rain in ponchos they'd spread over the low jungle vegetation. They funneled the water down through the hoods of the ponchos into their dry canteens. I prayed that "manna from heaven" in the form of food, ammo, and helicopters would arrive when the morning sun peaked over the A Shau's tangled horizon.

At the CP strategy pow-wow in the morning, the officers decided that we did not have enough firepower to fight our way back down the mountain. We were, in effect, trapped on Co Pong until extraction or resupply choppers could reach us. The captain decided to set tigers up a hundred meters down the trail on either side of our perimeter. We would then wait for the weather to give us a break.

At exactly 1320 that afternoon, the cracking of M-16 fire shattered the steady patter of gentle rain on the broad jungle leaves. The ambush on the November (north) side of the mountain had found a target. Spoiling for a fight, everyone on my side of the defensive circle grabbed their weapons and ran toward the shooting. We were anxious to balance the score from the previous five days. Beaten down but not defeated, we were eager for a fight with Sir Charles.

By the time we reached the first platoon squad that initiated the ambush, the shooting had stopped. The guys partially satisfied their passion for North Vietnamese blood when they dragged the uniformed body of a gook officer from the underbrush. The young NVA lieutenant had been shot twice in his chest. The squad carried the lifeless body halfway to the company perimeter before it dropped from their improvised poncho litter. After everyone had a chance to gawk at the corpse, they tossed it just off the trail and left it to the bugs and worms.

As always, after Americans had abandoned a site, Luke the gook had moved in to "police up" what we left behind. Believing the choppers picked us up the evening before, they returned to scrounge anything of value. Surprise! We had not vacated Co Pong, and Charlie paid the price for his careless assumption. This time we had caught him coming up the trail.

The next day, the slow-learning gooks repeated their same mistake. This time Sergeant Tew's squad caught the intruders trying to climb our hill. My guys were assigned as the immediate response team, so we were the first to reinforce third squad. Again we were too late to catch any of the action. In our search of the area, however, we discovered the positive results of Sergeant Tew's ambush, a well-executed *coup de grace*. Wilson and Blackwell each found AK-47s. Muskrat and I found a badly wounded gook.

The little NVA soldier couldn't have been more than four feet, five inches tall. Nor could he have weighed more than 70 pounds, but there was no doubt he was a bad guy. An M-16 bullet had hit him in the back as he attempted to run back down the mountain. The bullet shattered his spine.

The pain must have been intense, but the pale, waxy-faced soldier just lay there on his back and watched the giant Americans hover over him. He expected to be executed at any moment. His black eyes rolled from side to side as our numbers increased around him. An American grunt would have been screaming his head off for a medic if he had a similar wound. Like most wounded enemy, however, this one didn't utter a peep. His involuntary facial expressions told us he was suffering, and undoubtedly the little NVA soldier was wishing he were dead.

Five or six black M-16 bayonets tickled his throat waiting for the slightest provocation to thrust. It was not a good time for him to be defiant. I searched his uniform but found nothing that would identify him. Maybe, I thought, that would simplify things. A wallet with a picture of a girlfriend, or worse, a wife with kids, would transpose the soldier into a human being. As he was, anonymous, with no name, no age, and no family, he meant nothing to us. He bore his suffering and maybe his last moments on earth alone. None of us would care if or when he died. He would just be one less to fight another day.

Odds were that he was a shooter in the ambushes that destroyed so many of our friends. He may even have command-detonated the mine that killed Minnie. Sympathy and compassion were not warranted. I wanted to give in to the consensus of the men that he deserved to die, and order it done, "to put him out of his misery."

When our Kit Carson interpreter arrived several minutes later, the frightened prisoner talked up a storm. He was only 17 years old.

He claimed that it was his second day in South Vietnam after walking down the Ho Chi Minh trail. Under determined questioning, the boy identified the location of his base camp and two underground hospitals.

Doc Wursten was the first medic to arrive. He immediately began caring for the wounded soldier, something we had not considered nor cared about doing. When Doc had sufficiently patched the prisoner, we tossed him face-up on a sagging poncho litter. We carelessly dragged him toward our company perimeter. No one tried to avoid the tree stumps and protruding rocks that jutted up out of the trail. They often just scraped along the length of the guy's back, including his shattered spine. The improvised litter protected him from nothing. In a more civilized world, I'd seen trash collectors handle garbage cans with more care. The soldier's bare feet hung from the trailing edge of the poncho. They were often tromped on when they got in the way of the hard American boots. Halfway up the trail, the litter carriers purposefully dumped their burden off the sagging poncho. They rolled him on top of the stiff day-old corpse of the young soldier's platoon leader. The Kit Carson questioned him again.

Considering what we had just come through and our avenging attitudes, we felt it clemency enough that we allowed him to live. In our bitter minds, he deserved no additional pity. The medics gave him morphine and did the best they could to stop his bleeding and repair the wound. From the reports and rumors we'd heard of enemy care for captured Americans, I believed our treatment of the little Charlie was more than fair.

I asked Doc Wursten why he didn't just let the guy die.

"You don't have to kill him, just let him die." I suggested.

Doc said he thought about it every time he had to work on one of them.

"The thoughts come and go, Sergeant Rock; some thoughts are better off gone. It's what a man does, not what he thinks of doing, that counts. Doing the wrong thing can never be taken back; thinking it is just dust in the wind."

A medevac arrived and hovered for a few moments above us. It was trying to pick up the wounded prisoner to deliver him to the 18th Surg. The fog was back, however, and it was so thick the Navy could have floated a small ship in it. The pilot finally radioed down to us that, considering conditions, he would not risk his crew or the helicopter for a North Vietnamese soldier. He would attempt the impossible for an American, he said, but not for a gook.

We were almost as proud of the automatic rifles we captured as we were of the prisoner we held. Weapons were sometimes a better indication of the damage done than were the much desired body counts. It was a dangerous and time-consuming ordeal for a soldier to hand carry weapons down the long rugged Ho Chi Minh trail. Sir Charles expended great effort to keep from losing his prizes. They heaped much personal shame upon an NVA or VC soldier who lost his rifle. We knew we had hurt the enemy badly whenever we found abandoned weapons after a firefight.

The morning of our third day the weather still had us trapped on Co Pong's summit, and we were even more desperate for supplies. Our lifeblood, those little .223 caliber bullets, were rationed among us. Theoretically, we could live a week without any food, but when our ammo was gone we'd die shortly thereafter. The captain sent an edict around that he did not want to hear any automatic fire. You are just going to have to aim better, he said.

To our surprise, at about 1030 the clouds slowly began to move on. Most of the time, we had no idea where the stuff went. Unlike the swift eagle, however, this morning's fog seemed to creep back down the mountain on the spiral shells of rain-forest snails. It was a tremendous relief to finally look down off the summit and see Firebase Airborne still there. We knew we could now be airlifted back to the relative safety of the little sandbagged fortification. The manna I'd prayed for came several days late, according to my schedule, but I was still alive to enjoy it.

The medevac was the first chopper to arrive; it hauled our little captive away. In his 24 hours among us, our attitude toward him mellowed considerably. While we could have bayoneted him days earlier and not felt bad about it, most of us were now happy to see him evacuated to the hospital. Hueys quickly dropped out of the sky like olive-drab-colored guardian angles and lifted Alpha Company off the mountain six at a time. As the skids broke contact with the earth, we cheered and applauded ourselves for having survived the worst Co Pong had to give.

# CHAPTER 28

# I MADE IT!

Immediately upon Alpha Company's return from Co Pong, our little sandbagged home reminded us of its ever-present stench. Firebase Airborne smelled like an old yellow-stained urinal. Piss tubes, the common vernacular, were half-buried black urinal pipes—six-inch diameter, six feet long—that were scattered around the little base. The pipes were discreetly placed next to communications antennas or in slight ground depressions to provide maximum privacy. The idea was for a soldier to urinate down the angled screen-covered pipe instead of wherever he happened to be standing. I guess it was a good idea, except the concentrated smell around the piss tubes was intolerable. Not everyone was accurate, and the soil beneath the user's feet was usually saturated. Whenever it rained hard the urine rose to ground level, so many of the troops avoided soiling their boots by just urinating anywhere they pleased.

While the smell of the fire support base was the same, the appearance of Airborne had changed. The entire west end of the perimeter was either fire blackened or covered with a fine layer of grey mud. Excited bunker guards explained that during our absence a big twin-rotor Chinook helicopter had crashed onto the landing pad and burned to nothingness.

The huge bird had been lifting off after delivering supplies and taking on a load of GIs. Somehow a tire on the Chinook snagged a corner of the heavy perforated steel planking. The weight of the PSP overcame the lifting power of the rotors. The heavy ship, anchored by the one wheel, simply rolled over onto its side, broke open, and burst into flames. The four-man aircrew and seven of the twelve passengers burned to death. The fire spread to some just-delivered gasoline drums and then to a stack of fifteen 105 artillery shells. Evidently the resulting explosions and intense fire caused a spectacular show. We, less than two klicks away up on Co Pong, were completely oblivious to it all. I guess the wind and rain had washed away all the sound.

Within an hour of our arrival, Captain Knight and Lieutenant

Egginton strolled over to my bunker. I was helping Hansen clean the '60, and I had a dozen freshly oiled parts resting on a boonie towel in my lap. Hansen may have had an unwashed body, a defiled mind, and a filthy mouth, but his weapon was always clean. Standing when the captain addressed me would have been proper military etiquette but impractical at the time. Two officers visiting me probably meant that I was in some kind of trouble.

"Sergeant Rock, stow everything in your bunker except your rifle and a bandoleer of ammo. I'm sending you back to Camp Evans to a battalion promotion board."

The news completely surprised me. I had given up any thoughts of sergeant's stripes months before.

During the hour I waited for the Huey, Lieutenant Egginton coached me in proper military etiquette. I learned how to enter the room occupied by the board of officers, how to stand, and whom I should salute. I practiced standing at attention and the precise footwork required to execute an "about face." It seemed a long time ago that I had last practiced marching skills; there was not a great demand for that talent in South Vietnam. Of course I was the center of attention as I promenaded around the platoon area like a one-man parade. Silently I endured the many quips and jokes from the men; I didn't have the time to be embarrassed.

Just before I climbed aboard the chopper, the captain emerged from the command bunker. He yelled some breaking news that just came over Armed Forces Vietnam Radio. September 4, 1969: Radio Hanoi announced the death of Ho Chi Minh. Uncle Ho was dead; I wished it had happened 10 years earlier.

At Camp Evans later that afternoon, the chubby little clerk in the company office informed me that the review board would not convene for another two days. That was great news—I needed time. The way I looked and smelled would probably get me busted a rank rather than promoted.

My first stop was at the shower. The water draining from the overhead 55-gallon drums was cold, but it felt good to finally be washed clean of Minnie's blood. Spec 4 Karras, just returning from the hospital, came into the shower while I was there. It was good to see that my old squad leader had recovered from the AK bullet through his derriere. When he took his turn showering, he showed me the large scars on each side of his butt where the bullet had passed. Karras was fortunate he hadn't been killed. He was eager to hear all the news about the company, so I brought him up to speed on everything, including the assault on Co Pong. He washed his hair several times under the cascading water to hide his tears. We both lost good friends on the mountain. Karras was going home in 10 days, he told me, and so we would not see him in the field again.

I spent most of that day and the next memorizing facts from several military handbooks belonging to one of the senior NCOs: "The little ball on top of a flagpole is called a truck." "World War I began in 1914." "In 1941 the Germans launched the first successful paratroop invasion." "Alexander the Great of Macedonia organized the first known military supply system." "The Continental Congress created the U.S. Army on June 14, 1775." "The Army's motto is 'This We'll Defend'." "The official Army flag colors are blue, white, and red, with yellow fringes." The "fact" affecting me the most was "On March 3, 1863, during the Civil War, Congress passed the Enrollment Act." Thus began the draft authorization that eventually sent me to Nam.

Armed with my new "library" of facts, at 1800 hours I joined 29 other hopefuls outside the mess hall. I was dressed in brand-new, freshly pressed jungle fatigues. For at least two hours that morning I had spray-starched and ironed the jungle uniform until it was completely free of wrinkles and was as stiff as a sheet of balsa wood. I waited until 1745 hours before slipping into the fatigue pants that had been leaning up against the wall. I then walked with a stiff-legged gait, like that of a distance-walking athlete, to my appointment.

Although we all claimed indifference to being promoted, it was obviously not true. All 30 of us had spent a great deal of time and effort to make a good first impression. We tried to act casual as we milled around, working off our nervousness. Politely chatting, we gave little coaching hints to each other. The big secrets, which would hopefully make us stand out in the eyes of the board, we kept to ourselves.

One of my compatriots, bloated from chow, loudly passed gas with a great deal of satisfaction. He grinned from ear to ear. A few of us snickered; everyone fanned their screwed-up faces and walked a few paces away. The tension had been broken for just a few seconds. Only five slots were available; that meant 83 percent of us would go back to our jobs as cooks, clerks, infantrymen, etc., wearing the same Spec. 4 rank pins. Since most of us were already filling E-5 slots, new responsibilities were not the issue; it was the money.

My armpits were sweating like Niagara Falls in springtime. Infantry guys did not own luxuries such as antiperspirant. And now I was afraid it was what the panel of officers would remember the most about me. "Hey, remember that soldier with the sweat stains?" Why, I asked myself, did it have to happen just now? The more I worried about the problem, the worse it got.

"Specialist Olson, would you please come inside."

Upon hearing my name called, I felt the eyes of those still waiting to be interviewed fall on me. I knew what they were thinking: "Good luck, but we hope you blow it."

Entering the mess hall, I smartly displayed my much-practiced marching skills. I came to attention precisely 18 inches from the front center of the table. Opposite me were seven officers seated in high-mileage steel folding chairs.

"Sir, Specialist Olson reporting as ordered, Sir."

There, returning my salute was the battalion commander, Lieutenant Colonel Thompson. I was surprised to see him and wondered if he remembered me. It was just two weeks earlier that my squad had pulled that special ambush for him. I watched him for a little nod of recognition but none came. For all I could tell, he didn't know me from the man in the moon. A fresh haircut with proper military whitewalls, a warm shower, and clean starched fatigues had changed my appearance considerably. I'm standing two feet taller than he's sitting. I look down at him and he looks up at me but he doesn't seem one bit intimidated.

During the next 20 minutes, the board asked me rapid-fire questions. Not one question was about anything that I had so laboriously crammed into my head. They tested my knowledge of combat tactics and "what if" type problems: "What if your squad suddenly received heavy weapons fire from a fortified bunker above the trail you are on?" "What would you do if an officer gave you a direct order that you knew would result in the death of some of your men?" "What would you do if one of your men refused to fight in a combat situation?" "During a heavy engagement with the enemy, one of your men cowers and runs; would you shoot him?" "If a small child approached you with an armed grenade in hand, what would you do?"

None of the questions had easy "yes" or "no" answers. I knew that any hesitation in responding to the complex inquiries may reflect an inability to quickly make correct life-or-death decisions. I prided myself in my ability to think on my feet, but before the promotion board, the answers did not seem to come easily. While they fired the next series of questions at me, I thought of things I should have said to the previous ones.

At the conclusion of the "inquisition," I executed a precise salute, did a textbook about-face and marched across the hollow plywood floor to the mess hall exit. I carefully closed the spring-loaded screen door so it wouldn't slam. I had just taken an Army IQ test, and I was sure the results were going to expose me as the dumbest soldier in the United States Army. Over the years millions soldiers have heard it repeatedly said: "There is a right way, a wrong way, and the Army way." This time I hoped I had done everything the Army way.

The night air felt cool and refreshing as I stepped from the wooden porch of the mess hall. My waiting peers quickly surrounded me. "What did they ask?" and "What did they want to know?" were the most frequently asked questions. Not willing to offer an edge to anyone, I answered: "Know what the ball on top of the flagpole is called and what year World War I began."

Walking through the company compound toward my hootch, I wiped a stiff scratchy sleeve across my forehead. It soaked up little of the dripping perspiration. The obsidian shine on the toes of my new jungle boots collected dust, destroying the hours of spit-shining I'd done while sitting on my cot that afternoon. After time to rethink my words, I decided that maybe I had done OK with the promotion board after all. I certainly wished that I had been better prepared, however. Tactics—who would have guessed they'd ask an infantry guy about tactics? The *Manual of Small-Unit Tactics* is what I should have been studying. Stupid, stupid me.

Inside my hootch, I plopped down on the squeaky canvas cot and stared at the underside of the corrugated tin roof. I thought of the 11 replacements that had come with me to Alpha Company. I was shocked when I realized that I was now the only one left in the boonies. Three of us had been killed and seven others medevaced out of the country with serious wounds. That left only "screw-up" Major Poulsen, the official Camp Evans shit-burner, and me. The Army is a great trainer of fighters, but unfortunately it kills its students.

A "short timer's calendar" hung above the cot next to mine. A curvaceous nude female was sketched in ink like a character in a child's coloring book. She was divided into one hundred numbered sections. As the owner of the calendar counted down to DEROS, he colored in each section. Strategic portions of the female anatomy had lower numbers. If the calendar belonged to me, I thought, I would have colored over three-quarters of her by now. Because I didn't have a calendar and seldom even knew what day or week it was, time had just slipped by. I remembered guys like "Chief" Haskell, who thought of almost nothing but time. The only thing that seemed important to him was time in-country and time to DEROS. I wondered if I also would become obsessed with the passing of time as it grew shorter and shorter.

Rain began to plink against the tin roof, and a gust of cool evening air blew into the room. The screened walls filtered the breeze of its bugs and mosquitoes. I pulled my poncho liner up over my shoulders, and interlocked my fingers behind my head. Relaxing to the rhythm of the drizzling rain, I continued my daydream.

The guys at Airborne were wet, cold, and dirty, while I enjoyed the "luxuries" of rear-echelon life. Reminiscing about comforts back in the world, I swore I would never forget to appreciate the good life if I lived long enough to experience it again. Before coming to Nam, the American lifestyle was all I knew. The Vietnamese people, their country, poverty, and the war, had really opened my eyes.

Sleepily listening to the decreased *plinks* of the falling rain, I retrieved a thin spiral notebook from the old wooden 105 artillery box nightstand next to my cot and began writing a letter home. "Dear Mom and Dad . . ."

It was almost 0700 before the heat of the morning sun, shining through the screens, awakened me. I threw the poncho liner off and looked around. I was the only one left in the building. The other half dozen soldiers were probably already at chow. Slowly sitting up and pivoting to the left, I dropped my still-booted feet to the plywood floor with a thump. The old wooden cot groaned and squeaked its displeasure at every move I made. My writing tablet fell off my lap to the floor, so I slowly bent over and retrieved it. I reread the beginning of the message that I'd sleepily scrawled the night before, then shoved the rolled up tablet into a leg pocket.

"Well, I guess I'll wander over to the mess hall," I mumbled as I stood on my feet and did a few quick jumping jacks.

What I said to myself reminded me that the mess hall now had additional meaning to me. Besides food, it meant the possibility of sergeant's stripes.

Hot footin' it across the wet, oiled-dirt compound, I scanned the battalion bulletin board for a list of successful E-5 candidates. I quickly discovered, however, as did the two hopefuls after me, that the roster wasn't posted yet.

The magnetic quality of the bulletin board continued to draw anxious soldiers for the next four hours. My own half-hourly migration to the shrine of good fortune, ended at 1100 hours.

I was in the supply hootch shootin' the bull with Karras and several REMFs when I noticed a large gathering over at the board. Trying to act casual, I strolled over to join the gathering. The list we were all waiting to see had indeed been posted. Edging my way into the crowd, I finally got close enough to read the typewritten print. There it was! My name was in bold lettering. It seemed to jump off the paper! **SGT. ROCKY OLSON** was the second name on the short list of five. I made it!

# CHAPTER 29

# FINALE

No sooner had I hopped off the slick from Camp Evans and run from beneath the turning blades than I was surrounded. Isolated in the middle of the A Shau Valley, word of my promotion still reached the company at Airborne before I did. For the first 10 minutes, I felt like a politician after winning the big election. The handshaking and back slapping ended when Lieutenant Egginton ordered the men to return to their detail. In all fairness I think the guys were desperate for a work break and maybe anticipating some cool beer from the rear. They were chopping the green surrounding Firebase Airborne back another 20 meters to improve the fields of fire. It was an endless and boring task.

I managed to keep busy unpacking and stowing my gear for the last two hours of sunlight and avoided the sweaty jungle-clearing job. I still had my new starched fatigues on, and I thought I was lookin' pretty good.

When the squad returned at sundown, I passed around several cases of hot soda that I had brought from the rear. Most of the men might have preferred something much stronger, and a great deal of it, but I didn't think that this was the right time or place to host a big party. Being defended my first night back in the valley by a bunch of inebriates was the last thing I wanted.

While sitting my first guard that evening, the lieutenant stopped while checking the bunker line. He told me that Delta Company had attacked the enemy base camp that the little gook prisoner on Co Pong told us about. Although alert NVA scouts warned the camp in time for most of them to get away, some did not. Delta's riflemen killed five North Vietnamese defenders in a short but fierce firefight while suffering no casualties of their own. That was good news.

Charlie's living quarters was just 400 meters down the steep side of Firebase Airborne. Before interrogation of the captive, we had been oblivious to it. We had always been searching the high ground above us like Co Pong, and of course we had found nothing at any of those places.

During the week, Sergeant Tew, third squad's leader, got orders reassigning him to Fort Ord in California. Like me, Tew was one of the few old-timers left in the company. I was happy for him yet hated to see him go. Spec. 4 Jace Austin, one of Tew's fire-team leaders, took over his squad.

During my second week back, Alpha Company was replaced as security at Firebase Airborne. We were leaving the valley for good. Everyone greeted the news enthusiastically. The guys in the squad toasted our survival by passing around a canteen of Tang. Muskrat had kept it buried in the cool mud under his bunker for just such an occasion.

Before beginning operations in our new area, battalion gave us a two-day stand-down at Camp Evans. As usual, many guys spent their time drinking and standing in line for the boom-boom girls outside the base. Prostitution was not outlawed in Vietnam by either the government or the military. Health checks for the bar "ladies" were nonexistent. Consequently, gonorrhea and syphilis were almost as common among U.S. soldiers as the common cold back in the world. For many soldiers it was a sign of machismo to brag about catching the clap.

During the stand-down we finally had two straight days without rain. Blue daytime skies and clear nights peppered with millions of stars lifted everyone's morale. Staff Sergeant Wardle tried to convince us that this monsoon season had been quite short.

"When ya stop to think about it" he said, "we only got two rains. One lasted fer just three months, and the other one continued fer two more."

Speaking of Wardle, orders for him to return to the world came while we were on our two-day vacation. Captain Knight decided the platoon sergeant had seen enough combat during his two tours. He left the sarge behind when we moved out early in the morning of day three. Sarge's last 10 days in-country were spent as a REMF. I was very happy that the good ol' boy was leaving Vietnam alive, but at the same time I felt a little sorry for the NCO. He'd been in the Army for 16 years, two of them in Nam, yet he was still only an E-6. He deserved better.

We slowly humped three klicks due south the first day out of Evans. The rolling hills were covered in waist-high brush or short elephant grass, providing camouflage when we wanted to hide yet allowing us some vision. Luke the gook enjoyed the same terrain benefits; that is why we were taking our time. Our NDP was in a small clearing on the top of a hill that wasn't much taller than the others around it. Most of the guys felt it was safe to smoke, so they did. Cigarette smoke was always a dead giveaway—pun intended. The smell of a hundred sweating American soldiers and the pungent aroma of mosquito repellant also gently floated downwind. It was impossible to hide this many Americans from observant enemy soldiers.

At first light on the second day out of Evans we changed our direction of movement to west by northwest. Four klicks later, at 0945, we entered the abandoned *ville* of Thon Huynh Lien. Our search of the place produced nothing. No one had inhabited the little ghost-town for several years. There were just a few crumbling concrete foundations from by-gone hootches. Envisioning the layout of the *ville* was difficult. The narrow dirt road leading through the hamlet had been overgrown with vegetation for some time; so was almost everything else.

We hid in the shade of the trees. That night we formed a tight NDP; fewer enemies necessitated fewer guards, allowing more sleep. The darkness passed peacefully. The third day we continued the same directional coordinates toward another small village, Thon An Thon. This abandoned *ville* was only a klick away and on the banks of the Song O Lau. Thick groves of old banana trees and aged bamboo fields surrounded it on three sides. Just outside the *ville's* lush green barrier wall, Captain Knight halted the long column of soldiers. Several three-man teams from first platoon searched the perimeter for access roads or trails and for booby-traps.

Above the oasis of tall trees, we could see the masonry steeple of an old Catholic church. The yellowing sun-bleached tower stood in stark contrast to the variety of deep green that surrounded it. When the recon fire-teams returned, they guided us through a tunnel in the vegetation into the ville.

There were a half a dozen roofless concrete buildings encompassing the small but still majestic old church. While unloading our heavy rucks from our tired backs, many of us smelled smoke. We quickly fanned out around the *ville's* Catholic centerpiece and searched. Again we found nothing. Austin's squad discovered that the odor came from inside the building itself. The smoke's origin was high up in the bell tower.

Austin cautiously led his men up the creaky winding wooden

staircase to the tower's platform. Meanwhile, the rest of us were prepared to blow the steeple off the roof at the first sign of any resistance. Our excitement was unnecessary, this time. Austin's guys found a small tin pot full of warm rice among a few pieces of smoldering firewood. The tower was otherwise vacant, even of its bell. From his lookout post, Charlie had seen our approach and did a hasty escape, leaving his breakfast behind.

Common sense told us that an observation post would not be necessary unless there was something to protect. We diligently searched the old *ville* for the rest of the day. We found no tunnels, caches, or signs of recent gook activity. Whatever Sir Charles had there, it was hidden well.

Before night erased the long shadows of the trees, we set up two platoon-sized tigers in each end of the little ghost town. The remaining platoon, mine, "volunteered" to be obnoxious Americans and attempt to draw enemy attention during the night. We had the advantage of being inside the thick concrete walls of the old abandoned church. The disadvantage was that there was no way to escape the structure if we needed to.

While inspecting the interior of the church, I threw my heavy ruck up on the old concrete altar. The front of the once ornately painted altar displayed a sculptor's replication of the last supper. The heads of Jesus and the Twelve Apostles had all been broken off.

Three heavy wooden beams, about 10 feet apart, ran the width of the old structure and supported its faded red tile roof. Everything that could be used for firewood or was valuable as salvage was gone, except the spiral staircase. Obviously the enemy, probably Viet Cong, needed access to the bell-less tower. The three large window openings on each side of the chapel had been stripped of their stained glass. The frame at the front of the building where big double doors had once hung was now empty.

I assigned three squad members to each of my fire-team leaders, Sergeant Valdez and Sergeant Melaney. I told them to stand watch at the front two windows on the east side. Hansen, Smitty, Polansky, and I took the third window, up by the altar. Salvetti ordered his men to watch at the windows on the opposite side of the church. Austin divided his men between the front door and the tower.

We played loud rock music on our little 9-volt radios and built a smoky fire in the steeple until it was dark. We tried to be tempting targets. Our first lines of defense, besides the two ambushes, were our claymores. We strung the mines out about 10 meters and aimed them toward the surrounding bamboo and palm fronds. I told the men to stack their grenades under the windows and near the doorway. We put two machine guns in the steeple and the third gun at the chapel's entrance.

After dark our raucous behavior changed drastically. We were quiet as church mice and spoke only when necessary. Movement was minimal. Guards at each window intently watched and listened. Seeing anything that was more than a few meters away was difficult, but if by cunning or dumb luck the gooks were able to get past the trail ambushes on each end of the *ville*, we were prepared to make them pay.

Because I had placed my gear on the altar early in the evening, my sleeping accommodations were reserved. The top of the concrete platform was about a meter and a half off the floor, and the best bed the tiny church had to offer. Elevated off the littered floor, I would be safely above most of the bugs, rats, and other creeping crawling varmints.

Due to luck at drawing straws, I got fourth watch and slept well. Hansen's hand on my shoulder at midnight awakened me. He gave me a negative situation report.

"Everything's quiet, but it's real spooky out there."

Satisfied that I was alert, Hansen returned to the poncho liner that he had spread on the dusty floor in our corner of the room.

Leaning against the interior of the window frame, I strained to see into the darkness. I could see the dark bamboo wall 25 meters to my front, but not much else. The partly cloudy sky allowed moonlight to gently dance through the tops of the coconut palms. Periodically some of the soft light, passing in clouded patterns, fell onto the woody old bamboo fields. In turn, shapeless shadows from the trees seemed to very slowly creep closer and closer.

The thick dry bamboo groaned when the stalks bent and rubbed each other as slight breezes pushed their way through. To our advantage, the only thing darker than the exterior of the church was its interior. Since I could not see anyone inside with me, I was confident that Sir Charles couldn't either.

I laid my rifle on the window sill, knelt on the floor and folded my arms over the weapon. Resting my chin on my forearms, I stared at the bamboo as it seemed to close in. With a twitch of his finger, any gook with an RPG could instantly blow away my protective wall, so I had to see him first.

Shadows changed again; I held perfectly still and concentrated. I could have sworn something was moving out there, but it made no sound. Was something really creeping up on me, or was my over-stimulated mind creating the illusion again? I remembered back several months to that ambush just outside Camp Evans when I saw gooks in the fog that weren't really there. . . . There it was again! . . . Again! . . . Movement!

Silently, at the apex of my anxiety, a large black cat jumped from the ground outside up onto the window sill with me. Out of nowhere, warm fur pressed against my face. The animal caught me by complete surprise. Although its mother may have been domesticated, this creature certainly was not. Before my reflexes could send me reeling back in mortal terror, the surprised feline gave an ear-piercing screech and leaped back outside. My M-16 followed it off the window sill onto the ground below. Stumbling in hasty retreat, an involuntary cry of fright burst from my mouth, and I threw my arms up in defense.

"WHOAAA!"

As if my cry was a command to open fire, the alert guards instantly filled the outside blackness with red tracers. Brilliant white flashes of exploding claymores and grenades punctuated the night with bold exclamation marks as their shrapnel sought imaginary targets.

I did not immediately recognize that I had generated the eruption. I did recognize, however, that I was nearly helpless without my weapon. Realizing what had to be done, I chucked a frag as far as I could into the bamboo and with a running start jumped out of the window. This was the second time in a year that I had jumped out of a church window. Adrenaline pumped through my system as I scrambled around looking for my rifle. I found it right under the window. Feeling the weapon's heft in my hands made me feel safer, and I dove headfirst back into the building. I had accomplished my little mission without getting shot, and that made me happy.

The steady thunder of our detonating ordnance and chattering rifles echoed around the chapel's bare walls. Every blast amplified the previous one and stimulated the next. Most of the guys were violently awakened from their sleep. They thought we were engaged in a fierce firefight. It was a domino effect, everything just escalated into a deafening one-sided fight. My ears hurt from the concussions.

Regaining my composure and breath, I watched for incoming green tracers or other signs of gook activity. . . . Nothing.

"Cease fire! Cease fire!" I yelled.

After several repetitions of my screamed command the shooting tapered down to silence.

"Has anybody seen anything? Is anybody hurt?"

Silence answered both of my questions. No one seemed to remember what had initiated the eruption, so to save face, I volunteered absolutely nothing. I knew, however, that my confrontation with the cat had started the whole thing. I also knew that any admission of guilt would have resulted in a six-month detail to police up cigarette butts outside of some little observation post in the middle of the A Shau Valley. Lots of soldiers were going to be upset about this.

Lieutenant Egginton perched high up in the steeple called a negative situation report to Captain Knight. He explained that our outburst resulted from itchy fingers and moving shadows. He then apologized for the unplanned mad-minute and signed off. There was no chance that we'd surprise any VC now.

I was more than happy to see the light of the new morning. This business of purposefully offering ourselves as targets was just too risky, and I expressed that opinion to Lieutenant Egginton when we were alone. The lieutenant nodded his head and said that he understood, but he didn't comment beyond that. Another officer that quickly came to mind would have just waved me off, or worse, if I had dared to criticize any officer's ideas.

Midway through the day's unsuccessful re-search of the old *ville*, Captain Knight came looking for me. He announced that it was time he and I had a little man-to-man chat. I was quite sure it had something to do with my "bad attitude" concerning the church ambush. Motioning for me to follow him, he led me a little way from the main body of men, out of their hearing.

We sat together on the side of a large grass-covered mound containing an old family bunker. He got right to the point.

"Sergeant Rock, my time in the field is limited. I'm being rotated back to a rear job. There are a few changes I would like to see made, however, before I depart. One change involves you. As you are well aware, the company is desperately short of experienced leadership. I seem to be able to get plenty of Shake-N-Bake NCOs, but combat-educated leaders are few and far between. Staff Sergeant Wardle's departure has emptied a platoon sergeant slot that must be filled by a competent NCO who has been tested under fire. Sergeant

Rock, you're the man."

With those words, he opened his left hand, revealing two staff sergeant insignia pins.

"I will pin these on your collar right now, no review board necessary, if you give me a positive answer to one question. First, I want you to understand how important this is to you and your platoon. Should you choose, as I have, to make the Army your career, this promotion could be a tremendous advantage for you. Staff Sergeant Wardle will most likely retire from 'this man's army,' after 20 years of service, as an E-6. You, on the other hand, will have attained that same rank in less than a year and a half. With normal career advancement from here on you could have very healthy Army retirement checks and the leisure life before you turn forty-three. That's got to be a better option than your previous employer offered."

He was right. I was a ski salesman with limited future possibilities. I listened as he continued.

"The second point I want to make concerns your responsibility to the platoon. I've watched the men: they trust you and follow your lead, and that's important. As the platoon sergeant, you can continue teaching the tricks necessary for them to survive in this place. We need ya!"

The captain played on my sympathy, a good tactic.

"Now here's the deal," he said. "All I need from you right now is a verbal agreement that you'll extend your tour 'on line' for another three months."

I looked at the captain who had just given me his best sales pitch and then stared at the black dirt between my jungle boots. I slid my boots together several times, creating a little pile of dust as my future swirled through my head. I was almost sure what my answer was going to be, but I didn't want to make a mistake that I would later regret.

"Tell you what I'm going to do, Sergeant," he announced in one last effort to sweeten the pot. "If you want to return to civilian life, I'll see that you get a three-month early-out from your remaining active duty obligation. Vietnam will be your last duty station—no more Stateside garrison duty. What do you think?"

My head began to swell from the captain's compliments and his generous offer. I expressed appropriate thanks to him. After another short pause, I also told him that I respectfully declined the offer. My first 18 months in the Army were spent in Basic and

Advanced Infantry Training, followed by Vietnam. All were unpleasant experiences. My first impression of Army life was not good. Secondly, and by far the most important, were my poor odds of a healthy survival. I was the only one left in the field of my original group of 12 FNGs, and I didn't want to push those statistics any further. Against all odds I was still alive; I liked that. I had two weeks left to DEROS. If I made it, I'd thank God for protecting me and gladly endure spit-shining boots and harassment for the last six months of my Army obligation.

The company commander listened to and accepted my declination without any obvious signs of emotion. He ended the conversation with words to the effect that he really didn't blame me for not wanting to stay. As we stood to rejoin the company, he casually pulled a folded official manila envelope from his back pocket.

"Oh, by the way, we've received orders for your next duty station," he said, as he handed me the document.

I ripped open the sealed envelope and unfolded the paperwork. "Well, what did you get?" he asked.

The answer was typed in bold capital letters about halfway down the sheet.

"I've been assigned to the 3rd Cavalry, at Fort Lewis, Washington."

My new orders were officially taking a big burden off my back; they were relieving me of the unwritten responsibility to die or get maimed for my country.

The Vietnam War had changed a great deal since my arrival a year earlier. The Viet Cong main force army was seldom seen by us in war-torn South Vietnam anymore. Those soldiers had been devastated by superior American weapons, tactics, and logistics. A great manpower advantage had belonged to the VC several years earlier, but they had lost every major engagement with us, generally at a 10-to-1 ratio. The much ballyhooed six months' Tet Offensive (including our Counter Offensive) for instance, was a military disaster for the VC. In their last grand effort they had attacked well over a hundred cities and *villes*, but they were able to keep none of them, not one. The popular uprising that the communist north's leader, Ho Chi Minh, had predicted did not happen. All politics is local, and it was the average everyday rice farmer and shop keeper who had rejected the communist blueprint for their future. Everyone in Vietnam, North and South, except the anti-war news media knew of the communists' failure. New recruits for Victor Charlie from South Vietnam were now hard to come by, since we "owned" all of the population centers.

The Viet Cong had committed so many atrocities during Tet that the South Vietnamese civilians were more afraid of that leadership than they were of their own corrupt leaders. There was little support among them for a barbarous communist government. Only small local units and mostly part-time soldiers in black pajamas remained. And we would find them. It was God's job to forgive them for the atrocities committed during Tet. The 101st Airborne just arrange the meeting, every time we could.

To beef up the war headlines back in America, and possibly win the all-important public opinion battle, Hanoi was now pouring her own better-trained and -armed NVA soldiers down the many Ho Chi Minh trails and across the Demilitarized Zone. It was a last-ditch effort, since both the Soviet Union and China were getting tired of the long, expensive war. They were also having some military conflicts (border disputes) between themselves. I was not going to be here to personally witness the next phase to the Vietnam War, and that left me with mixed emotions.

News of my imminent departure and new duty station quickly spread through the company. Some of the guys had been through basic training at Ft. Lewis. They tried to convince me that the new assignment was good duty. Any duty station, in my mind, would be good after South Vietnam. I had no complaints.

With just one week left for me in beautiful Southeast Asia, the entire 2/506th was transferred to a new AO. We were going to be part of the 101st Airborne's new assignment, to replace the 3rd Marine Division up near the DMZ. The demilitarization zone was supposed to be no man's land, neutral ground between the warring North and South Vietnamese countries. The "secret" presence of U.S. and communist troops inside the zone was common knowledge, however. It was a lousy and very dangerous place to spend my last week of the war.

The 3rd Marines were the heroes of Khe Sanh (just a few miles from our new AO.) They had valiantly turned back three divisions of NVA soldiers in their historic meeting. In a several-months-long firefight in early 1968, the Marines, aided by massive air power, killed between 10,000 and 15,000 North Vietnamese troops. They had managed to change a little part of the communist's prearranged history.

President Nixon had announced that 250,000 U.S. troops

would be withdrawn, and the South Vietnamese military would assume more, and eventually all, of the war effort. The plan was called "Vietnamization" of the war. The 3rd Marine Division was among the first of the large units to be withdrawn.

The proud Marines were not going home due to poor performance or because they had "capitulated" to the North Vietnamese. The president, urged by a vocal minority, had decided it was time to bring our part in the war to an end. In the next few years we were all scheduled to go home; that was our government's mandate to us. If anyone should eventually get tagged with the "we lost the war" anchor around their necks, it should be the politicians or the far-right war protestors, not the soldiers.

Many of the front line ground-pounders fighting the war in late 1969, like me, were conscripts, yet we did what was thrust upon us and when our turn came we returned home honorably. I just hoped that U.S. soldiers in future wars would be treated fairly by the news media, prayed for, and thanked for a job well done when their time of service was up. Those honors had slipped by us. We were not the aggressors in this war, we were defenders. We had no intention of keeping the country or its wealth. Unlike the communists, we were not in the global acquisition business.

Because we were "Air Mobile," the plan called for us to make lightning-fast assaults on the North Vietnamese by air, something the Marines were unable to do. In theory, the new tactic would surprise the gooks, and allow us to disrupt their organization and logistics. The success of this operation depended upon our ability to get on the ground without being compromised by the enemy, however. It only took one trail watcher to see the insertion and run to his comrades.

Right after our move into the DMZ, Sergeant Melaney was given his own squad in the first platoon, and he deserved it. Valdez stayed with me; he would most likely get transferred to another infantry company or be reassigned to the rear and given the title of REMF. I do not know how he ever graduated from Instant NCO School, as common combat sense was not his strong suit. He was dangerous to us, and I knew he would never be an infantry squad leader in Alpha Company.

Our transfer to the new area of operation was uneventful, and we began an air and ground recon of the area immediately. Every night we made several faults assaults into small clearings, bomb craters, or mountaintop landing zones to distract any gook trail watchers before the real insertions were made. Hopefully the gooks were running all over the DMZ, expending a great deal of energy chasing 101st airborne shadows. After total darkness the company would then move several hundred meters and set up an NDP on the selected mountainside. We spent our days searching the jungle in company size patrols exploring high-speed red ball trails for activity, and then humping to an extraction point for helicopter pickup.

Except for periodic long-distance sniper fire, we made no contact with Sir Charles during my final days in Nam. That suited me just fine. My last few hours in the jungle seemed to creep by. I guess I was getting anxious.

I spent all the time with the squad. Time was running out. There were many tricks of the trade and "Sgt. Rock's laws of combat" that I wanted the newer soldiers to benefit from before I left, whether by freedom bird or body bag. If someone didn't teach them, many would undoubtedly learn their lessons the hard way. And I didn't think I could take any more of that.

"Contrary to what some may tell you," I said, "always have a round chambered. Never walk flat-footed in the mud—always heel-to-toe, heel-to-toe. Look for loosely coiled vines across the trail, not just the obvious taut trip wires. During the hot season never wear underwear; the fewer clothes the better. Don't try to stuff guts back into a belly wound; just cover the mess as best you can with compress bandages. Never smoke a cigarette in the open at night. The tiny illumination will light up a sniper rifle's crosshairs from three hundred meters away and guide a 7.62 mm bullet right to your face. Like it says on the side of the package, 'Smoking can be hazardous to your health.' Always leave the safety pins in your grenades bent over, to prevent them from inadvertently slipping out." I even taught an FNG how to protect himself from the blistering sun by making shade from his M-16 and a poncho.

I tried to pass on a year's worth of the combat experiences that had kept me alive. I didn't want to receive letters from anyone telling me of suffering or death that could have been avoided had I properly trained them.

"Keep your weapon clean; never forget that it was made by the lowest bidder. And a clean weapon will give you a better bang for the Army's buck."

On my final day, the guys gave me a small going-away party. We shared some C-rations, funny stories and promises to get together again once it was all over. I gave away my little 9-volt transistor radio, rifle-cleaning kit, last two tins of peanut butter, and a full canteen of water. It was during that tear-filled jungle farewell that I said my last goodbyes. I was going back to civilization, back to the world, and they were not.

On October 15, 1969, in a small unnamed clearing in the demilitarized zone that separated the North and South Vietnam countries, I wished the guys good luck and took some last photographs of the squad. Tony Salvetti followed me to the turbulence of the chopper blades, where we looked at each other for maybe 10 seconds without saying a word. "Well, I guess this is it," was all of my grand goodbye speech that I could remember. I'd been preparing the farewell address to Tony for a week, but it didn't come. We embraced and firmly slapped each other on the back three times. I wanted to hold my best friend a little longer, but it wasn't the manly thing to do. Tony's final words to me were "Sgt. Rock you just would not die would ya?"

I climbed aboard the waiting logistics bird. It rose up, lifted its tail, and I flew away. I gave the split fingered V sign to everyone from the air, as I had done so many other times when I was the one being left behind.

The gooks had had more than their fair share of opportunities to kill me, but thankfully they couldn't get it done. No, I would not die in Vietnam. Within three or four days, I'd be safely back in the world. My brothers would, however, remain in Vietnam, to suffer and die.

# EPILOGUE

The feelings of relief shared by the soldiers on my freedom bird were obvious. We were going back to the world. It was almost as if we were condemned penitentiary inmates who had just received a last-minute reprieve from the electric chair on Terminal Island.

The Pan American DC-8's wheels squealed as they touched the runway in Oakland, California. The sound evoked a great cheer from the war's veterans, shoe-horned inside the plane. Hats flew around the interior of the giant aluminum tube as it braked to a stop. Along with many other soldiers, immediately after deplaning, I fell to my knees and kissed American soil (actually, it was black asphalt.) I had successfully deprived some eager communist soldier the opportunity of giving me an early release.

Home in Utah, I received a hero's welcome from friends and family. Some Vietnam survivors from other parts of the country were treated like heartless baby killers. Utah was not a Mecca for those of the antiwar movement. My mind left Vietnam long after my body did. Best friends were still sweating and dying in the forbidden jungles while I was not, and I felt guilty about it.

I longed to hear from the guys, but when their letters came they nearly always told of pain and suffering. The following two letters, written by "Muskrat" Brostrom, were of particular interest to me.

*Hi Rock,* *Oct 23, 1969*

*How's it going old buddy? We're all fine here. A lot of interesting things have happened since you left. One night two gooks walked into our LP's trip flare. LP2 saw them coming up the ridge with flashlights but didn't call anyone to tell them about it. Sergeant Valdez and 3 FNGs were on LP for us and by the time they blew their claymores and threw a frag, the gooks had gotten away clean. We did get one of their helmets though. I would imagine the gooks had to stop and clean their pants out before they got very far though.*

*After that we had a hot LZ, so everyone that was there is getting an Air Medal. We'd been receiving fire from the ridge lines just about 800 meters to 1 klick on both sides. Most of the time they were firing AK's and SKS's. We had an air strike called in on them and two Cobra's fired their loads at them. The gooks were firing their AK's at the Cobra's. After that we started our CA but still received fire from both sides of the ridge. If they weren't afraid of the Cobra's you know our small company wouldn't have scared them. I believe if we would have stayed there another night we would have gotten a ground attack.*

*Night before last, 5 guys and Lt. Holjes from 1st platoon were out on a recon mission. Their medic was having convulsions so they set up a perimeter and tried to have him medevaced. A gook walked through their perimeter and scared the guys to death. About 15 min. later one of the new guys was coming in to the middle to get his poncho liner. Another FNG there fired up the new guy with a 60 and killed him. They were fogged in so bad they never did get the medevac out that night. The medic is OK now, but the other GI lost his life on a hum bug.*

*What's happening back in the world? Did you get that fried chicken dinner you wanted your first night home? I hope you did, you deserved it.*

*Well, I've got to go. Take Care!*

*Muskrat*

*Hi Rock, Oct 29, 1969*

*Things have really been going rotten here Rock. We lost Tony Salvetti on the 27th. He took over your squad when you left and only had a few days left to DEROS. We'd been out on a six man recon. Lt. Egginton got a job at Brigade and so they sent a new Louie to us. I had met him about 45 min. before we made another CA. Our platoon and the company CP made it alright. There weren't any gooks around, but it was a bad LZ. We had driven just about everyone off the LZ. Tony came up to me from a stream 20 meters below the LZ and said, "Here Muskrat try some of this water, it's outta sight."*

*A chopper landed and the guys unloaded. It started to lift off and tilted like it was making a turn. I heard some popping and jumped into the bushes. Tony and the Louie died instantly along with 4 other guys. Tony was decapitated as were 3 others. The Louie had his arm, leg and head cut off. Blackwell from 1st platoon was cut clean in half at his waist line. It even tore his pants off. There were parts of bodies scattered all over the place. It took us 3 or 4 hours to get everything squared away.*

*I said a prayer for Tony and the guys that night. Rock, I'm sure glad you got out of here. If it be the good Lord's will, maybe I'll get to come home too.*

*Keep in touch Pal.*

*Muskrat*

The same experiences I had learned to live with in Southeast Asia suddenly tore at my twisted guts. I wanted to fight back, but could do little more than punch my bed pillow and shed tears. Maybe if I'd have been there, maybe . . .

I wondered how many more of my buddies would die in the defensive war game we continued to play. Would the politicians ever allow U.S. soldiers to attack North Vietnam and cut the head off the dragon, or would we forever just try to dodge its fiery breath? The best thing perhaps would be to just give up, sheathe our well-worn swords and go home. Soldiers, and the armies they serve, cannot just fight forever. We had gone to war, after all, to force a peace in Southeast Asia. If the fanatical Communist North would not come to the peace table (or honor the previous Geneva Conference treaty) the solution must be bought with the blood of warriors. The reason for a valiant soldier's death must be of such worth that the yielding of his life is justifiable to him personally. I wondered if the world was going to be a better place because of Tony Salvetti's honorable sacrifice.

So many bright, talented young American men had been killed *(average KIA age was about 23)* or maimed *(75,000 would be permanently disabled).* I could see little progress being made toward our goal of peace and democracy in this faraway land. A few successful military and political careers were being launched, but many other men and women had to bear the physical and emotional weight of those terrible days. Winning a war is not determined by who is right, but who is left.

Early in the Vietnam War the enemy was not afraid to bring mayhem to the Americans. But by late in 1969 we often had to travel great distances into remote jungles to find sizeable enemy units to fight. Pushing Sir Charles away from population centers was a positive thing, but the deaths of friends made me circumspective, I guess.

Yes, we had won every big conflict, but those extended firefights at company and platoon level were not so one-sided—we lost many of them. And because our foe most often chose when and where the engagements would happen, we were not always able to utilize the awesome firepower available to us (an important concept not lost to the enemy) before they had melted back into the terrain from which they had suddenly emerged.

As a result of officers not witnessing specific acts of heroism, I know many valiant NCOs and enlisted men never received the recognition they deserved, had the officers been on the scene during the fight. Those were injustices. It was my experience that there were no formal medal presentation ceremonies, or citations read, to which we ground-pounders were invited. We were always too busy, far away from the rear, fighting the war.

During Vietnam out-processing, I found a typed sheet of onion paper in my personnel file that identified numbers and kinds of medals I had been awarded. With the exception of one write-up, I did not know where or when any of the other noteworthy events had taken place—I just had to guess.

Listed among the Vietnam War's dead were many of my very best friends: Pearson, Washington, Jacobs, Peterson, Hernandez, Thurman, Morris, and Martinez. Now I must add Blackwell and Salvetti to the still-growing death roll. There is heaviness in my heart that I will have to carry for the rest of my life. When would the bad news from Vietnam ever end? It was always darkest for me just before it got black.

I believe when anyone, young or old, is about to die and life is being reflected upon, two questions beg to be answered: Will anyone remember me after I'm gone? and Have I made a difference? In the case of the American soldiers killed fighting this war, both questions are a resounding YES. Friends and family who died in war-torn South Vietnam have made a difference, a significant impact in the termination of the communist's rock-hard goal of global domination. The monumental accomplishments of many individual soldiers changed the world. The domino theory did not happen. Communism was stopped in Southeast Asia. The people in Thailand, Indonesia, Singapore, and the Philippines stayed free due to the sacrifices of brave Americans and our gallant allies.

Other friends who did not die, survivors like me, managed to make it home. For many of them, however, their bodies and/or minds will never again look or function as God intended. There are Lieutenant DeWitt, Jakes, Sonognini, Haskell, Cannon, Bennett, Martindale, Peterson, Zorn, Bayne, and many others. I know that I will always remember them. I might forget some names over the years, but I will always remember their determined spirit, individual courage, and loyalty to me and America. For the most part, they were great guys, and they served their country valiantly.

# GLOSSARY

**Actual**: A call sign used to distinguish a unit commander from his radio operator

**AK-47**: Soviet-designed 7.62 mm military assault rifle commonly used by the VC or NVA soldiers

**AO**: Area of operation: a geographical area of responsibility for a military unit

**APC**: Armored personnel carrier (M-113)

**ARVN**: (Arvin) Army of the Republic of Vietnam or a South Vietnamese soldier

**ASAP**: As soon as possible

**Bird**: A helicopter

**C-Ration:** Also C-Rats. An individual box of canned food; also contained cigarettes, toilet tissue, coffee, gum, Tabasco sauce, etc

**CA**: Combat assault. An infantry assault initiated with troop bearing helicopters

**Charlie:** Also 'Sir Charles.' A nickname given to VC, and often the NVA, soldiers; slang for Viet Cong

**Chu hoi**: Vietnamese for "I surrender"; not a literal translation

**Chopper**: A helicopter

**Claymore**: Command detonated antipersonnel mines used by the US and NVA, throws shrapnel parallel to the ground, toward the enemy

**CO**: Commanding officer

**Cobra**: The Army's primary attack helicopter It was equipped with rockets, 40 mm grenades, and 7.62 mm Gatling-type machine guns

**Concertina**: Coiled barbed wire used as a defensive obstacle

**Contact**: A hostile engagement with the enemy

**CP**: Command post

**Cordon**: To surround

**DDP**: Day defensive position

**DEROS**: Date of estimated release from overseas
**Deep serious**: The worst possible position to be in
**Didi mau**: Vietnamese for "to run" or "go"
**Ditty-boppin**: Slang term for carelessly moving about
**DMZ**: Demilitarized zone; the 17th parallel, dividing North and South Vietnam
**Dust-off**: A medical evacuation helicopter
**E-4**: Specialist fourth class
**E-5**: Sergeant
**E-6**: Staff Sergeant
**ETA**: Estimated time of arrival
**FAC**: Forward air controller; a small observation airplane
**Firebase**: A forward artillery and support base
**FNG**: F---ing new guy
**Frag**: Fragmentation grenade
**Fatigues**: U.S. Army standard green combat uniform
**Gook**: A derogatory slang word for a VC or NVA soldier
**Ground pounder:** A common nickname for the American infantryman
**Grunt**: See "Ground pounder "
**Head**: A slang term for soldiers using marijuana or drugs
**Hootch**: A small Vietnamese dwelling, or simple living quarters for American soldiers
**HQ**: Headquarters
**Huey**: UH-1 helicopter, the primary helicopter for troop transport
**Hump**: Labored march, usually with heavy rucksacks
**Juicer**: A slang term for soldiers who drank alcohol
**Khong biet**: Vietnamese for "I don't know"
**KIA**: Killed in action
**Klick**: Kilometer, one thousand meters
**Lai day**: Vietnamese for "Come here "
**LAW**: Light anti-tank weapon. A single-shot, disposable rocket launcher
**Lifer**: A career soldier
**Log bird**: A Huey logistics resupply helicopter

**LP**: Listening post; a nighttime forward "look-out" position

**LZ**: Landing zone

**M-16**: Standard rifle used by U.S. infantrymen after '66: 5.56 cal

**M-60**: Standard light machine gun used by U.S. infantrymen: 7.62 cal

**M-79**: Single-shot grenade launcher used by U.S. infantrymen: 40 mm

**Mama san**: Older Vietnamese women

**Medevac**: Medical evacuation helicopter

**NCO**: Non-Commissioned Officer

**NDP**: Night defensive position

**NVA**: North Vietnamese Army

**OJT**: On the job training

**OP**: Observation Post; a daytime forward look-out position

**Papa san**: Older Vietnamese man

**PFC**: Private First Class

**Piaster:** The basic monetary unit of South Vietnam

**Point, Point man**: The units lead man on a combat operation

**PRC-25**: (Prick-25) The portable American communications radio used by combat troops

**Prick-25**: Slang pronunciation for PRC-25

**PSP**: Perforated steel planking Used to surface landing pads/strips, muddy roads, and to fortify sandbagged bunkers

**Red ball express:** A heavily used enemy road or trail

**REMF**: (rim-ph) Rear echelon mother f---er A derogatory slang term infantrymen used for cooks, clerks, truck drivers and other non-combat support personnel

**RPG**: Russian acronym for "Ruchnoi Proteevotankovee Granatomet"—"Rocket Antitank Grenadelauncher": U.S. forces called it a "Rocket Propelled Grenade." The standard VC/NVA shoulder-fired antitank rocket launcher with a shaped charge projectile

**RTO**: Radio/Telephone operator
**Rucksack:** A backpack (with frame) used by U.S. infantry soldiers
**Sapper**: A VC or NVA commando, usually armed with satchel explosives, specially trained to penetrate U.S. military installation perimeters
**Slick**: A Huey helicopter stripped of external weapons
**Squad:** A basic fighting unit usually comprised of eight to ten soldiers led by a Specialist 4 or Sergeant
**Starlight scope**: A device that uses reflected light for nighttime observation
**Tiger**: Ambush
**Triple canopy**: A term used to describe three layers of jungle growth that generally blocked out the sun
**U S A F** : United States Air Force
**Ville**: A French word for city or hamlet
**VC**: Viet Cong. A communist guerrilla in South Vietnam
**WIA**: Wounded in action
**The world**: An American soldier's term for home, civilization, and the United States

# ABOUT THE AUTHOR

Photograph by Tamera Wursten

Rocky Olson was drafted into the United States Army in 1968 and sent to Vietnam as an infantry soldier. He was awarded the Bronze Star Medal; the Army Commendation Medal for valor (with Bronze Oak Leaf Cluster) and the Air Medal. The South Vietnamese government presented him with the Vietnamese Cross of Gallantry (with Palm Unit) and the Vietnam Campaign Medal. On his uniform above them all is the Combat Infantry Badge.

Rocky is a graduate of Utah State University and spent a career working for the United States Department of Defense. He served in USAF Aircraft Simulation and Intercontinental Ballistic Missile management positions. His travels have taken him to every state in the union and many foreign nations.

A native of northern Utah, he is married and has four children. After hundreds of speeches about Vietnam and thousands of "When are you going to write a book" questions, he can now answer "Here it is."

Personalized books can be ordered at
**www.sgtrockbook.com**

Please send correspondence to:
**Zeroed-In Press**
**P.O. BOX 122**
**Roy, UT 84067-0122**

Or by email to:
**Sgt.Rock0@yahoo.com**

For speaking engagements, please call
**(801) 731-9228**